THE BIBLE DOCTRINE OF THE HEREAFTER

THE BIBLE DOCTRINE OF THE HEREAFTER

By
C. RYDER SMITH, B.A., D.D.
*Formerly Professor of Theology in the
University of London*

'This is life everlasting, that they should know thee the only true God, and him whom thou didst send, Jesus Christ.' (JOHN 17^3)

WIPF & STOCK · Eugene, Oregon

Wipf and Stock Publishers
199 W 8th Ave, Suite 3
Eugene, OR 97401

The Bible Doctrine of the Hereafter
By Smith, C. Ryder
Copyright©1958 Epworth Press
ISBN 13: 978-1-60899-782-4
Publication date 7/6/2010
Previously published by Epworth Press, 1958

Copyright © Epworth Press 1958
First english edition 1958 by Epworth Press
This edition published by arrangement with Epworth Press

TABLE OF CONTENTS

	ABBREVIATIONS	vii
	INTRODUCTION	ix
1.	PROLEGOMENA	1
	THE OLD TESTAMENT	10
2.	THE RULE OF GOD—PAST, PRESENT, AND FUTURE	10
3.	DEATH AND SHEOL	32
4.	THE HEBREW TERMS RENDERED 'FOR EVER'	51
5.	THE *CHASID* AND SHEOL	55
6.	THE OLD TESTAMENT APOCALYPSES	66
	THE SEPTUAGINT	80
7.	THE RULE OF GOD—PAST, PRESENT, AND FUTURE	80
8.	DEATH AND HADES	86
9.	*AION* AND *AIONIOS*	96
10.	THE RESURRECTION	104
	THE NEW TESTAMENT	112
11.	THE RULE OF GOD	112
12.	THE TWO AGES AND THE PAROUSIA	117
13.	GEHENNA AND PARADISE	129
14.	THE DATE OF THE PAROUSIA	135
15.	THE STATE OF THE DEAD	157
16.	THE PAROUSIA: RESURRECTION	174
17.	THE PAROUSIA: JUDGEMENT	187
18.	AFTER THE PAROUSIA: THE FUTURE OF THE WICKED	211
19.	AFTER THE PAROUSIA: THE FUTURE OF THE RIGHTEOUS	221
20.	THE EVIDENCE FOR UNIVERSALISM	250
	INDEX OF HEBREW, GREEK, AND ENGLISH TERMS	261
	INDEX OF SCRIPTURE REFERENCES	265

ABBREVIATIONS

for the names of

BOOKS OF THE BIBLE

Old Testament

Gn—Genesis
Ex—Exodus
Lv—Leviticus
Nu—Numbers
Dt—Deuteronomy
Jos—Joshua
Jg—Judges
Ru—Ruth
1 S, 2 S—1 and 2 Samuel
1 K, 2 K—1 and 2 Kings
1 Ch, 2 Ch—1 and 2 Chronicles
Ezr—Ezra
Neh—Nehemiah
Est—Esther
Job
Ps—Psalms
Pr—Proverbs
Ec—Ecclesiastes
Ca—Canticles
Isa—Isaiah
Jer—Jeremiah
La—Lamentations
Ezk—Ezekiel
Dn—Daniel
Hos—Hosea
Jl—Joel
Am—Amos
Ob—Obadiah
Jon—Jonah
Mic—Micah
Nah—Nahum
Hab—Habakkuk
Zeph—Zephaniah
Hag—Haggai
Zec—Zechariah
Mal—Malachi

Apocrypha

1 Es, 2 Es—1 and 2 Esdras
Ad. Est—Additions to Esther
Wis—Wisdom
Sir—Sirach or Ecclesiasticus
Bar—Baruch
Three—Song of the Three Holy Children
To—Tobit
Jth—Judith
Sus—Susanna
Bel—Bel and the Dragon
Pr. Man—Prayer of Manasses
1 Mac, 2 Mac—1 and 2 Maccabees

New Testament

Mt—Matthew
Mk—Mark
Lk—Luke
Jn—John
Ac—Acts of the Apostles
Ro—Romans
1 Co, 2 Co—1 and 2 Corinthians
Gal—Galatians
Eph—Ephesians
Ph—Philippians
Col—Colossians
1 Th, 2 Th—1 and 2 Thessalonians
1 Ti, 2 Ti—1 and 2 Timothy
Tit—Titus
Philem—Philemon
He—Hebrews
Ja—James
1 P, 2 P—1 and 2 Peter
1 Jn, 2 Jn, 3 Jn—1, 2, and 3 John
Jude
Rev—Revelation of John

For other Jewish books (arranged alphabetically):

2 Bar—Apocalypse of Baruch
En—Ethiopic Enoch
Jub—The Book of Jubilees
Ps Sol—The Psalms of Solomon
Sibs—The Sibylline Oracles
Test—The Testaments of the Twelve Patriarchs: Test Jud standing for the Testament of Judah, Test Lev for the Testament of Levi, and so on.

INTRODUCTION

In this book an attempt is made to trace the development of the doctrine of the Hereafter in the Bible. In that book it is everywhere taken for granted that there *is* a Hereafter, the idea of extinction being nowhere found, unless it be in a verse or two of Ecclesiastes. The doctrine falls naturally into two parts—the doctrine of the future of the individual man and the doctrine of the future of the race, or of the society called 'mankind'. For the individual the Hereafter begins at death. When does it begin for mankind? Strictly speaking, in the earlier Hebrew writings there is no doctrine of the Hereafter of the race, for it is just assumed that it will continue, much as it is, indefinitely—that is, the 'Hereafter', if the word is to be used, is just the continuation of the 'Here'. But, when the doctrine of 'ethical monotheism'—or better, the belief in a single, personal, almighty, righteous, and merciful God—emerged with the Prophets, the belief that the world of men would just go on as it is, could not survive. Man is sinful, and a righteous God cannot tolerate the perpetuity of sin. There are evils in the universe too—the universe for the biblical writers being the home of man—and a perfect God cannot be content with an imperfect world. In consequence there arose a doctrine of a 'Hereafter' for mankind and mankind's world which would take the place of the sinful and imperfect 'Here'. This took the form that history is sharply divided into two 'Ages'— the Present Age of sin and sorrow and imperfection, and the Future Age of righteousness and joy and perfection. There is nowhere a doctrine that the first will merge into the second by gradual improvement. It is through the act of God that the Present Age ends and the Future Age begins, and it is for Him to decide at what point in history this will happen. For mankind the Hereafter begins at the division of the two Ages, often called 'The Day'. But here another question arose: 'Are the righteous dead to have no part in the Future Age of bliss?' It was not until the latest Old Testament period that this question was clearly asked. When it was asked, the answer was 'Yes, the righteous have a place in the Future Age, for they will rise from the dead to share in it'. Only so could the righteousness of God be vindicated. The rise of this doctrine meant that the state into which a good man passes at death is only an intermediate state. For him the ultimate Hereafter was the same as for mankind and began on the Day. To complete the doctrine a further question needed to be answered: 'What happens to a wicked man, first when he dies, and second at the End of the Age?' In this book an attempt is made to describe the development of the biblical doctrine of the Hereafter both for the individual and mankind. It will be found that the mankind of the future is to dwell, not in an undefined 'heaven', but in the present world re-made.

But what is the future mankind? Here the answer is individualistic, for the future mankind consists of righteous men, and righteousness is intrinsically individualistic. At this point the concept of 'judgement' emerges. The Day is a Day of Judgement, or rather, the Day of final Judgement. In an earlier book, *The Bible Doctrine of Sin and of the Ways of God with Sinners*, two meanings of the words 'judge' and 'judgement' were distinguished. To 'judge' may mean either 'to decide whether a man is good or bad' or 'to decide whether a man is good or bad *and* to reward or punish him accordingly'. In modern law-courts rewards have no place —but in ancient times the king was the judge, and, when he judged, he not only punished the bad, but often rewarded the good. In the earlier book the first definition of 'judge' is predominant, for, in the Present Age, God is always deciding whether a man is good or bad; in this book the second definition is usually relevant, for on the Day of Judgement, the dominant idea is that God rewards the good and punishes the wicked. There are passages, however, where the word 'judgement' means 'condemnation' or 'condemnation and punishment', and relates only to the wicked. It is on the Day of Judgement that the righteous and the wicked are finally separated, the righteous forming the new mankind. Today many Christians are 'universalists', believing that at long last every man who has ever lived will become righteous and be 'saved'. Often this takes the form of a belief in a 'second chance' after death. I have examined the biblical evidence on this subject at appropriate points, particularly in Chapters 18 and 20.

Among other things, the Bible is a book of religious ethics. In it the high calling of man is to do the will of God, and His will is righteousness. In the Bible, accordingly, men fall into two classes, the righteous and the wicked, the good and bad. It is remarkable that those who can hardly be called either good or bad appear so rarely. Yet under this division there is a difference between the two Testaments. In the Old Testament the normal axiom is that a man can be good or bad as he will—even though the number of the good may be few. In the New Testament all men are sinners —that is, wicked, and the division takes a new form. Those who believe in Christ were once bad men but through Him are becoming good. In New Testament terminology they are 'saints' (*hagios*) who are 'being sanctified' (*hagiazein*), and after the great Prophets 'sanctification' or 'holiness' includes righteousness. On the other hand, those who refuse to believe the Good News, the 'dis-believers', are bad men, for in the New Testament to reject Christ is the Sin of Sins. It is clear that this is a division within the limits of the 'hearers of the word', with whom the New Testament writers are immediately concerned, not within the whole race of men. None the less the term 'believers' is sometimes used below for 'the good', and, less often, 'disbelievers' for the bad. Of course, however, the first Christians were aware that there were multitudes, both of Jews and Gentiles, who had not yet 'heard the word'. Were these men, even though they were all sinners, to be reckoned at last among the wicked? In a famous passage Paul replies 'No; every man will be judged by the use he has made of the knowledge of good and evil that he has'—the Jews by 'the law of Moses' and the Gentiles by 'the law written on the heart' (Ro 2^{12-16}). There are theologians, who, rightly as I think, maintain that those who pass the test of 'the use of opportunity', are saved for Christ's sake, even though they do not know this. Indeed, even those who 'believe in Christ' are judged by the criterion of opportunity, for the Gospel is the greatest of opportunities. I have here epitomized the full discussion of the subject in *The Bible Doctrine of Sin* because of its bearing on the present subject. The point may be put paradoxically. Even though all men are sinners, every man whose 'conversation' or way-of-life accords with the knowledge that he has—whether through what Paul calls 'conscience', or through the Old Testament revelation, or through the Gospel—is here called 'good', and every man whose conversation does not is here called 'bad'. In the biblical account of the Hereafter there is indeed a long early period when there are no ethical distinctions in it, but ultimately ethics dominates the doctrine of man in the future as in the present.

As in earlier volumes, the Greek translation of the Hebrew Canon (LXX) has been included, together with the books of the

Greek 'Apocrypha'. For the present subject the Jewish Apocalyptic literature, both within and without the Canon, is peculiarly important. In New Testament times Apocalyptic was 'in the air', what may be called 'the Apocalyptic period' stretching roughly from 200 B.C. to A.D. 150. It was largely concerned, of course, with the Hereafter, and New Testament Apocalyptic teaching needs both to be compared and contrasted with it. To meet this need it seemed best to deal at some length with two Apocalypses, the Books of *Enoch* and *Second Esdras*, referring to other books as occasion required. At the beginning of almost all chapters on the New Testament, therefore, there is an account of the teaching of these two books on the subject treated. In this way I have tried, not only to examine particular New Testament passages, but to illustrate contemporary ideas. I have taken for granted the usual accounts of the two books named. Under *Enoch* this means that the book is a collection of a number of different documents, which, while they belong to one school of writers, do not always agree on particular points. The various documents are sometimes quoted under their several names—'Parables', 'Dream Visions', and so on. Under *Second Esdras* the prevalent opinion is that it is the work of a single Jewish writer, with Christian interpolations. Except at one point, the puzzling verses in 7^{28-32}, it seems to me that on the subjects pertinent here the scattered passages may be gathered into a consistent account and that this may be ascribed to one Jewish writer. The passage named, on the other hand, seems to be an interpolation belonging to a second Jewish writer, into which a Christian has intruded the word 'Jesus'. As to the rest of the book, the writer explicitly states that in his 'visions' some subjects left obscure or incomplete in one 'vision' are resumed in another (e.g. 6^{34}, 13^{56}; cf. $6^{12\text{ff}}$). By '*Enoch*' Ethiopic Enoch is meant, and by '*Second Esdras*' the Latin version, though under the latter I have sometimes preferred the Syriac rendering in particular texts, as given in the margin of the English Revised Version. For *Enoch* I have used R. H. Charles's translation, though I do not always agree with his exegesis.

As in earlier volumes I have not included references to other scholars' works—both for reasons of space and because there seems to me to be value in an independent examination of the original sources. But, as it fell to me to lecture on the subject of this book for twenty years and as I have been studying it for more than fifty, it is probable that I owe more to others than I am aware of.

As already implied, the book is one of a series on great Bible Doctrines, former volumes dealing respectively with Salvation, Man, Sin, and Grace. Where I need to mention a subject discussed fully in an earlier book, I have referred the reader to it, but I have kept these references as few as possible. Where a difficult passage is in question—e.g. the reference in 1 Peter to 'spirits in prison'—I have not hesitated to give considerable space to it. Under the Old Testament I have taken passages as they now stand, without inquiring into their composition, for it is as they now stand that they passed into the Hebrew Canon. Where the tetragrammaton, YHVH, occurs in the Old Testament, I have followed the English Revised Version and used 'the LORD', printing the word in capital letters. In biblical references I have followed the English Versions, except that I have used 'Sirach' regularly for Ecclesiasticus, and sometimes 'Koheleth' for Ecclesiastes. Under the discussion of terms I have often given the number of the uses of a term in brackets, generally under its first mention. If only because of 'variant readings', the number, especially under terms of frequent use, may not be accurate to a digit. Hebrew and Greek terms have been transliterated. For those who do not read those languages it may be noted that in Hebrew *ch* is to be pronounced as in *loch* and in Greek as in *chaos*. In Hebrew the signs ' and ' represent gutturals that are often left unpronounced in English. The contractions *HDB* and *ERE* denote Hastings's *Dictionary of the Bible* and his *Encyclopaedia of Religion and Ethics*.

I am very grateful to four of my friends—the Rev. G. W. Anderson, M.A., and the Rev. T. Francis Glasson, M.A., D.D., for reading the typescript and making a number of valuable comments, and the Rev. Frank H. Cumbers, B.A., B.D., and the Rev. J. Alan Kay, M.A. Ph.D., of the Epworth Press, for their ready help in the publication of yet another book. My thanks are also due to the Rev. F. A. Tomlinson for making a 'fair copy' of a rather tangled typescript, and to Mr William Jackson for preparing the very long Index of Texts.

September 1955   C. RYDER SMITH

NOTE

It was not Dr Ryder Smith's habit to quote rival authorities or to indicate where his views differed from those of other scholars. It has therefore seemed right, in preparing this book for printing, to restrict editorial comment to an absolute minimum. But a few footnotes have been added, drawing the reader's attention to relevant data not mentioned in the text or to points on which the author's view differed markedly from that commonly held.

T. F. G.
G. W. A.

CHAPTER ONE

PROLEGOMENA

THE Bible Doctrine of the Hereafter cannot be understood except in relation to three other biblical beliefs—the concept of the universe, the concept of history, and the concept of the various elements that together constitute a man. Some account of these is given in this chapter. Fortunately, apart from details, all three concepts are uniform throughout the Bible.

Both the Hebrew and the Greek, like other men, began by assuming that things are what they look like, and then added other ideas that seemed consonant with this one. This applies to their concept of the universe. Around them there lay a great stretch of land and sea, both of which looked approximately flat—and they believed that it *was* flat. Above them there was a blue dome that looked hard, and they believed that it was a 'firmament' in the literal sense of the word. Underneath the dome there was air, and moving across or below it there were bright things—sun and moon and planets and stars. Some of these, and probably all of them, were thought to be alive (e.g. Job 38[7], Ps 19[1-6], 104[19]), for a postulate of early thought was that there was life in anything that seemed to move of itself. So, for instance, the Hebrew called running water 'living water' (e.g. Jer 2[13], Jn 4[10]), and used a term for 'wind' (*ruach*) that connotes life. The wind, however, unlike the stars, cannot be seen. For some reason both Hebrews and Greeks came to believe that the regions between the flat earth and the hard dome were the habitat of unseen living beings, who may be conveniently called 'spirits'. Some of these, the 'demons', lived near the surface of the earth, practically among men. Some others lived higher up but they could visit the earth when they wished. The sun, moon, and stars lived very far up indeed, and did not descend to earth, but none the less played a part in the lives of men—or, to use the word that derives from this very idea, they 'influenced' men (e.g. Jg 5[20], Ps 121[6]). In New Testament times, at any rate, and probably earlier, different kinds of 'spirits' were supposed to have their usual habitat at different heights above the ground—i.e. in different *strata* of 'the heavenlies', to use Paul's word. Some of these spirits were good and some bad. Of course, for monotheists like the Jews, God was master of them all, even though He often allowed them, as He allowed men, to do as they liked. For the present purpose it is not necessary to discuss the Old Testament answer to the question: 'Under this view of the universe, where was *God*?' He was always thought of as being 'above', and in the final Hebrew account of the universe (Gn 1), He is outside the world that He has created, though He can visit any part of it, if He wishes, in a flash. Such ideas are the stuff out of which the doctrine of Divine transcendence is elaborated by philosophers. Probably the New Testament concept of God was half-way between the final Hebrew account and the philosophical idea. While the earth was flat, it was not a mere crust but a very thick mass. How else, for instance, could it carry the heavy dome of the firmament? The sea was a part of the *Tehom* ('deep', *36*) of waters that lay below and around the irregular mass of the earth. In Hebrew the word usually rendered 'sea' is applied to two seas. These would be the Mediterranean toward the west and the mysterious sea to the south, of which the Red Sea and Persian Gulf were parts. But the two seas were only a part of the one *Tehom*. In the Mediterranean and the Red Sea it covered parts of the earth, but its mass lay underneath the earth, which floated on it. It might be said to 'couch' like a wild beast (Gn 49^{25}, Dt 33^{13}). It was only by God's decree that the *Tehom* did not 'again cover the earth' (Ps 104^9)—i.e. that the heavy earth did not again sink into 'the deep'. At the flood God not only poured down rain from heaven, but 'broke up the fountains of the great *Tehom*' (Gn 7^{11} P). Usually, as Job put it, He 'hung the earth upon nothing' (Job 26^7) lest it should sink. While today we know that everywhere there is earth beneath the 'deep', in the Bible the 'deep' is everywhere beneath the earth. 'The bottoms of the mountains' lie far down in the *Tehom* (Jon 2^6), like the bottom of an iceberg. Under the Mediterranean and the Red Sea and doubtless elsewhere there were a number of chasms through which the mass of waters surged up and showed themselves. Each of these chasms might itself be called a *Tehom*. Those under the Red Sea were frozen over when Israel crossed (Ex 15^8; cf. Isa 51^{10}, Ps 106^9, etc.). When a Psalmist compares himself to a drowning man, he hears one 'deep' (*tehom*) calling to another (Ps 42^7; cf. 107^{26}). Even a lake no deeper than the Sea of

Galilee (less than 200 feet), opened into the Abyss (Lk 8[31]), as doubtless did the Dead Sea. As this has no outlet, the ancients would think that the water that pours into it went down into the *Tehom*. Probably even such swamps as are found at parts of the angle where the coast turns north from Egypt to Gaza, were thought to surge up from the *Tehom*, for might not men be sucked down into them? Again, at springs the *Tehom* burst up through the earth (Dt 8[7]). Rivers, therefore, came from the *Tehom*, and Assyria, whose capital Nineveh was watered by the Tigris, was 'nourished' by 'the deep' (Ezk 31[4]). This was a blessing (cf. Gn 49[25], Dt 33[13]), as people who neighboured the waterless desert knew, but normally the *Tehom* struck landsmen like the Jews with fear and horror. Had it not overwhelmed all men but eight at the flood? The word *Tehom* always refers to this mass of waters, except in one text (Ps 71[20]). This speaks of 'the *depths* (*tehom*) of the *earth*', but here the true Hebrew reading is probably the word rendered 'lower parts', as in parallel texts (e.g. Ps 63[9]). While drowning men perished in the *Tehom*, it was not thought of as a realm of the dead, but of living things from Leviathan and deadly serpents to the smallest fish (Ps 104[25f], Am 9[3]). *Abussos* ('abyss') is the regular LXX rendering (*29*) for *tehom*, and occurs eight times in the Apocrypha (e.g. Sir 1[3], 24[5], Wis 10[19]). For the Hebrew the *tehom* was not a place of punishment, but the 'deep' where, for instance, Leviathan, 'king of all that are in the waters' (Job 41[34] LXX) gambolled in his grotesque might. The 'waters above the firmament' (Gn 1[7]) were a part of the *Tehom* but have no bearing on the present subject.

It was also believed that in the middle of the vast mass of the earth there was a huge cavern, or series of connected caverns. This was called 'Sheol' in Hebrew and 'Hades' in Greek. Here again it is best to begin with men's experience and work from it. Both Palestine and Greece are lands of limestone hills and mountains. In these there are many caves. Most of these have no exit except to the open-air, but there are a few from which irregular passages lead away into the 'heart of the earth'. Only recent spelaeology has shown how far these may go and how deep they may sink—or, rather, their extent is unknown even yet, as in the Pennines. They lead to other caves, large and small. Streams and even water-falls are frequent in them. The best biblical example of such a cave is Engedi (1 S 24). David and his men, seeking to escape from Saul, hide in the cave, and, when

Saul enters, lurk in 'the sides (*yārēk*) of the cave' (verse 3). Probably this means 'in the smaller caves or passages' that lined its sides, for it is unlikely that the mere shadows in the main cave would hide a number of men. Of course, no one would voluntarily dive into the dark and awesome maze beyond. If anyone somehow got lost there, it is unlikely that he would return. It is probably from the knowledge of such caves that the Hebrews developed their concept of Sheol and the Greeks of Hades. While most of these caves were dry, in some there would be running water. At least one stream bursts from a cave at Engedi. It is likely enough that there was a stream through the Cave of Adullam, for a stronghold needs a safe water-supply. The Greeks believed that a river called Styx flowed through the nether regions and Hesiod says that it was as large as one of the nine great rivers found on the earth's surface. All this water in caves must have come from the *Tehom*, or Abyss. How? Almost certainly the ancients believed that there were channels into Sheol or Hades from the 'bottoms of the mountains' in the sea (Jon 2^6). This means that they thought that water sometimes rises above the level of its source, but this is what it *seems* to do, as the English phrase 'a *spring* of water' shows. Sheol, however, is so deep in the earth that it lies lower than the surface of the sea (Job 26^5). But, while streams from the *Tehom* break here and there into Sheol, to break out again somewhere on the surface of the earth, the *Tehom* is quite distinct from Sheol. At first sight the earlier part of the Psalm of Jonah seems to contradict this (Jon 2^{2-6}), but this is not really so. Jonah describes in verses 3-6a how he tumbled down to the 'roots of the mountains'. There the earth swallows him and his *nephesh* (verse 5; cf. Ps 69^1) passes into 'the belly of Sheol' (verse 2). From *there* he cries unto the LORD, and He brings the Prophet back, *nephesh* and body, through the *Tehom*, and so delivers him from the Pit (verse 6). He exchanges 'the belly of Sheol' for 'the belly of the fish', where he is safe (verse 1).[1]

This account of the structure of the universe persists throughout the Bible. Two other ideas appear for the first time in the centuries just before Christ. Both of them relate to fire. One was a belief that somewhere within the earth there is a place of fire; and the other that there are huge fires in the far East and the far West. It

---

[1] It is generally held that the poem in Jon 2 did not originally belong to the story of Jonah, but is a psalm of independent origin. It is a thanksgiving for a deliverance already experienced rather than the prayer of one in need. [G.W.A.]

is probable that the first belief arose from the phenomena of the volcano, for in these fire rushes out from 'the bowels of the earth'. If, as is likely, the Sinai of the Exodus was an active volcano, it might be supposed that the Israelites then first learnt of the subterranean fire, but it seems certain that they believed that God came *down* in smoke and fire on the top of the Mount (Ex 19[18-20]; cf. Dt 5[4f]), and not that these burst up from beneath. It is in Sirach, as will appear below, that the idea of a fire within the earth first appears in Hebrew literature. Probably the Jews learnt it from the Phoenicians and Greeks. Both these peoples sailed the Mediterranean, and they would know of the three volcanoes of Vesuvius, Stromboli, and Etna, which neighbour each other. It was almost inevitable that they should deduce that thereabouts there was a vast cave of fire within the earth, of which the three volcanoes were mouths. Clearly this cave might either be a part of Hades or separate from it. Probably the Hebrews had learnt of this fire long before it appears in Sirach. As to the belief in the Eastern and Western fires, it is easy to suggest its origin, for often, at sunrise and sunset, it *looks* as if flames from fires beyond the horizon were leaping into the sky. One may surmise that this belief was ancient in Israel, but it does not appear in her literature until the Book of Enoch.

Under the structure of the universe, therefore, five regions are to be distinguished. First, there was the *Tehom* or Abyss of waters, which enveloped the whole creation described in Genesis 1. Second, there was the vast mass of the earth itself. This floated in the *Tehom*, the latter somehow encroaching on it and covering parts of it in the Seas. Third, the earth held up a vast, hard dome, which kept the *Tehom* from overwhelming the earth. Below this there were the heavenly regions, the habitat of spirits, good and bad. Fourth, there was the surface of the earth, the home of man. Fifth, within the earth there was a vast series of interconnected caverns, called Sheol or Hades. Along with these five, in the Hellenistic period, there appears a belief in three great fires, one within the earth, the other two at the far East and the far West. It needs to be emphasized that, while the universe had several parts, it was *one* universe. The phrase 'the heaven(s) and the earth' does, indeed, occur, but, as the context regularly shows, these are not separate things, but parts of one thing, as, say, the parts of a gun are in the phrase 'lock, stock, and barrel'. Under the Hebrew phrase, again, 'the earth' includes Sheol, for this is in the middle of the earth's mass. It need hardly be added that the concept of a 'spiritual universe', which, being non-spatial and non-physical, is independent of the 'universe of things', is not biblical.

From this account of the universe it follows that, whether the Hebrews had any concept of empty 'space' or not, it was in the concrete contents of 'space' that they were interested. It was the same with 'time'. The Hebrews' interest lay in the concrete contents of 'time'—that is, if the word be used to cover the future as well as the past and present, in *history*. Today this appears in the claim that for the Hebrew, God was primarily 'God of history'. For him the chief questions about the LORD were 'What has He *done?* What is He *doing?* What is He *going to do?*' This doctrine of history also prevailed in the Hebrew doctrine of *man*. Primarily man is 'man in history', for, to use a modern phrase, it is history that 'has value'. For societies, therefore—especially the nation and the family—the desirable thing was that they should live on and on and on in history; for centuries, similarly, the desirable thing for the individual was that he should live *long*, for, until late Old Testament times, it was believed that, when he died, he dropped out of history. He 'slept' unendingly in Sheol, and a sleeper is a man who does nothing—i.e. has no part in the activity that is history. At a certain stage in Hebrew history—with the Prophets and Apocalyptists—the concept arose that history falls into a number of 'ages', to use a later word, and this concept crystallized into the belief that there are two Ages, separated by the Day of the Lord. Before it there was the Age of Sin, after it the Age of Righteousness—but both of them were parts of history, even though the second belonged wholly to the future. At a very late stage in the Old Testament story the belief arose that good men would return from Sheol to take their part in history once more. Only so could they be true 'men' again. This belief, of course, continues in the New Testament. The details of these ideas will be examined later. The immediate point is that the concept of history and its value forms part of the permanent background of this study.

At this point it should be noted that Biblical Symbolism is what may be called '*historical* symbolism', and is therefore to be distinguished from other kinds. In Jotham's parable, for example, 'the bramble' (Jg 9[14]) does not stand for 'pretentiousness', but for a particular pretentious man, Abimelech, who is part of history.

Similarly, when Jesus 'spoke in parables', His symbols did not stand for theoretical principles, but for concrete, historical action. 'The sower', for instance, was Himself at work in history. The use of symbolism has a supreme example in Apocalyptic, and, as Apocalyptic has a large part in this book, it is important to note that the Apocalyptists' symbolism is also 'historical'. When, for instance, Daniel sees a 'ram with two horns', this does not merely symbolize 'brute force', but an actual empire (Dn 8^{20}); or, when Esdras sees 'a lion roaring out of the wood' he is not merely symbolizing 'might', but the Messiah who is to take a part in history (2 Es 12^{31f}); or, when John of Patmos accumulates symbols in describing his vision of 'one like unto a son of man', none of them is to be taken literally, but all are symbolic of the characteristics of a real, historical person, Christ (Rev 1$^{13-16}$). In Apocalyptic it is not always possible to be sure which details are symbolic and which literal; indeed, it is likely that the Apocalyptist himself did not much consider the point; but this matters comparatively little, for the symbol always stands for something more real than itself. It is not to be dismissed, as it sometimes is today, as 'merely symbolic'—that is, something imaginary—that is, something that may be ignored. It is possible, for example, and even probable, that when John of Patmos wrote of 'the lake of fire' and 'the gates of pearl', he was speaking symbolically, for he has some claims to be the greatest symbolist in history—but both phrases symbolize the actual, the concrete, the historical (the last word, as already explained, including past, present, and future history). In the Bible there are no symbols either for *mere* ideas or *mere* ideals. In this situation there is no need, even if there were space, to ask below whether any particular phrase is symbolic or not. It is enough that it stands for something 'real', in the modern sense of that word.

The belief that death is by dissolution appears to be universal, the word 'dissolution' implying that a man is a composite whole of which the parts fall asunder at death. But different peoples give different accounts of the several parts. The Hebrew distinguished four parts or *elements in a man*. There was the *neshamah* ('breath'), which comes and goes in the act of breathing. There was the *nephesh*, a word that has no exact English equivalent but which combines the ideas of 'life' and 'soul'. *Nephesh* is sometimes used to describe the whole man (e.g. Ex 1^5), for 'My *nephesh*' may be used as equivalent for 'me' (e.g. Ps 6⁴), and, when a woman 'binds her *nephesh*' in a vow, she 'binds herself' (Nu 30³¹)—and so with the other personal pronouns. In other words, while there are passages where a man *has* a *nephesh*, there are others where a man *is* a *nephesh*. Then there was the *basar* ('flesh') which denotes the 'stuff' of which the different parts of the body are made—the term for the whole body (*geviyyah*) being rare. The fourth element in man is *ruach* ('spirit'). The word, which originally meant 'wind', occurs often in the phrase 'The *Ruach* of the LORD' and parallel phrases, and this *ruach* sometimes 'came upon' particular men and possessed them (e.g. Jg 15¹⁴, 2 K 2¹⁵), but the use of the word to describe an element in *every* man's nature, rare before the Exile (e.g. Gn 4¹⁸), becomes common with Ezekiel (e.g. 21⁷, 36²⁶). Animals, like men, have a *nephesh* (the phrase rendered 'living creature' in Gn 2¹⁹ being '*nephesh* of life'), but men, like God, have a *ruach*. It should be noted that, so long as a man is alive, each of the four constituents of his nature, including 'flesh', is alive too.

In LXX there are regular Greek renderings for all these terms, and the New Testament inherits these. For *neshamah* the term is *pnoē*, but, as it happens, this element in man's nature is only once named in the New Testament (Ac 17²⁵). For *nephesh* the regular word is *psychē*, which is sometimes translated by 'life' and sometimes by 'soul' (e.g. RV text and margin in Mt 16²⁵). An animal has a *psyche* (e.g. Rev 8⁹). 'My *psyche*' sometimes stands for 'I' (e.g. Mk 14³⁴), and the plural may mean 'men' (e.g. Ac 2⁴¹). The term for the whole body, *sōma*, is commoner than *geviyyah* in the Old Testament. *Sarx*, the term for *basar* ('flesh'), has four distinguishable meanings in the New Testament, but, so far as is needed under the present subject, these are distinguished later. For *ruach* the regular word is *pneuma* ('spirit'), which, like *ruach*, originally meant 'wind' (cf Jn 3⁸). *Pneuma*, of course, is also used for 'the Spirit of God'. This is a very summary statement, made in preparation for the question: 'What happens to the various parts of a man when he dies?' For a full discussion of a very complicated subject, the reader is referred to *The Bible Doctrine of Man*.

A note may be added about the use of the terms 'judge' and 'judgement' in this book. In the Bible every king is judge, for judgement was a function of kingship. When a king judged a man, he did two things: (*a*) decide and declare whether the man's ways were good or bad, and (*b*) reward or punish him accordingly.

Often, of course, the two went together, but they are none the less distinct. The range of a king's judgement was much wider than in a modern criminal court, which confines itself to a particular crime. The word 'judge' might be used either of (*a*) or (*b*)—or of both. Since God is King, it follows that He is also Judge and the final Judge. The passages relevant to the Divine judgement under (*a*) have been examined in the writer's earlier volume on the *Bible Doctrine of Sin and of the Ways of God with Sinners*. While the two functions cannot always be kept separate, in this book it is the second concept—God's assignment of rewards and punishments, particularly at the Last Judgement (e.g. Mt $25^{31\text{ff}}$, 2 Cor 5^{10})—that is the main subject. There are passages where the assignment of punishment only, and not of reward, is in mind (e.g. Jn 3^{18}, Rev 17^1). In these passages 'to judge' means 'to condemn'.

THE OLD TESTAMENT

CHAPTER TWO

THE RULE OF GOD—PAST, PRESENT, AND FUTURE

THE Hebrew doctrine of the Future has been put in a few simple words: 'They shall be my people, and I will be their God.' The saying belongs to Jeremiah and Ezekiel, but, like other such epitomizing phrases, it had long antecedents. Its roots were in the history of Israel. The antecedents may be briefly considered.

It is generally agreed that, while the earliest extant Hebrew documents, denominated J and E, were not written till somewhere round 850-750 BC, they contain traditions, whether oral or already written down, from a much earlier time. These traditions fall into three groups—the traditions of the period from Adam to Noah, the traditions of the Three Patriarchs, and the traditions of Moses and the Exodus. It is not pertinent here to ask how far these traditions are historical, for the present subject is Hebrew *doctrine*, and, as with other ancient peoples, the doctrines or beliefs of Israel are embodied in their traditions, whether historical or not.

The first group of traditions is contained in Genesis 1-11. A large part of these chapters is assigned to the document P, which belongs to a much later period than J and E. Broadly speaking, the parts assigned to P are the later story of Creation (Gn 1) and the genealogies. The remainder, which belongs to J and E, is a series of stories. One subject links them all—sin. There is the story of the sin of Adam and Eve, then of the sin of Cain and of the fate of the Cainites, then of the universal sin that spread from the intercourse of the angels with women, and finally, of the universal fate of sinners in the Flood and the salvation of 'righteous Noah'. But the group of stories also exhibits the ways of God with sinners, and to do this is their motif. Adam and Eve deserved to die, but God condemned them instead to the fag of the field and the pains of child-birth—and their descendants with them. Cain deserved to die, but, instead he was 'driven out from the presence of the LORD' (Gn 4^{14-16})—that is, God would have no more to do either with him or his descendant peoples.

This is a dire punishment, but not the worst. In the Flood the uttermost punishment is, indeed, inflicted—but God forthwith binds Himself never to 'smite every living thing' again (Gn 8^{21}). All the stories illustrate the ways of the Lord of History in a world of sin. It is presupposed that God can do what He will with mankind. While early Israel believed that there were other gods (e.g. Jg 11^{24}), here they are ignored, for they do not count when the LORD takes a decision. Again, all the stories assume that the LORD made men to be 'righteous', like Noah (Gn 7^1)—i.e. He made all mankind to be 'his people'. The story of the Tower of Babel (Gn 11$^{1-9}$) is a kind of appendix to this group. After the Flood, it is assumed, all mankind has again turned to sin and there is no knowing what evil it will do if it remains united. God, therefore, dooms it to be many-tongued and scatters it. *Dividit et imperat.* The early Hebrews believed that God had long ago decided that the nations that filled their world should survive, even though they were sinful—that for the most part He let them go their own way—but that, when He chose, He could do what He would with them. This is a doctrine of God in history.

The next group of traditions (Gn 12ff) contrasts with the first group. It tells, on the one hand, of three men who live in 'covenant' with God and always do His will, and on the other hand, of His continuous faithfulness to them. They are 'wandering Arameans' (Dt 26^5), who seem helpless, but God redeems them from all evil (Gn 48^{16}), and it is 'well with them'. It is taken for granted that they are righteous, as Abraham's question in the story of Sodom shows—'Wilt thou consume the righteous with the wicked?' (Gn 18^{23}). (To say that Jacob was a knave, for instance in his dealings with Laban, is to judge him by the ethics of a later time.) The story of Sodom shows too that God could do what He would with 'sinners of the Gentiles'. Though He usually let them alone, He could make an exception when He would. It seems to the present writer that there is another reference to the 'nations' in the repeated phrase 'In thee (and thy seed) shall all the families (nations) of the earth be blessed' (or 'bless themselves') (Gn 12^3, 18^{18}, 22^{18}, 26^4, 28^{14}). This requires that the word '*eretz* in the passage is to be translated 'earth' and not 'land (of Israel)'. Jeremiah took it so (Jer 4^2) as did Sirach, who defines the phrase as 'all men' (Sir 44^{21f}). If this be right, then the Hebrews believed that God had another purpose for 'the nations' than just to let them alone. The idea lay fallow century after century, but it did not die. It is beside the point to say that Israel 'did nothing about it', for it was something that God was to do, not Israel. This, however, is not the main message of the tradition. The burden of the Stories of the Patriarchs is that God keeps covenant with the men who keep it with Him, and 'blesses' them *in this life*, and will prosper their 'seed' after them by giving them a land of their own. This is a doctrine of the future.

In the traditions of ancient peoples there is no mention of periods of disaster except when they are the prelude of triumph. This was so with Israel. The third group of traditions, which tells of the triumph of the Exodus, begins with the sorry plight of Israel in Egypt, *sans* explanation of the centuries of her slavery there. For the present writer this sojourn lies behind the passage where the LORD uses the much-discussed phrase: 'I will be what I will be' (Ex 3$^{13-15}$). Moses expects that, when he tells the captives that 'the God of (their) fathers' will now deliver them, they will ask: 'What is his name?' For the Hebrew the 'name' of a God was the organ of his power—as, for instance, in the sentence: 'The name of the God of Jacob set thee up on high' (Ps 20^1). The Hebrews say to Moses, in effect: 'We have heard what great things our God did for our far-away fathers, but He has done nothing for us for many, many years. Why should we expect that He will manifest His name in power now?' God replies, 'I will be what I will be'—that is: 'You shall learn what I am by what I am now going to do.' And they do so learn! Their God proceeds to show that, when He will, He can do what He will with the empire of Egypt—not to mention such smaller peoples as the Amalekites and the Amorites of Og and Sihon. The next focal point is at Sinai. Its significant word is: 'Ye have seen what I did unto the Egyptians, and how I bare you on eagles' wings, and brought you unto myself. Now, therefore, if ye will obey my voice indeed, and keep my covenant, then shall ye be a *segullah* unto me from among all peoples: for all the earth is mine' (Ex 19^{4f}). The Hebrew word *segullah* means 'a precious, personal possession'. For instance, while David was lord of all Israel, he had a *segullah*, a private treasure (1 Ch 29^3). Similarly, while 'all the earth' (with its many nations) is God's, Israel is to be His *segullah*. In reply to God's challenge 'all the people answered together, and said, All that the LORD hath spoken will we do' (Ex 19^8)—a pledge that is repeated when the LORD has spoken further (24$^{3, 7}$). What He says on Sinai, as the Hebrews believed when J and E were written, is gathered in the Decalogue and the so-called 'Book of the Covenant'. The ethical element is pronounced in the first and far from absent in the second. At the end of the latter God pledges Himself to give Israel Canaan (23^{20-33}), if only they do not 'transgress' (verse 21). In brief: 'If ye will be my people, I will be your God.'

So far the third group of traditions does hardly more than apply the beliefs of the other two to a new situation. But, even while Moses is still 'in the mount', the people, led by Aaron, its priest, commits the sin of the Golden Bull (Ex 32). But for Moses' intercession the LORD would have 'consumed' Israel—a first instance of the belief that God will spare His people when they sin because of the faithful in it (cf. Nu $14^{11\text{ff}}$). After this the story is of sin after sin. For instance, in the Story of the Spies (Nu 14), the people do not believe that the LORD is master of nations and can wipe out the Canaanites before them, even to the Sons of Anak. He therefore condemns every one of them to die in the Wilderness (verses 29ff), a sign that while the emphasis is on the nation (i.e. on a societary unit), individualism is not absent. There is no need to recapitulate the story of the Forty Years in the Wilderness. One pattern runs through almost the whole of it—the people rebel, Moses saves them. But Moses is 'the servant of the LORD' (Ex 4^{10}, etc.). God fulfils His purpose and brings them to Canaan in spite of themselves. The Wilderness is the first instance of the typical Old Testament situation—there is the sinful mass; there is Moses, and a handful of others (Joshua, Caleb, and, for the most part, Aaron) who are faithful; and there is the LORD, master of history all the time.

It is the Deuteronomists who, starting from the various groups of traditions, first enunciated a clear doctrine of the future. It is assumed here that this school of teachers took its rise before the time of Jeremiah, won a victory under Josiah, and went on with its work undespairingly till the middle of the Exile. The primary work of the school is the Book of Deuteronomy, but it also edited, to a greater or less degree, all the books from Joshua to Kings apart from Ruth. It would be easy to show how it resumes the various doctrines expressed or implied in the early traditions. For instance, Moses, the ostensible speaker throughout the book, reminds Israel of her 'Fathers', the Patriarchs, over forty times (e.g. Dt $4^{31,\ 37}$). Or again, Israel is the LORD's *segullah*, whom, if she keeps His commandments, He will 'set on high above all the nations which he hath made' (Dt 26^{16-19}; cf. 7^6, 14^2). But it is the doctrine of the future that the Deuteronomists developed that is significant. It is expressed, for example, in 30^{15-20}, from which some phrases may be quoted: 'Behold, I have set before thee this day life and good, and death and evil. . . . If thine heart turn away; . . . I denounce unto you this day that ye shall surely perish. . . . I call heaven and earth to witness against you this day that I have set before thee this day life and death, the blessing and the curse: therefore choose life, that thou mayest live, thou and thy seed: to love the LORD thy God, to obey his voice, and to cleave unto him; for he is thy life and the length of thy days, that thou mayest dwell in the land which the LORD sware unto thy fathers, to Abraham, to Isaac, and to Jacob, to give them.' This is the burden of a number of other passages—for instance, of the tremendous sermon of Chapter 28, with its final picture of a return to the Egypt from which the LORD had delivered the Israelites under Moses, but with the new horror that they shall be glad to 'sell themselves' into a new slavery but are denied even this last refuge of the miserable (28^{68}). This is the last word in a cumulative curse of fifty-four verses. Before it (verses 1-14) there is an account of the blessings of a faithful people. Both blessing and curse relate wholly to a future in this life and this world. The curse comes last and is so prolonged because the chief purpose of the Deuteronomists is warning. It is their answer to an implicit claim, which might be put into a few words—'The LORD is the God of Israel, and He will save His people, whatever they do as, indeed, the story of the Exodus itself shows. Did not the LORD give the land to our fathers, though through the forty years they sinned and sinned?' It could be claimed too that the 'saviours' whom God had raised up in the days of the Judges had delivered Israel, good or bad. To this the Deuteronomists replied by putting these stories into a 'Deuteronomic frame-work', wherein they say 'It was to a repentant people that God raised up saviours' (e.g. Jg 3^9). In brief, the Deuteronomists preached from this text: 'The LORD will be your God *if* ye will be His people,—and not else.' But this is not their last word. In 30^{1-10} they expect that Israel, now in Exile, will 'return unto the LORD', who will 'circumcise (her) heart' and pour His boons on a loyal people. Completing their book in the Exile, and looking at Jehoiachin, the forlorn scion of the House of David (2 K 25^{27-30}), they declare that, while God will discipline that House, its 'throne shall be established always' (2 S 7$^{12-16}$ D), and, where there is a king, there is a people. In the days when Bel of Babylon seemed to have crushed Jahveh of Israel, these men amazingly passed from the old assumption that 'other gods' are helpless before the LORD to the assertion that there are no such gods and that, on Israel's return to Him, He 'will not fail (her)' (Dt 4$^{30f, 35, 39}$). Like Hosea, the Deuteronomists believed that, while the LORD declared that his people ('*am*) were now 'No people of mine' (*lo-'ammi*), He would again call them 'My people ('*ammi*) (Hos 1^9, 2^1). All this Jeremiah and Ezekiel, contemporaries of the Deuteronomists, gathered into the simple phrase: 'They shall be my people, and I will be their God' (Jer 11^4, 24^7, 30^{22}, Ez 11^{20}, 14^{11}, 36^{28}). There is no need to say that He would do for them all that a god should do. This doctrine of the future persists throughout the rest of the Bible.

The doctrine that the Deuteronomists drew from the past, the Prophets applied to the present. Their line stretches from Amos to Trito-Isaiah, a period of two centuries and a half. It was a time of World Wars, the 'world' of those days stretching from Nineveh and Babylon to Egypt. Every nation within it, small and great, was swept into the swirl of war after war. In it the little kingdoms of Israel and Judah would seem like mere flotsam. Their Prophets declared, however, that 'the LORD', being God of History, was master of all the nations all the time, deciding which should triumph and which should fall. In earlier days He had, for the most part, let other nations alone, even though they were all sinful. Now He lets none of them alone. In discussing the Prophetic evidence there is no need here to deal with the problem of the authorship of particular passages, for it is the doctrine of the Prophets as a whole that is under examination. The Apocalypses (Isa 24-7, Joel, Zec 9-14, Dn) are taken later.

The Prophets' teaching might be gathered under one word: 'Day.' Its use to describe a victory was old in Israel. For instance, the Hebrews called Gideon's victory 'The Day of Midian', and Jehu's victory 'The Day of Jezreel' (Isa 9^4, Hos 1^{4f}). These were 'Days of the LORD'. No doubt it was also used of other victories of the Lord's past. It is quite likely, for instance, that the Hebrews used the phrases 'The Day of Sodom' and 'the Day of Sisera'—just as the early Muhammadans used such phrases as 'The Day of Ohod'. In Amos's time the Northern Hebrews used the word, not only of the LORD's past victories, but of a *future* victory (Am 5^{18}), as Prussian officers drank to 'the Day' in the Kaiser's time. Probably, living in the time of the second Jeroboam's temporary success, they meant a 'Day of Aram'. The Prophets use the term to denote a coming 'Day of the LORD' about a hundred and fifty times. It may be used also of oracles where it does not happen to occur—for instance, the Book of Nahum tells of the 'Day of Nineveh', and, in the collections of oracles against nations gathered in Isaiah, Jeremiah, and Ezekiel, every oracle describes a 'Day of the LORD'. The word only occurs in two texts in Deutero-Isaiah, but they are significant. In one the time of the prophecy is a 'Day of Salvation' (49^8). This does not merely mean that the Exiles are now to return to Palestine, but that, when they reach it, they will enjoy a 'salvation' that shall be everlasting (51$^{4-6}$; cf. 55^{13}). Similarly, in the other passage, which declares that in the coming 'day' of deliverance God will cry to His people 'Behold, here I am', He also declares that 'henceforth' Jerusalem shall be holy, strong, and glad (52$^{1-6}$). Deutero-Isaiah expected a 'Day of the LORD' in the full sense of the phrase and expected it to follow immediately on the Return. Trito-Isaiah does not use the word 'Day' in this sense at all, but who can deny that such passages as Isa 60 and 66$^{10-24}$ describe the Day of the LORD? Or, to take a single sentence, surely the words 'Behold, the LORD hath declared unto the end of the earth, Say ye to the daughter of Zion, thy salvation cometh' (62^{11}) announce a Day of the LORD. The truth is that *all* the Prophets think in terms of 'the Days of the LORD'. The words 'time' and 'year' are occasionally used as synonyms (e.g. Jer 46^{21}, Isa 61^2). In a period of World Wars the LORD was once more 'a man of war' (Ex 15^3). This is what 'I will be what I will be' means now.

When a Prophet foretells a Day of the LORD, he always expects it *soon*. Here, as in some other ways, Amos leads the line. His hearers did not deny that there would some time be an 'evil Day', but they 'put it far away' (Am 6^3), saying, in effect, that it did not concern them, and claiming that the Day that was near would be a Day of Victory (5^{18}). Amos's reply is that the next 'Day of the LORD' will be 'darkness and not light' and that it will come 'now' (6^7; cf. Nah 1^{13}). Other Prophets use such phrases as 'yet a little while' (Hos 1^4, Isa 29^{17}) and 'at hand' (Isa 13^6, Zeph 1^7). Here too of course, the idea may be present without the word. The Prophets were preachers and preachers do not threaten punishments to their hearers that will not arrive for centuries! Ezekiel speaks for the whole line when he cries: 'An end is come, the end is come . . . the time is come, the day is near' (Ezk 7⁶ᶠ).

The Prophets applied their doctrine in a kind of ascending scale, as history demanded. While Amos speaks of such little peoples as Edom and Moab (1³–2¹⁶), later Prophets deal with 'world empires'. For instance, Isaiah, to whom mighty Assyria is a mere tool in the hands of God, declares that its Day is near (10¹², ²⁷), and Jeremiah, for whom Nebuchadnezzar is no more than the 'servant' of the LORD's anger, tells that 'the time of his own land' will come (27⁶ᶠ). Ezekiel extends the teaching to Tyre, the mistress of the seas, and to Gog, a name for the hordes that roamed beyond the bounds of civilization (26²ᶠ, 38²ᶠᶠ). As Assyria and Babylon carried war through the world of that time, there are references to 'many nations' (*10*—e.g. Mic 4¹¹; Ezk 26³), and many more to 'all nations' (*31*—e.g. Am 9⁹; Isa 14²⁶, 34²). Both phrases are especially frequent in Jeremiah (e.g. 22⁸, 25¹⁵, ¹⁷). This Prophet's oracle of 'the Cup of the Fury of the LORD' may be specially noted (25¹⁵⁻³¹). Here there is a list of 'all the kingdoms of the world, which are upon the face of the earth' that far outstretches the empire of Assyria or Babylon, and the synonym 'all flesh' (verses 26, 31) is used to denote that all mankind is weak before the LORD. A victory over 'all the nations' is *ipso facto* the last of the 'Days of the LORD', and might be called *par excellence* '*The* Day of the LORD'. Similarly the oracle of Isa 66¹⁰⁻²⁴, where 'all flesh' significantly occurs (verses 16, 23), is an oracle of the last of the series of Days.

The Days of Doom are all Days of punishment for sin. In war, as in other things, the LORD's 'ways are not as man's ways'. As Amos says again and again, a Day is the LORD's reply to a people's repeated 'transgressions' (1³–2¹⁶). A Day of Doom is sometimes called a 'Day' or 'Time' or 'Year of Visitation' (e.g. Hos 9⁷, Isa 10³, Mic 7⁴, Jer 46²¹, 48⁴⁴). This means that the LORD has come to see what a nation is doing, finds that she is sinful, and punishes her. Usually, as in the whole Bible, it is just taken for granted that the 'Gentiles' are sinful, but the sins of Israel and Judah are often mentioned. For instance, Hosea speaks of 'the multitude of thine iniquity' (9⁷); for Isaiah the sins of Judah are as 'scarlet' (1¹⁸); Jeremiah stands in the gate of the Temple to arraign the sinners who crowd into it' (7¹⁻¹¹); and so on. This is why a Day is a 'Day

18   THE RULE OF GOD—PAST, PRESENT, AND FUTURE

of Wrath' and 'Trouble' and 'Destruction' (e.g. Zeph 1^{15}, Jer 2^{27}, Ob 12).

For a Gentile nation a 'Day of the LORD' was an 'end'. Here there are two Hebrew words. The first is *qētz*, which comes from a root meaning 'to cut off'. It occurs first in Amos—'The end is come for my people Israel' (8^2)—and, for instance, Jeremiah cries to Babylon: 'Thine end is come' (51^{13}). Its best illustration is in Ezk 7^{2-6}, where it occurs four times as a kind of interjection. The other word is *kalah*, from a root meaning 'complete', and well rendered by 'a full end'. In twenty-one passages Prophets declare that the LORD will make a 'full end' of one nation or another (e.g. Jer 5^{18}, Ezk 11^{13}, Nah 1^8, Zeph 1^{18}). Here a verse in Jeremiah is notable. He declares that the LORD will '*not* make a full end' of Judah, but *will* make a full end of all the nations whither (he) has scattered (her)' (30^{11}; cf. 46^{28}). It should be noted that to announce the 'end' of a people does not mean that every man belonging to it will perish, but that, considered as a 'nation' or 'kingdom' or what is today called a 'state', it will perish. A 'day of the LORD' is, indeed, a 'Day of Slaughter' (e.g. Isa 10^{20}, Jer 12^3, Ezk 21^{28}, Ob 9), but not of extermination. For instance, while Amos expects that the 'end' of Israel is near, he expects too that there will be 'wandering' survivors (8^{11f}; cf. 7^8). Similarly, Ezekiel expects that in the Day of Jerusalem, there will be those that 'escape' (Ezk 24^{25f}; cf. Isa 17^6, Nah 3^{18}, etc.). When Jeremiah says that the LORD will 'make a full end of all the nations' (30^{11}), he does not mean that God will exterminate mankind, but that there shall no more be any kingdom but His own.

For *Israel* there was to be a 'Day' of Punishment but not an 'End'. It is true that Amos expects an 'End' for Northern Israel (Am 8^2), and some think that Micah foretold one for Judah (e.g. Mic 3^{12}), contradictory oracles in both books not being genuine —but these Prophets are exceptions. A few examples of the idea that Israel will survive her 'Day' may be mentioned. Hosea ends an oracle of hope (2^{16-23}) with the words, 'I will say to *Lo-ammi*, Thou art my people, and they shall say, My God'; Isaiah, followed by two other Prophets, declares that a 'remnant shall return, even the remnant of Jacob, unto the mighty God' (10^{20-3}; cf. Zeph 3^{10-13}, Zech 8^{11-13}); Jeremiah foretells what may be called a 'Day of Salvation' (cf. Isa 49^8); Ezekiel promises faithful exiles that the LORD will again give them 'the land of Israel' (11^{17}). Other

THE RULE OF GOD—PAST, PRESENT, AND FUTURE

pertinent texts will be quoted later. A note may be made about the doctrine of the 'remnant' or 'residue'. *It* is the true Israel, and it is *this* Israel that will survive; the remainder of so-called Israel perishing. But the 'remnant' does not merely survive; it becomes a great people—a new Israel. For instance, in Zeph 3^{11-20} the LORD 'takes away' the 'proud and haughty' majority, leaving only a 'remnant' of poor and afflicted people' (verses 11f), but, with this nucleus, He will show Himself 'mighty' in Jerusalem and 'make (Israel) a name and a praise among all the peoples of the earth' (verses 17, 20). Similarly, Ezekiel declares that the LORD will 'judge between the fat cattle and the lean cattle' (36^{20}), and Trito-Isaiah, in his oracle of the final Day, after describing the joy of the faithful, tells of the horrible fate of 'the men who have transgressed against me' (66^{24}). Here God deals with Hebrews one by one, i.e. in a series of oracles about nations taken societarily, individualism intrudes (cf. Jer 31^{30}, Ezk 18^{20}).

On a Day of the LORD's anger, whether for ruin or 'visitation', war had its usual grim fellows—fire and sword, pestilence and famine (e.g. Am 1^4, Hos 8^{14}, Jer 24^{10}, Ezk 7^{15}, Isa 51^{19}, 66^{15f}). Often there was exile too for survivors (e.g. Jer 15^{2-4}). In Isa 34 there is an unparalleled picture of the desolation of a dis-peopled land. But the God of Nature also took action, for He and the God of History are one. In the Day of Egypt the Nile dries up and becomes stinking and in the Day of Babylon her own streams overwhelm her (Isa 19^{5-7}, Jer 51^{36-44}). There is 'thunder and earthquake and whirlwind and tempest' (e.g. Isa 29^6). The sun itself will set at noon (Am 8^9; cf. Jer 15^8, Mic 3^6). All this is just a vast illustration of the way in which, in Hebrew thought, the universe is the framework of history, or, in abstract terms, 'space' the arena of 'time'. 'Behold, what desolations He hath made in the earth.' The Hebrew, looking down on Sodom from his hills, knew what a Day of Doom was.

The phrase 'Day of Salvation' will serve to denote the oppositive concept, for, though the phrase is rare, the idea is everywhere. The phrase 'in that Day' occurs about twenty times with this connotation (e.g. Hos 2^{16}, Isa 10^{20}, Jer 30^8, Ezk 29^{21}, Mic 7^{12}, Isa 52^6), 'the days come' occurs seventeen times in Amos and Jeremiah—sometimes of doom (e.g. Am 4^2, Jer 7^{32-4}), and sometimes of hope (e.g. Jer 16^{14f}, 33^{14-18}); 'in those days' (*9*) on the other hand, is confined to oracles of hope (e.g. Jer 3^{16}, 50^4, Zech 8^{23}

except in one text (Ezk 38^{16}), the longer phrase, 'in the latter days', when used by Prophets (*8*), always occurs in similar oracles of hope, which are not confined to Israel (e.g. Hos 3^5, Jer 23^{20}, 48^{47}). In one passage, indeed, it is used of 'all nations' (Isa 2^2). Its literal meaning is 'in the end of the days'—that is, 'in the final period of history'. Hence LXX often renders by 'in the last days' (*eschatos*). 'The Day of Salvation' is always the *final* 'Day of the LORD' (cf. Hos 2^{18}, Jer 31$^{35-7}$, Ezk 37^{25f}, Am 9^{15}, etc.). It ends the Era of Sin and begins the Era of Righteousness. For the Hebrew these were the two parts of history.

The 'Day of Salvation' is primarily the Day of *righteous Israel*. A few examples out of many may be quoted—in Hosea God promises 'I will betroth thee unto me in righteousness' (2^{19}); Isaiah declares that Jerusalem is to be called 'The City of Righteousness' (1^{26}), and for Jeremiah 'The LORD is our righteousness' (33^{16}); in Deutero-Isaiah the LORD has glad tidings for those who 'follow after righteousness' (51$^{1, 7}$), and Trito-Isaiah declares 'Thy people shall be all righteous' (60^{21}); Zechariah sums all up in the phrase 'They shall be my people, and I will be their God, in truth and in righteousness' (8^8). Malachi's postscript to prophecy may be mentioned here. On the Day the LORD will purge Israel from dross by fire as a refiner purges silver (Mal 3^2), but first another Elijah will preach repentance, not without effect (4^{5f}), and the faithful will be safe, for they are the LORD's *segullah* (3^{16f}).

Most of the Prophets, making the usual Old Testament assumption that a man or a race can be righteous if it will, are content to leave it there. With Jeremiah and Ezekiel this is not so. For them Israel will sin again unless she is a different Israel. They declare that God will therefore change her nature—'After those days, saith the LORD, I will put my law in their inward parts, and in their heart will I write it; and (so) I will be their God and they shall be my people' (Jer 31^{33}); 'A new heart also will I give you, and a new spirit will I put within you. . . . And I will put my spirit within you . . . and (so) ye shall be my people, and I will be your God' (Ezk 36$^{26-8}$). There is no need to say that the Prophecies of the New Covenant and the New Spirit are among the great Old Testament oracles.

Of 'the latter days' the prophets have left many descriptions, but all these display the same characteristics. Five terms may be used as titles—'the LORD', 'Peace', 'the Land', 'the King', and 'the City'. The fundamental idea, *fons et origo* of all the rest, is religious. Israel will be *the* LORD's *people*. This has already been illustrated in the texts quoted under 'righteousness'. A few other phrases will further interpret the concept—'(Ye are) the sons of the living God' (Hos 1^{10}); 'They shall worship the LORD in the holy mountain at Jerusalem' (Isa 27^{13}); 'One shall say, I am the LORD's . . . and another shall write on his hand, Unto the LORD' (Isa 44^5); 'Thou shalt delight thyself in the LORD' (Isa 58^{14}); 'They shall walk up and down in (my) name, saith the LORD' (Zech 10^{12}). Jeremiah has the summary word in the prophecy of the New Covenant—'They shall all know me (as person knows person), from the least of them unto the greatest of them, saith the LORD' (Jer 31^{34}). Here is both an individual and what is now called a 'spiritual' religion. All the rest of the Prophets' account of 'the latter days' describes happiness, but for them happiness is just God's response to holiness.

For a people over whose land war after ruthless war has passed generation after generation the first boon is *peace*. This appears in such texts as Mic 5^5, Jer 29^{11}, Ezk 34^{25}, and Zech 9^{9f}, but it may be sufficiently illustrated from oracles gathered in the present Book of Isaiah. Here the Coming King is 'Prince of Peace' and the future Son of Jesse will reign over a realm where 'the wolf shall dwell with the lamb' (Isa 9^{6f}, 11$^{6-9}$). Elsewhere there are the familiar phrases, 'The work of righteousness shall be peace' (32^7), 'How beautiful upon the mountains are the feet of him that . . . publisheth peace' (52^7), 'Ye shall go out with joy, and be led forth with peace' (55^{12}), 'Behold, I will extend peace to her like a river' (66^{12}), 'Neither shall they learn war any more' (2^4).

Israel was an agricultural people, and for her, granted peace, prosperity depended on the land. Long ago the LORD had given Palestine, *the Land*, to her fathers; in the Era of Sin there had often been drought and famine and desolation; in 'the latter days' 'the land that was desolate shall become like the Garden of Eden' (Ezk 36^{35}). As under Days of Doom, nature and history go together, and what is now called 'miracle' is just a rare act of God. There is, for instance, a promise that 'the corn and the wine and the oil' shall all cry '(We were) God-sown!' (Hos 2^{21f}); sun and moon are to shine as never before (Isa 30^{26}); there is to be joy for sorrow because of the overflowing plenty (Jer 31$^{10-14}$); it will take so many months to gather the harvest that the reaper of one year's yield will find the sower of the next year's seed treading on his heels (Am 9^{13}); a trickle of water issuing from 'the sanctuary' shall deepen and deepen as it teems down the steeps of Jeshimon to sweeten the Sea of Salt (Ezk 47$^{1-12}$); peace is the seed and prosperity the fruit (Zech 8^{12}). As so often, Trito-Isaiah puts the crown on the series—'Behold, I create *new heavens and a new earth*; and the former things shall not be remembered, nor come into mind. But be ye glad and rejoice always in that which I create; for, behold I create Jerusalem into a rejoicing and her people into a joy' (Isa 65^{17f}). Here the word *bara'* ('create') is used three times. It does not always mean 'create out of nothing' (cf. Ezk 21^{19}), and here it means 're-fashion', as is clear in the phrase 'create ... her people a joy'. These are the same 'people' transformed (cf. Ps 51^{10}). As the context shows (verses 16-19), the meaning is that the universe, the city, and the righteous remnant in it, shall all be rid of the 'troubles' of the former days and burst into joy, for the LORD Himself now 're-joices in Jerusalem and joys in (his) people'. 'The joy of the LORD' thrills in all the passages of prosperity. Yet there is no hint anywhere that in the Latter Days men would live for ever. There can be no doubt that it was taken for granted that 'in those days' every righteous man would live a long, prosperous and happy life and then be 'gathered to his fathers' in peace (cf. Isa 65^{20}).

The main subject of the Oracles of the Future is the Future Nation, for the nation was the chief society of the world of the Prophets. *Ipso facto*, too, every nation had a god and a king—that is, a divine king and a human king, who, in one way or another, 'went together'. It is rare for the LORD to be called 'king of Israel', since, as He was Israel's God, He was, of course, Israel's king. Occasionally, however, a Hebrew writer calls Him 'king' for some special reason (e.g. 1 S 12^{12}, Isa 6^5). This is sometimes so when Prophets are looking to 'the latter days' (e.g. Isa 33^{22}, 43^{15}, 44^6, Zeph 3^{15}), their purpose being to encourage their hearers. As one of them says, their 'Redeemer; the King of Israel', is 'the LORD of hosts', who is 'the first and the last', and beside whom 'there is no god' (Isa 44^6). Another says that 'the LORD shall reign' over the future 'strong nation for ever' (Mic 4^7). But in the Old Testament the word is normally used of human kings. The Prophets speak of the Future King about twenty times. Several of them mention such a king in order to say that, almost of course, he will be of David's line (Hos 3^4, Isa 16^5, 55^{3f}, Jer 30^9, Ezk 34^{23f}). Probably they all thought so. But there are six passages that might be called 'Oracles of the Coming King', for they describe him and his rule at some length.

Three of these oracles are found in the present Book of Isaiah. One of them (Isa 32^{1-8}) does not say that the Coming King is of David's line, but this is perhaps assumed. It gives itself to a description of the way in which a true king will judge his people. There are two chief ideas—first, 'a king shall reign in righteousness' and therefore, for those who are wronged by mightier neighbours, he will be 'a hiding-place from the wind' and 'as rivers of water in a dry place'. Here, in contradiction to such texts as Isa 60^{21} (cf. 65^{20}), there are still evil men in the coming realm—but they will no longer prevail. The ruling idea is that of a righteous *State*. The rest of the oracle appears to describe a king who will infallibly distinguish between suitors. In modern law-courts it is often hard to find out the truth, but it was much more so when disputants came before an Eastern king, disputing and pleading and lying and vituperating. But there will be no deceiving the king that is to be. His rule, therefore, will astonish, vindicate, and delight the 'meek and needy'.

A second oracle (Isa 9^{1-7}) gives an instance where a Prophet starts from contemporary history, passes to the Day of the LORD, and then, without pause, to the Coming King. Galilee, the most distant part of the Land, is to be delivered either from a long 'darkness', or a recent disaster, or both, by a victory as decisive as in 'the Day of Midian'—and then a king of the House of David will reign. He had already been 'born'. He will have four names —'Wonderful Counsellor' (i.e. he will know how to rule), 'Mighty God' (i.e. he will have the power of God behind him), 'Everlasting Father' (i.e. he will always be the 'Father of his People'), and 'Prince of Peace'. His 'rule' will spread and spread and last for ever in righteousness. Finally, no might of man, but 'the zeal of the LORD of hosts shall perform this'—an axiom sometimes just taken for granted.

The third oracle (Isa 11^{1-9}) is placed just after a prophecy of the LORD's destruction of Assyria (Isa 10^{33f}). Here the Davidic king is called 'a shoot (*chōter*) out of the stock of Jesse and a branch (*nētzer*) out of his roots', as when an old stump of a tree puts forth a young sapling. Four characteristics mark this Son of Jesse. First, 'the spirit of the LORD shall rest upon him', equipping him with every gift that a perfect king needs. Next, delighting in 'the fear of the LORD', he will rule with insight and righteousness.

Here, as in 32^{1-8}, there are still wicked men left, but the king will 'slay them with the breath of his lips' and vindicate the 'meek'. But third, 'girt' with righteousness and faithfulness, he will so rule that there will be no more wicked men, the wolf and leopard and lion and bear dwelling in peace with the lamb and the kid and the calf and the cow, with 'a little child' to lead them all, while babies make friends with asps. This is perhaps the most famous picture of peace in literature. Finally, the reason for this transfiguration ends the oracle—'They shall not hurt nor destroy in all my holy mountain (i.e. Palestine), for the Land shall be full of the knowledge of the LORD as the waters cover the sea'. Here, of course, 'knowledge' means, after the Hebrew fashion, such knowledge as issues in life. The Shoot of Jesse is to rule the LORD's people in the LORD's peace.

The 'Bethlehem Ephrathah' Oracle (Mic 5^{2-4}) is part of a longer passage (Mic 4^6–5^9), which seems to be composite, since it expects both Assyrian attack and the Babylonian Captivity. The Coming King will drive Assyria back and lead Israel to overthrow her and the 'many nations' of her empire (5^{5-9}). This is a prophecy of a Day rather than of the Latter Days. It is peculiar because the human king takes part in a Day (cf. 2^{13}). Under Babylon the Prophet foretells exile but declares that it is to be the 'travail of Israel' ($4^{10}, 5^3$)—that is, an agony that ends in joy. Now she has no true king (4^9), but one is to be born—not, however, from the *City* of David (for cities are anathema to this Prophet—cf. $3^{12}, 5^{11}$), but from his old *village*, Bethlehem, that seems so feeble. This Coming King will be the true Shepherd of Israel 'in the strength of the LORD, in the majesty of the name of the LORD his God', and '*now* shall he be great unto the ends of the earth' ($5^{2, 4}$).

There remain Jeremiah's two prophecies of the 'Branch' or 'Sprout (*tzemach*)' from the 'root' of David (Jer $23^{5-8}, 33^{14-26}$). Here the Babylonians have already taken their captives into exile, and Jeremiah foretells their return. As appears elsewhere, he expected this in 'seventy years' (25^{11f}). Apparently the Prophet expected the king, whose name is to be 'The LORD our righteousness', to begin his reign as soon as the exile is over. North and South are to be one again (23^6). The wonder of the deliverance is to exceed the wonder of the Exodus itself (23^{7f}). From henceforth David 'shall never want a man to sit upon the throne of the house of Israel' (nor Levi a priest to offer sacrifices) (33^{17-24}).

THE RULE OF GOD—PAST, PRESENT, AND FUTURE 25

God pledges Himself to this by a covenant as unbreakable as His 'covenant of day and night' (33^{25f}). It is clear that, while each of the several oracles has its own emphasis, their general message is the same. The Coming King, being the LORD's true vicegerent, will fulfil perfectly the two chief functions of an Eastern king— he will rule his people in righteousness, mercy, and peace, and he will be mighty against other nations. Therefore the coming line of David will rule for ever. The term 'Messiah' does not occur in any of the six passages, but it is clear that the Coming King is 'the LORD's Anointed'.

In the Old Testament there are references to Hebrew 'cities' (e.g. 1 S 18^6, 1 K 12^{17}), but the Hebrew word (*'ir*) denotes any settlement, large or small. There is no doubt that, from the time when David took the Ark to Zion and Solomon built the Temple, Jerusalem was *par excellence* the City of Israel, and that it was the City of Israel because it was the City of the LORD. Yet, by the time of Jeremiah at latest, it had become the Capital of Israel's sin (e.g. Jer 7^{1-15}). Ezekiel, indeed, begins his prophecies with a vision of the LORD's speeding on a moving throne from sinful Jerusalem to the faithful by the Chebar (Ezk 1). None the less, the Prophets, except perhaps for Micah, believed that on the Day Jerusalem would again become the City of the LORD, with all that this meant. In the Prophetic books there are at least seventy references to the Future Jerusalem (or Zion). Of these some forty-five fall in the various parts of the present Book of Isaiah. A few typical examples may be given—'Thou shalt be called the City of Righteousness, the faithful city' (1^{26f}); 'Thine eyes shall see Jerusalem a quiet habitation, a tent that shall not be removed' (33^{20}); 'The ransomed of the LORD shall return, and come with singing unto Zion; and everlasting joy shall be upon their heads' (35^{10}); 'O thou that tellest good tidings to Zion' (40^9); 'A *go'el* shall come to Zion' (59^{20}). There are similar texts in other Prophets—e.g. 'At that time they shall call Jerusalem the throne of the LORD, and all the nations shall be gathered unto it' (Jer 3^{17}); 'And the name of the city from that day shall be, The-LORD-is-there' (Ezk 48^{35}); 'Saviours shall come up on mount Zion . . . and the kingdom shall be the LORD's' (Ob 21); 'Be glad and rejoice with all the heart, O daughter of Jerusalem' (Zeph 3^{14}); 'In this place will I give peace, saith the LORD of hosts' (Hag 2^9); 'Sing and rejoice, O daughter of Zion: for, lo, I come, and I will dwell in the midst of thee, saith the LORD' (Zec 2^{10}). Even in

Micah, whether by interpolation or not, there is the text 'Arise and thresh, O Daughter of Zion, for I will make thine horn iron . . . and thou shalt devote the gain (of many peoples) unto the LORD' (4^{13}). In two or three cases the text quoted is the Prophet's last word. Two longer passages may be mentioned. When the cleansed Temple is ready, Ezekiel sees 'the glory of the LORD' return to it (and therefore to the City), and the word rings: 'This is the place of my throne . . . where I will dwell in the midst of the children of Israel for ever' (43^7). In a complementary and splendid passage (Isa 60), Trito-Isaiah, addressing Jerusalem without naming her (cf. verses 10f), hails her as the light to which all mankind will throng—'Arise, shine, for thy light is come, and the glory of the LORD is risen upon thee'. All the passages, of course, depict a Jerusalem *on earth*.

The last passage named, with its picture of the gathering of peoples and their kings to the 'light' at Jerusalem (Isa 60^3), as well as two or three of the quotations just made, raise the question: 'What of the *Gentiles* in the Latter Days?' As already indicated, no independent Gentile *State* would be left, but there would be multitudes of survivors. These would still fall into separate 'peoples, and even their kings might be among the survivors. The Prophets have two replies to the question raised. Some of them teach what may be called 'the future Servility of the Gentiles', and others 'the future Salvation of the Gentiles'.

One of the most extreme examples of the doctrine of Servility, and perhaps the earliest, is found in Micah (7^{16f}). In it the fugitive nations, startled into silence by the happy fate of Israel, 'shall lick the dust like a serpent; like crawling things of the earth they shall come trembling out of their close places: they shall come with fear unto the LORD our God, and shall be afraid because of thee'. Here the frightened fugitives creep to the feet of Israel and so far worship her God as fear allows. Something approximating to this, of course, would happen whenever one Eastern king conquered another, as, for instance, the Black Obelisk of Shalmanezer III shows.

Another exponent of the doctrine of Servility is Deutero-Isaiah, the 'Servant Songs' being omitted. For instance, in one oracle (Isa 45^{14-17}) the Prophet, turning both to Egypt, the great rival of every empire in the biblical East, and to the further Ethiopians and Sabaeans, whom even Persia never conquered, declares that *they* shall come cringeing to their Hebrew masters, laden with chains and tribute. Even *they* will have learnt at last that the 'God of Israel', who has so long been a 'God that hideth (himself)', has all the time been the almighty God. In the oracle that follows next (45^{18-25}) the LORD calls the survivors, who have 'escaped of the nations' in the Day of Doom, to worship at His feet. He has sworn that they *shall*! In the Old Testament there is a worship of sincere dread. For Deutero-Isaiah there is another example in 49^{22-6}.

Trito-Isaiah has the same doctrine. For instance, he declares that the Gentiles, seeing that the LORD is the God almighty, will worship Him with the worship of sincere dread (59^{17-19}). Again, they are to serve His people under *corvée*, for they will bring all her sons that still remain in exile to Jerusalem from the ends of the earth 'on horses' and 'in chariots' and 'litters' (66^{20}). They are to fill the city with tribute and rebuild her walls (60^{5-10}). There is no exception in 56^{1-8}, for here the 'eunuchs' and 'sojourners' have chosen the worship of the LORD before the Day. This Prophet ends his book with a prophecy of the perpetual worship of 'all flesh' when they see the horrible fate of the enemies of the LORD (66^{23f}).

The doctrine of the Salvation of the Gentiles appears in Jeremiah. 'At that time,' he says, 'all the nations' are to forsake 'their evil heart' and gather to the name of the LORD, to Jerusalem' (3^{17}); they are to 'bless themselves' and 'glory' in him (4^2); they are to 'come from the ends of the earth', saying 'Our fathers have inherited nought but lies', and the LORD will teach them once for all the 'name' of the true God (16^{19-21}). In Ch. 18 this Prophet lays down the principle on which the LORD acts. If *any* nation, at the very instant of doom, turns from evil, God will spare it.

There is another oracle of salvation in Isa 2^{2-4}. Here the 'many nations flow to the mountain of the LORD's house' as naturally as rivers to the sea. He, now the universal God, rules mankind, and there is therefore universal peace—the Prophet using a figure drawn from a time when iron was scarce (cf. 1 S 13^{19-22}). The same oracle is included in Micah, though a contradictory verse is added (Mic 4^{1-5}).

In contrast to the rest of Deutero-Isaiah, the doctrine of the Salvation of the Gentiles is a chief burden of 'the Servant Songs'. In the first (42^{1-9})[1] the preacher foretells that when the Gentiles

---

[1] The First Song is usually taken to be 42^{1-4}; but some scholars would include the following five verses. [G.W.A.]

see the way in which the almighty LORD has saved the truly righteous Israel, even though its light was only a 'dimly burning wick', 'light' will burst upon them! They will amazedly learn that the righteous LORD is ready to make 'covenant' with *any righteous* people—and they will walk out of the dark prison of their ancient blindness to rejoice in His light. He will 'set His justice in the earth' by taking *them* into Covenant. In the second Song (49$^{1-6}$), while the phrase 'a *light* to the Gentiles' recurs, an old symbol is used in a paradox. From of old the LORD has drawn His '*sword*' to *destroy* (Jos 5^{13}; Jg 7^{20}), and Jeremiah had cried out because it seemed that He would never thrust it into its scabbard again (47^6; cf. Ezk 21^5). Now the Servant's 'mouth' is to be God's 'sword' so that He may *save* the Gentiles! Similarly, the Servant is depicted as the LORD's smoothed arrow, whose target is 'salvation' for the Gentiles! As the present writer thinks, the last and greatest Song (Isa 52^{13}–53^{12}) should be added. In Chapter 53 he would assign verses 1-6 to the nations and kings of 52^{15}, verses 7-10 to the Prophet, and verses 11f to the LORD Himself. On this account it is the Gentile peoples and kings who, 'startled' by the 'prosperity' or success that is now the Servant's lot (52^{13}), cry: 'Surely *he* hath borne *our* sickness . . . and with *his* stripes *we* are healed.' If this exposition be accepted, this is the climax of the doctrine of the Salvation of the Gentiles.

Isaiah 11$^{1-9}$ has often been included here. It has been interpreted above of the salvation of Israel, but the verse that follows the oracle, 'And it shall come to pass in that day that the root of Jesse, which standeth for a rallying-standard for the peoples, unto him shall the nations seek; and his rest (after victory) shall be glory' (11^{10}), shows that, at least sometimes, the wild beasts were taken to be symbols of the Gentile nations, who are now at peace with Israel under the righteous rule of the LORD. This means that it is the 'earth', not 'the land', that is 'full of the knowledge of the LORD'.

The next passage is Zechariah 2$^{10-13}$. Here the meaning is clear. Foretelling that *Israel* will no longer follow 'iniquity' (3^9), and calling the daughter of Zion to 'sing and rejoice' because the LORD will now 'dwell in the midst' of her, the Prophet declares that 'many nations will join themselves to the LORD' and become His 'people', for will not 'all flesh' fall 'silent' as they see what the LORD does when He 'rouses' Himself in His holiness to bless Israel (2$^{10-13}$)? Later (8$^{18-23}$) the same Prophet declares that Israel will turn her 'fasts' in feasts when she sees 'many peoples and strong nations' hastening in harmony to Jerusalem 'to intreat the favour of the LORD'. They 'lay hold of the skirts' of any Jewish exile who is on pilgrimage to Jerusalem, to follow him there, for they have 'heard' that 'God is with' the Jews to make them 'a blessing among the nations' (verse 23).

After Malachi there were no more Prophets in Israel until the Baptist came.[2] It does not follow, however, that their message was forgotten. There are two Psalms (2 and 110) which, while they may have been written to celebrate some Hebrew ruler's victory, were probably applied to a future king when put into the Psalter. Another Psalm (72), while it does not mention a Day, describes the universal rule of a righteous and faithful king. But the chief evidence lies elsewhere. It was in this period that the oracles of the Prophets were collected, edited, and finally put into the Canon. This means that their account of the Future became authoritative for Israel. The belief in the Day and with it the belief in the splendid future of a righteous Israel was an integral part of the Hebrew creed. The editors even added oracles of hope where they were missing—e.g. they gave Amos a happy ending (9^{11-15}). Probably the Canon of the Prophets was complete by *c.* 250 BC. By then the Oracles of the Doom of the Nations had been fulfilled—not, indeed, in every Prophetic detail, but in their main import. For instance, the empires or States of Assyria and Babylon and Pharaonic Egypt were no more. At one point there was indeed a problem of which the Canonists could not be unaware. The Prophets had foretold a Day for this nation and that, which would come *soon*, and, however far the meaning of 'soon' were stretched, this had not always happened. For instance, it was not until Alexander's time that Tyre fell. Israel learnt that the postponement of a Day did not invalidate a prophecy. Probably the ultimate fulfilment of other prophecies helped in face of the postponement of the final Day. It had not come in either of its parts. There were still heathen States—in particular, the Seleucid and Ptolemaic Empires—and the triumph of Isael tarried and tarried. Jewish teachers seem to have explained the delay on the ground that Israel was not yet righteous (cf. Ezr 9^{6-15}, Tob 3^{2-6}). But, whatever the puzzle, they

---

[2] There were prophets after Malachi (e.g. Neh 6^{14}); and parts of the prophetic literature are assigned to later dates. [G.W.A.]

put the oracles of *the* Day into the Canon. However inscrutable the ways of the LORD might be, in this way or that, Israel held resolutely to the belief that the God of History at last would get His way in history. 'They shall be my people, and I will be their God.'

Though this is not the place to argue the point, the present writer would maintain that the Hebrew Doctrine of the Future is unique. It is too often put among secondary things, as though a belief that at last God's name will be hallowed, His kingdom will come, and His will done, *on earth*, could be a minor matter. Is it not pertinent at a time when world-wars again rack mankind? There is in it a social message, for it may be summarized under the words 'Let a nation be righteous, and God will do the rest', and as is shown at length in *The Bible Doctrine of Society*, the concept of righteousness is intrinsically social. But the Old Testament Doctrine of the Future is incomplete. It tells of the future of societies and, by implication, of the future of individuals so long as they are alive, but it says nothing of the future of the multitudes of individuals who, having lived their lives on earth, die. As will appear in the next chapter, for by far the greater part of the Old Testament writings, these multitudes just drop out of history and have no future. This, indeed, is so nearly taken for granted that the evidence for the belief has to be laboriously collected from references and allusions. Yet, in the last Old Testament period there began to be protests against it. This is shown in the chapter on 'The *Chasid* and Sheol'. Their plea, in brief, is: 'Surely the God with whom we are in fellowship will not leave us out of His future realm.' In the last chapter on the Old Testament it will be found that Apocalyptists began to give the confident answer: 'He will not; He will bring you back from the dead to share His kingdom.' Meanwhile, it is to be noted that the Hebrew doctrine of the Future is a doctrine of future *History*.

A note may be added on the use of the phrase 'Kingdom of God' and its synonyms in the Old Testament. They occur about twenty times. There are four Hebrew terms and one Aramaic, but they are all derived from the root *malak*, and it is difficult to make any distinction in their meanings. The original idea is 'kingship' (and therefore 'rule',) not 'realm', but, as the *Oxford Hebrew Lexicon* shows, the meaning 'realm' occurs under at least three of them— 'realm' sometimes denoting 'the *people* ruled'. For instance, this is the meaning in the phrase, 'Ye shall be unto me a kingdom of priests' (Ex 19^6 E). It is assumed from first to last that the LORD is 'king of *Israel*', for they are His 'people'. The first appearance of the phrases is in Hezekiah's prayer when he is facing the seemingly omnipotent Assyria—'Thou art the God, even thou alone, of all the kingdoms of the earth' (2 K 19^{15}). Here 'kingdoms' means 'realms', as also in a similar passage in 2 Ch 20^6, and, under the phrase 'rule in the kingdom of men', in Dn $4^{17, 25, 32}$, 5^{21}. This is probably so too in 1 Ch 17^{14} and 28^5. On the other hand, the original meaning appears in 'Thine is the kingship, O LORD' (1 Ch 29^{11}; cf. 2 Ch 13^8), and in such phrases in the Psalter as 'The kingship is the LORD's', 'His kingship ruleth over all', 'Thy kingship is an everlasting kingship' (Ps 22^{28}, 103^{19}, 145^{13}; cf. 45^6, 145^{11}). The culminating example is in the Aramaic part of Daniel, where it is the watch-word of the writer as he faces Epiphanes. He uses the phrase 'His kingship is an everlasting kingship, and his dominion is from generation to generation' or a closely similar phrase seven times (Dn $4^{3, 17, 25, 32, 34}$, 5^{21}, 6^{26}). Here, of course, 'everlasting' covers all history, past, present, and future. In 7^{27}, as the context shows, a like phrase is used of the Everlasting Kingship of God *after* the Judgement. Here 'the saints' are His vicegerents. In 7^{14}, where the vicegerent is 'one like unto a son of man', it is he who is to exercise everlasting kingship and universal dominion. Of course, in all the passages the ideas of 'kingship' and 'kingdom', 'rule' and 'realm', are both present, for the words are correlative. Where there is a king there are subjects, and where there are subjects there is a king.

CHAPTER THREE

DEATH AND SHEOL

IN THIS chapter seven subjects are considered—the Hebrew attitude to death, the dispersal of the constituent parts of a man when he dies, the burial of the body, Sheol, the 'sleep' of death, oracles of dead nations, and the relation of God to Sheol. Sometimes—for instance, in the New Testament—the word 'death' is used, not only for the event called 'death' that ends a man's life, but for this *and* the state that follows it, or even for the state only. Here it is used solely of the event in history that closes a man's life.

Death, of course, considered as an event in history, is universal. 'The hour and article of death' comes to every man—that is, death is an individualistic phenomenon. Even in the Flood each man died alone. What did the Hebrew believe about this phenomenon? In the story of Adam and Eve he had an account of its origin which taught that it came by the will of God because man sinned. Yet the event called 'death' does not occur in the story, for Adam and Eve are spared. Further, in the next story Cain, the first murderer, is spared. God does, indeed, drown all sinners in the Flood—but only to declare that He will not do so again. He confines Himself to limiting the life of sinful man to a hundred and twenty years (Gn 6³ J). This means that, while a sinner deserves to die and to die at once, God does not usually exact this penalty. Here is the beginning of the doctrine of the 'long-suffering' of God. As to the belief that 'in Adam all die', it is not found in the Old Testament, but belongs to the period of Second Esdras and Paul. The terms 'death' (*maveth*) and 'die' (*muth*), of course, are very frequent in the Old Testament (*930*), but when they describe 'natural' death, as they usually do, they simply denote the common lot of man. It is taken for granted that 'it is appointed unto man once to die'. Even in Ps 90 this is so, for its burden is that a miserable *life*, not death, is the punishment of sinners, just as in the next Psalm a long and satisfying *life* is the guerdon of the saint (Ps 91¹⁶). To read the Ninetieth Psalm at funerals is to misinterpret it.

In the Book of Genesis there is the suggestion that, while death is the lot of all men, *righteous* men live unusually long lives. This idea lies behind the genealogy of the descendants of Seth before the Flood (Gn 5⁶⁻³¹). This list of multi-centenarians means little to a modern reader, but it is a list of the *good* men who linked Seth with Noah and so with Abraham, and its message is that these *good* men lived very long lives, rejoicing in abundance of 'sons and daughters', and died in a good old age. As it stands the chapter belongs to the Priestly document, but no doubt the Priests were here using very old traditions. Illogically they include Adam—but they do not mean to suggest that, when he died at the age of nine hundred and thirty, the primeval curse at last slew him! After his expulsion from Eden he is treated as a good man. The idea is that the LORD gives good men the blessings of a long life. The recurrent phrase 'and he died' has no hint of punishment about it nor any suggestion that a good man ought not to die at all. In the later Old Testament the question 'Why do the righteous *suffer?*' is clamant, but the question 'Why do righteous men *die?*' is never asked. Of course, too, the idea that good men, as such, live extraordinarily long lives could not survive. The three Patriarchs, indeed, out-lasted the 'hundred and twenty years' named in the text already quoted, and Moses reached that limit, but men would soon learn that the most that a man could expect was seventy or eighty years. They would learn too that a life of this length is not the monopoly of good men. Some Psalmists protested that bad men ought not to live so long, but, no doubt, most men just accepted the facts. 'Natural' death in old age was no more than the moment when a man ceased to live. There is no suggestion that God slew him then. As will be found later, when at last some Jews began to cry out that death was not the fit end for a righteous man, they did not ask to escape death, but to live again after it.

It is otherwise under *premature* death, especially when it is sudden and violent. Here the passages fall into three classes. First, there are the instances of murder. Here, of course, it is men who kill, not God. Second, there are the passages where God is said to slay men, and third, those where some man, acting on God's behalf, slays another—as when Joshua slew the Canaanites, or Samuel slew Agag, or Jehu slew Jezebel, or a king, being 'the LORD's anointed', executed a criminal (cf. 2 S 12⁵). The third class may be treated as a sub-division of the second. There are instances where it is simply said that 'the LORD slew' or 'smote' a man, as with Er (Gn 38⁷) and Uzzah (2 S 6⁷). In other stories the LORD uses nature to slay men, as when He 'caused it to rain upon the earth' at the Flood or 'rained brimstone on fire' on Sodom (Gn 7⁴, 19²⁴). In the earlier documents God may slay men merely because they are His and Israel's enemies, but when the Prophets and Deuteronomists 'moralized' Hebrew religion, 'enemy' became 'sinner', and the idea emerged that when God inflicted sudden death, it was punishment for sin. When a man 'died by the hand of God', two deductions were made—first, that, whether other men knew it or not, the man had sinned exceedingly; and second, that sudden death *per se* (without any question of what followed it in Sheol) was punishment for sin, because it deprived men of a part of man's normal life. Under the doctrine of the value of history, it was held that it is good to live a long life and evil to lose part of it.

There is a passage where the whole man, body and all, is 'swallowed' by Sheol (Nu 16²⁸⁻³³ JE; cf. Pr 1¹², Ps 55¹⁵, Isa 5¹⁴), but normally, of course, when a man 'went down to Sheol' (e.g. Gn 37³⁵, Ezk 31¹⁵, Job 7⁹)—still more when he went down into its 'depth' (e.g. Isa 14¹⁵, Ps 71²⁰, Pr 9¹⁸)—it is clear that it is not meant that the *whole* man did so, for his body remained in the grave and could be dug up. When a man died, the four constituent parts of the living man—the body, the *nephesh*, the breath, and the spirit—fell asunder. What happened to each of them? The body, of course, now a corpse, remained on earth. The *nephesh* passed to Sheol, as appears, for instance, in the following texts—'Thou hast loved my *nephesh* (so as to save it) from the pit of worthlessness' (Isa 38¹⁷), 'Thou wilt not leave my *nephesh* to Sheol' (Ps 16¹⁰), 'Thou hast delivered my *nephesh* from Sheol beneath' (Ps 86¹³). There are four such phrases in one passage in Job (33¹⁸⁻³⁰). A father's vigilant rod will 'deliver (his son's) *nephesh* from Sheol' (Pr 23¹⁴). The other two elements in man, the 'breath' and the 'spirit', may, for the present purpose, be taken together, it being remembered that the 'breath' was drawn from the air and that the original meaning of *ruach*, the word for 'spirit', was 'wind'. They are put together in Job 27³: 'For all the while my breath is in me, And the *ruach* of God is in my nostrils.' Similarly, a man dies when God 'gathers unto himself (the man's *ruach* and breath' (Job 34¹⁴). To lose 'the breath of the *ruach* of life' is to die (Gn 7²² J). Koheleth, describing death, says that 'the dust returns to the earth as it was, and the *ruach* returns to God who gave it' (Ec 12⁷)—i.e. both the body and the *ruach* return to that from which they came. Similarly, a Psalmist, in one of the very rare passages where *ruach* is ascribed to animals, declares that they die or live as God 'takes away' or 'sends forth' *ruach* (Ps 104²⁹ᶠ). It seems clear that the underlying idea is that God has a kind of great fund of air and wind from which He gives men 'breath' and *ruach* while they live, restoring both to the same fund when He wills that men shall die. Koheleth's phrase 'the *ruach* shall return to God who gave it', of course, does not mean that a dead man's *ruach* 'goes home to God', for in the next verse he takes up his refrain, 'Vanity of vanities; all is vanity', and he believed that men and animals have 'all one *ruach*' (Ec 12⁸, 3¹⁹). While *neshamah* and *ruach* are very different at other points in Old Testament teaching, at this point they go together. During a man's life-time God continually gives him both; when the man dies, God takes both away. It should be noted that the *ruach* does not pass to Sheol at death. The Old Testament knows nothing of 'spirits' there.

The Hebrews had a distinctive verb *qabar* (*72*) with a cognate noun *qeburah* (*14*), to denote the right way to treat a dead body. English words 'bury', 'burial', and 'grave' suggest digging, and this is not implied in the Hebrew words, though it is not excluded (cf. Lk 11⁴⁴). When they could, the Hebrews laid the bodies of their dead in caves. They were used, as a rule, for a number of bodies, each being laid in a niche cut in the sides of the cave. There was no coffin (cf. 2 K 13²⁰ᶠ). Sometimes the caves were 'hewn out', in whole or in part (e.g. 2 Ch 16¹⁴). The openings were closed sometimes having 'thresholds' (Ezk 43⁸). It seems unlikely that there were enough caves for all dead bodies, especially near the larger cities. At Jerusalem there were 'graves of the sons of the people' for common folk (Jer 26²³). It is at least possible that these were dug in the modern way (cf. Lk 11⁴⁴). This would suit such post-Exilic phrases as 'I shall lie down *in the dust*' (Job 7²¹; cf. 20¹¹, Isa 26¹⁹, Dn 12²), and 'the *worm* covereth them' (Job 21²⁶), for these do not apply so readily to a body on a shelf in a cave. It is clear, however, that to be buried in a cave was the desirable way. As with many other peoples, a corpse was 'unclean' (e.g. Nu 19¹⁴, Ezk 44²⁵).

Usually a people's beliefs, or some of them, may be inferred from the *ritual* of burial, but here Old Testament evidence is scanty. There would, of course, be the shrill 'lament' of the East (e.g. 1 S 28³, Jer 25³⁴). At a king's funeral men cried 'Woe! lord!', and one prophet, bewailing another, cried 'Woe! my brother!' (Jer 34⁵, 1 K 13³⁰). Men and women put on sackcloth and 'wallowed' in ashes (e.g. 2 S 3³¹, Jer 6²⁶). It would be wrong to infer that the mourners sorrowed because they believed that something evil awaited the dead any more than when one Christian mourns another. The wailing and so on would betoken their own loss. Another burial custom was the 'burning' of incense at kings' funerals. The most detailed text occurs at the burial of Asa, which shows that the body was also laid in spices— 'And they . . . laid him in the bed which was filled with sweet odours and divers kinds (of spices) prepared by the apothecaries' art; and they made a very great burning for him' (2 Ch 16¹⁴). On the other hand, of Jehoram, one of the worst Judean kings, the Chronicler writes: 'And his people made no burning for him, like the burning of his fathers. . . . And he departed without being desired' (2 Ch 21¹⁹ᶠ). There is no evidence that the 'burning' was a religious ceremony. Probably it is to be interpreted by the word 'honour' in the phrase 'And all Judah and the inhabitants of Jerusalem did honour to him [Hezekiah] at his death' (2 Ch 32³³). It is possible that the custom arose at some early date, and that at first it was an attempt to placate the dead man's 'spirit' (though this does not suit the use of *ruach* among the Hebrews), but this idea, if ever it existed, had died out by Jeremiah's time, for *he* refers to the custom as an innocent one (Jer 34⁴ᶠ), as does the Chronicler. Again, those who touched the body, like all others who were ritually unclean, would be purified by 'the water of impurity'. A whole chapter describes the preparation and use of this water (Nu 19). This shows that, while the priest prepared the water, which was kept for use when it was needed, any 'clean person' (verse 18) could sprinkle it upon the unclean man and so purify him. Finally, there was 'the breaking of bread' and the giving of 'the cup of consolation' to the mourners (Jer 16⁷). Here again it is clear that, whatever the far-away origin of the custom, by Jeremiah's time its use in Israel was wholly innocent. As a scornful reference of Sirach shows, outside Israel 'messes of meat' were uselessly laid upon graves (Sir 30¹⁸ᶠ), but these were not eaten by the mourners. Apparently 'eating in mourning' might cost a good deal (Dt 26¹⁴), perhaps because the poor gathered to share in the mourning and the meal (To 4^{16f}). It is to be noted that, so far as the evidence goes, there was no religious ceremony of any kind at funerals, unless the layman's sprinkling with the 'water of impurity' be called one.

Anthropological research shows that 'primitive' men *selected* the way in which it was 'proper' to get rid of a dead body and there would be some reason for the selection. In the Old Testament three ways of disposing of the dead are mentioned—burial, exposure, and cremation. The Hebrews practised burial, and, as the story of Machpelah shows, they believed that this was the right way from their earliest days. Probably they inherit the custom from still earlier times. Burial, unlike exposure and cremation, secured the continuance of the 'bones'. The Hebrews did not embalm, like the Egyptians, and so seek to preserve the whole body. Probably they lacked the skill to practise this highly technical and difficult art. But, when a corpse is buried, the bones, as distinct from the rest of the body, will go on existing indefinitely, as archaeological discoveries abundantly show. Some archaeologists claim that there are prehistoric skulls a million years old! While the men of Jabesh Gilead burnt the rest of the remains of Saul and Jonathan, they *buried* their bones (1 S 31^{12f}). Joseph's body was embalmed, but the Hebrew writer says that it was his *'bones'* that the Israelites carried to Canaan (Gn 50^{26}, Ex 13^{19}). In slaying a man the worst that one could do was to 'break his bones' (Nu 24^8; cf. Ps 34^{20}). The Hebrew idea of the right way with a dead body was to lay it on a niche or 'bed' in a cave, leaving the flesh to its slow decay and the 'bones' or skeleton in perpetual rest. Here the sense of the continuity of the family in history would be strong. In the cave of the family's 'burial place' the remains of its fathers for generations past lay in their separate niches, testifying to its age.

On the other hand, exposure and cremation were reckoned as dishonour and disaster. The men of Jabesh Gilead risked their lives to save the bodies of Saul and Jonathan from exposure (1 S 31^{11-13}). An exposed body would be the prey of beasts and vultures. Within a meal-time the dogs ate the whole body of Jezebel except her skull and hands and feet according to the curse of Elijah (2 K 9^{34-7}). Jeremiah foretold that the tombs of the men of Jerusalem from the kings downwards would be rifled and their bones spread abroad like dung (8^{1f}; cf. 16^{3-6}, 25^{33}). He also foretold (wrongly) that Jehoiakim should be 'buried with the burial of an ass'—i.e. should *not* be buried, but 'cast out, to the heat in the day and to the frost in the night' (22^{19}, 36^{30}). When an ox or sheep or goat grew unserviceable, it would be killed and eaten, but an ass, which was not eaten, would be worked till it died, and then its body flung into the open. Other examples could be added (Isa 22$^{16, 18}$, Ezk 6^5, Ps 141^7). Cremation was worse than exposure. Amos denounced the king of Moab 'because he burned the bones of the king of Edom into lime (Am 2^1; cf. 6^{10}, 2 K 23^{16}). Ezekiel, in a horrible oracle, depicts Jerusalem as a rusty caldron in which the LORD will boil its people and, when the flesh is well boiled, send the bones to be burned (Ezk 24$^{1-11}$). Finally, there is a passage, written soon after the Exile, where exposure and cremation go together (Isa 66^{24}). Here, when the Day of the Lord is over, men will 'go forth and look upon the carcasses of them that have transgressed against (him): for their worm shall not die, neither shall their fire be quenched; and they shall be an abhorring unto all flesh'. This refers to the great garbage heap or midden that would be outside Jerusalem as outside other ancient cities. A fire, kept perpetually burning, would slowly eat into it. Meanwhile worms would continually breed in it. The text does not describe worms and a fire *in Sheol*, but *on earth*. The phrase 'they shall be repulsive to all flesh' seems to be a reference to the nausea of the *effluvium* that would rise from the heap. It is possible that from the days of Josiah the midden at Jerusalem had been at 'Tophet in the valley of the children of Hinnom' (2 K 23^{10}). If so, it seems to have adjoined the crowded burial-places of the common people of the city (Jer 7^{31f}, 19$^{6-14}$). As shown later, at some unknown date the Hebrew phrase for 'valley of *Hinnom*', *gēy hinnom*, was Hellenized as *Gehenna*, and used of 'hell', the last words in Isaiah being then associated with it as a description of its torments. But *in the Old Testament* the 'valley of *Hinnom*' is a spot near Jerusalem, as is Trito-Isaiah's pile of corpses (cf. Isa 66^{24}). Whether they are to be identified or not in the Old Testament neither has anything to do with Sheol.

Why did the Hebrews so sedulously practise burial and loathe exposure and cremation? There were certainly four reasons. First, there was the power of immemorial custom, which is especially strong in the treatment of the dead. Second, there was the need to put away defilement. Even to touch a bone of the dead defiled a man (Nu 19^{16}; cf. Ezk 39$^{11-16}$). Third, there was the Hebrew respect for the body. It was a God-given and integral part of a man (e.g. Gn 2⁷), and should be honoured even when dead. The Hindu, despising the body, burns it; the Hebrew, valuing the body, kept it as long as might be. Fourth and chiefly, burial in a family grave expressed the sense of history. But was there not a fifth reason? Taken as a whole, the passages seem to imply that somehow burial was a boon to a dead man and exposure or cremation somehow a curse. In particular, the vehemence of the Prophetical passages seems to require this. It would follow that the ordinary man had believed from of old that burial was *somehow* a boon to the dead, and exposure or cremation a disaster, and that the Prophets moralized the doctrine —not, however, in general but in particular instances. They declared that certain bad men would *suffer* by exposure or cremation or both and that certain good men would be *blessed* by burial. Of course, it might be asked 'Can a corpse feel?', but it is quite usual for peoples to entertain feelings about the dead which are illogical. The word 'feelings' is appropriate for the ideas in question are not based on reason. When cremation was introduced into England there were those who shrank from it as though they 'instinctively felt' that it was cruel. It is said that, while Mussolini's corpse lay unburied, there were people who riddled it with bullets. Of course this was a sign of intense hatred, but was there not also some obscure feeling that somehow the bullets might hurt the dead dictator?

The Hebrew concept of Sheol has already been briefly described. What the word itself originally meant is not certain. It occurs sixty-five times in the Old Testament, and always in reference to the dead. The Hebrews had no other interest in the series of caverns within the earth. The idea that the dead go to these caverns is very ancient and widespread. Cave-burial can be traced as far back as Neolithic times, and its first Old Testament example, at Machpelah, is far from an early instance. Anthropologists have no agreed answer to the question: 'What was the origin of the idea that some part of a dead man went down into the cavern within the world?' In the Old Testament there is no attempt to explain it. Like their neighbours, the Hebrews inherited the idea from pre-historic times *sans* explanation. In the Authorized Version Sheol is sometimes rendered 'hell' (*31*) sometimes 'the grave' (*31*), and sometimes 'the pit' (*3*). The first two renderings are mistranslations. It is best to use 'Sheol' itself, as in the Revised Version (text or margin).

In consonance with the hoary antiquity of the idea, the term Sheol occurs six times, as a well-understood term, in the earliest Old Testament documents (e.g. Gn 37^{35} J, Nu 16^{30} JE). Men, however, often preferred to use such a euphemistic phrase as 'to sleep with his fathers'—just as today people sometimes avoid 'die' and say 'pass away'. In consequence the term 'Sheol' only occurs eleven times in the Books from Genesis to Esther, and three of these are in psalms (e.g. 1 S 2^6). It is more frequent in the heightened language of the Prophets (*19*), the Psalter (*16*), and Job (*8*), and even in the earnest speech of Proverbs (*11*). Examples are given later.

From Ezekiel onward two synonyms for 'Sheol' occur. Both have to be translated 'Pit'. One, *bōr* (*68*), can be used to mean a 'well' with water in it, but it is used also for empty wells (Gn 37$^{20-9}$; cf. Jer 38^6), and this is the use pertinent here. The other word, *shachath* (*23*), corresponds to 'pit' in English. It describes, for instance, the pit dug to trap animals (e.g. Ps 9^{15}, Ezk 19^4). When an animal was caught in one, it would be dragged out by ropes, even though they drag a man into the pit and not out of it (Ps 18^{4f}, 116^3, 94^{13}). The English Versions sometimes use 'destruction' or 'corruption' for *shachath* (e.g. Ps 16^{10}, 103^4). Here they follow LXX, but the Greek translators seem to have connected the word with a wrong Hebrew root. There can be little doubt that it describes something concrete, for it denotes a place into which men 'go down' (Job 33^{24}, Ps 30^9), and, in texts where it does not refer to death, it undoubtedly means 'pit' (e.g. Job 9^{31}, Ps 7^{15}, Pr 26^{27}). The famous text in Ps 16, therefore, should be rendered, with RV margin (as elsewhere): 'Thou wilt not leave my soul to Sheol, Neither wilt thou suffer thy holy one to see the Pit.' 'Pit' is used below both for *bor* and *shachath*.

There is yet another synonym, '*Abaddon*' (*6*). This late word occurs six times of Sheol (e.g. Job 26^6, Ps 88^{11}, Pr 15^{11}). It means 'destruction'. A thing is destroyed, or 'perishes', when it no longer fulfils its proper function. So, when asses or sheep stray, it can be said that they 'perish' (1 S 9^3, Ezk 34^4) even though they are still alive. What use are lost animals? A *man* is destroyed when he no longer lives, for 'to live' is just to fulfil his function. While 'Abaddon' does not occur until after the Exile, its verb, '*abad* is occasionally used earlier, as well as later, to mean 'die'.

In the earliest instance of this the context requires 'perish in Sheol' (Nu 16^{33} JE). Other examples, where Sheol is not named, are Mic 4^9, Jer 40^{15}, Job 31^{19}, Pr 31^6. In translating the various forms of *'abad*, three English terms, 'destroy' and 'lose' and 'perish', all need to be used.

A particular form of sudden and untimely death, drowning, may be considered at this point. It involves the *Tehom* or 'deep' as well as Sheol. The greatest instance of drowning, of course, is the Flood (Gn 6^9–9^{19}). Next there comes the drowning of the Egyptians in the Red Sea. Here the chief evidence comes from one of the oldest of Hebrew songs (Ex 15$^{1-18}$, ^{21}). The subject of this taunt-song surges up in its refrain: 'The horse and his rider hath (the LORD) thrown into the sea' (verses 1, 21). One element in the joy would be 'Hallelujah! Unburied!' The *Tehom* is mentioned three times (verses 4f, 8, 10). Here the prose story varies from the Song. In the prose story the Israelites cross on 'dry land' and their enemies' corpses are flung on the beach (verses 29f). In the Song, not only are the waters 'piled up' on either side for the Israelites' passages, but 'the deeps are *frozen* in the heart of the sea' lest they should sink into the *Tehom*. *Israel* walked through on ice! On the other hand, the Egyptians 'sank like lead in the noble waters' beneath them. They are engulfed in the *Tehom*. But then comes the phrase: 'The *earth* swallowed them.' This is Sheol without the word, for, as shown earlier, the Hebrews believed that there were passages between it and the *Tehom*. Similarly, Ezekiel prophesies that Babylon and her allies shall 'bring (Tyre) down to the Pit' by flinging this mistress of the ocean into 'the *heart* of the seas' (Ezk 28^8)—i.e. the depths of the *tehom* (cf. Ex 15^8). One way to Sheol was through the *Tehom*. In the next relevant passage (Ps 69) a faithful and forlorn Psalmist, crying out for God's help against the neighbours that never ceased to persecute him, begins with the words, 'Save me, O God, for waters have come as far as (my) *nephesh*'—that is, he is like a man sinking in a morass whose waters have risen as far as his lips (verses 1f). Another moment and his *nephesh* will be gone! Later he repeats the cry, adding: 'Let not the water-flood overwhelm me, Neither let the deep (*metzulah*) swallow me up; And let not the Pit shut her mouth upon me' (verses 14f). The term *metzulah* is used in the Song of Miriam for the *Tehom* (Ex 15^5; cf. Jon 2^3). Here again, drowned men pass through the *Tehom* to Sheol. When a man was drowned, his *nephesh* passed to Sheol like other men's. The calamity of drowning was that the *body* was not buried, but tossed about in the *Tehom*. In the Psalm of Jonah there is a vivid description of this horror (Jon 2$^{3-5}$).

While it is the dead man's *nephesh* that 'goes down' to Sheol, the word is not used to describe its inhabitants. No name is found for them before the Exile. This may be because the word was *tabu*, or because there was no occasion to mention these beings. When a name does occur it is used as if it were well-known—for instance, in Proverbs (2^{18}, 9^{18}, 21^{16}). The name is 'the *Rephaim*' (*8*). This derives from a Hebrew verb *rāphāh*, which means 'to be sunken' or 'slack'. The Rephaim are the Weaklings. The Revised Version margin renders the word by 'the shades', but the comparison of the dead to shadows is not Hebrew but Greek. Here again it is best to transliterate the Hebrew word, for there is no true English equivalent. 'Ghosts' will not serve because this word means 'spirits' and because its perspective is wrong. Today 'ghosts' normally 'walk' in this world; in the Old Testament the *Rephaim* helplessly sleep in Sheol. In one of the special passages discussed in a later chapter (Isa 14^9) they do indeed look and speak, but this is mentioned just because it is abnormal. In the discussion of another passage, the story of the Witch of Endor (where the name does not occur), it will be argued that it is possible for them to appear *outside* Sheol, but this too is abnormal. Again, even these Weaklings 'tremble' before God (Job 26^5), and can be called a 'congregation' (Pr 21^{16}), but the emphasis, as their name implies, is not on what they do but on their impotence. In a psalm where 'the *Rephaim*' and 'the dead' are synonyms, it is implied that, if God Himself 'showed wonders' to them, it would be useless (Ps 88$^{5, 10}$; cf. 115^{17})! Koheleth (9$^{1-6}$), declaring that a 'living dog is better than a dead lion', is thinking of dead men who do not even 'know anything'.

The comparison of death with sleep is very ancient and very common. A text in Job (3^{13}) gives the points of likeness: 'Now should I have lien down and been *quiet*; I should have *slept*; then had I been at *rest*.' It is an instance of 'emotional belief'. A dead man is as still as a sleeper; therefore he too is at peace. The comparison survives in modern poetry—e.g. in

> *Little he'll reck if they let him sleep on*
> *In the grave where a Briton has laid him.*

It concentrates on 'the good side' of death and is an optimistic account.

For the verb 'to sleep' (*yāshēn*) there is a synonym 'to lie down (to sleep)' (*shākab*), and they are here taken together. The phrase 'he slept with his fathers, and was buried', with slight variations, occurs about twenty times in the Books of Kings (e.g. 1 K 11^{43}, 14^{31}). It had perhaps become the conventional phrase for 'died and was buried', but a convention need not be merely formal. The phrases meant 'died a natural death'; for instance it is not used of Josiah, since he was put to death (2 K 23^{29f}; cf. 2 Ch 34^{28}). There is no ethical distinction made under the phrases, for they were used alike of good Judean kings and bad (e.g. 2 K 15^{38}, 16^{20}), and the first part of the phrase, 'to sleep with his fathers', is used even of the worst kings of the North (1 K 14^{20}, 22^{40}). This shorter phrase has earlier instances. It is used in suggesting to a man that the time will come when he will die (e.g. Dt 31^{16} JE, 2 S 7^{12}, 1 K 1^{21}). A third alternative phrase is 'to be gathered (*'asaph*) unto his people', which perhaps arose from a comparison with a shepherd folding his flock. This is used by the Priestly writers in the Pentateuch in speaking of the death of the Patriarchs and Moses (e.g. Gn 25^{8}, Dt 32^{50}). An earlier document has 'go to thy fathers in peace' (Gn 15^{15} JE). Much of the emotional force of the phrases depends upon the words 'thy fathers', and illustrates the same sense of family continuity as 'buried with his fathers', but here the idea of quiet and rest and peace is added.

Was the account of death as a kind of sleep constant in Israel? It will be found later that after the Exile some 'saints' reckoned it misery to abide in Sheol. Did the ethically neutral account continue alongside the new one? There is evidence that it did. The word 'sleep' is not often used to describe death in the Psalms, but it does occur to denote the *violent* death of sinners. For instance, it is used ironically when the phrase 'The stout-hearted have drowsed off to sleep' is used to describe slaughter (Ps 76$^{3-6}$; cf. Nah 3^{18}). Or again, one Psalmist complains that he is already 'like the *slain* that *lie down* in the grave' (Ps 88^{5}), and another cries out for God's rescue from his enemy lest too soon he 'sleep the (sleep of) death' (Ps 13^{3}). In contrast to the historical books there are writers who use 'sleep' when speaking of premature death (Jer 51$^{39, 57}$, Isa 43^{17}, Job 20^{11}). Again, at least in some of the Psalms where God's 'holy ones' cry out against their 'oppressors', they appeal to Him to put things right *here*, with the silent axiom (expressed in Ps 13) that there are no ethics where all sleep (e.g. Pss 44, 55, 74). Again, when, long after the Exile, the Chroniclers wrote their history of Judah, they were content to say that David, their favourite, 'died in a good old age, full of days, riches, and honour' (1 Ch 29[28]), and eleven times they followed the editors of the Books of Kings in saying that kings, good and bad, 'slept with their fathers' (e.g. 2 Ch 32[33], 33[20]), though they boggled when it came to the loathsome Joram (2 Ch 21[20]). They would perhaps write the phrase with some nostalgia, for there had been no king to bury in the ancient tombs for three hundred years. Similarly, the post-Exilic editors of the Pentateuch were content to say that Abraham, Ishmael, Isaac, Jacob, Aaron, and Moses, when they died, were 'gathered to their people' (Gn 25[8, 17], 35[29], 49[29, 33], Dt 32[50]—all P). For them good and bad fared alike in Sheol. It seems clear that, until the rise of Apocalyptic, this continued to be the common belief. It perhaps survived among the Sadducees even in New Testament times (Mk 12[18], Ac 23[8]). The 'saints' themselves, when they cry out against the misery of Sheol, assume that all are alike there, and long, not for a different lot in Sheol, but for a return from it. The normal Old Testament belief is that there are no ethical differences in Sheol.

Did the Hebrews think that the dead 'slept' in the grave or in Sheol or in both? If, as is likely, it was from the quiet of a corpse that the word was first used of the dead, the earliest answer would be 'in the grave'. Again, when a man's body was carried into the cave of his forefathers, the mourners might easily think, as they looked round it, that each ancestor lay asleep in his niche. The phrase 'lie down *in the dust*' occurs three times (Job 7[21], 20[11], 21[26]), and 'sleep *in the dust*' once (Dn 12[2]). On the other hand, Ezekiel seems to picture the dead as lying down in Sheol (Ezk 31[18], 32[27-30]), and it might be argued that as Abraham, Moses, Aaron, and David were not *buried* with their fathers, the phrases 'gathered to his people' (Gn 25[8] P, Dt 32[50] P) and 'slept with his fathers' (1 K 2[10]) must refer to Sheol. Jacob uses the same phrases to denote something that happened *before* burial (Gn 47[30] J, 49[29] P). To stress this use of the phrases, however, is perhaps to be logical overmuch. Yet a Psalmist passes easily from 'lie in the grave' to 'laid in the lowest pit' (Ps 88[5f]); in Job two longer passages, one describing the grave and the other speaking of Sheol, lie side by side (Job 14[7-15]); and an Apocalyptist unites 'dead bodies', 'ye that dwell in the dust', and *Rephaim* in a single promise of resurrection (Isa 26^{19}). There is a 'bed' both in the grave and in Sheol (2 Ch 16^{14}, Job 17^{13}; cf. Ps 139^{8}). Two conclusions are possible. The first is that the Hebrew believed both that the body slept in the grave and the *nephesh* in Sheol—though there is no hint how the two ideas were integrated. The other and more likely conclusion is that, like many other 'emotional beliefs', this one was both various and vague. If someone were to ask the question 'Where—in the grave or elsewhere?' reading the inscription '*Requiescat in pace*', could anyone say that there is a uniform and clear answer?

There is evidence that some Hebrews, at any rate, believed that certain people knew how to control the dead and bring them back 'here'. Under the doctrine of 'sleep', this would mean that necromancers could *wake* the dead. This belief probably lingered long (cf. Isa 65^{4}), but, at least as early as the days of Saul (1 S 28^{3}), necromancy was forbidden in Israel. The dead were to be left to sleep. Again, both the Egyptians and the Babylonians and probably the Canaanites, as archaeology shows, deposited in the grave articles for the use of the dead in their activities hereafter—i.e. they supposed that what was done for a dead man 'here' made a difference to him 'there'. If the archaeologists should some day prove that this was done in some Hebrew graves, this would only exhibit another heterodoxy. Sleepers have no use for tools, nor even, so long as they sleep, for food. The negative Hebrew belief was that the dead did nothing.

The Hebrew attitude to the dead was peculiar and perhaps unique. Israel was so obsessed with history—i.e. the life of man on earth—that for long centuries she all but ignored what happened outside it. Under the word 'sleep' the Hebrews united two beliefs, that a dead man was at rest, body and *nephesh*; and that it was the LORD's will that he should never do anything more. He had passed out of history.

Every man dies alone, even if others die at the same time, as in a battle or a shipwreck. All that has been said so far in this chapter illustrates this. But much of it also suggests that, when the *nephesh* has reached Sheol, it is solitary there. For instance a man is solitary when he is asleep. But there are two oracles which, taken literally, imply that there are *nations* in Sheol. On examination, however, it emerges that they are not to be taken literally, but symbolically, and that it is a mistake to generalize from them and deduce that the Hebrews believed that there are societies of some kind in Sheol. The bodies of a family might lie together in one grave, as at Machpelah, but there is no corresponding idea, either for the family or the nation, in Sheol.

The first of the two oracles (Ezk 32$^{17-32}$) purports to be a description of Sheol. Seven nations, great and small, which have already fallen before Babylon and 'lain down' in the Pit, greet Egypt on her arrival there—and 'Pharaoh' is 'comforted' to find them in Sheol! (verses 21, 31). In this oracle there are 'graves' *in Sheol* and 'bones' and 'weapons'! (verses 22f, 27). Clearly Ezekiel is transferring to Sheol what happened, not to the *nephashoth* of individuals when they 'go down to the Pit', but to the *bodies* which they leave on earth—in this case the *unburied* bodies on a stricken field. This gives a meaning to the phrase 'they have laid their swords under their heads' (verse 27). A soldier on service, when he slept, put his sword under his head, ready to his hand on any alarm—but this time the swoop of the foe is too quick for him. Ezekiel *pictures* Sheol as if it were a battle-field, for this will drive home his message: 'Dead and *done with!* Dead and *done with!*' Being a great symbolist he casts logical consistency to the winds. A nation with a carcase? An army of *corpses* strewn in the Pit? At some points he borrows from the normal Hebrew ideas about unburied bodies and the grave and Sheol, but it is quite wrong to take details from his abnormal descriptions and supposes them to illustrate the ideas of the ordinary Hebrew. For instance, if his dead warriors lie in Sheol with a soldier's weapons about them, it does not follow that the ordinary Hebrew thought that, when a dead man's *nephesh* passed to Sheol it took with it the tools of his particular craft. Nor does it follow that the ordinary Hebrew believed that men formed nations there. As well take Milton's description of Hell literally and deduce that his contemporaries believed that the fiends wear armour!

With a nameless Prophet of the later Exile it is Babylon that is to perish (Isa 14$^{3-23}$, especially verses 9-20). Here too an empire, personified in its king, goes down to Sheol (verse 9); here too its carcase lies un-buried on a battle-field (verses 19f). While Ezekiel says ironically that it 'comforts' Egypt to see the slaughtered heaps of her forerunners, here a personified Sheol awakes the 'he-goats' or kings of the dead nations to greet Babylon, describing her king the while as covered with 'worms' (verses 9-11)! In Ezekiel *no* nation has a grave, but here Babylon *alone* is grave-less (verses 18f). The other kings have 'houses'[1] and sit on thrones! But Sheol is king of kings. He says, in effect: 'Get up, ye kings, and come along! There's another of you here!' In the gloom the kings peer into the face of the newcomer with a startled: 'Is it you, Babylon? You? You?' It does not at all follow that the ordinary Hebrew believed that there were thrones in Sheol, with sleeping kings sitting(!) on them, or that the sleepers there sometimes awoke to walk and look and speak and listen. These two symbolic oracles do not prove that the Hebrew believed that nations preserved their unity in Sheol. There are only individuals there.

There is no doubt that, according to the Old Testament, it is for God to decide when a man is to die—that is, God is the master of the *event* called 'death'. It is true that men may interfere with His will here, as Cain did when he killed Abel, but this is only the extreme example of the Old Testament doctrine that man has a realm of freedom, and that he can so use it as to interfere with the sovereign will of God—that is, he can sin. The Hebrew believed that, just as it is for God to decide that a man shall be born, so it is for Him to decide when a man shall die—i.e. when he shall pass to Sheol. But has God anything to do with him *in Sheol?* What evidence there is shows that, while the LORD usually leaves men in Sheol, this is not because He must, but because He so wills.

The first passage is the story of the Witch of Endor (1 S 28[3-25]). It has often been compared to the Spiritualist *séances* of today, but it has not so often been asked: 'Which kind of *séance?*' Today, if A wishes to communicate with his dead friend B, he usually visits a medium. The latter then gets into touch with a 'control'—that is, someone 'in the beyond' with whom she or he is accustomed to confer. Then 'the control' gets into contact with B, and A and B reach each other *through* the 'control' and the medium. In this type of *séance* the dead man is not *seen* either by the medium or by the inquirer. In the story of Endor the woman 'cried with a loud voice' when she *saw* 'a god coming up out of the earth' (verse 13), as though she had not expected this. One purpose in the technique of magicians has always been protection from their visitants. If the technique fails, they are in great danger. Perhaps it is to the risk of losing mastery over her *'ob*,

---

[1] i.e. mausoleums. [G.W.A.]

to use the Hebrew word, that its 'mistress' refers when she says: 'I have put my life in my hand' (verse 21).

What is meant by *'ob* (*16*)? The derivation of the word is uncertain, but in Job 32^{19} it denotes skin 'bottles'. Here the impatient Elihu says: 'Behold, my belly is as wine that hath no vent; like new wineskins it is ready to burst.' Here the reference is to the *sound* that would come out of a distended skin bottle when its mouth was untied. *'Ob* might perhaps be rendered 'gurgler'. In twelve texts, including the instances in the story of Endor, LXX translates by *engastrimuthos*. This means 'one that speaks out of the belly'—that is, a 'ventriloquist'. Of old time an interview with a ventriloquist was counted a form of what is now called a *séance*. The ventriloquist himself, as well as his clients, thought that he heard the voice of some deceased man, or supernatural being, whom he called up by the contortions of his belly. In early times, at any rate, neither he nor his inquirers would think that the voice was *his* voice.[2] All this suits the *setting* of the story of Endor. The phrase 'mistress of an *'ob*' might be rendered 'a woman that had a familiar', using the last word in the old way as a noun, but not 'a familiar *spirit*', since, as noted above, for the Hebrews, the dead Samuel, like other dead men, would have no *ruach*. The woman would probably need to *interpret* the sounds. The *'ob* would be the 'control', who spoke for the dead man. But, to the woman's terror, she *saw* something as ventriloquists do not. *Saul*, on the other hand, like the clients in one kind of *séance*, saw nothing. When, however, Samuel spoke, Saul both heard and understood him. Apparently he had hoped that Samuel would help him even though 'the LORD had departed from him'. But Samuel, asking 'Why hast thou disquieted me? (i.e. disturbed my sleep)', speaks for the LORD. Would he do so unless the LORD had bidden him? Whatever the earlier answer may have been, there can be no doubt that, when the Deuteronomists left the story in the Book of Samuel, they took it to mean that the LORD had over-ridden the ventriloquist and her *'ob*, and Himself called up Samuel to tell Saul his doom. In other words, the story implies that the LORD could take action in Sheol if He would. Whatever in fact happened, this is what the Hebrews believed.

Among the stories of Elijah and Elisha four are relevant here. Three of these describe a resurrection—that is, the return of dead people to life here; the other tells how Elijah, instead of going

---

[2] For the facts about ventriloquism see the article in the *Encyclopaedia Britannica*.

down into Sheol, was 'taken up into the heavens'. There is no need to say that all four are miracles—that is, unusual acts of God.

Two of the resurrection stories are alike. The first tells how Elijah brought to life the dead son of the widow of Zarephath (1 K 17$^{17-24}$). He prayed and stretched himself on the child three times. God answered his prayer and the child's lost *nephesh* 'returned into his inward part' and 'he lived' (verses 17, 21f). In the longer story of Elisha (2 K 4$^{18-37}$), one of the most vibrant in the Bible, it seems clear that the child suffered from sun-stroke (verses 18f). Elisha 'prayed unto the LORD', who answered him by two stages. When the Prophet first stretched himself upon the boy, 'the flesh of the child waxed warm'. Then Elisha 'walked to and fro in the house', apparently to gather further power, and, on again stretching himself on the child, the boy 'sneezed seven times' (on one rendering of the Hebrew) and 'opened his eyes'. So Elisha 'made him to live' (2 K 8$^{1, 5}$). The child's *nephesh* is not mentioned, but its return is implied, especially in the last phrase. Similarly, in the third story (2 K 13^{20f}), when a dead man's body touched 'the bones of Elisha, he lived and stood up on his feet'. In all three stories it is implied that it was the LORD who worked the miracle through a notable 'man of God'. In him there was a God-given power, which to some degree was present even in his staff (2 K 4^{29}). What this power was is not stated, but only in the third story is the miracle a mere *monstrum*. In the other two the LORD, in answer to prayer, raises from the dead the two little children of two nameless but faithful women. The Hebrew axiom again is that God *can* raise the dead if He *will*, though this is not His usual way. If the Prophets' power be called *mana*, it only shows itself when the LORD will. The fourth story is that of Elijah's ascension (2 K 2$^{1-18}$), with which Enoch's may be taken (Gn 5$^{21-4}$ P). They show that the LORD can cheat Sheol if He will. They also imply that there are men for whom Sheol is not a fitting end, so anticipating the claim of the *Chasid*. It may be added that if 'the Servant of the Lord' be taken to be an individual, Isa 53^{9f} implies that he will rise from the dead.

To the stories of resurrection there may be added Ezekiel's oracle of the Valley of Dry Bones (37$^{1-14}$), for its basis is the belief that the LORD could raise the dead if He would. The Prophet is answering the exiles' cry of despair—'our bones are dried up, and our hope is lost; we are clean cut off' (verse 11)—i.e. 'We are like a dead man of whom there is nothing left but dry bones'. 'But', replies Ezekiel, using their own symbol, 'the LORD can make dry bones live, if He will.' In his vision there is first an earthquake that shakes the scattered bones into skeletons; then 'flesh' and 'skin' cover the skeletons, and they are corpses; and then the *ruach*—the dominant word, which has to be rendered both by 'breath' and 'wind' and 'spirit'—enters into the corpses and they stand up alive! Though neither the *nephesh* nor Sheol is mentioned, the burden of the vision is that the LORD can do anything He will, even to the raising of the dead. Similarly, on the exposition given above, the return from the Exile is symbolized under the resurrection of Jonah.

There are a few passages which show that God can not only bring the dead from Sheol, but is *Master of Sheol itself*. Amos declares that even if frightened sinners dig their way into Sheol, God will pluck them out of it (to punish them *here*) (Am 9^2). In a Deuteronomic song 'the fire of (God's) anger' 'devours the earth', 'burns into the lowest Sheol' and even 'sets on fire' the deeper 'foundations of the mountains' (Dt 32^{22}). This, of course, does not denote a perpetual fire in Sheol, an idea foreign to the Old Testament, but it does denote that Sheol is under God's sway. Again, Sheol is open to God's glance and the *Rephaim* 'tremble' before Him in its depths (Job 26^{5f}). He knows everything about it (Pr 15^{11}). He *could* 'hide' Job in Sheol for a while, though He *will* not (Job 14^{13-15}). Psalm 139 teaches that if He will, God can be in Sheol, as He can be anywhere else, in a flash. The Psalmist at first cries out because God 'besets (him) behind and before' to 'search' him, but at last *asks for* such 'searching' (verses 1, 5, 24). He says that wherever he goes, God speeds there before him. This is in accordance with the Old Testament doctrine that God can be anywhere He will in a flash (and not that He is everywhere at once.) The Psalmist says that if, *per impossibile*, he were to flee to Sheol while still alive, God would forestall him there (verses 8-10). The implication is that, if God were to decide to visit Sheol, even though this is not His way, He could do so. Yet it is not His use to 'work wonders' there (Ps $88^{10, 12}$). Until the latest of Old Testament periods the Hebrew belief was that normally God just leaves Sheol and the dead alone because that is what He chooses to do. The dead are outside history.

CHAPTER FOUR

THE HEBREW TERMS RENDERED 'FOR EVER'

HERE THERE are three Hebrew 'compound' words, each consisting of the preposition *le*, meaning 'to' or 'for', and a noun. One of the three is *lānetzach* (*39*), rendered by 'for ever' twenty-four times. The noun *netzach*, which only occurs by itself four times, is derived from a root that denotes 'prevailing-ness'. Samuel calls God 'the *netzach* of Israel' when he wants to assert that in His choice of David instead of Saul He will prevail (1 S 15²⁹; cf. 1 Ch 29¹¹, Isa 63⁶). That which prevails is that which lasts, and 'lastingly' would often be a good rendering for the adverbial phrase. In the great majority of passages the phrase refers to something that lasts *in 'this life'*—i.e. in history. There are examples in Abner's question, 'Shall the sword devour continually?' (2 S 2²⁶), and in Amos' declaration that Edom has 'kept his wrath lastingly' (Am 1¹¹; cf. Jer 3⁵, Ps 103⁹). When used with a negative, it may be rendered 'never', as when the wicked man says that God 'will never see' his sin (Ps 10¹¹). There are a few passages where the context refers to death. In all of these the reference is to the historical *event* called 'death' that makes an end of life—not to the state of the dead in Sheol. At the moment when God takes life away, His withdrawal of it 'prevails' lastingly in the sense that now there is no more *life* (Job 14²⁰, Ps 52⁵). When a man dies and 'goes to the generations of his fathers', he *never* again 'sees the light' any more than a dead 'beast' does (Ps 49¹⁹ᶠ). The idea is 'no life'. Except in this negative way, *lanetzach* is never used of the dead. It always refers to history—that is, to events on earth.

The fundamental idea of the second noun, *'ad*, is 'going on and on'. The adverbial phrase *lā'ad* (*49*) means 'continuously', though it is generally rendered 'for ever' (*42*). In twenty of these instances it occurs along with a similar phrase formed from the next word, *le'ōlām*, the combined phrases being rendered 'for ever and ever'. 'Always' would be a better translation, for this English word, like *lā'ad*, but unlike 'for ever', has various 'universes of discourse' and therefore various meanings. For example, in 'he always talks like that now', 'always' means 'in his present phase';

in 'When the Houses have passed a Bill, the King always signs it', it means 'since the death of Queen Anne'; in 'the sun will always rise in the east', it means 'for many, many trillions of years'. Such variations are not less real because they are made unconsciously. When a speaker is challenged, he admits them. In most texts *la'ad* is used of *God* and His actions *in history*. Here the notion of 'endlessness', however vaguely conceived, occurs. Yet the notion is not that God is 'eternal' because He transcends 'time', or even that 'time' is endless, for 'time' is an abstract term. The concrete term is 'history', and the idea is that God and history 'go on and on' together endlessly—and relatedly. For instance, in Isa 57^{15}, the meaning is that God, because He 'abides perpetually', abides continually 'with him that is of a contrite and humble spirit'. 'That inhabiteth eternity', the rendering of the English versions in this text, is a great phrase, but it does not express the Hebrew concept, for 'eternity' does not suggest history. The phrase 'the LORD shall reign for ever and ever' (e.g. Ex 15^{18} E) means 'the LORD shall always reign'. Psalm 111, with its threefold *la'ad* (verses 3, 8, 10), is an exposition of this idea. The passage where God says 'I create new heavens and a new earth' is addressed to people who will live through that crisis and thereafter 'rejoice *always*' (Isa 65^{17f}). Even here 'rejoice for ever' gives the wrong idea, for it is presently assumed that some time these men will die. It is their '*seed* and name' that is to 'remain' as long as the new creation (Isa 66^{22}). *La'ad*, when used of God, refers to His endless activity in history, and when used of Israel refers to its perpetuity in history, but when used of *a man* it means 'as long as he lives'. For instance, while Zion is to be the LORD's lasting 'resting-place' (Ps 132^{14}), and while *Israel* is to 'walk in the name of the LORD (her) God perpetually' (Mic 4^5; cf. Ps 61^8), when a particular righteous man pledges himself to 'observe (God's) law continually' (Ps 119^{44}), he means 'as long as I live'. The Davidic kingship is to last as long as history (Ps 89^{29}). When a Prophet, speaking of a newly born king, calls him 'Father of '*ad*' (Isa 9^6), he does not mean that he is 'Father of Eternity' (*RV* marg.), with its supratemporal suggestion, or even that he is to be 'an everlasting Father', but that he will *always* be a father to his people. When a Psalmist declares that 'all the workers of iniquity' will be 'destroyed *la'ad*', he means, as with parallel phrases under *lanetzach*, that God, by a decisive act of premature death, will end their part in history (Ps 92^7; cf. 9, 11, 14).

The third noun '*ōlām* is much the commonest (*439*). It has some twenty renderings, the most frequent being 'ever' or 'for ever' (*270*), 'everlasting' (*64*), and 'perpetual' (*20*). It is a very elastic term, probably more so than any of the relevant English words, though the varying 'universes of discourse' under 'ever' in such English questions as the following may give some hint of its range —'Was there *ever* such a thing?', 'Shall I *ever* finish?', 'Will war *ever* cease?', 'Will the stars *ever* burn out?'. '*olam* is occasionally used of long *past* history (*42*), the best rendering being 'ancient'. Sometimes its reference is to God's ways 'of old' (e.g. Isa 46^9, Ps 25^6). Here the phrase 'from everlasting' (Ps 93^2; cf. Pr 8^{23}) probably implies that for *God* there was somehow history before the creation. The hills, 'gates', the *Nephilim*, the line of prophets and a nation, are all 'ancient' in varying senses (Gn 49^{26}, Ps 24^7, Gn 6^4, Jer 28^8, 5^{15}). 'The days of old' may be used vaguely (Ps 77^6; cf. 143^5) or refer to 'the days' of Moses or of David (Isa 63^{11}, Am 9^{11}). When used of the past the term always refers to distant history.

When used of the future it means 'endless' *in history* even when it describes God (e.g. Gn 21^{33} J, Isa 40^{28}). For instance, the phrase 'His mercy (endureth) for ever' (*33*) means that it is 'everlasting' in this sense as its contexts show (e.g. Ps 136, *passim*). Similarly, His covenant and laws and promises and so on are 'everlasting' (e.g. 2 S 23^5, Ps 119^{89}, Isa 40^8). There is the same reference to the history of the far future when '*olam* is used of the earth (Ps 78^{69}), the Davidic house (1 K 2^{33}, Ps 72^{17}), 'the righteous' as a class (e.g. Ps 37^{27-9}, Mic 4^5), and a righteous nation or family (e.g. Isa 47^7, 1 S 13^{13}; cf. Lv 25^{34}). But where '*olam* is used of the future of *an individual man*, it means no more than 'as long as he lives'. The very few exceptions (Jon 2^6, Dn 12^{2f}) are discussed in a later chapter. They belong to the latest Old Testament period. Until then 'during his life time' is the uniform meaning (e.g. 1 S 1^{22}, 27^{12}, Dt 15^{17}, Ps 15^5). There is an exception that proves the rule when Bathsheba uses the conventional phrase 'May the king live for ever' for she is asking David to arrange for a successor (1 K 1^{31})! The rendering 'always' sometimes occurs, but it too means 'as long as life lasts' (e.g. Ps 41^{13}, 61^8, 121^8). The phrase '(God) hath set '*olam* in (men's) heart' (Ec 3^{11}) seems to mean, as the context suggests and as suits Koheleth, that men can look a long way both into the past and into the future, but that, as this gift of God is useless, a man's wisdom is to make the best of the immediate present. In another passage this writer says sarcastically that 'the living do know that they will die' but 'the dead know nothing', for they have no more 'portion for ever under the sun'—i.e. in history (Ec 9^{5f}; cf. verse 10). In the last chapter of the book the Hebrew phrase rendered 'his long home' means 'the house of his '*olam*', and denotes 'the (lasting) grave' to which an old man, as the many signs of his physical decay show, is 'going' (Ec 12$^{1-8}$).

The prevalence of the translation 'for ever' in the English versions for this term, as for the other two, gives a wrong impression. While they rarely describe the state of the dead because it was just taken for granted that the dead had done with life, occasionally they occur for the sake of emphasis, as in 'they sleep a *perpetual* sleep and do *not* wake' (Jer 51$^{39, 57}$). It would not be inaccurate to use the paraphrase: 'They have no further part in history.' In their positive use, at any rate, the three phrases always refer to history. It follows that, when the overtones of the words are considered, the rendering 'always' suits the three phrases better than 'for ever'. It is true that in English 'for ever' may be used in reference to the events of history, as in 'Will they go on quarrelling for ever?', but usually there is the suggestion, however vaguely, of a realm beyond history, and this is not so with the Hebrew terms. On the other hand, 'always' regularly has this historical connotation. The word 'everlasting', if it be used in its literal sense, is sometimes admissible. On the other hand, 'eternal', if it is used, as it should be, to mean 'transcending history', is not admissible. Even when the Hebrew used the phrases about God, *he* did not mean 'transcendent'. A philosopher, examining the implications of the use, rightly argues that a doctrine of transcendence is involved, but the Hebrew did not examine the philosophical implications of his thought any more than 'practical men' do in any period. For him God controlled history, both before and after the Day, and that was enough.

CHAPTER FIVE

THE *CHASID* AND SHEOL

'AND GOD created man in his own image, in the image of God created he him; male and female created he them' (Gn 1^{27} P). This is the Hebrew form of the doctrine of 'personality' and 'the value of the individual'. It is individualism full-grown. The writer has drawn out the long story of the emergence of individualism in the Old Testament in *The Bible Doctrine of Society*. Here the chief point is that the doctrine, finally formulated in the Priestly Document, corresponded to experience—the experience of the *chasid*. In the plural this word is used to describe a certain class of man in the Books of the Maccabees (e.g. 1 Mac 7^{12f}), but the singular occurs frequently in the Old Testament (*32*), particularly in the Psalms (*27*), and it is in the original sense that the word is used here. The most frequent and best rendering is 'saint', but no English word is satisfactory. A *chasid* was a man between whom and God there was mutual *chesed*, which has been translated 'leal love'.[1] He was a man who lived in conscious fellowship with God. He appears in many places where the term *chasid* does not happen to occur. For instance, the great Prophets were *chasidim*, the unknown writers of most of the individualistic Psalms were *chasidim*, Koheleth would have been a *chasid* if he could, it is a likely surmise that the writer of Job was a *chasid*.

It was inevitable that sooner or later the doctrine of Sheol delineated above should become a stumbling-block to the *chasid*. It might suffice so long as the individual was little more than a part of the family, it being enough that the family should survive, but not when there arose a belief in the value of every individual man. In particular, however subconsciously, the *chasid* would begin to be restless under the doctrine. Could it be that the God with whom he lived in fellowship would end by abandoning him? He would shrink from the loss of God. For the *chasid* the evidence, examined below, suggests that there was a plaint, 'Am I to perish at last?', and a plea, 'Wilt Thou leave me to perish?', before he

---

[1] There is a full discussion of the meaning of *chesed* and *chasid* in *The Bible Doctrine of Grace*.

groped his way at last to the confident faith: 'Thou wilt not leave me in Sheol! Thou wilt not!' As already shown, he believed all the while that God *could* deliver him from Sheol if He would. *Would* He not?

The changed attitude to Sheol appears in terminology. Four of the terms enumerated above begin to appear, alongside earlier ones, at about the time of the Exile. The two terms for 'pit', *bor* and *shachath*, first occur then as synonyms for 'Sheol'. The phrases 'to go down into the pit' or 'the dust' or 'silence' (*24*) have not the same flavour as 'to sleep with one's fathers'. Similarly, it is significant that the term '*Abaddon*', 'Destruction', now first appears as a synonym for Sheol, and the name *Rephaim*, or 'Weaklings', for its denizens. There is a longer example of the new attitude in Ps 88$^{3-6, 10-12}$. The writer has drawn so near to Sheol that he can write as if he were already there (verses 3, 6). He says, 'I am counted with them that go down into the Pit', a phrase that has a shudder in it. It is the same with the accompanying phrases for the dead—'A man that hath no help', 'Cast off among the dead', 'Whom thou rememberest no more', 'Cut off from thy hand', 'Laid in the lowest Pit' (verses 4-6)—and with the questions that follow (verses 10-12) which all imply a kind of complaint because God does nothing for the *chasid* when dead, neither 'showing wonders' nor 'lovingkindness' nor 'faithfulness' nor 'righteousness' in the dark *Abaddon* of 'forgetfulness'. This is not a picture of the peace of sleep, but of misery, the root of the misery being that *Rephaim* cannot 'praise' God (verse 10).

On the other hand there are now texts which suggest that for the *wicked* Sheol, under its new meaning, *is* an appropriate place (Ps 9^{17}, 22^{29}, 88^{4f}, Pr 5^5, 7^{26f}, 9^{18}), though the idea that they suffer there, still less suffer torment by fire, is not found. It is the impotence or nullity of perpetual 'sleep' that is meet for them and not for the righteous. A number of passages, which describe Sheol as a prison with 'bars' and 'gates' add the idea that there is no escape from it. In 'The Psalm of Hezekiah', for instance, the writer begins by crying out that before his time he is reaching 'the gates of Sheol' that will shut him off both from God and man (Isa 38^{10f}, cf. Job 17^{16}). In the Psalm in Jonah too, when a man passes into the 'Pit', 'the earth with her bars (closes) upon (him) once for all' (Jon 2^6). In a synonymous phrase 'the gates of death', within which men cannot praise God, are set over against the joyful 'gates of the daughter of Zion' (Ps 9^{13f}; cf. 107^{18}, Job 38^{17}).

The impotence of a prison is meet for sinners, but is the *chasid* too to be shut up in impotence? Is he just to pass to a place where 'there is no work nor device, nor knowledge, nor wisdom' (Ec 9^{10})? Could the *chasid* go on hopelessly accepting such a doctrine?

It is agreed that there are passages which show that he could not, but there is dispute about their number. Here it may be recalled that, on given expositions, there are examples of resurrection in the last Servant Song and the Psalm in Jonah. These, however, ascribe resurrection to particular people, as in the Elijah-Elisha stories, and do not fall under the present question: 'Are there any passages that teach that a *chasid* will rise from the dead just because he *is* a *chasid*?'

There is a passage in Hosea (13^{14}) that is sometimes quoted, but almost certainly mistakenly. It may be rendered: 'Shall I ransom (these sinners) from the hand of Sheol? Shall I redeem them from death? O death, where are thy plagues? O Sheol, where is thy pestilence? Repentance is hid from mine eyes.' Here the context requires a threat of premature and painful death, and the text may be so taken. God calls 'death' to bring its 'plagues' and Sheol its 'pestilence' to punish the sinners of the North, for He will not repent of His determination to doom them. In the eighth century before Christ, when Hosea wrote, a reference to a resurrection—and, in particular, a resurrection of *sinners*—would be an anachronism.

It is in Job and the Psalter that the really relevant passages occur. Of the first text sometimes quoted in Job it is widely recognized that the Authorized Version rendering, 'Though he slay me, I will trust in him' (Job 13^{15}), is a mistranslation, and that whichever of the two Hebrew readings for the second clause (meaning, respectively, 'I will wait' and 'I will not wait',) be preferred, the meaning of this and the next verse is: 'He is going to slay me ... so I will take my chance and argue now.' The next text (14$^{13-15}$) is embedded in one of Job's earlier speeches (Chh. 13 and 14), and falls between two descriptions of the misery of man here and of his hopeless state after death (14$^{1-12,\ 16-22}$), the second description applying this to Job. In the text itself Job cries: 'Oh that thou wouldst hide me in Sheol, That thou wouldst keep me secret until thy wrath be past!' If, as had never happened to any other man, he could spend a fixed period in Sheol—until the time that God had 'set' for the ending of His wrath—and *then* return to earth, how willingly he would go to Sheol and how eagerly listen for the 'change' or 'release' of God's recall! There is no question here of a far-away resurrection of all righteous men —but of the return of a particular man from a temporary interruption of his normal life on earth. But—as the tone of the passage itself shows, and as the passages before and after it state expressly this cannot be! The writer uses Sheol to bring out the misery of Job's plight *here*. Better a spell in Sheol itself than this agony! The next passage emphasizes the hopelessness—that is, the finality —of existence in Sheol (17^{10-16}). There are again difficult phrases, but the main purport is clear. Job says, in effect, to his three friends: 'You are three fools! And as for me, I shall very soon be dead (verse 1) and in the Pit of Sheol, where there is no "hope"— and so the injustice of God's ways with me will remain.' In a later passage (21^{16-34}) he says this to them more briefly (verses 23-6). 'Whether men live "at ease" or in "bitterness" here, they are all alike when it comes to the "worm" and the "dust" ($17^{14,\ 16}$)—and therefore there ought to be that difference between the lot of the righteous and of the wicked *here*, which you three keep on saying wrongly that there *is*.' These verses fall between two accounts of what his friends say (verses 16-22, 27-33), seeking, forsooth, to 'comfort' Job with 'vanity' (verse 34).

The remaining passage, beginning 'But I know that my Redeemer (*go'el*) liveth', is a famous *crux interpretum* (Job 19^{25-7}). Taken alone it may mean either 'I shall recover from my dire sickness' or 'I shall die but I shall rise from the dead'. Since an interpretation that suits the whole book is to be preferred to one that does not, something needs to be said about its writer's purpose. Its subject is the problem of undeserved suffering in *this* life, not the problem of the fate of the righteous in Sheol. Both the poetic conclusion and the prose epilogue (Ch. 42) show that the writer thought that the problem was solved *before* Job's death. Again, if the exposition of the earlier passages just given be accepted, to interpret this one of a resurrection is to make it a kind of 'erratic boulder'. This interpretation while not impossible, should not be preferred to one that harmonizes with the rest of the book. In the three verses neither Sheol nor 'the grave' is mentioned. The term 'worms' is not in the Hebrew, but the words 'skin' and 'flesh' (and perhaps 'eyes') show that Job is thinking of his *body*. The 'destruction' of his 'skin' would quite well describe a loathsome symptom of his disease *now*. The rendering 'without (or 'apart from') my flesh I shall see God', if it refers to a return to earth from *Sheol*, requires the idea of the return of the *nephesh* to life *without a body*. Since a man without a body was *not* a man for the Hebrew, this is a very unlikely rendering. The Platonic belief in 'the immortality of the soul' when it is once rid of the encumbrance of the body, is quite alien to the Hebrew mind. This means that even if the passage be *taken by itself*, the preferable interpretation is that Job declares that though he is so loathsome, his loyal Kinsman (*Go'el*) will come to him and, taking his stand 'in the dust' where he grovels, will do a kinsman's part and rescue him—not from Sheol, but from his sufferings *here*. 'From his flesh'—that is, before he leaves his body and his *nephesh* passes into Sheol where he will have no hope at all—'he will behold (*chazah*) God'. In verse 27 there is, in effect, a three-fold 'I'—first the term 'I' itself is emphatic, then it is repeated under the phrases 'for myself', and 'not another'. Job cries 'I, I, I shall behold my Kinsman! And my own eyes will *see* (*ra'ah*) him— even though my skin is perishing and "my reins are consumed within me" ' (cf. Ps 73^{26}). This is consonant with another passage that speaks of 'seeing' God (33$^{23-8}$). Here Elihu describes, not only the saving of a sick man's *nephesh* from the edge of the Pit, but the perfect restoration of his 'flesh', and his '*seeing* (God's) face with joy'. This passage corresponds almost point by point with 19$^{25-7}$—except, of course, that Elihu declares that Job must first repent of his sins—and here there is no doubt that recovery, not resurrection, is meant. In this passage the four-fold use of the word *shachath*, with its connotation of 'destruction', for 'pit', as well as the use of *Abaddon* elsewhere in the book (Job 26^6, 28^{22}), exhibits the new concept of Sheol as a place from which men shrink, but in Job there is no evidence—or, at any rate, no clear evidence—that the *chasid* had come to believe that God would redeem him from it.

The remaining group of passages belongs to the Psalter. Here there are sometimes difficulties about the Hebrew text, but these problems cannot be discussed here. As a rule, the present text is accepted. It needs also to be remembered that Hebrew phrases rendered by 'for ever' or 'for evermore' are no proof that there is any reference to what happens after death. As already shown, they mean 'always' and vary in meaning with the 'frame of reference' like that English word.

It is only under one of the few Psalms in question that it is possible to reach a certain conclusion. Where there is doubt, the only criterion is the context of the whole Psalm and its 'universe of discourse'. When Wyclif was thought to be dying 'before his time' and said, 'I shall not die but live, and declare the evil deeds of the friars', he clearly meant 'I shall not die *yet*'—not 'I shall not die *at all*'. Perhaps the chief help in interpreting these Psalms is to ask: 'Is the Psalmist thinking of premature death, either at the hands of "adversaries" or through sickness?' The Psalms where it is least likely that there is a reference to a life after death will be taken first.

Three of these use the word 'awake' (17, 73, 139). This term suggests the passing of night into day and would suit the idea of a 'morning' after the 'sleep' of Sheol. But elsewhere in the Psalter 'morning' is used to describe the passing of sorrow, or rather terror, into joy without any reference to resurrection. For instance, in Ps 59^{16} the *chasid* who is being persecuted by wicked men and whom God will deliver, is like a man who is abroad in the night but will live till 'morning'. In Ps 143, again, the writer's 'enemy' has all but killed him and he is on the edge of the Pit (verses 3, 7), but he cries 'Cause me to hear thy lovingkindness in the morning' (verse 8)—that is, turn my sorrow into joy *here*. 'Morning' is just a symbol for gladness after trouble, and is not to be taken literally. Similarly, there are passages where 'night' stands for a 'troublous time' (Ps 17^3, $77^{2, 6}$, 119^{55}). In Ps 30 the *chasid's* 'foes' are the tools of God's 'anger' (verses 1, 5); he too has been on the brink of Sheol (verse 3); but while 'weeping may come in to lodge at even', there is a 'cry of joy in the morning' (verse 5) —i.e. when God turns from His anger. In Ps 88 the writer, describing Sheol at length (verses 3-6; cf. 10-12), writes *as though* God had already 'laid him in the lowest Pit' (verse 6), but when he cries 'In the morning shall my prayer come unto thee' (verse 13), he means that God will save him from this *untimely* death. Two Psalmists cry out to God to 'awake' and rescue them from the enemies that are closing in upon them *now* (Ps 35^{23}, 59^4; cf. Job 8^6). It is tempting to call these Psalms 'Maccabean' because we know that the loyal Jew went in peril of his life under Epiphanes, but it is likely enough that in parts of the Persian Empire there were the far-away beginnings of the local pogrom, and that in Palestine itself Sanballat's attempt to 'do Nehemiah mischief' (Neh 6²) had lowlier parallels. Where these Psalms say that the *chasid* has 'drawn near' to the Pit the reference is to violent and premature death, and not to 'natural' death in old age. Their writers do not ask to be delivered from the latter. None the less, they illustrate the new emotional reaction to the old doctrine of Sheol described above. They betray the sub-conscious feeling that the Pit is a fit end for the wicked but not for the *chasid*, even though they acquiesce in the doctrine that Sheol is the inevitable end for all men.

This examination of the uses of the words 'morning' and 'awake' in other Psalms raises a presumption that they are similarly used in Ps 17, 73, and 139, and do not refer to a resurrection. This presumption is confirmed in each case when the whole Psalm is considered. Ps 139 may be summarized under the word 'continually'. First (verses 1-12), the Psalmist declares that God has been *continually* with him, 'searching' him, and that, even if he fled from this scrutiny to regions to which no man can flee, he would find that God has sped there before him. Next (verses 13-18), on remembering with what loving care God created him and what God's purposes for him now are, his fear turns into trust and he is glad to be *continually* with God here, even under affliction. Finally (verses 19-24), since it is the wicked whom God will 'slay' prematurely, and since he himself is not one of them, he asks God to go on 'searching' him and leading him *continually* in the right way to the end of his life. The fundamental idea is that continual fellowship with God, even when it means 'winnowing' (verse 3), is *the* boon of the *chasid*. The particular phrase, 'I awoke, and I am still with thee' (verse 18), may be interpreted in three ways—(*a*) 'Every day when I awake, I am still with thee'; (*b*) 'I awoke from my bad dream about God's "searching" to discover that it had not separated me from Him'; (*c*) 'I awoke from the sleep of death to find that I had not lost God.' The last interpretation requires that 'to awake' was a well-understood synonym for 'to rise from the dead'. So far as the evidence goes, this was not so until after the rise of Apocalyptic, if even then. To the present writer the interpretation under (*a*) is easily the most likely for it suits both the whole Psalm and parallels in other Psalms. The succinct use of 'I awoke' to mean 'whenever I awake' suits poetry.

In Ps 73 it is God who awakes, banishing an evil 'dream'

(verse 20). In the English Versions the crucial phrase is rendered 'And afterwards receive me to (or with) glory' (verse 24). The verb used (*laqach*), however, does not mean 'receive' but 'take'. God is said to 'take' in many different senses (e.g. Gn 2^{22} J, Jos 24^3 E, Dt 4^{20}, 30^4, 1 K 11^{37}, 2 K 2^3, Hos 13^{11}, Isa 47^3, Nu 8^{18} P). It is the context that decides the meaning. The phrase in the Psalm describes the end of a process *here*: 'Thou *holdest my right hand*; thou wilt *guide* me with thy counsel, And in the end *lead* me (to) honour.' The Psalmist is a preacher (verses 15, 28), and announces his theme in the first verse—'Surely God is good to Israel—(that is) to such (Israelites) as are pure in heart'. To take 'glory' to mean they will rise from the dead would entail both that the word was current in this sense, of which there is no evidence, and that the writer gave only one phrase to the main message of his Psalm!

In Psalm 17 the last verse runs: 'As for *me*, I shall behold thy face in righteousness: I shall be satisfied, when I *awake*, with thy form.' As elsewhere, fellowship with God is the *chasid's summum bonum*. He has been passing through a 'night' of trial, and, claiming that he has met the test, appeals confidently to God to 'hide (him) under the shadow of (his) wings' and so save him from the enemies that 'compass (him) about with hungry greed' (verses 3-9). He then compares the wicked to a lion lurking in wait for his prey (verses 10-12)—that is, they are seeking to kill him before his time. He cries: 'Arise, O LORD, forestall (the lion), lay him low in death' (verse 13; cf. Ps 78^{31}). This seems to be the key to the interpretation of the difficult verse that follows (verse 14), the underlying idea being: 'Why dost Thou let the wicked live a long and prosperous life? Cut them off before their time as they seek to cut me off before mine.' The contrast implied in the English Versions between their fate in '*this* life' and 'the next life' depends wholly on the word 'this', which is not in the Hebrew. In consonance with the theme of the whole Psalm, the phrase 'When I awake' (verse 15) means 'When I wake from this nightmare' (cf. verse 3)—or, more broadly, 'When I pass from this darkness into light'—'I shall behold thy face'. It repeats an earlier verse that describes the writer's certainty that presently God will deliver him (verse 6). If 'when I awake' meant 'when I awake from the sleep of death', the hope of resurrection is strangely left to lurk in a single adverbial Hebrew word. In LXX, which has 'But *I* shall see thy face in righteousness, I shall be satisfied when I have seen thy glory', the phrase 'When I awake' is either omitted or interpreted by 'satisfied'. Neither the word 'Sheol' nor any of its synonyms occurs in this Psalm. As in Ps 139 and 73, the writer is speaking of the premature and violent death which is the appropriate fate of the wicked but not of the righteous.

Some have found a promise of resurrection in the phrases, 'Though I walk through the valley of the shadow of death, I will fear no evil, for thou art with me' and 'I will dwell in the house of the LORD continually' (Ps 23[4, 6]). 'The shadow of death' renders one Hebrew word *tzalmaveth* (*17*), taking it as a compound noun. As such compound words are very rare in Hebrew, scholars think that the original word was *tzalmūth* ('gloom'). The Hebrew copyists, however, always have *tzalmaveth*, and this way of understanding the word is at least as early as LXX, which renders it by *skia thanatou* eleven times, including all the instances in Psalms (23[4], 44[19], 107[10, 14]). But the phrase 'in the shadow of death', like the English phrase 'on the brink of the grave', does not *per se* imply death itself. The phrase is used, for example, to describe 'night' (Am 5[8], cf. Jer 13[16]), and a people's dwelling-place here (Isa 9[2]; cf. Jer 2[6]). The word occurs ten times in Job. In six of these the context precludes a reference to Sheol (3[5], 12[22], 16[16], 24[17] (*bis*), 28[3]), and in another such a reference is unlikely (34[22]). It is true that in three the word describes Sheol (without the term) (10[21f], 38[17]), but this means no more than that Sheol is *a* place of darkness. In the Psalter *tzalmaveth* occurs twice. In one it is parallel to 'the place of jackals' and describes the evil plight of Israel when God punishes her here (44[19]). In the other passage (23[4]), now under consideration, the word *tzalmaveth* does not *per se* imply 'death' as appears abundantly above. As for the last phrase in the Psalm, rendered 'for ever', the Hebrew words mean 'for length of days'. Elsewhere this phrase means 'as long as life lasts' or 'for a long time' (e.g. Dt 30[20], Job 12[12], Ps 91[16], Pr 3[2], La 5[20]). Even in Ps 21[4], where the phrase rendered by 'for ever and ever' is added, the meaning is not that the king who trusts in God will never die, as the discussion above of 'for ever and ever' shows, but that he will live a long, long life. In Ps 23 the singer means that God is his 'shepherd' both beside 'still waters' and, if the way leads there, in a dark, dark valley; then, by a change of figure, that he will be a guest in God's house as long as he lives, as the parallel phrase 'all the days of my life' suggests. The phrase 'the house of the LORD' means 'the Temple' elsewhere (e.g. Ps 116^{19}, 122^{1}; cf. 42^{4}), and other Psalmists speak of 'dwelling' there (Ps 27^{4}, 84^{4}; cf. 92^{13})—meaning, not necessarily that they stay in the Temple all the time, but that it is their haunt (cf. Lk 2^{37}).

The sixteenth Psalm rises to the climax: 'For thou wilt not leave my soul to Sheol, Neither wilt thou suffer thy *chasid* to see the Pit. Thou wilt shew me the path of life: In thy presence is fulness of joy; In thy right hand there are pleasures enduringly' (*netzach*) (Ps 16^{10f}). While the verdict has here to be *non liquet*, the 'universe of discourse' makes it at least possible that this Psalmist expects life after death. There is nothing about 'adversaries' or premature death, for the writer only refers to the wicked to say that he has nothing to do with their idolatries (verse 4). There is nothing about trouble of any sort, but, on the contrary: 'Yea, I have a goodly heritage' (verse 6). The Psalmist begins 'Keep me, O God, *for in thee do I put my trust*' and the rest of the Psalm is a glad exposition of the italicized phrase. To take 'Thou wilt not leave my soul to Sheol' to mean 'Thou wilt not *yet* leave me to Sheol (though I know I am to go there at last), does not suit the 'universe of discourse' at all. Here the *chasid's* 'emotional *reaction*' to the new concept of Sheol as misery seems to pass into the 'emotional *conviction*' that God will be faithful to a man that 'trusts' Him even when he dies. As with other 'emotional convictions', there is no exploration of all that this means, but just '*one* thing I know'— but the 'one thing' is enough, for it is a truth about *God*.

In the remaining Psalm (49) there are a number of difficulties in the Hebrew, but its main message is clear. In it the writer does not pray, but calls all men to listen to his song (verses 1-4), for he has 'solved a riddle' (verse 4, LXX, *problema*). The 'riddle' is posed by the wicked and is implied in verses 10-12. In effect they say: '*Chasid*, you and we alike know that the same chill Sheol awaits *every* man, good or bad. The only thing to do, therefore, is to follow the way to wealth and prosperity in *this* life. As you will have noticed, it is the wicked that prosper here and leave fortunes when they die. So we choose to be wicked, for it "pays". What can you say against this?'[2] The preacher's answer appears twice (verses 6-8, 12-20), but it is in the second passage that it is drawn out. It is a *new* answer. Unlike some other Psalmists this one does

---

[2] In verse 11 the first phrase in LXX runs 'their *graves* (i.e. the graves *both* of wise men *and* fools, as verse 10 shows) are their houses always'. This is probably correct. It sustains the paraphrase above, for it is part of what the wealthy wicked say that *they* 'see' (verses 6, 10) and draw their own conclusions.

not say 'God will slay the wicked *before their time*', for he knows that often wicked men do, in fact, live long and prosperous lives. His answer is, in effect: 'The righteous do not pass permanently to Sheol when they die. This is the fate of the wicked, and of the wicked only, as it ought to be.' What then happens to the righteous? This Psalmist's answer is 'God will ransom (*padah*) my soul from the hand of Sheol, for he will take me' (verse 15). The context requires that 'take' here means 'take me to himself' (cf. Gn 5[24]). The 'emotional reaction of the *chasid* to the new concept of Sheol passes clearly at last in defiance of the ancient creed, into the *conviction* that Sheol is not the final destiny of righteous men. Its basis is 'When the man who is faithful to God dies, God will still be faithful to him. God can no other.' Whatever may be true of other Psalmists, this one had 'solved the riddle' (verse 4).

If this exegesis is correct, it follows that in *this* Psalm the words 'morning' and 'light' (verses 14, 19) are to be interpreted of the resurrection. Then 'the righteous will have dominion over (the wicked)', or better, with LXX, 'lord it over them' (*katakurieuein*). It would follow too that, in spite of the difficult details in verses 7f, the general sense is that while God Himself will 'ransom' the righteous, no propitiatory sacrifice (LXX *exilasma*) will avail to rescue a wicked man's *nephesh* from Sheol. The Psalm is noteworthy too for the shudder in its account of Sheol (verses 14, 17, 19f). Here is no question of quiet sleep! For this *chasid*, at any rate, Sheol is a fit end for the wicked, but not for the righteous. It is only the former who 'perish like beasts' (verses 12, 20). For the latter there will be life after Sheol.

The two passages in Apocalypses that teach unmistakably that *chasidim* rise from the dead are taken in the next chapter under Isaiah 24-27 and Daniel.

CHAPTER SIX

THE OLD TESTAMENT APOCALYPSES

It is usual to distinguish four Old Testament Apocalypses—the Book of Joel, Isaiah 24-27, Zechariah 9-14, and the Book of Daniel. It is possible that the first, and probably that the third, come from more than one author. Apart from Joel, they all belong to the Hellenistic period. The Apocalyptist took up the task of the Prophets, but with a difference. There is no need to explore the difference here. Anyone who compares, for instance, the Prophecies of Hosea and Jeremiah with the Books of Daniel and Enoch, will be aware of it. But it is also agreed that there is an Apocalyptic element in Prophecy and a Prophetic element in Apocalyptic, and that the Prophetic element is so pronounced in the first three Old Testament Apocalypses that they might be called Prophetic-Apocalyptic. Indeed, when the Canon of the Prophets was drawn up the Jewish editors included these three Apocalypses in it. With the Apocalyptists the subject of the second chapter, 'The Hebrew Doctrine of Future History', is resumed. It needs to be repeated that this is the chief Old Testament doctrine under the present subject—and not 'the future of the individual'. While the collection and integration of the evidence under the latter subject has required much space, in the Old Testament it is quite subordinate to the societary doctrine of the future of Israel and mankind.

Apart from Joel, the Apocalyptic literature, like the Prophetic, belongs to a time of World Wars. Under Alexander's attack the world, as the Hebrews knew it, fell to pieces in a mere matter of three or four years. The wars of the Diadochi ensued, and, when these ended, Palestine was left as a 'bone of contention' between the Seleucid and Ptolemaic Empires. There was, indeed, a brief interval or two of peace between them, but these only punctuated wars. For the Hebrew all this raised the old Prophetic question: 'What is the LORD doing, and going to do, now?' As with the Prophets, it is just assumed that He is Lord of History, even though His own people were now no more than a seemingly insignificant fragment of an alien empire. The answer of the

THE OLD TESTAMENT APOCALYPSES 67

Apocalyptists to the question was: 'All these wars are just the prelude of the Day of the LORD.' In their writings there are many textual and exegetical difficulties, but for the present purpose these can usually be ignored, only the salient points, about which there is rarely dispute, being mentioned.

While the Book of Joel may be by two authors, the dividing point being at 2^{28}, it is here taken as a unit. The probable date is in the latter part of the rule of Persia. The book gives two accounts of the Day of the LORD, one in 1^1–2^{27} and the other in 2^{28}–3^{21}. In the first the Day (1^{15}, $2^{1, 11}$) is a Day of Judgement on Israel, and in the second (2^{31}, 3^{14}) a Day of Salvation for Israel, but of Judgement on 'all nations'. In the first part the Apocalyptist, preaching in the midst of a plague of locusts ($1^{4, 6-12}$), warns the Jews that the LORD is calling up His 'army'—whether of further swarms of locusts or of men, is not clear—to execute His 'great and terrible Day' (2^{11}). The terrors of this 'army' are described in 2^{1-11}. With this warning Joel mingles a call to repentance (1^{13f}, 2^{12-17}), asking: 'Who knoweth whether (the LORD) will turn and repent and leave a blessing behind him?' (2^{14}). It is implied that the people respond, for '*Then* was the LORD jealous for his land and had pity on his people' (2^{18}), pledging Himself to give them a blessing of untold prosperity (2^{19-27}) that will even include the harvests of 'the years that the locust hath eaten' (2^{25}). This oracle gives an instance of a threatened Day that does not come, or rather, of a Day of Judgement that turns into a Day of Salvation. But, with the second part, more is added: 'And it shall come to pass afterward that I will pour out of my spirit upon all flesh' (2^{28}). The last phrase does not mean 'all mankind' but 'all Jews', as the ensuing words, '*your* sons and *your* daughters', '*your* old men' and '*your* young men', show. Next there is promise that the LORD will 'bring again the captivity of Judah and Jerusalem' (3^1). At this point the judgement of 'all the nations' is described (3^{1-14}). The LORD gathers them to the Valley of Jehoshaphat—i.e. 'the Valley of the LORD's Judgement'. Two ironical passages follow. First, the LORD 'pleads' with the nations to do what He Himself is going to do, 'deliver his people whom they have exiled and oppressed' (3^{2-8}). Then (3^{9-14}) He calls all the nations to come up to war against His people that He may be able to decide what to do with their 'multitudes', 'decision' being an ironical term for 'slaughter'. When the Lion of Judah 'roars from Jerusalem' 'the

Heavens and the earth will shake', but He will be a 'refuge unto his people' (3^{16f}), and 'in that day' 'a fountain shall come forth from the house of the LORD' and the whole land shall abound in fruitfulness (3^{16-18}). At three points in the book there are 'wonders in the heavens, the sun and moon being darkened' and 'the stars withdrawing their shining' ($2^{10, 30f}$, 3^{15f}). Jerusalem is the centre of interest throughout.

The LORD's pledge that He will 'pour out of (his) spirit' on every Jew, even to the slaves (2^{28-32}), is, of course, the crown of the Book of Joel. In effect, 'every Jew' means 'every Israelite', for, in practice, Israel had shrunk to the Jews. The gift of the Spirit is the proper prelude to the Day and not its sequel. Ezekiel has a like prophecy (36^{25-7}), but there is a contrast. He, himself an ecstatic, took ecstasy for granted, and stressed ethics; Joel, taking ethics for granted, stresses ecstasy. To suppose that he did not take ethics for granted but ignored them, is just an anachronism. Indeed, the Apocalyptist himself presently speaks of the 'remnant whom the LORD is calling' and who 'call upon the name of the LORD' (verse 32)—and 'remnant' always means 'righteous remnant'. The general postulate that before the Day comes there will be a people ready for it has here an outstanding example. As always when the Spirit is named, the gift is individual in origin and societary in outcome. Men who have the same Spirit are one.

The Apocalypse found in Isaiah 24-27 is a mixture of oracles and songs. It is remarkable that the phrase 'The Day of the LORD' does not occur. On the other hand, the phrase 'in that day' occurs seven times (24^{21}, 25^9, 26^1, $27^{1f, 12f}$). Clearly this was now a well-worn and well-understood phrase. The first Song (25^{1-8}) epitomizes this *chasid's* message. He is one of a faithful group who, as in Malachi and some Psalms, have been 'waiting' and 'waiting' for the LORD to vindicate Himself and them (25^9; cf. 26^{16-18}). *Now* He is beginning to do so (24^{1-12}), for it is *He* who, through Alexander, is 'making the earth empty and waste and turning it upside down'. All the Gentiles are sinners, so 'the curse' is on one and all (24^{5f}). Here the writer concentrates on some 'city' (perhaps Persepolis, which Alexander burnt). This, for him, is the capital of Sin (24^{10-12}). It is to be 'destroyed', 'left desolate', and fall back into the primeval chaos. The feet of the LORD's 'poor' are to trample it under foot (26^{5f}). God is still disciplining Israel

THE OLD TESTAMENT APOCALYPSES 69

—not to destroy her, like other nations, but to 'purge her iniquity' (27⁷⁻⁹). This Apocalyptist does not neglect ethics. But after the purging, 'the LORD of hosts shall reign in Mount Zion and in Jerusalem and before his ancients (shall be his) glory' (24²³). The City of Righteousness fronts the City of Sin.

What is to happen when the Day comes? The LORD will first reduce the clamour that now fills the earth to the silence of an Eastern noon (25⁵⁻¹²). Then, as the writer says ironically, He will gather 'all peoples' to a strange feast at a 'mountain' that flanks Jerusalem, and will there 'destroy' the veil that has hidden from them the truth that it is He, the LORD, who has all the time been Master of them all, and then—'Death hath swallowed (the Gentile nations) once for all—i.e. they are dead and done with.¹ When they are gone, the LORD's long-suffering people dry their tears—or rather, He dries them. 'His people' are those who have suffered 'reproach' because they have been loyal to Him through all the years when He *seemed* to be helpless, as verse 9 shows. Next (26¹⁻⁴, ¹², ¹⁵, 27¹²) 'the righteous nation that keepeth truth' gathers at its 'strong city',—strong because 'Jah Jehovah is its Rock of Ages', who can and will go on to keep His *chasidim* 'in perfect peace'.

The most famous verse in this 'book' remains to be quoted: 'Thy dead shall live; my corpses shall rise. Awake and cry out for joy, ye inhabitants of the dust: for thy dew is the dew of herbs [or, 'of the light' that brings life], and the earth shall cast forth the Weaklings' (26¹⁹). The verse is to be taken in contrast with verse 14—'The dead shall not live; the Weaklings shall not arise'— spoken of the 'many lords' that have ruled over Israel for centuries. As verse 14 requires, there is no idea that *all* the dead will rise, but only the faithful. *Their nephashoth* in Sheol are to rejoin their bodies, 'spirit' is to return to them, and they will live again *on earth*. While the verse is triumphant, it does not play the large part in the 'book' that an altogether new idea surely would. It is possible that the belief in resurrection was not altogether strange and that the writer of Psalm 49 was not singular (cf. Pr 15²⁴, 23¹⁴). In any case, even though the verse is quite subordinate to

¹ The English Versions, following the Massoretic vowel points, render: 'He hath *swallowed up* death' (RV, 'for ever'; AV, 'in victory'). This would mean that the taking away of the 'veil' at the 'feast' describes the conversion of the Gentiles. This idea, however, is not consonant with the tone of this Apocalypse, and LXX has: 'Death in its might swallowed (them) down.' Cf. I Co 15⁵⁴. When Paul 'christianized' an Old Testament text, he was not always careful of its historical context. Like Philo he believed that a passage might have a deeper meaning as well as a literal one.

the main theme, there is here at last an indisputable[2] assertion that the righteous will return from Sheol to glad life on earth.[3]

Zechariah 9-14 falls into three parts, probably by different authors—Chh. 9-11, 12 and 13, and 14. Two of them are called 'burdens' (*massah*—9¹, 12¹). They all probably belong to the time of the Maccabaean revolt and just after. The first 'burden' itself falls into two parts—the one (9 and 10) telling of a great 'hope' (9¹²) and the other (11) of a great disappointment. In the latter the *chasid* represents himself as a true 'shepherd', as over against the false 'shepherds' (i.e. the high priests). His 'flock' are the 'most miserable of (the) sheep', whom the false shepherds are slaying (11⁵). The comparison with Ezekiel 34 is obvious. But even *this* 'flock' rejects its 'shepherd', treating him as if he were 'a hireling and not a shepherd'. At length he, half ironically and half broken-heartedly, cries, 'Pay me off then, if you will', and they weigh him out the price of a slave (11¹²). Here, 'in that day' (11¹¹) denotes this Day of Despair. It only remains for this 'fool of a shepherd' to foretell that the LORD will give faithless Israel such a 'shepherd' as they deserve, who shall himself perish by the sword (11¹⁵⁻¹⁷). This is perhaps the classic instance of the postponement of the Day until there is a people worthy of it.

The oracle of hope (9-10), falls into four parts. The main message (9¹¹⁻¹⁷), marked by the phrase 'in that day' (verse 16), tells that the LORD Himself will lead the 'Sons of Zion' in war and triumph against 'the Sons of Greece'. Here the 'Sons of Zion' include both Judah and Ephraim, the latter apparently being the so-called 'Samaritans'. To this War of the LORD there is a prelude and two sequels. In the former (9¹⁻⁸) the LORD, 'having his eye' upon Israel and the small peoples that ring her round, subdues them to her. In one of the sequels (10⁶⁻¹²) the LORD gathers the exiled Northerners home from the four corners of the earth; in the other (9⁹ᶠ). He gives Israel a new king whom He has 'saved' until now. The description of this king approaches the unique. The War of the LORD is a war that ends war. The coming king is

---

[2] Not indisputable; it has in fact been disputed. [G.W.A.]

[3] The present writer does not think that the very difficult passage in 24²¹ᶠ refers to the resurrection of the 'kings of the earth' (and their counter-parts in the lower 'heavens'—cf. Isa 14¹², Dan 10¹³). Here the 'pit' (*bor*) is defined by *masgēr*, which is the dungeon of a fortress on earth (LXX: *ochurōma*; cf. Gn 41¹⁴). Probably the verses are an interpolation and symbolize the fact that during the struggles of the Diadochi there were no 'world powers' that dominated Palestine, but that after 'many days' these revived in the Seleucid and Ptolemaic empires.

not only 'righteous' and has therefore been 'saved' against this Day, but 'lowly'. Unlike the king of Jeremiah 17^{25}, he will not ride into his city with the 'horses and chariots' of war, but will come 'riding upon an ass', the symbol of meekness and peace. As he rides into Zion, the City of David, there is little doubt that he is of David's line, though this is not mentioned (cf. 12^{12}). At long last 'he shall speak peace unto the nations, and his dominion shall be from sea to sea, and from the River unto the ends of the earth'.

In the second 'burden' (Zec 12 and 13) the phrase 'in that day' occurs ten times (12$^{3, 4, 6, 8, 9, 11}$, 13$^{1, 2, 4}$). The oracle is unique because its main theme is that the Day will be a Day of Judgement for Jerusalem and Judah, in which two-thirds of the inhabitants will perish and the other third will only be saved as by a refiner's fire (13^{8f}). There are idols in the City and it is infested by prophets with an 'unclean spirit' (13^{1f}). There is a faithless 'shepherd' (13^{7}). There seem to be factions, 'the House of David', 'the House of Nathan', and 'the House of Levi' fighting each other. Jerusalem is full of 'sin and uncleanness' (13^{1}). In this situation the LORD Himself summons 'all the nations round about' to assault His own City! Being Master of the Universe and of 'the spirit of man', He puts the spirit of a drunkard into the nations so that they are mad enough to think they can overcome His City (12^{1f}). This will prove impossible (verse 3) and in the end the LORD will smite the assailants (verse 4), the Jews winning a desperate victory (verses 5-9). But as a brief recapitulation at the end of the oracle shows, in the horrors of the siege the LORD has been 'smiting' His own people with its false 'shepherd' (13^{7f}). When, however, the victory is won, the 'remnant' (12^{14}) that survives will turn to a universal repentance; to save his life, a man who has been a false prophet will deny that he ever was one (12$^{10-14}$, 13$^{2-5}$); and 'a fountain shall be opened to the House of David and to the inhabitants of Jerusalem for sin and for uncleanness' (13^{1}). In a very brief epilogue the preacher describes the future. The purified remnant shall not pray in vain; God will say 'It is my people' and they will reply 'The LORD is my God'. It is an adequate epitome, but the main message of this Apocalyptist is that the Day will be a Day of Judgement for 'Israel' (12^{1}) and that only few will be saved and the few 'as by fire'. Though the House of David is named again and again, nothing is said of a future king.

The third passage, an oracle of 'spoil' (14¹), begins with the words, 'Behold, the Day of the LORD cometh', and the phrase 'in that day' occurs eight times (14¹, ⁴, ⁶, ⁸, ⁹, ¹³, ²⁰, ²¹). This Apocalypse is complementary to the last, for it says less of the fate of the Jews and more of 'all the nations'. The City has not repelled their attack, but fallen and suffered the horrors of an ancient sack —houses rifled, women raped, half of the inhabitants carried captive, spoil ready to divide (verses 1f). At that moment the LORD sets to His hand. Standing with His angels on the Mount of Olives, He cleaves it asunder, and the Jews that remain in the City flee through the cleft as from an earthquake (verses 4f).

For the Jews, pillaged and captive and fugitive, the Day, therefore, begins in darkness, but it will end in light (verses 6f), for perennial waters shall pour forth east and west from Jerusalem and 'all the land' will become as fertile as the Jordan Valley and the 'curse' put upon the 'ground' when Adam sinned will be gone (verses 8-10). Next there follows a horrible account of the virulent 'plague' with which the LORD will smite 'all the nations', apparently even as they are dividing the spoil (verses 12-15). Here the Apocalyptist describes simultaneous details. The flesh of the armies of the victors rots on their bones (verse 12); eager to hurry from this terror in the City they quarrel over the spoil (verses 13f); but none of it will ever be carried off, for the same 'plague' falls upon the beasts of burden waiting to be loaded (verse 15). Nothing is left but the vast heap of spoil. All this is because the LORD is now showing that He is the one 'King of all the earth' (verse 9). The remaining verses (verses 16-21) describe the sequel. Jerusalem, now the Holy City (verses 20f), will be the capital of the world. To it all the nations will throng every year at Tabernacles to 'worship the King, the LORD of hosts' (verse 17). If any refuse, drought will fall upon their land—but upon Egypt, since she does not need rain but lives by the waters of the Nile, the 'plague' (verses 17-19). Finally, everything in Jerusalem (and not merely the Temple), from the 'horses' to the 'seething-pots', will be 'holy unto the LORD'.

The Book of Daniel is the first of the pseudepigraphic Apocalypses, that is, it is ascribed to an ancient *Chasid* but written by a later author. Its readers may have understood the device. It meant that the LORD had foreknown and controlled everything in the centuries when He had seemed inert. The ostensible writer is

'Daniel', who belongs to the sixth century B.C., but the real writer belongs to the second—that is, the four centuries from Nebuchadnezzar to Epiphanes lie between them. God is said to reveal the history of these four centuries *beforehand* to Daniel, but in fact they were already past. As the present subject is the real writer's account of the Future, as little as possible is said of these four centuries, but a preliminary note is needed. They are described twice—once under the symbol of an idol with four parts (Ch. 2), and once under the symbols of four 'beasts', or, better, 'brutes' (Ch. 7). In both cases the symbols stand, in the Hebrew fashion, for the actual, not for ideas. The latter part of the four centuries is described a third time, under an account of the struggle between three 'Princes'—the Prince of Persia, the Prince of Greece, and Michael, the Prince of Israel (Ch. 10). These Princes, unlike the Idol and the Four Brutes, are 'heavenly' or aerial persons and not symbols. They belong to the manifold inhabitants of the air, of which 'angels' are most frequently named. They may be called 'societary persons', since each of them and a nation go inseparably together, just as in earlier days a Hebrew king and his people were identified. The date of the real writer of the book is the time when the three Maccabees rose against Antiochus Epiphanes, and probably 165-164, when Judas rededicated the Temple.

It needed the protracted study of modern scholars to fix this date, for the writer himself never names Epiphanes or the Maccabees, but leaves the interpretation under the implicit rubric: 'Let him that readeth understand.' It is for this reason that in later times, beginning with the New Testament century, it has been possible to ascribe the 'End' named in Daniel to one historical crisis after another. While for the real writer, as for the earlier Apocalyptists, the Day is near, for the ostensible writer it is distant. This phenomenon recurs under the extra-Canonical Jewish Apocalypses. There is another contrast too. The earlier Apocalyptists were passionate preachers, making their urgent appeals. Daniel, receiving his revelations in 'dreams' and 'visions of his head upon his bed' (e.g. 7^1), just describes them. Men do not make urgent appeals four centuries ahead! In great measure Daniel is here too typical of later Apocalypses.

It is with this background that 'Daniel's' doctrine of 'the last things' is to be considered. He has such phrases as 'latter days' and 'end of the days' (2^{28}, 10^{14}, 12^{13}), but for *the* Day he prefers the word 'end' (*qētz, 10*), though it does not occur before Chapter 8.

He has the phrases 'the time of the end' (8^{17}, $11^{35, 40}$, $12^{4, 9}$), 'the appointed time of the end' (8^{19}; cf. $11^{27, 35}$), and 'the end', *simpliciter* (9^{26}). Part of the book is in Aramaic (2^4–7^{28}) and part in Hebrew, but both parts use this characteristic word. Here the Hebrew part is considered first.

In Chapters 8-12 there are three 'visions', of which two (8 and 9) may be taken together. The writer begins with an account of the period from the reign of Nebuchadnezzar to the desecration of the Temple by Antiochus Epiphanes (8^{3-12}). He reckons its length mistakenly as four hundred and ninety years taking Jeremiah's prophecy that the exile would last seventy years to mean 'seventy *weeks*' of years—that is, seven times seventy ($9^{2, 24}$). Others seem to have thought much the same (2 Mac 15^{14-16}). This means that the End will come in the writer's day. It will close the four hundred and ninety years of Israel's discipline and purging (9^{24}). There is no need here to go into the details of 9^{25-7} and their relation to the history of the writer's day, though it may be noted that 'the anointed (one)' is a High Priest. The worship of an abominable idol in the Temple (cf. 1 Mac 1^{54}), which is the crisis of crises for this writer, is to last 'half a week', or three years and a half (168–165 B.C.), and then there shall be a 'consummation' (*kalah*) that God has 'determined'—i.e. the kind of 'end' that means the destruction of evil (cf. Isa 10^{23}). While the writer's centre of interest is the *contemporary* date of the End, he conceives it ethically, all but taking it as read that at the End God will, of course, 'make an end of sins ... and bring in everlasting righteousness' (9^{24}). Nothing is said of the peace, joy and prosperity that will accompany righteousness.

The third 'vision' (10-12) begins with an account of Daniel's meeting with 'a man clothed in linen, whose loins were girded with pure gold of Uphaz' (10^5). This 'man' is clearly an angel. The whole 'vision' comes through him. In the middle of it there is an account of the period from Daniel's supposed day to Epiphanes (11^{2-39}), which is not pertinent here, though it may be noted that the writer ironically sets the phrase '(Epiphanes) shall do (what he will)' over against the words 'appointed' and 'determined' ($11^{27-30, 36}$). But the phrase 'the *man* clothed in linen' is an example of one of the leading characteristics of the book—the writer's use of the term 'man', in a variety of phrases, to describe angels. In 9^{21} Gabriel, who 'touches' Daniel, is explicitly called 'the man Gabriel'. In Chapter 10 Daniel is similarly 'touched' three times—once by a 'hand', and twice by angels under the phrases 'one like the similitude of the sons of *men*' and 'one like the appearance of a *man*' ($10^{10, 16, 18}$). If verses 5, 9f, 13, 16, and 18-20 in the same chapter are taken together, it is clear that these are alternative names for 'the *man* in linen'. The last phrase is borrowed from Ezekiel ($9^{2, 4ff}$), where this 'man' sets God's mark on the saints who mourn because of 'all the abominations' done in Jerusalem. The phrase 'clothed in linen', of course, means that this aerial person is 'pure', as being one of 'the holy ones'. He is sent to Daniel because the latter is one of God's 'greatly beloved' ($10^{11, 19}$)—i.e. the typical *chasid*. The implication of the use of the term 'man' is that the angel and men of the true kind have much in common. As will appear below, in the Aramaic portion of the book, under yet another of these significant phrases, this idea develops into their societary unity.

The last part of the vision (11^{40}–12^{13}) falls into two sections, the first running from 11^{40} to 12^4. Only a few leading details need be mentioned. It is now 'the time of the end' (11^{40})—i.e. the 'time of trouble' (12^1) that began when Epiphanes set himself to root out the religion of the Jews. The writer distinguishes two classes of Jews, the worst and the best (11^{30-5}). When Epiphanes 'does' (what he will), even to the setting up of 'the loathsome thing that appals' (LXX, 'abomination of desolation') in the Holy Place, there are, on the one hand, the apostates who 'do wickedly against the covenant', and, on the other, 'the wise', or better, 'the discerning' (*sakal*). Some of them will die for their faith and thereby will purify their people against the imminent 'time of the end'. Others who 'know their God', will 'do' (what *they* will)—i.e. will rebel against Epiphanes who is 'doing' (what *he* will). All this describes what was already happening in the true writer's time. In 12^{1-4} he passes to what is going to happen. Through 'the time of trouble' Michael, the 'prince' of Israel, taking the side of the 'man clothed in linen', has been fighting the 'prince of Greece' (10^{20f}). He will prevail and 'every one' of 'the people' whose name is 'written in the book' will be 'delivered'—that is, salvation is to be *individual*. 'Many of them that sleep in the *earth of dust*' are then to 'awake'—that is (as in Isa 26^{19}) there is a resurrection of the body, the *nephesh* and *ruach* returning to it. Here, however, 'many' of the bad are to rise as well as 'many' of the righteous. Whether the claim that 'many' sometimes means 'all' can be made good in other passages or not, it is not so here, as the use of the word in 12$^{3, 4, 10}$ shows. Probably the apostates and martyrs are meant. The 'many', both good and bad, are to return to live *on earth*, the righteous enjoying 'perpetual life', and the wicked enduring 'perpetual contempt'—which is not true 'life'. The word rendered 'contempt' occurs also in Isaiah 66^{24}, but, while the reference there is to the nausea of corrupting and burning corpses, here it is to the loathsomeness of apostates. These are to exist like lepers under the perpetual 'abhorrence' of their fellows. No other punishment is named. The 'discerning', on the other hand, are to share the perpetual glory and dominion of the stars 'who live in the firmament'.

The last paragraph of the book (12$^{5-13}$) centres in the question '*how long* will the "time of trouble" last?' The 'man clothed in linen' takes a great oath that it will last 'for a time, times, and an half'. Daniel, living long before, does not understand that the phrase means three years and a half for 'the words are shut up and sealed till the time of the end'—i.e. till *the writer's* time. The figures in 12^{11f} are puzzling, but the meaning clearly is that for the men who have known how to 'wait', it will be a happy thing to be alive at the End. Daniel is to share their happiness after 'resting' for hundreds of years in the grave (12^{13}). The promise of resurrection, as in Isaiah 26^{19}, plays a surprisingly small part in the book if it were a *new* belief. Probably it was current in more than one form, at least under the question 'Can it be?' It was a *settled* belief of the Pharisees in the time of Jesus and this probably implies a long period of discussion (cf. 2 Mac 7). It is the same with the phrase 'everlasting life'. It occurs now for the first time, but it is used as if it denoted a well-known concept. To say that after the End a man will live always is, of course, quite different from saying that after it there will be a realm of 'everlasting righteousness'. In Daniel the opposing phrase 'everlasting loathing' seems to mean that the specially wicked will also go on existing always on earth, unless this be taken to mean that for any wicked found for a while on earth there will always be loathing.

In the Aramaic part of the book there are two relevant passages (Chh. 2 and 7), both furnishing instances of symbolized facts. In the former of them two verses describe the End (2^{44f}). Here Daniel tells Nebuchadnezzar that, at a certain time in the distant future, the 'God of heaven' will set up a final kingdom, whose 'people' shall break in pieces and rule the other peoples, and shall 'stand for ever'. The Idol of the Four Empires is to crash at last because 'a stone cut out of the mountain without hands' will 'break it in pieces' (2^{45}; cf. 8^{25}). Probably the 'mountain' is the holy mountain of Zion (cf. Isa 28^{16}) and the 'stone' is the faithful in Israel. Here God is compared to a slinger who does not miss His mark. The writer takes it for granted that the 'people' who are to rule in the final kingdom are righteous and that *therefore* their rule is to be everlasting. The idea is not that in the final kingdom *all* peoples will be righteous, but that the *one* righteous 'people' will rule the rest.

The second passage (Ch. 7), the Vision of the Four Brutes and their End, is more detailed. Epiphanes, who is 'the little horn' (verse 8), is not only boasting 'great things' but 'prevailing' in war against the 'saints' (verse 21). The chapter falls into two parts. In the first (verses 9-14), there is a universal judgement (verses 9-12) and then the appointment of the future vicegerent of God (verses 13f). Under the Judgement the writer borrows from Ezekiel the image of a fiery throne speeding on 'wheels' wherever God will. It speeds from heaven to earth, and the 'Ancient of Days', girt with the myriads of His 'ministering' Holy Ones, sits to judge the Brutes. The fourth Brute, now embodied in Epiphanes, is destroyed and burnt, but the other three, unthroned (verse 9), endure for a while. Then the vicegerent of the Future is named. He is an aerial person, who is 'like unto a son of man' —i.e. as the phrase means in Aramaic, 'like a man'. Then there follows the famous description of his universal and everlasting rule (verse 14). In the second part (verses 15-28), Daniel is disquieted after this vision, for there is something missing. What is to happen to the 'saints (*qaddish*) of the Most High' over whom Epiphanes had formerly 'prevailed'? The answer is that they will 'receive and possess the kingdom' and rule the whole world for ever as God's vicegerents (verses 18, 27). Probably it is implied that those whom Epiphanes had slain will rise from the dead, for how should *they*, of all the 'saints', fail of victory? The declaration that both the 'one like unto a son of man' and 'the saints' are to rule for ever are not contradictory but complementary, for the former is both an individual and a societary person. It is as if one were to say both 'Darius ruled a vast empire' and, speaking of the same period, 'the Persians ruled a vast empire', for, in a sense, Darius *was* the Persians, or, again, to say that the aerial person called 'the Prince of Persia' (10^{20}) *is* the Persians. The 'one like unto a son of man'—like the 'man clothed in linen' of the Hebrew part of the book (10^5)—and the faithful Hebrews fall under the societary principle of identification. He and they are one.

In the Book of Daniel one contrast is drawn in three ways. Near its beginning a 'stone made without hands' (i.e. by God) is set over against a colossus with four parts; at its end the 'man clothed in linen', under various names, is set over against 'the princes' of four empires; in the middle 'one like unto a son of man' is set over against four 'brutes'. It is clear that the colossus, the 'princes' and the 'brutes' all stand for the same four empires. It seems to follow that the 'stone', the 'man clothed in linen' and the 'one like unto a son of man' all stand for the same agent of God— and, in particular, that the *last two* are to be identified. It has often been pointed out that in Aramaic the phrase 'one like unto a son of man' is equivalent to 'one like a man'. Is not this so too with the Hebrew phrases 'one like the similitude of the sons of men' and 'one like the appearance of a man' ($10^{16, 18}$), which, as has been seen, describe the 'man clothed in linen'? If so, the 'one like unto a son of man' of 7^{13} is no otiose angel 'out of the blue', but the victor in the fight against Persia and Greece ($10^{18, 20}$) to whom the vicegerency in the everlasting kingdom is entrusted. He first wins a final victory, and then rules the final kingdom. His glory is like God's glory (10^{5-8}), yet he is also like a man (cf. Ezk 1^{26-8}). The Davidic line is ignored.

There is abundance of evidence that for the last of the Apocalyptists, as for the other three, the Future City is a dominant concept. This suits a period when Jerusalem was the centre of Hebrew worship even for the Dispersion. In one chapter (9) the writer of Daniel names Jerusalem six times (cf. 6^{10}). He speaks twice of 'the land of beauty'—probably with the implication of 'desire' (*tzebi*) ($11^{16, 41}$)—once of 'the holy mountain of beauty' (11^{45}), and once of the 'beauty' *simpliciter* (8^9), thinking always of Jerusalem as the jewel of God. It is *there* that 'the abomination that maketh desolate' is set up, and *there* that it will perish when 'all these things shall be finished' and the horror is over (11^{31}, $12^{7, 11}$). For the Prophets and Apocalyptists the Future Kingdom without the Future City would have been like a circle without a centre.

With Daniel there begins a change of emphasis in the concept of 'the Day'. With his three predecessors the focus of the complex concept had been 'victory', rather than judgement, as with the Prophets, but now 'Judgement' begins to be the focal concept.

The word is sometimes used (Dn 4^{37}, 7$^{10, 22, 26}$), and sometimes implied (e.g. 5^{27}, 9^{12}, 11^{45}, 12^{2}). The phrase 'The judgement was set and the books were opened' (7^{10}) announces the period in which the Day is primarily 'the Day of Judgement'.

It will be seen that, while the four Old Testament Apocalyptists vary greatly in details, they all held a common creed. They all believed that, since God is master of history, the Day of the LORD, will inevitably come, and that it will divide the Era of Sin from the Era of Righteousness. The Day is societary, for on it the rule of sinful nations ends and the rule of God over a universal society begins. It is also individual, for the wicked—that is, all the Gentiles and some part of the Hebrews—will either perish or sink to servitude, and the righteous Hebrews will flourish as none had ever flourished before. They all believed too that the Era of Righteousness, like the Era of Sin, is part of the *history* of man on earth. The two Eras fall within *the same universe*, and both belong to the realm of *time*. There can be little doubt that, however greatly opinion varied on points of detail, this creed was normal in Israel, and remained so in New Testament times. Why else should Daniel have then found its way into the Canon?

THE SEPTUAGINT

CHAPTER SEVEN

THE RULE OF GOD—PAST, PRESENT, AND FUTURE

For the present subject the LXX is important in two ways. First it gives the current Greek renderings of Hebrew words in New Testament times. Here it is to be remembered that the first Christians normally quote from LXX, this being their customary 'Bible'. Second, the books added to the Hebrew Canon, now called 'Apocrypha', show the ways in which the Jewish doctrine of the Future developed. Very occasionally the Greek version of Hebrew books also helps here, either because it is based on a different Hebrew text or because the translators did not translate literally, but interpreted. The background of the Books of the Apocrypha is the Hellenistic Age, which has already been described.

The mere acceptance of the Hebrew Canon shows, of course, that the Greek-speaking Jews accepted the doctrine that all history, past, present, and future, is under the Rule of God. This carries with it the belief that He also controls the universe, which is the sphere of history. This appears very clearly in the Song of the Three Holy Children (the *Benedicite*), where the writer first calls at length upon the whole universe to 'bless, praise, and exalt the Lord', then upon 'the children of men', then on Israel and the righteous, and finally on the Three Children themselves (Three 35, 60, 61, 64, 66). Men do not exult in a God who is not master of the situation.

The belief that God has ruled throughout the history of the *past*, and especially throughout the past history of Israel, appears in the Apocrypha as well as in the Old Testament. For instance, it underlies the whole Book of Baruch. But there is nothing added to the doctrine. Under the belief that the Lord rules the *present*, the Apocrypha emphasizes two particular points. First, in a period when, for His own purposes, God is leaving His people under alien rule, the belief takes the form: 'In spite of our seemingly helpless plight, He is *saving* us *now*.' In one way or another this belief lies behind every book in the Apocrypha. It will suffice to give an outstanding example. In the Book of Judith, an Ammonite (5^{5-24}) having rehearsed to Holofernes the story of the Lord's ancient deliverance of His people from Egypt, and of the way in which He has since given them victory when they were righteous but punished them when they sinned, concludes that Holofernes will conquer because they are sinners now—with the implication that the Hebrew God will settle the business as He will. To this Holofernes replies: 'Who is God but Nebuchadnezzar?' (Jth 6^2). The whole book of Judith is an answer to this challenge. It is a vindication of 'the Almighty Lord' (16^6). Yet He does not deal with the universe of men. All He chooses to do for the present is to save Israel. It may be noticed that Judith is both an individual and a societary person.

The second outstanding instance of the belief that God is God of History now is that in some of the Books of the Apocrypha God saves individuals—whose life, of course, is part of history. It has already been shown that in the period after the Exile individualism came to its zenith in Israel. Correspondingly, God saves righteous individuals—Tobit and Tobias, the Three Holy Children and Susanna—and even gives Daniel a dinner (Bel 33-42). Further, He can save them wherever they are— e.g. Tobit in Assyria, Sarah in Ecbatana, and Tobias on his journey from one to the other. Every fictitious story in the Apocrypha presupposes that the Lord is master of history now.

In the Old Testament the belief that He is also master of *future* history belongs principally to the Prophecies and Apocalypses— and there are none of these in the Greek Apocrypha (where Second Esdras has no place.) They were 'Crisis Books'. The First Book of Maccabees is history and the Second claims to be. None of the books of the Apocrypha gives the impression that it was written at a moment when the Day of the Lord seemed near. Yet there are texts which show that the canonical doctrines were current. In 'the Rest of Esther' Mordecai dreams a dream (11^{2-11}) of 'a *day* of darkness and gloominess, tribulation and anguish, affliction and great uproar upon the earth' (verse 8). In a passage which is placed first in this book in the English Versions but ought to be placed last, this dream is interpreted (10^{5-12}). In it God prefers the 'lot' of Israel to the 'lot' of 'the nations' at a certain 'hour and time and day of judgement' (verse 11). This was to be *a* Day of salvation for Israel and of 'visitation' on the Gentiles which would befall at a given point in Persian history, not '*the* Day' that would end the present kind of history, but it illustrates the belief that the Lord controls future history. At the end of Judith's Song there is a clear reference to '*the* Day' even though here there is no article in the Greek—'Woe to the nations that rise up against my race: the Lord Almighty will render them retribution on Judgement Day, To put fire and worms in their flesh; And they shall weep and feel their pain for ever' (Jth 16^{17}). This, of course, recalls Isaiah 66^{24}. It is the unburied bodies of the slain *on earth* that are in mind, not their 'souls' in Hades. Now, however, it is explicitly stated that these corpses can feel and weep! Behind the whole Song there is the conviction that God, having just vindicated Israel on *a* Day, has thereby pledged Himself to give her a final victory on '*the* Day'. The corpses are not those of all the wicked who have died in the past, for nearly all these would have been buried, but of the wicked who fell on 'the Day'. There is another reference to 'the Day' in the Book of Wisdom, under the phrase '(the) Day of Decision' (*diagnōsis*) (Wis 3^{18}). The writer is saying that, even if a wicked man dies before his time, this will not be his only punishment, for another will follow on 'the Day'. The noun *diagnosis* does not occur elsewhere in LXX, but the cognate verb, *diagnōskein* (*9*), sometimes means 'to decide to act (after considering a situation)' (e.g. Jth 11^{12}, 2 Mac 9^{15}, 15^6). Both in Judith and Wisdom the writers just take it for granted that their readers will understand their allusions and that they believe that some time 'the Day' will inevitably come. This means that, even for faithful Jews who did not date the Day soon, the idea was by no means otiose. It is not unlikely that the writer of Second Maccabees believed that 'the Day' *would* have come quickly if the Jews had remained faithful to God as Judas did (cf. 15$^{14-16}$), but if so he writes at a time when that hope has failed and the Day is again distant. While he believes that the Resurrection of the Righteous which is an element in the concept of the Day, is *certain* (2 Mac 7), he does not say that it is *near*. There were Jews then, as there are Christians now, who, accepting a Canon which taught, here and there, that the Day was near, yet believed that it was distant, though sure. There would come a time when God the Lord of future history, would put an end to the Era of Sin. This, of course, is very different from the belief that sin will gradually disappear as man progresses.

In rendering such phrases as 'the Day of the LORD' LXX regularly uses the ordinary Greek word for 'day', *hēmera*. It has been shown above that, particularly in the Book of Daniel, the Hebrew word *qetz*, 'End', is synonym for 'Day'. In LXX there are fifteen renderings for *qetz*, but only four are anything like frequent. These are *telos* (*7*), *peras* (*17*), *kairos* (*6*), and *sunteleia* (*15*). In these numbers the renderings of *qetz* both in LXX version of Daniel and Theodotion's are included, the two versions being distinguished below.

Of the four terms named the first two, *telos* and *peras*, are peculiar to Theodotion, who uses *telos* twice for *qetz* (9²⁶, 11¹³) and *peras* seven times (8¹⁷,¹⁹, 11²⁷,³⁵,⁴⁰, 12⁶,⁹). *Telos* denotes a completed purpose. For the *differentia* of *peras* perhaps 'goal' gives the best idea. It renders *qetz*, for instance, in 'Let me know mine end' (Ps 39⁴), and Ezekiel uses it seven times—e.g. in 'an end! the end is come!' and 'the time of the punishment of the end' (Ezk 7², 21²⁵). It is not unlikely that Theodotion, who was a careful translator, had the idea 'goal' in mind when he used it in Daniel.

Of the other two renderings both Theodotion and LXX use one, *kairos*, in a single text 8¹⁷)—'The vision belongs to the time of the end'. The word means 'season'—i.e. it denotes the end of a process—as in 'the end of all flesh is come before me' (Gn 6¹³), and 'Her seasons have come! Open her barns!' (Jer 50²⁶ LXX). In LXX translation of other books than Daniel the fourth word, *sunteleia*, is common (*54*), rendering twelve Hebrew words, but it never renders *qetz* except in Daniel. Here Theodotion has it three times (12⁴,¹³) and LXX no less than fifteen times (8¹⁹, 9²⁶, 11⁶,¹³,²⁷,³⁵ᶠ,⁴⁵, 12⁴,⁶ᶠ,¹³). It is the LXX translator's favourite word for *qetz*. Among the terms that it translates elsewhere *kalah* is the most frequent (*22*), a word that means 'to finish' or 'complete'[1]—for example, in the phrases 'smite unto completion' (2 K 13¹⁷ LXX), and 'I will not make a full-end' (Jer 4²⁷). *Sunteleia* renders *kalah* (as well as *qetz*) in Daniel itself, both in Theodotion's translation (9²⁷) and in LXX (9²⁷, 12⁷). Under *kalah* 'completion' is a better translation than 'consummation', for 'consummation',

---

[1] The verb *kalah* means 'to be complete', 'to be at an end', and, in the Pi'el, 'to complete', 'to bring to an end'. The noun *kalah* means '*completion*'. [G.W.A.]

GBDH

strictly speaking, denotes the perfecting of a *harmonious* whole, and the texts in Daniel, as the context of 9^{27} in particular shows, denote the end of a period in which bad men and good live very *inharmoniously* together. This applies too to the texts where *sunteleia* renders *qetz*—e.g. there is to be 'war unto the *sunteleia*' (9^{26}; cf. $11^{13, 27}$), and the *sunteleia* is the end of a period where good men and bad are mingled (11^{35f}). All four terms denote 'completion', and all signify that at an 'appointed' time (Dn 8^{19}, 10^1, $11^{27, 29, 35}$) God will complete His plan for the first part of the history of mankind.

The four terms are common enough in the Apocrypha (*telos*, *20*; *peras*, *11*; *kairos*, *113*; *sunteleia*, *19*). All four may denote the 'end' of a man's life (e.g. Wis 3^{19}, 19^4, Sir 5^7, 33^{23}). This is the meaning in Sirach's phrase: 'Be mindful of wrath in (the) day of death (*teleutē*), and (the) season of retribution in (the) turning away of (his) face' (18^{24}). There is only one text where any of these terms refers to '*the* Day' or 'End'—'In the season (*kairos*) of their visitation (*episcopē*) (the righteous) shall shine forth' (Wis 3^7). The phrase is unusual, but the meaning is clear. For the 'souls' of the righteous in their quiet resting-place there will come a Day of Resurrection and of Dominion (verses 7-9).

It will be noticed that both under the few passages where the Apocrypha speak of 'the Day' and under the four terms just examined the central idea is now that 'the Day' is a Day of Judgement rather than, as with the Prophets, a Day of Victory. God does not now need to go forth to war in order to prevail over the wicked; the Almighty does not need to strive. The 'appointed' End is *ipso facto* the Day of Judgement. Further, 'Judgement' must not be taken to imply that there is a question 'Guilty or not?' with a scrutiny of evidence as in a law-court today. The Omniscient knows already who is righteous and who is wicked. On the Day of Judgement the Judge does nothing but *act*.

The term *basileia* ('kingship' or 'kingdom') is not common in the Apocrypha, but there is sufficient evidence to show that the phrase 'Kingdom of God' was current, even though there is no instance of this precise phrase. Tobit (13^1) begins his 'prayer for rejoicing' with the words, 'Blessed is God that liveth for ever and his kingship', going on to claim confidently that He only 'scourges' Israel now in order that He may 'exalt' her—not after an Apocalypse, apparently, but in the course of ordinary history. It is much the same in Baruch 5^6, where one reading describes the returning exiles as 'children of the kingdom' (cf. Ad. Est 16[16]). Here either 'rule' or 'realm' gives good sense, because the words are correlative. There are texts that illustrate the principle that kings, even heathen kings, rule by God's appointment (Wis 6[4, 20], Ad. Est 16[16]). When God gives the Maccabees victory, He has 'restored ... the kingdom (or kingship)' to Israel (2 Mac 2[17]). When Jacob fled from Esau Wisdom 'showed him God's kingship', apparently at Bethel—i.e. she showed him that God was ordering everything all the time. Under the word *basileia* in the Apocrypha there is no reference to the everlasting kingship that will follow the End, but in the Apocalyptic passage in Wisdom (4[18]–5[23]) the phrase '(The righteous) shall receive the *basileion*, or kingly (crown), of dignity' (Wis 5[16]), implies both that there will be a 'kingdom of God' after the End and that the 'righteous' will reign in it. Except in Tobit's 'prayer', the texts in the Apocrypha bear witness to the currency of ideas that they do not expound.

CHAPTER EIGHT

DEATH AND HADES

UNDER THESE subjects LXX, so far as the translation of the Hebrew Canon goes, repeats, of course, the Old Testament teaching and it is sufficient to give the usual Greek renderings of the leading terms. Where the writers of the Apocrypha merely carry on the tradition, a reference or two will show this. At the points where there is development of thought more will be said.

For the Hebrew word for 'die' (*muth*), by far the commonest rendering is *apothnēskein* (*412*). In the Apocrypha, as in the Old Testament, a quiet death, after a long and prosperous life, is the proper end of the righteous (e.g. To 14^{11-15}, Jth 16^{23}). Premature death, especially when it is sudden and violent, on the other hand, is a disaster. Sometimes it is punishment for sin, whether the sinner is killed 'by the hand of God' (e.g. 2 Mac 9^5) or by an agent of His (e.g. Sus 60-62, 1 Mac 2^{24f}). At other times it is murder. Sirach has a long passage of praise because God has saved him from this (51^{1-12}). The commonest renderings for the Hebrew words that denote 'to kill' or 'slay' may be given. In the texts where 'fire' or 'sword' is said to 'eat' or 'devour', the Hebrew *'akal* is sometimes rendered literally by *esthiein* or *katesthiein*, and sometimes by *analiskein* or *katanaliskein* (*16*). Whatever the etymology of the second pair of words, they mean 'consume' (e.g. Dt 4^{24}, Wis 16^{16}). For *shachath* ('to ruin'), the commonest renderings are *diaphtheirein* and *kataphtheirein*, with their cognates (*110*). While the original meaning of the Greek root seems to have been 'to waste away', these words are used, like *shachath*, to denote *any* kind of ruin, and not only ruin by 'corruption'. In the Apocrypha *diaphtheirein* and its cognates, while they may denote violent death (e.g. Sir 47^{22}, Wis 18^{12}, 2 Mac 8^{35}), never denote the physical decay of 'corruption'. It follows that 'destroy' and 'destruction' are the right English renderings and not 'corrupt' and 'corruption'. It is true, indeed, that in two of the three places where the adjective *phthartos* occurs the rendering 'corruptible' rightly describes the kind of destruction in question (Wis 9^{15}, 2 Mac 7^{16}), but this is not so with the third (Wis 14^8), and its opposite adjective, *aphthartos*, in its two instances (Wis 12¹, 18⁴), describes the 'spirit' of God and 'the light of the law', neither of which is destructible in *any* way. In view of all the evidence it is best to render *phthartos* by 'destructible'. In the one example of this word outside the Apocrypha (with the variant *phtharma*) foreigners' sacrifices are not called 'corruptible', for all sacrifices are this *ipso facto*, but destructive of Israel (Lv 22²⁵). Finally, the term *'abad*, the most important in the list, is almost always rendered by *apollunai* or its noun *apoleia* (*183*). As with *'abad*, English needs three terms to render *apollunai*—'destroy', 'lose', and 'perish'. *Apollunai* also renders *karath* ('to cut off') —*94*), *shamad* ('to exterminate by slaughter'—*43*), and *shachath* ('to ruin'—*33*). None of these three Hebrew words means 'to annihilate'. It is the same where the term renders *'abad* (e.g. 1 S 9³, Ezk 34⁴). As with *'abad*, the underlying idea always is that a person or animal or thing has ceased to fulfil its proper function. Under *apollunai* there are examples from the Apocrypha in 1 Es 8⁸⁸, To 3¹⁵, Sir 10¹⁶ᶠ, Wis 12¹⁴, 1 Mac 3⁴². The two commonest words in the whole list are *apollunai* and *diaphtheirein*, with their cognates. If any distinction is possible between them, it would be that under the first a thing, or the use of a thing, is 'lost', while under the second the thing is 'spoilt', either through deterioration or disintegration. After the Prophets had done their work, when God destroys men it is always wicked men—i.e. for them sudden death is punishment.

The Hebrew believed that death came by dissolution, the four parts of a man falling asunder. The usual Greek renderings for these have been mentioned in the Prolegomena, but further details may be given. For the rare Hebrew word for 'body' (*geviyyah*) *sōma* is usual, and for the far commoner term 'flesh' (*basar*) *sarx*. The usual word for *neshamah* is *pnoē* (fifteen times out of twenty). For *nephesh* there are seventeen Greek renderings, but sixteen of these are rare and sporadic. The regular rendering is *psyche*, which translates *nephesh* some six hundred and fifty times. Like *nephesh*, *psyche* combines the meanings of 'life' and 'soul'. Similarly, *ruach* has no less than twenty-four renderings, but one of them *pneuma*, occurs about two hundred and seventy times. The next most frequent word is *anemos* ('wind'), but this is only found forty-nine times. *Pneuma*, like *ruach*, combines the concepts of 'wind' and 'spirit'. In the texts where the *nephesh* is related to

Sheol LXX always renders it by *psyche*. Similarly, where *ruach* occurs in relation to death, the Greek term is always *pneuma*.

As the continued use of the four Greek terms shows, the belief that death is dissolution continues in the Apocrypha. Here only a note or two need be made. The belief that the corpse of a dead man ought to be buried has an outstanding example in the Book of Tobit. Here Tobit risks his life to bury an unburied Jew (1^{17ff}; cf. 2^{3ff}), and begins his Charge to Tobias with the words: 'My child, when I die, bury me' (4^{3f}; cf. 14^{10-13}). The belief that at death a man's *pnoe* passed into the air has a dramatic instance in the phrase 'at the last gasp' (2 Mac 3^{31}, 7^9). The idea that at death the *pneuma*, like the *pnoe*, rejoins the air is explicit in 'The *pneuma* shall be dispersed as thin air' (Wis 2^3). It is true that this is what the wicked say, but it is not under *pneuma* that the writer challenges them but under *psyche* (2^{22}, 3^1). In the description of Tobit's death (14^{11}) the Greek does not mean 'He gave up the ghost' (i.e. 'spirit'), as both English Versions translate, but 'His *psyche* failed' (*ekleipein*), as in Jon 2^8 LXX. This introduces the fourth of the constituents of a man, *psyche*. Outside Wisdom there is no novelty in its use. At death it passes to Hades (Sir 51^6), as in Hebrew books. In Wisdom, on the other hand, there is new teaching at this point, as will appear below.

The Hebrew word *sheol* is rendered by *hades* except in three texts where *thanatos* ('death') is used (e.g. 2 S 22^6). Hades was the natural translation, for the Greeks, like the Hebrews, believed that the dead passed into a vast cavern within the earth and Hades was their name for this. The word occurs twenty-two times in the Apocrypha, of which ten are in Sirach. In the Revised Version unfortunately it is sometimes translated by 'the grave', for this term is appropriate to the body, not to the *psyche* but usually the Revisers use the Greek word itself. 'To send a man to Hades' is used as a synonym for 'to kill' (2 Mac 6^{23}; cf. Ad. Est 13^7). Baruch (3^{9-19}) warns 'Israel' that, like the 'princes of the heathen and such as ruled the beasts', she will 'go down to Hades' (verses 11, 19) unless she repents. On the surface this seems to teach that nations, like individuals, may die and pass to Hades, but an appeal for repentance, of course, is an appeal to individuals. One of the words for 'the Pit', *bor*, is rendered by *bothros* (a 'hole'), eight times; by *hades* three times; and by *lakkos* (a 'cistern'), six times. Where the other term, *shachath*, means 'the Pit', *thanatos* occurs five times, *apoleia* or a cognate three times, and *diaphthora* ten times. *Abaddon*, except in one text where LXX does not refer it to Hades (Job 31¹²), is always rendered by *apoleia*. The word *gava'* ('to expire'), unfortunately Englished by 'to give up the ghost', is rendered seven times by *ekleipein*, six times by *apothneskein*, and four times by *apollunai*.

There is one term, *repha'im*, under which LXX introduces a new idea. As earlier noted, this word is first used to describe *dead* men in Sheol in Isaiah 14⁹. But it had been used earlier (e.g. Gn 15²⁰ JE) to describe some of the ancient inhabitants of Canaan, who were giants (Dt 2¹⁰ᶠ, 3¹¹). In five texts (e.g. Gn 14⁵) LXX renders the word by *gigantes*. It uses it also for the *gibborim* (*17*), 'mighty men of valour', for the *Nephilim* (*2*), and for such a man as Nimrod (Gn 10⁸ᶠ). The word *Nephilim* describes the offspring of the 'sons of God' and the 'daughters of men' in Genesis 6⁴. These are counted a certain kind of *man*, as the phrase 'men of renown' shows. Apparently all the ancient giants were of the race that sprang from this unholy union (Nu 13³³). The race had long been extinct (Dt 3¹¹). In Ezekiel 32²⁷ the Greek translators take the phrase *gibborim nōphelim* ('the mighty that are fallen'), to refer, not to fallen monarchs, but to the Fallen Giants, assuming that the *Nephilim* were so called because they were now 'fallen'. In LXX the verse runs: 'And (the kings) sleep with the giants fallen of old, who went down into Hades with warlike weapons, and laid their swords under their heads, and their iniquities were upon their bones because they terrified all men in their life-times.' Similarly, it is the giants who say unto the Pharaoh 'Take thy place (*ginou*) in (the) depth of (the) pit!' (verse 21). The parallel text in Isa 14⁹ᶠ runs: 'Hades below is provoked to meet thee (Babylon)! All the giants who ruled the earth are roused for thee! These rouse from their thrones all kings of nations! All shall make answer and say to thee, Thou too caught! Even as we also (were)! And thou art reckoned among us!' In these two pictures the Giants seem to be the Watchmen of Hades, who, seeing the mighty Egypt or Babylon on the way to the Pit, rouse even its slumbering denizens to 'see this great sight'. It will be noticed that the Giants give orders in Hades and are not mere watchmen. These passages furnish the first instance of a belief about the Giants that played a large part in such books as Enoch. The word *gigantes* does not occur in the New Testament.

It has been seen that in the Hebrew Old Testament the earliest idea about Sheol was that it was a place of 'sleep' and peace and rest and that this idea persisted to the end, but that, in the later period another idea grew up alongside it among the *chasidim*—that Sheol was not a place of rest but of misery, which, while it might suit the wicked well enough, was not a fit account of the future of the righteous. In the Old Testament relief was found from this situation in the beginnings of a belief that the righteous would rise from the dead and return to earth to join in the life of happiness that would follow the Day. All these ideas recur in the Apocrypha. The subject of the Resurrection is taken in another chapter. But in the Apocrypha a new idea was added—that the old account of Sheol or Hades was too good for the wicked but not good enough for the righteous. This means that their fates differed *immediately after death*. The evidence for the survival of the two old accounts of Sheol will be taken first, and then that for the emergence of the new belief.

Under the concept that death is 'sleep', LXX has five terms—*hypnoun* ('to sleep'), *koimasthai* ('to lie down (to sleep))', *nustazein* ('to nod') (in satire—Nah 3[18]), *katheudein* ('to slumber'), and *anapauein* ('to rest'). With *koimasthai* and *anapauein* there go the nouns *koimesis* and *anapausis*. *Hypnoun* occurs in the Apocrypha to describe death (e.g. Sir 46[20]), as do *koimasthai* (e.g. 2 Mac 12[45]), *koimesis* (e.g. Sir 46[19]), *anapauein* (e.g. Sir 47[23]), and *anapausis* (e.g. Sir 38[23]). The LXX rendering of Job 3[13f] is a good example of the use of three of the words. If, says the Patriarch, he had died at birth, he would 'now have lain down to sleep (*koimasthai*) and been at ease, And, having fallen asleep (*hypnoun*) he would rest (*anapauein*)'. The meaning of *anapauein* is 'to rest', not 'refresh', for the original sense is 'leave off'. When the context requires it, it may imply 'refreshment'—as, for instance, when an ox or ass is given 'rest' on the Sabbath (Ex 23[12]), a text where 'refresh' (*anapsuchein*) occurs as a synonym—but, when used of death, this implication is, of course, excluded.

Many of the texts just quoted are taken from Sirach because the Sage is a good representative of the faithful Jews in humdrum days when there was no crisis. There are passages, however, where he shows restlessness under the orthodox doctrine, and probably here too he was representative. In a passage (14[11-19]) where, as he loved to do, he is giving advice to a 'young man', he says, in effect: 'Live a good and pleasant life here, for, when you die, all chance of this is gone.' 'Give and take, and beguile thy soul, For there is no seeking of luxury in Hades. . . . For the covenant from the beginning is, Thou shalt die the death' (verses 16f). Behind the passage there is a kind of protest against the helplessness and hopelessness of Hades, very different from the concept of 'rest'. This comes out in another way in 17^{27-30}, where the Sage reminds his hearers that in Hades one cannot even 'give praise to the Most High'! In a third passage (41^{1-4}), where Sirach apostrophizes 'Death', he describes two kinds of aged men. To an old man who is happy and prosperous and has a good appetite, the thought of death is 'bitter', but to a grey-beard who is poor and weak and worried and bad-tempered it is another matter. One suspects that the Sage himself fell under the first class. He concludes: 'Don't fear or try to refuse death, for it is the good pleasure of the Most High that it should be the lot of every man, and, at any rate, even in a millennium, in Hades there are no rebukes' (*elegmos*). One seems to hear the Sage meditating discontentedly on the orthodox creed, and even to catch a slightly bitter note in the word 'good pleasure' (*eudokia*).

There are other texts where Sirach, however inconsistently, silently repudiates the normal creed. In one he declares, 'It is an easy thing in the sight of the Lord to reward a man in the day of death according to his ways' (11^{26}), implying that after death there is a difference between the righteous and the wicked. In another (41^{9f}) he tells the 'ungodly' that for them there is a 'curse' in this life and 'destruction' (*apoleia*) after death, implying that this is not so with the righteous. Another text (7^{17}) is more specific—'the punishment of the ungodly man is fire and the worm'.[1] There is a clear reference here to Isa 66^{24}, but with a significant change. The Isaianic text describes what will happen *on the Day* to the corpses of the enemies of the LORD *on earth*. It is unlikely that Sirach is referring to the Day, for he does not seem to have expected it soon, and in the previous verse he has said: 'Remember that wrath will not tarry.' If, however, he is thinking of 'natural death', the phrase 'fire and the worm' cannot refer to the fate of unburied bodies on earth, as in the Prophet, for, of course, the corpses of the wicked were not left unburied. Sirach

---

[1] It should be noted that we now have two thirds of Sirach in the original Hebrew. In this verse, 7^{17}, the Hebrew has no reference to fire; the word 'worm' does not take us beyond Old Testament conceptions. This is not the only instance where the Greek translation, made by the writer's grandson, shows an advance in doctrine on the original. What is stated in the present work concerning the book of Sirach is true of the Greek translation (made about 130 B.C.); it does not necessarily apply to the original Hebrew. [T.F.G.]

is writing as if a dead man took his *body* to Hades—just as multitudes of Christians, knowing that a dead body remains in its grave, have none the less believed that a sinner's body is tortured by fire in Purgatory or Hell. It is an instance of the 'blurred psychology' that is not infrequent in beliefs about the dead. With this text there goes another—'The congregation of wicked men is (as) tow wrapped together; And the end of them is a flame of fire. The way of sinners is made smooth with stones (i.e. is an easy road); And at the last end thereof is the pit of Hades' (21^{9f}). Yet there are two texts which, taken in their context, seem to describe the fate of unburied corpses *on earth*—'For when a man is dead, he shall inherit creeping things and beasts and worms' (10^{11}), and 'Moths and worms shall have him to heritage' (while his 'Soul' is 'taken away'—to Hades) (19^3). Here Sirach adds other gruesome details to the picture of the slowly burning heap of refuse outside an ancient city. It seems to follow that in his time the Isaianic phrase 'Their worm shall not die, neither shall their fire be quenched' was sometimes used in its original sense (cf. Jth 16^{17}) and sometimes applied to the state of the wicked in Hades from the day of their death. It is unlikely that Sirach was the first to make this application, for he does not need to explain his two references to it. This concurrent use of a phrase in two ways has parallels. For instance, Christians have sometimes spoken of 'heaven' as if it were a saint's destiny at the moment when he dies, and sometimes as though he, with all other saints, passes there at the Resurrection—with a similar dual use of 'hell'. It is to be noted that Sirach nowhere describes the better fate of the righteous in Hades. Possibly he took it for granted that according to the orthodox creed, *they* would 'sleep' there, for, while he was not content with this prospect, it was very different from 'fire and the worm'. In none of the texts in Sirach does he write as though he were saying anything novel. His *role* throughout his book, indeed, is not that of an innovator but of a sage who speaks for the righteous. If this is so under the present subject, it follows that some, at least, of his contemporaries shared his inconsistent beliefs.

What Sirach suggests in a text or two, the writer of Wisdom asserts. It is a chief point in his book that, immediately after death, there is a difference between the fate of the righteous and of the wicked. The evidence lies almost wholly in the long passage (Wis 1^{12}–5^{23}) in which he argues his case with certain Epicurean neighbours, who are plotting to kill him (4^{10}). He sets out their doctrine at some length (2^{1-20}), but it is his own beliefs that are pertinent here.

His doctrine of creation needs first to be noted, for it is the background of the doctrine now under discussion. He believed that 'God created man for indestructibility (*aphtharsia*), and made him an image (*eikōn*) of his own proper being (*idiotēs*)', or, as some MSS read, 'of his own everlastingness (*aidiotes*)' (2^{23}). Again (1^{13-15}), God, of course, created man to be righteous, and 'righteousness is immortal'; He 'made not death'—i.e. He meant man to live on this earth for ever; He made the world too to exist for ever for He 'created all things' without any 'poison of destruction in them'. This writer, accepting the Hebrew doctrine that everything that God created is good, concluded that He meant it to last for ever.

But (2^{24}), 'by the envy of the devil death entered into the world, and they that are of his portion put (death) to the proof' (*peirazein*)—i.e. sinners will discover what death is. 'Ungodly men', though created for immortality, 'call Hades unto them as though it were a friend' (1^{15f}). It is they who 'court death' and 'draw destruction (*olethros*)' upon themselves (1^{12}). When they reach Hades, they will find out what 'fools' they have been on earth (5^{3-14}; cf. 3^{10-17}) and that their lot now is to be 'torture' (*basanos*) (3^1). There is nothing here about the rest of sleep, nor anything about the misery that the *chasid* had found in the hopeless helplessness of Sheol. A doctrine of torture in Hades for the souls of the wicked has emerged.

But (3^{1-4}) 'the souls (*psyche*) of the righteous are in the hand of God, And no torture shall touch them'. They only '*seem* to have died'. For them what men call death is properly no more than a 'departure' (*exodos*); their 'hope is full of immortality' for 'The righteous live for ever' (5^{15}); 'they are in peace' and 'at rest (*anapausis*)' (3^3, 4^7); 'in the Lord is their reward, And care for them is with the Most High' (5^{15}); 'there is a prize for blameless souls' (2^{22}). Do these phrases describe a pleasant part *of* Hades or a realm *outside* Hades? It is all but certain that the latter is meant for 'Hades' seems to be the distinctive 'portion' of the ungodly ($1^{12, 16}$), and there is the text 'To give heed to (wisdom's) laws confirmeth indestructibility, And indestructibility bringeth *near unto God*' (6^{18f}). Again there is a passage about a 'righteous man' who 'dies before his time' (4^{7-14}). Throughout it he is compared to

Enoch, though the Patriarch is not named and the implication is that when a righteous man dies untimely, God 'snatches' (*harpagein*) him from the world of sin and 'translates' (*metatithenai*) him into a haven of 'rest' (*anapausis*) (verses 10f, 7). The whole point of the brief record of Enoch (Gn 5^{23f}) is that, though he died untimely (for an antediluvian), this was not punishment but reward, for God did not dismiss him to Sheol, but 'took him' to Himself. 'They that are faithful' will not pass to Hades but 'abide with (God) in love' (3^9).

Yet this 'rest' is not the final state of the righteous dead. For them 'the day of decision' (3^{18}) is 'the day of their visitation', when they will return to earth, and 'the Lord shall reign (*basileuein*) over them for ever' (3^{7f}). The 'rest' of 'the souls of the righteous in the hand of God' is not the final but an intermediate state.

It has sometimes been said that the writer of Wisdom held the Platonic doctrine of 'the immortality of the soul', but there are a number of differences. For Plato the 'souls' of all men, whether good or bad, are intrinsically immortal; in Wisdom immortality is confined to the good. Plato could not have held that Enoch was 'translated' body and soul. He would have agreed that 'a destructible body weighs down the soul' (9^{15}), but for him the body *per naturam* is destructible, while in Wisdom it *becomes* 'destructible' through sin. The statement that, when 'all things' (including the body) came into being, there was 'no poison of destruction in them' (Wis 1^{14}) does not belong to a Platonist. For him the destructibility of matter was not poisonous but natural. Again, when the writer of Wisdom apocalyptically declares that the righteous will return to earth to share in God's rule, it is all but impossible that he should mean that it is only their 'souls' (*psyche*) that return, bodilessly to 'hold dominion'. 'Apocalyptic' and 'bodilessness' are contradictory terms. While the writer of Wisdom does not *say* that, when a man's *psyche* returns to earth, it will be equipped with an 'indestructible body' like that with which God equipped the first man at the creation, He implies it. In the intermediate state the righteous are incomplete men, for, in the perennial belief of the Hebrews, a man without a body is not a complete man. The writer of Wisdom does not say this in set terms, but it harmonizes, as the Platonic creed does not, with all that he does say. On this subject, at any rate, the writer of Wisdom was not Platonist but Hebrew.

There is a passage in LXX version of Daniel that seems to

harmonize with the teaching of Wisdom (Dn 12¹¹, ¹³). Where the Hebrew says no more than that Daniel is to 'rest' during the centuries between his death and the resurrection at 'the end of the days', when he will 'stand in his lot', LXX enlarges considerably. In English the words of 'the man clothed in linen' run: 'And *thou*, come hither (*deuro*) and rest (*anapauein*). For there are yet many days and many hours unto the fulfilment of the completion . . . and thou shalt rise again (*anistanai*) into thy lot at (*eis*) the completion of the days.' The 'man in linen' calls Daniel to join him in the aerial realm, but none the less tells him that he will 'rise again'. Men do not rise from above! It is probable that the passage means that Daniel's *psyche* is to pass into the 'heavenly places', where it will 'rest in the hands of God', while his body will lie in the grave until the resurrection.

It has been shown that under the subject 'God and Sheol' the Hebrews believed that God could take action in Sheol but did not choose to do so. He just lets the 'sleepers', good and bad, alone. Even when the *chasid* began to cry out against this doctrine, he does not ask that there should be differences in Sheol itself, but that God would bring back the righteous into a happy world, and, as has been seen, there are two passages that teach a resurrection. Of these one teaches that the righteous only will rise again, and the other that 'many, both of the righteous and wicked, will return and that *after* this return, not in Sheol itself, there will be difference between them. But the teaching of Sirach, just detailed, is that God takes action *in Hades itself*, 'rewarding a man *in the day of death* according to his ways' (Sir 11²⁶). Again, the writer of Wisdom, teaches that *at death* God saves good men from Hades and punishes bad men in it. It is at least possible too that, when the LXX translators rendered *repha'im* by *gigantes*, they believed that it was God who appointed the Giants to watch and ward in Hades. The belief that He does nothing there is gone.

CHAPTER NINE

AION AND *AIONIOS*

For one of the Hebrew terms rendered 'for ever' (*leʻolam*), the Greek phrase *eis ton aiōna*, or a synonymous phrase, occurs two hundred and seventy-seven times, and for another, *laʻad*, thirty-six. In both cases these are far the most frequent renderings. Under the third term, *lanetzach*, it occurs five times—the usual rendering being the literal one, *eis to telos*, 'unto the end' (*21*). The adjective *aiōnios* occurs a hundred and five times. The examination of the use of the Greek phrases will show that the same conclusions may be drawn as for the Hebrew phrases. The chief of these are that they refer to time, or rather to history, past and future, and not to an 'eternity' that transcends time; and that their meaning depends upon the 'universe of discourse' or 'frame of reference' of the context. The *aion* phrases will be taken first and then *aionios*.

The phrases are not Apocalyptic for they occur in every part of LXX—history, law, poetry, Wisdom literature, as well as prophecy and Apocalyptic. This appears too from the use of the phrase *apo tou aionos*, which refers to the past and is rightly rendered 'from of old'—e.g. in: 'From of old men have not heard' (Isa 64[4]; cf. Ps 25[6], 119[52]). The phrase 'from age to age' means 'from generation to generation' when used of men (e.g. Ps 41[14], Neh 9[5]), but 'from everlasting to everlasting' when used of God (Ps 90[2]). In the phrase 'before (*pro*) the *aion*' the reference is to the creation (Jl 2[2], Pr 8[23]). 'The days (or day) of the *aion*' denotes vaguely ancient times (e.g. Am 9[11]. Mic 7[14]) and *aion* is used in the genitive to denote 'long ago' (e.g. Isa 51[9], Ps 143[3]). It is clear that, when a phrase containing *aion* refers to the past, it does not always mean 'from the beginning of the world', but is to be interpreted by the 'universe of discourse'.

Of the phrases referring to the future *eis ton aiona* is far the most frequent. It occurs about two hundred times, more than half of them in the Psalter. Except in eleven texts it renders *leʻolam*. To anticipate the results of the examination of instances below it does not bear its literal meaning, whether this be 'unto (the end of) the (present) age' or 'unto (the beginning of) the (future) age', or 'for the (present) age'. In use it is one word and might be written *eis-ton-aiona*. There are parallels in such English phrases as '*to*day', 'al*to*gether' and 'here*to*fore'. Often its best rendering is 'always', both because, as with *eis ton aiona*, in use the original and literal meaning of this English word—that it is a variant of 'always' and meant 'all the way'—is forgotten, and because the scope of its meaning varies greatly with the 'universe of discourse' of the context. This appears, for instance, in the phrases: 'The sun always rises in the East' (where 'always' denotes 'for many millenniums'), and 'he has always talked like that' (where 'always' means 'during the time that I have known him').

In the historical books (*47*), which are innocent of Apocalypticism, there are texts, for instance, that declare that God's covenant with Israel and His gift of the Land will last 'always' (e.g. 1 Ch 16^{15}, Ex 32^{13}), as will David's line and the Temple and the Aaronic ritual (e.g. 2 S 7^{16}, 1 K 9^3, Ex 40^{15}). When used of an individual the term means 'for life' (Ex 21^6), but in the two texts where it is used of God (Ex 15^{18}, Dt 32^{40}), and in the passage where Adam is shut off from everlasting life (Gn 3^{22}; cf. 6^3), the rendering 'for ever' is appropriate. In the Prophets there are similar uses (e.g. Isa 33^{20}, Jer 3^5, Ezk 26^{21}), but the phrase is not used of individuals. It occurs in various ways in passages that describe 'a Day' or 'the Day'—about 'smoke' in Isaiah 34^{10}; about the future Covenant of Love in Hosea 2^{18f}; cf. God's 'salvation' (Isa 51^6); and, under the phrase 'always and beyond (*epekeina*)', of the future way-of-life of Israel (Mic 4^5). In these texts the rendering 'ever-lasting' is justified, for God is involved. It is the same with passages in the two Apocalyptists that use the phrase. Joel has it three times (2^{26f}, 3^{20}), as has Daniel (4^{34}, 5^{10}, 12^7). Of Daniel's texts the first and last describe God Himself. In Isaiah *aion* occurs in a negative phrase that means 'never' (25^2). In the Wisdom Literature (*14*) the phrase only occurs in ways already indicated (e.g. Job 7^{16}, Pr 10^{30}; cf. La 5^{19}). In the Psalter (*123*) there are similar texts (e.g. 29^{10}, 72^{19}, 110^4, 119^{44}), but some notes may be made. The first is the use of the phrase for *individuals*, especially in Psalms of the *Chasidim*. In Psalm 37, where the phrase occurs eight times, the writer promises the righteous that their families shall inherit *the land* always (verses 18, 27). In Psalm $73^{12, 26}$ the writer, speaking of this life, says that, while the wicked rich are 'always at ease' in it, for him God is his lasting 'portion' *now*. Other Psalmists declare that the 'poor' will praise God *eis-ton-aiona* in *this* life (e.g. 5^{11}, 52^{8f}, 71^1, 145^2). In the Psalm of Resurrection the phrase occurs ($49^{8, 11}$), but of this life. The phrase 'for his mercy (endureth) for ever', found in the ritual of the Temple (e.g. 2 Ch. 5^{13}, Ezr 3^{11}, Ps 118^{1-4}), has its greatest example in the refrain of Psalm 136. This Psalm, after rehearsing the 'great wonders' (verse 4) God has wrought in the past, goes on to praise Him for His mercies now (verses 23-5). It is foreign to its theme and tone to suppose that, as the 'congregation' intoned the refrain, they were thinking of the Day and beyond. The Priests controlled the ritual, and they were far from Apocalyptist. Here, even though God is in question, it is His ways in the present 'age' that are in mind. Under the phrase 'I am the first and the last', where the Hebrew word for 'the last' is *'acharōn* ('following'), LXX uses *meta tauta*, 'after these things' and *eis ton aiona* as synonyms (Isa 44^6, 48^{12}; cf. 41^4).

The next most frequent phrase containing *aion* is *heōs (tou) aionos*, which occurs over fifty times under *'olam*. *Heos* sometimes means 'until' and sometimes 'while' or 'as long as'. It is tempting to render the phrase as 'until the (future) age (comes)' or 'as long as the (present) age (lasts)', but these Apocalyptic phrases are not in place. The meaning of the phrase is 'perpetually', and, as with *eis ton aiona*, it occurs in every kind of book and its scope varies with the 'universe of discourse'. There are examples for the historical books in 1 Samuel 20^{41}, 2 Samuel 7^{16}, and 1 Chronicles 15^2 (where the reference is to the continuity of families) and Genesis 13^{15} and Deuteronomy 28^{46} (which refer to the perpetuity of the nation). In the one use of the phrase in the historical books about an individual it means 'for life' (1 S $1^{22, 28}$). When used of God, the 'universe of discourse' is, no doubt enlarged (2 S 7^{26}, 1 Ch 29^{10}). The phrase is rare in the Prophets (*9*), but the uses are the same (e.g. Jer 7^7, 35^6, Mal 1^4). In the Isaianic Apocalypse LXX refers the phrase to the past (Isa 26^4). The Psalter has fifteen examples—e.g. 18^{50}, 28^9, $106^{31, 48}$, 121^8). In the Psalm of Resurrection the phrase is used to denote the 'perpetual darkness' in which the dead dwell (49^{19}). For the phrase rendered 'From everlasting to everlasting' and used of God LXX has *apo tou aionos heos tou aionos* three times (90^2, 103^{17}, 106^{48}) and *apo tou aionos kai eis ton aiona* once (41^{14}). As the English rendering shows, even here it is difficult to take the word *aion* literally. In any case, under *heos tou aionos* there is no other passage where the original meaning of *aion* survives. The phrase *heos eis ton aiona*, which renders *le'olam* three times (e.g. Dt 23³), shows that *eis ton aiona* was used as a single word. To use impossible English, it means 'as long as always'.

The plural phrase 'the ages' (*aiōnes*) occurs ten times, six of them in Daniel. Here English has a parallel use, perhaps borrowed from the Bible, the meaning varying with the 'frame of reference'. For instance, in 'O God, the Rock of Ages' the word means a period very different from that in the colloquial phrase: 'I haven't seen you for ages.' In the Old Testament the Davidic line of kings and the Temple worship are to last 'for ages' in present history, but the rule of the 'saints' is to last 'for ages' after the End (Ps 72¹⁷, 2 Ch 6², Dn 2⁴⁴). *Eis tous aionas, eis ton aiona*, and *eis ton aiona tou aionos* can be used as synonyms (Ps 48¹⁴; cf. 9⁶, 45¹⁷). The last phrase illustrates emphasis by reduplication, as in such English phrases as 'for ever and ever', 'on and on and on', and 'through and through'. In one passage the Greek phrase denotes the everlasting rule of God and in another no more than the span of a man's life (Ps 10¹⁶, 145¹; cf. 37²⁹). It may be noted that *pro tōn aiōnōn*, 'before the ages', may render *qedem*, 'of old time' (Ps 55¹⁹), and that 'all generations' may be rendered 'all the ages' (Ps 145¹³). *En tois aiōsi tois genemenois*, where the plural of *'olam* occurs in the Hebrew, means 'in the ages before our day' (Ec 1¹⁰). *Heos aionos ton aionon* ('until (the) age of the ages') describes the future rule of the 'saints' (Dn 7¹⁸). Throughout the whole gamut of phrases an Apocalyptic reference is only found when the context requires it and this is relatively rare. The use of the word *aion* is not *per se* Apocalyptic.

The same conclusions follow from some of the rare texts where *'olam* is not rendered by a phrase containing *aion*. For instance, in Leviticus 25³² it is translated by *dia pantos* with the meaning 'at any time', and in one passage the rendering is *aei* ('ever') (Isa 42¹⁴). *Aenaos* (literally 'ever-flowing') is found four times in three of them for *'olam*, with the meaning 'everlasting', for the word describes the 'sands', 'the hills', and 'the arms of God' (Gn 49²⁶, Dt 33¹⁵, ²⁷). Under these renderings, as under *aion*, the context decides the scope of the terms. The common word for 'always' in classical Greek, *pantote*, does not occur in LXX. It is displaced by *eis ton aiona*. If this phrase does not mean 'always', what did LXX use for this common word?

Like results follow if the use of *eis ton aiona* and similar phrases are examined in the Apocrypha (*III*). They are specially common in Tobit (*24*) and Sirach (*43*). Only a few examples need be given. Within three verses 'truth' is said to exist *eis ton aiona* and *eis ton aiona tou aionos*, and to be 'the majesty of all the ages' (1 Es 4$^{38-40}$), the word 'truth' requiring the rendering 'everlasting'. In 1 Esdras 8^{85} *heos aionos* is used as a synonym for 'all the time' (*chronos*). In Tobit, on the one hand (6^{17}), Asmodeus is not to return to vex Sarah *eis ton aiona tou aionos*—that is, as long as she lives—but, on the other, where similar phrases are used in 'Blessing' God, their meaning is 'everlasting' (e.g. 3$^{2, 9, 11}$). Tobit uses *aion* to mean 'a period in history' when he speaks of 'the seasons (*kairos*) of the *aion*' between the Destruction of Jerusalem and the Rebuilding of the Temple (14^{4f}), but he means 'through all future history' when he calls God 'Our father unto all the *aiones*', who will love faithful Jews 'unto all the generations of the aion' (13$^{4, 10}$). When the Jews call down the Almighty's blessing upon Judith *eis ton aiona chronon* the phrase means 'as long as thou livest' (Jth 15^{10}). In the books of the Maccabees (*8*) the phrases may be rendered by 'always' in every instance (e.g. 1 Mac 2^{57}, 2 Mac 14^{36}).

The practical Sirach almost always uses the phrases about 'this life'. In a number of passages they mean 'for life'—e.g. in 1$^{13-15}$, where the RV has 'eternal', the context shows that he means that 'wisdom' is the foundation of the whole present life of a man who 'fears the Lord'. Again, there are 'covenants' that last as long as the race (14^{17}, 17^{12}). Similarly, the 'seed' of the righteous may last as long as time (44^{13}). 'Time' is a good rendering elsewhere (1^2, 42^{18}). In the one text where Sirach uses *aion* to describe the state of a man after death he means that Samuel's 'sleep of *aion*' is lasting (46^{19}). When he says that 'wisdom' is 'with God *eis ton aiona*' the 'universe of discourse' begins when time began, but never ends (1$^{1, 4}$, 24^9; cf. 36^{17}, 42^{21}). In the Book of Wisdom *aion* usually denotes 'the course of time' or 'history' (e.g. 4^2, 12^{10}, 13^9), but once it is used of 'the generation of Israel that received the law' (18^4), and once of the 'lasting' shame of an un-buried corpse (4^{18}). But in the text 'righteous men live *eis ton aiona*' (5^{15}), the context requires the rendering 'everlasting'. In the Song of the Three the repeated doxology, 'Praise and exalt (the Lord) above all *eis tous aionas*', calls men to praise God as long as there are any men—which to the Jew would mean 'everlastingly'.

As already seen *eis ton aiona* only renders *lanetzach* five times. A paragraph about its other renderings may be intruded here, for, under the most frequent rendering, *eis (to) telos* (*21*), the findings are not unlike those under *eis ton aiona*. The word *telos* means 'end', and there are texts where it may be taken literally, the reference being to the 'end' of this life (e.g. Job 14[20], Ps 13[1]), but there are others where the literal meaning seems to be forgotten and the phrase means, like *lanetzach*, 'enduringly'. In one Psalm, for example, the phrase occurs five times with this meaning (74[1, 3, 10f, 19]). If Psalm 16 be taken to teach a resurrection, its last phrase would mean, not 'to the end (of life)', but 'for ever', as in Psalm 49[9]. The phrase *heos eis (to) telos*—which shows that *eis to telos* was used as one word—occurs seven times. In Numbers 17[13] it means 'until we die to our full number'. In seven texts *lanetzach* is rendered by *eis nikos* ('unto victory'—e.g. Jer 3[5], Job 36[7]), and once by *eis chronon polun* ('for much time'—Isa 34[10]). There are examples from the Apocrypha under 'utterly' in Sirach 10[13] and 'wholly' in 2 Maccabees 8[29]. It will be seen that the renderings need to vary according to the 'frame of reference' of the context, but this hardly ever justifies the rendering 'for ever' in its exact sense, frequent though this is in the English Versions.

The same results follow when the use of the adjective *aionios* is examined, except that, relatively to the number of occurrences, it denotes 'endlessness' more often than *aion*. It always renders either *'olam* or its Aramaic equivalent (*105*). By derivation it means 'belonging to (an) *aion*'. Except when the word describes God, the best rendering is 'enduring' or 'lasting', for the scope of the meaning of these English words is defined by the context, and it is the same with *aionios*.

Examples may be taken first from the use of the word by the Greek translators outside the four Apocalypses. In a few texts *aionios* refers to the *past*, with the meaning 'enduring of old'. For instance, Job speaks of the old, old path that the righteous have trod (22[15]; cf. Jer 6[16]), and a Psalmist says: 'I considered ancient (*archaios*) days and the years of yore (*aionios*)' (77[7]). Where Isaiah 58[12], 61[4] use the phrase 'wastes of *'olam*' to describe 'wastes that were only a century or so old, LXX renders by *aionios*. In reference to the future the word is used of mountains, the Covenant, statutes, generations, and so on (e.g. Hab 3[6], Gn 9[16], Ex 27[21], Gn 9[12]). There are, of course, texts that speak of God as 'everlasting' (e.g. Gn 21[33], Ex 3[15], Isa 40[28]). In the rare texts where *aionios* refers to individual men the meaning is 'lasting as long as life', as when Elihu speaks of a 'constantly righteous' man (Job 34[17]), or Jeremiah wishes that his 'conception' had been 'lasting'—i.e. that he had never been born (20[17]). Hades is the 'land of enduring darkness' and 'enduring sleep' (Job 10[22], Jer 51[39]). In one manuscript of Job the inhabitants of Hades are called 'the *aionioi*', the meaning being that they are enduringly rid of the 'task-master' (3[18]).

In the Old Testament Apocalypses *aionios* is confined to Isaiah 24-7 and Daniel. In the former it occurs of the 'covenant' and 'the Lord Jehovah', neither passage being Apocalyptic (24[5], 26[4]). In Daniel three texts describe the 'dominion' or 'kingdom' of 'the Most High', *aionios* being parallel to 'from generation to generation' (4[3, 34], 7[27]). These texts are not, strictly speaking, Apocalyptic. Four other texts, however, refer to the Apocalyptic 'Day'. After it 'one like unto a son of man' is to exercise 'an everlasting dominion that shall not pass away' in a 'kingdom of everlasting righteousness' (7[14], 9[24]). The other two instances occur together—'Many of them that sleep in the dust of the earth shall awake, some to everlasting life, and some to shame and everlasting abhorrence' (12[2]). The phrase 'everlasting life' is unique in LXX, though there is a synonymous phrase, 'the enduring re-living of life' (2 Mac 7[9]). It is with Daniel that the Apocalyptic use of *aionios* emerges.

In the Apocrypha *aionios* occurs twenty-six times. In Baruch 4[8]–5[2] God is six times called 'the Everlasting'. The term is also used of 'joy' (Bar 4[29]), of the Covenant (e.g. Sir 45[15], Bar 2[35]), of the Law (To 1[6]), the Aaronic priesthood (1 Mac 2[54]), and the Davidic kingship (1 Mac 2[57]). In this list the Apocrypha repeats the Old Testament. The term is used seven times to denote the 'enduring' memory of ancient heroes (e.g. Jth 13[20], Sir 15[6], Wis 8[13]). It only occurs twice of the future existence of individuals (To 3[6], 2 Mac 7[9]), the first passage calling Hades 'the everlasting place', and the second referring to an 'everlasting renewal of life' at resurrection. Throughout LXX *aionios* means 'everlasting' more often than the phrases containing *aion* do, but this is because the context requires it—not because this is the only meaning of the word.

If now it be asked, 'Why did the translators use *eis ton aiona* (with its companion phrases) and *aionios* in this way?', a surmise may be ventured. It may be taken for granted that the translators did not invent the use, but borrowed it from their Hellenistic contemporaries. With the latter a distinction may be made between the original meaning of the terms and their *current* meaning. There can be no doubt about the original meaning. The Greeks, like many other ancient peoples, believed that the movement of time (and history) was circular and repetitive, like that of the seeming movement of the sun day after day or the movement of a wheel spinning about its axis. This, for instance, was one of the tenets of Stoicism, a prevalent philosophy in Hellenistic times. The Stoics held that there were four 'Ages of the World'—i.e. that each of the recurrent circles of time may be divided into four parts, each part being called an 'age'. They believed too that each of the Four Ages was very long. Aratus, for instance, who belonged to the third century BC, fixed the length of each of them at 60,000 years. Unless, therefore, it was expected that the present Age was about to pass into the next, the phrase 'the Age' would mean, in common use, 'the present Age', and *eis ton aiona* (and *aionios*) would mean 'as long as the present Age lasts'. But this is the kind of phrase that people cease to use in its exact sense, using it to mean 'as long as matters and longer', like the English phrase: 'Ever so long.' Often it would be used without any remembrance of its exact and original meaning. This, of course, is quite common—as, for instance, with the English words 'nice' and 'presently' and 'understood'. It seems to be with this inexact meaning that LXX borrowed the Hellenistic terms. Of course, *eis ton aiona* and *aionios* might still be used sometimes in the literal sense. In due time the Hebrews borrowed the literal use too. It is true that they did not believe that the course of time (and history) is like a circle, but like an endless line. None the less, when the belief arose that history is divided into two parts, they found the word *aion* apt for each part, and came to use such phrases as 'the Present Age' and 'the Coming Age' as will appear later. In LXX, however, this use does not appear—such phrases as *eis ton aiona tou aionos* and even *eis tous aionas* being merely emphatic synonyms of *eis ton aiona*. There are, therefore, two biblical uses—one where the original meaning is lost, and one where it is in mind, the latter use emerging long after the former.

CHAPTER TEN

THE RESURRECTION

UNDER THIS subject the chief evidence falls under the Apocrypha, but some points may first be noted under the translation of the Hebrew books.

The LXX rendering of Job 14[13-15] seems to refer to a *possible* return from Hades. The writer has just been saying that a man who has 'fallen asleep' will not return so long as 'the heaven is not rent asunder' and that men 'shall not be awakened out of their sleep'. But the LXX version goes on: 'If only thou wouldst keep me in Hades, And hide me until thy wrath should cease, And appoint me a time in which thou wouldst remember me! For, if a man die, having completed the days of his life (*bios*), shall he live?' (i.e. 'Is it not possible after all that he shall live again?'). 'I will wait until I come to be again. Then thou wilt call, and *I* shall give heed to thee, And with the works of thy hands do not thou away.' Here, rather confusedly, three ideas emerge—first, Job asks God to grant him rest in Hades, but only for a while; second, he asks that when God's wrath is spent, He will call him back to earth; third, for a moment he seems confident that God will do this. He is asking for a miracle like the 'rending of the heavens', but cannot God work even such a miracle? For a moment Job hopes that He will.

In the LXX translation of Job 19[25-7], on the other hand, whether it was made from the present Hebrew text or not, it is probable, though not certain, that there is no reference to a resurrection. It runs: 'For I know that everlasting is he that is about (*mellōn*) to set me free on the earth, (and) to raise up (*anistanai*) my skin that is enduring these things—or, to set me free (and) raise up on the earth my skin that is enduring these things. For from (the) Lord these things are completed (*suntelein*) to me, which things *I* for myself understand, things which my eye hath seen and not another, and all things have been completed in (my) bosom.' The probable meaning is: 'I know that God is about to restore me from my sufferings because I know that they are now complete.' It is a question of recovery, not resurrection.

In the frequent phrase 'the latter days' the Hebrew word for 'latter' is *'acharith*. The word occurs fifty-three times in the Hebrew Bible. It has sixteen renderings, but in thirty-five of the fifty-three texts *eschatos* (literally 'last') is used (e.g. Nu 24[14]). There are examples of the use of the phrase 'the last days' in Hos 3[5], Mic 4[1], Jer 23[20], Ezk 38[16], Dn 10[14]. In LXX *eschatos* renders eleven Hebrew terms, but out of 109 instances *'achar* and its cognates (including *'acharith*) claim eighty-nine. In the Apocrypha *eschatos* is common, but the passages that are at all relevant to the present subject do not describe the End. They fall into two classes—passages that refer to a man's death (e.g. Sir 1[13], 7[36], Wis 2[16], 2 Mac 3[31])—i.e. his passage to Hades (cf. Sir 21[10]); and passages where the meaning is 'at last' or 'at length' (e.g. Sir 6[28], 12[12], Wis 3[17]). As the phrase *to eschaton* is used so often now to mean 'the End', usually with the meaning 'the End of *history* (and so of 'days' in the ordinary sense of the word)', it may be noted that there is no antecedent for this in LXX. It is true that a phrase containing *eschaton* renders *qetz* (Ezk 35[5]), but here 'the end' meant is the Destruction of Jerusalem. To use 'the last days' to denote 'the time that follows the Day', which is what the Hebrew phrase means, implies that the translators, unlike their Gentile neighbours, believed that there would only be *one* future 'age'.

In one of the two Apocalypses that teach a resurrection, Isaiah 24-7, there are three passages where LXX renderings may be noted. In one of them (25[8]) the translators prefer the Hebrew vowels that relate the text, not to a resurrection, but to the destruction of the Gentiles. In another passage (26[19ff]) the Greek runs: 'The dead shall rise again (*anistanai*), and those in the tombs shall be awakened (*egeirein*), and those in the earth shall be made glad. For the dew which is from thee is healing to them, and the land of the ungodly shall fall . . . and the earth shall uncover her blood, and shall not cover up those that have been taken away (to burial).' Of the variations from the Hebrew here the only one notable falls under 'the land of the ungodly shall fall'. The Hebrew has 'the earth shall cast forth the Rephaim'. The translators, for whom the Rephaim were the Giants, would not say that *they* rise. In the third passage (24[21-3]) the Greek renders *bor* by *desmōterion* and *masgēr* by *ochurōma*, two words for 'prison'. The former word occurs eight times in LXX and the latter thirty-seven, but neither of them ever stands for the Underworld. While LXX here omits 'on that day' in verse 21, it is clear from the context that the Day is in question. When it comes God will 'put (his) hand upon the world (*kosmos*) of the heaven and upon the kings of the earth, and will gather its company into a prison and shut (it) up into a jail. Through many generations shall their visitation be.' 'The world of the heaven' renders a Hebrew phrase meaning 'the host of the height' and describes an ordered hierarchy of evil spirits. On the Day they, and with them 'the kings of the earth' (presumably their earthly counterparts), are to be shut up in a prison *on earth*, which is to be their habitat 'for many generations'. They do not pass to Hades.

Finally the rendering of the word *chasid* may be noted. It was seen earlier that this Hebrew word denoted the man between whom and God there was the fellowship of *chesed* ('leal love'), and that the revolt of the *chasid* from the misery of Sheol was the root from which a belief in the resurrection at last grew. Of its thirty examples it is rendered by *hosios* twenty-six times (e.g. Ps 16^{10}). It is to be distinguished from *hagios*—which never renders *chasid* —for this word describes the *result* of the fellowship with God that the *chasid* enjoyed rather than the fellowship itself. If 'holy' be kept for *hagios*, 'devout' may be used for *hosios*, as for *chasid*. For the present subject the word links the LXX of the Hebrew Bible with the Apocrypha, for many of the books of that collection are 'Books of the Devout' and the word *hosios* (with the variant 'elect') occurs twice in the greatest passage in the Apocrypha about the Resurrection (Wis 3^9, 4^{15}). Of its sixteen instances in the Apocrypha eleven are in Wisdom. Sirach has it twice (39^{13}, ^{24}), in the first text describing the 'devout' as 'sons of God'— just as Wisdom calls them 'friends of God' (7^{27}). God is loyal to His friends, not just till they die, but for ever.

In the Apocrypha there are three books that speak of the Resurrection—Sirach, Wisdom, and Second Maccabees. In the first of these there are three references, all found in the 'Praise of Famous Men' (Sir 44-50). Two of the three may be taken together. Both about the 'judges' and 'the twelve prophets' Sirach has the peculiar phrase: 'May their bones bloom out of their place' (46^{12}, 49^{10}). While this might possibly be taken to refer to the posthumous influence of these 'famous men', this is not likely with such a writer as Sirach, and the phrase seems to mean 'May they rise again!' It would follow that Sirach *hoped* that there would be a resurrection, at least for the heroes of Israel. The third passage belongs to the 'praise' of Elijah and Elisha (48^{1-16}). Here Sirach refers to the stories that tell of these two Prophets' raising of children from the dead and of the resurrection of the corpse that touched Elisha's bones. Evidently he has resurrection in mind. He tells too of Elijah's 'rapture' and of his expected return—quoting Malachi 4^{5f}. Immediately after this, apostrophizing Elijah (48^{11}), he writes: 'Blessed are they that saw thee, And they that have been adorned with love, For *we* also shall surely live' (literally, 'live with life'). Whether the verse, or part of it, is an interpolation or not, it seems plain that its writer expected that, when Elijah returned 'before the great and terrible Day of the Lord' (Mal 4^5), there would be those who would rise from the dead, the writer and his group being among them. It is strange that outside the 'Praise of Famous Men' nothing is said of a resurrection and that within it the curiously phrased references should be so rare and allusive. It looks as if the problem of the resurrection were being canvassed among the Jews at the time, the majority denying its possibility, but a certain group expecting it.

In the Book of Wisdom, written at least a century later than the original Hebrew of Sirach, the situation is very different. The prelude of the writer's passionate argument with the 'ungodly' runs, 'righteousness (and therefore the righteous man) is immortal' (Wis 1^{15f}), and the two *foci* of the whole argument (2-5) are (*a*) that immediately after death there is a vast difference between the fate of the 'righteous' or 'devout' on the one hand, and of the 'ungodly' on the other, and (*b*) that there will at last be a 'day of decision' (*diagnōsis*) (3^{18}), which will be the 'season of visitation' (*episcope*) for the righteous (3^7). Clearly this is a 'season' of blessing. The argument is passionate, even vehement, and, as often with such arguments, it is not pursued with orderly logic and the writer intermingles his two subjects. None the less, the word *episcope* in 4^{15}, under the text 'There is a visitation among (*en*) his devout ones', marks the point where the *main* subject ceases to be the state of men immediately after death and begins to be the final Day—even though the earlier part of the argument gives three verses to the ultimate fate of the righteous, and the latter part opens with a parenthesis about the fate of a righteous man, not at the End, but when he dies (4^{16f}). The writer's teaching about the fate of men immediately after death has already been examined. Under the second subject, now in question, the writer rises to a climax in 5^{17-23}, where the Lord, clad in His panoply of 'righteousness' and 'judgement' and 'holiness' and 'wrath', uses for His 'weapons' 'the whole creation'—with its lightnings and hailstones and floods and tempests—to sweep away 'lawlessness' and 'evil-doing' from the earth. Before this climax there is a description of the Lord's ways with the wicked and the righteous on the Day, intermingled in the fashion of this writer (4^{18}–5^{16}). Under the fate of the wicked he borrows from the earlier part of Psalm 2 (and from the later part, under 'kings', in 6^{1-11}), using such phrases as 'laugh to scorn' and 'dash to the ground' (4^{18f}). With this he mingles a reference to Isaiah 66^{24}—speaking of 'dishonoured corpses' and the 'contempt (*hybris*)' heaped upon these as they lie 'in anguish' exposed 'among the dead for ever' (4^{18f}). On the other hand, the 'righteous' 'stand in great boldness' on the Day, for they will 'live for ever', receiving from the Lord their protector the 'reward' of 'the crown of royal dignity' and 'the diadem of beauty' ($5^{1, 15f}$). So far all seems clear. But the question arises: 'Is the writer speaking here *only* of the men who are alive on the Day, or does he include those who have died before it and who rise again when it comes to meet their different dooms?' There is no doubt that he believes that the *righteous* dead rise again, for earlier he says that 'at the season of their visitation' they will 'shine forth', sweep over the earth as 'sparks among stubble', 'judge nations and have dominion over peoples', the Lord 'reigning over them for evermore' while they 'abide with him in love' (3^{7-9}). It is for this that they have been 'kept' until God 'visits them' (4^{15f})—like Enoch, who is described, though not named as the word 'translated', in particular, shows (4^{10-14}). For the wicked the question is more difficult to answer. Much depends upon the temper of the whole argument. It is not a quiet disquisition, but a vehement *argumentum ad homines*—the writing facing the persecuting 'ungodly' men of his time with a persistent undertone of 'You!' 'You!' 'You!' To the present writer this word seems to underlie the very vigorous description of the repentance of the wicked on the Day (5^{3-8})—as though this persecuted man were saying: 'This is what *you* will come to!' It seems to be his final rejoinder to the challenge of the 'ungodly' (2^{6-20}). If the wicked dead do not rise again, their 'souls' presumably remain for ever in the 'torment' of Hades. As has already been argued, it is implied that when a righteous man rises, his 'soul' is given an 'indestructible body'. The writer of

Wisdom believed that there is to be a Day of Judgement, that the righteous will rise in triumph from the dead when it comes, and, though less certainly, that the wicked too will rise to meet their final doom.

For the doctrine of the Future the Second Book of Maccabees goes with the Book of Wisdom as the most important in the Apocrypha. Its writer too is both a *chasid* and an eschatologist. In his book, as in First Maccabees, the word '*chasidim*', transliterated as 'Hasideans', describes the men who took their lives in their hands to fight for their faith under Judas (1 Mac 2^{42}, 7^{13}, 2 Mac 14^6), but it must not be inferred that there were no other *chasidim*. The mother and seven sons of 2 Maccabees 7 do not fight, but they are *chasidim* indeed. The book falls under a text quoted from a Psalm of the *Chasidim* in First Maccabees (7^{17}): 'The flesh of *thy devout ones* (did they cast out), And their blood did they shed round about Jerusalem, And there was no man to bury them.'

The meaning of a unique and obscure passage (2 Mac 12^{39-45}) may be taken first. It tells of a costly sacrifice offered by Judas Maccabaeus. Apparently there were two accounts of its nature. On one (which is suggested in a parenthesis) it was a 'pious' *thank*-offering for the Jews who had 'fallen' in Judas's campaigns and were now 'asleep'; on the other it was a '*sin*-offering' and 'propitiation' (*exilasmos*) for secret apostates who had been killed in battle. Under the second account their comrades believed that they had perished because of their secret sin, and prayed that 'the sin that had taken place might be wholly wiped away'—i.e. the sin-offering was made that these sinners might escape the consequences of their sin—not in Hades but at the Resurrection, for Judas was 'taking thought for a resurrection', the comment being added: 'For if he were not expecting that they that had fallen would rise again, it were superfluous and idle to pray for the dead.' It is perhaps not by accident that the second account would suit the Pharisees, who believed in a resurrection, while the first, in which it is a thank-offering, would suit the Sadducees, who rejected the belief.

In another Resurrection passage (2 Mac 14^{45f}), the dying Razis calls upon 'the Lord of *zoe* and *pneuma*' to 'restore him these[1] again'. But it is in the story of the Mother and her Seven Sons

---

[1] 'These' (*tauta*) probably refers to his bowels (*entera*) flung to the crowd, as mentioned in the same verse. [T.F.G.]

(2 Mac 7) that the belief in the resurrection of the faithful blazes in full splendour. In face of torture unto death a believer in a righteous God *must* believe also in resurrection or lose his faith (cf. verses 6, 20). The Second son says that 'the King of the world shall raise us up (*anistanai*) unto everlasting (*aionios*) re-living (*anabiosis*) of life (*zoe*)' (verse 9); the Fourth adds that for such a one as Epiphanes 'there shall be no resurrection (*anastasis*) unto life' (verse 14); the Youngest speaks of 'a short pain (that brings) everflowing life' (verse 36); the Mother expects that 'the Creator' will give their '*pneuma* and *zoe* back' to her sons, and that she herself will 'in the mercy of God recover' them (verses 23, 29) —that is, there is to be re-union in the Resurrection. The word 'torture' or 'torment', *basanos*, and its verb, describe their present sufferings (verses 8, 13; cf. 1^{28}). Epiphanes is to be 'tormented' in this life as he has 'tormented' others (7^{17}; cf. 9^{5f}). Nothing is said of his plight in Hades. It is assumed that Hades is misery. It is only in Second Maccabees that LXX uses *anastasis* to mean 'resurrection' (7^{14}, 12^{43}). The Third Son expects that he will 'receive back' his tongue and hands even though they are cut off —i.e. he expects a resurrection of the *present* body.

Some conclusions may be drawn from this survey. First, a belief in the Resurrection does not appear before Alexander's conquest. There is a possible exception in Psalm 49, for its date is uncertain, but is usually assigned to the Hellenistic period. Next, the belief almost always appears in an Apocalyptic context, even in books that are not Apocalypses. Third, there is no set argument under the question 'Is there a resurrection?' as there is, for instance, in Paul's argument in 1 Corinthians 15. On the contrary, the belief either appears as an assured part of what happened on the Day, or almost incidentally, as in Sirach. It seems to follow that the belief was already held either by the Jews in general or by the readers for whom the books were written. The present writer, as the account given above shows, accepts the second alternative. For him the Isaianic Apocalypse, Daniel, Sirach, Wisdom and Second Maccabees, with all their differences, are all 'Books of the *Chasidim*', written by and for 'the devout'. He thinks that this is so even with Wisdom, though so much of it is directed against the 'ungodly', the writer providing the 'devout' with their answer to their persecutors. On this showing some Jews believed in a resurrection and some did not. No doubt there would be some who said 'We do not know'. Among believers some confined the resurrection to the righteous, others including the wicked. It looks as if the number of believers grew between the time of Sirach and of Wisdom and Second Maccabees. The New Testament shows that the Pharisees, whose guidance the people normally followed, were eager upholders of the doctrine (Ac 23[9f]). The absence of references to a resurrection in the other 'Books of the *Chasidim*' arises from their subject-matter, for this does not require any reference to it.

THE NEW TESTAMENT

CHAPTER ELEVEN

THE RULE OF GOD

I<small>N</small> <small>THE</small> New Testament the idea that history is divided into two Eras, or, to use the word that was now common, two Ages—the Age of Sin and the Age of Righteousness—is universal. The Old Testament doctrine that God is ruler, both in the present and future Ages, is, of course, the doctrine of the New Testament too. Otherwise He would not be God. He rules in the Age of Sin, even though, through His 'forebearance' or 'long-temperedness' (*makrothumia*), He tolerates sin. This doctrine is generally just taken for granted—for example, in prayer. In order to show that God has followed a 'purpose according to election' (Ro 9^{11}), Paul describes a large part of His ways in the Age of Sin in Romans 9-11. Now, however, 'the fulness of the times'—or 'the end of these days'—has 'come' and God has 'sent forth his Son' and 'spoken unto us in a Son' (Gal 4^4, He 1^2). This, of course, introduces the *differentia* of the New Testament. The Incarnation is the beginning of the End. While the word 'Day' usually refers to the Parousia and the Day of Judgement, it now and then refers to the Incarnation. Paul declares 'Now is the day of salvation' (2 Cor 6^2), John has the text 'Your father Abraham rejoiced to see my day' (8^{56}), and the author of Hebrews writes 'He again defineth a certain day', identifying it as 'Today' (4^7). The Day of Salvation is the prelude of the Day of Judgement and falls within the Present Age. While there are passages in the Old Testament where Israel is called to repent before the Day, there the Day of Salvation and the Day of Judgement are simultaneous because 'salvation' denotes the full enjoyment of a perfect world in which there is no sin. In the New Testament the word 'salvation' can be used in this sense (e.g. Ro 13^{11}), but there a man who believes in Christ is already 'saved' in the fundamental meaning of the word, for he is 'a new creature' (2 Co 5^{17}). All the rest is sequel. The Prophets had taught that on His chosen Day, God would break into the Era of Sin to make an end of it. At the Incarnation He 'broke in', but not yet to make an end. It is at the Parousia that the End of the Age comes. While it is true that from the point of view of creation the Incarnation is consummation, from the point of view of sin it is inruption. In this first inruption 'the Son of Man came'—first 'in the flesh' and then 'in the Spirit'—'to seek and to save that which was lost' (Lk 19^{10}).

But there is to be a second inruption. Here too the Christian *differentia* appears. For the Christians the Day was the Day of the *Parousia*, the Second Coming of the Son of Man. Then the full 'salvation', which has been 'nearing' all the time, will be realized (Ro 13^{11}). This does not only mean that believers will themselves be altogether saved from sin and wholly loyal to God, but also that they will dwell in a *kosmos* that will itself be altogether rid of sin and teem with the blessings that belong to the saved. This implies, of course, that all that dwell in it will also be wholly loyal, for one sinner would spoil their harmony. In other words, the eschatological prayer that Jesus gave His disciples will be answered, and God's name will be hallowed, His kingdom have come, throughout the *kosmos*, His will be done. As in the Old Testament, all this is to come to pass 'on *earth*'. The ways of the angels 'in heaven' will be the ways of men here (Mt 6^{9f}). Most of the subjects named in this summary statement will be dealt with later in detail. In this preliminary chapter they are mentioned to show that there is a present 'rule of God', and that it has its culminant examples in the Incarnation and the Parousia and all that lay between them. The most poignant example in all history is Jesus' words in Gethsemane—'Howbeit, not what I will, but what thou wilt' (Mk 14^{36}). It was in loyalty to 'the rule of God' that Jesus died.

But, if God is king (*basileus*) now and rules (*basileuein*) now, why pray 'Thy kingdom (*basileia*) come'? Men do not ask for what is, but for what, as they hope, will be. This introduces the distinctive New Testament use of the phrase 'the *basileia* of God' or 'the *basileia* of heaven'. Clearly it denotes a future *basileia*, which differs in some way from the present *basileia*. As has been seen, in LXX there is no plain example of this use of the phrase, though there are anticipations of the idea. It has been seen that the primary meaning of *basileia* is 'kingship' or 'rule', that it may be used in the secondary sense of a 'kingdom' of people, and that, whichever is the meaning in a particular text, the other is implied, for 'king' and 'subjects', 'rule' and 'realm', are correlative terms. This is why it is sometimes difficult to be sure in which sense the word is used, and sometimes likely that it is used in both senses at once. For instance, the phrase 'the *basileia* of God' occurs thirteen times in the Gospel of Mark. Of these it seems to the present writer that in two texts *basileia* clearly means 'kingship' (Mk 9[1], 10[15]), and 'kingdom' in five (Mk 9[47], 10[14, 23-5]), while in six no certain decision can be reached, unless it be that the word means both 'kingship' and 'kingdom' (Mk 1[15], 4[11, 26, 30], 12[34], 14[25]). Under the English word 'kingdom' another distinction needs to be made. The phrase 'the kingdom of England' denotes kingship in a certain *land*—and therefore of the *people* in it. With *basileia* it is rather the other way, the word denoting kingship over a certain kind of people, and therefore over the whole world. It is the same with 'realm'—unless, as suggested earlier, this be given the unusual meaning 'the people ruled'. This leads to the novelty in the New Testament use of the phrase 'the *basileia* of God'. Under God's rule in the Age of Sin, there are rebels as well as loyalists; in His rule in the Age of Righteousness all are loyal. The difference does not lie in the Ruler, but in the ruled. The prayer 'Thy *basileia* come' means 'May the day of universal and complete loyalty come'.

With Jesus, and with Jesus only, there was already a complete loyalty even in the Age of Sin, and even unto the Cross. As the writer thinks, this is what is meant by the word 'The *basileia* of God is in the midst of you' (Lk 17[21]). It is to be explained by the Synoptic texts 'Thou art my beloved Son; in thee I am well pleased' (Mk 1[11]), 'No one knoweth the Father save the Son' (Mt 11[27]), 'the kingdom of God is come nigh unto you' (Lk 10[9, 11]), and by such Johannine sayings as 'Which of you convicteth me of sin?' and 'I know the Father' (Jn 8[46], 10[15]). Under this absolute loyalty it may be said that in Jesus there was a 'realized eschatology'. Even in Him, however, it was only partly realized, for a complete eschatology includes, not only utterly loyal men, but the environment that is the complement of loyalty. Apart from Jesus, the phrase 'realized eschatology' has no instance in the Age of Sin. The usual phrase for believers is that they are 'entering into the *basileia*' (e.g. Mk 9[47], Jn 3[5]). None of them is ever said to be '*in* the *basileia*'. For them it will begin at the Parousia, when they are 'made perfect'. The text 'He that is but little in the kingdom of God is greater than (John)' (Lk 7[28]) means that the least in the future kingdom is greater than John is now. Similarly, the Beatitudes—more obviously in Luke, but also in Matthew—are eschatological. While there is now an *arrabon*—an instalment of the blessings and a guarantee of their fulfilment—the fulfilment is future (Lk 6^{20-6}, Mt 5^{1-12}). Here, of course, the writer is only giving his own opinions on a much canvassed subject, which is far too large for anything like full discussion here. Similarly, it is not pertinent here to examine the many 'Parables of the Kingdom', though a number of them are used in later chapters to illustrate various points. To the writer, it seems that, when Jesus said 'The kingdom of God is like . . .', He meant 'I will tell you something, generally *one* thing, about the perfect Kingdom of God', the 'one thing', for the most part, relating to the interval between the beginning of the coming of the Kingdom in the Son of Man and its full coming at the Parousia. For instance, the Parable of the Leaven describes Jesus' method of teaching in that interval, and the Parable of the Talents the right way for disciples to live in the interval. Under 'the Rule of God' the New Testament, while it takes over the Old Testament doctrine that God is ruling now, speaks much more largely about a future Kingdom in which all men will be 'His people' and therefore, in the full sense, He 'will be their God' (cf. Rev 21^3).

As already seen, in the period from Alexander to Barkokhba the kind of literature called 'Apocalyptic' flourished among the Jews. Its one purpose was to teach the truth about the Rule of God—and especially His future rule. Some Apocalypses had found their way into the Hebrew Canon before the days of Jesus, and one, the *Book of Daniel*, was finding its way in. But there were other Jewish Apocalypses, which failed to do this, but were written within the period to which the New Testament belongs. It will appear below that some, at least, of the New Testament writers refer to these books—which means that they were acquainted with them. But it seems to the present writer that this is only a manifestation of something much wider. He thinks that Apocalyptic teaching was 'in the air' in the First Christian century, and that it was a large element in the 'universe of discourse' of the whole of current Jewish thought. This requires that the Apocalyptic teaching was not a secret doctrine in the sense that certain circles kept it to themselves, as, for instance, with the Freemasons, but a teaching that was meant to spread, and did spread, among the Jewish people generally. No doubt it was kept from their rulers, both Hellenistic and Roman, as far as possible, and it may be that it took the peculiar form that it did because this would puzzle Gentiles. It is likely, too, that if Gentile rulers came across an Apocalyptic book and made out something of its meaning, they would dismiss it as 'a dreamer's vapourings'. However this may be, the important point here is that Apocalyptic ideas were *current among the Jews generally*. If it were not so, how did some of them find their way into the Canon, which was certainly what may be called a 'public book'? Jesus and His disciples knew what the contents of the *Book of Daniel* were (Mk 13^{14}), and the members of the Sanhedrin were quite well acquainted with the phrase 'the Son of Man' (Lk 22^{69}). Again, is it likely that the esoteric teaching of secret sects would survive in Ethiopic and Slavonic translations? Did the Christians need to steal a secret book before they annexed and interpreted *Second Esdras*? The whole question is too large to discuss here, but it is *taken for granted* below that in the first Christian century every Jew, whether he accepted Apocalyptic teaching or not, and whether he accepted it in one form or another, *knew* of it. While this assumption has often been made, its results have not always been fully drawn out. It must always be borne in mind in considering New Testament teaching about the Rule of God. This explains why the teaching of the Jewish Apocalypses is given so large a place below.

CHAPTER TWELVE

THE TWO AGES AND THE PAROUSIA

IN THIS and the succeeding chapters an attempt will be made to show that the first-century Church held a common doctrine of the Future. To show this the readiest way is to examine the use of the relevant terms, gathering examples from the various writers. The doctrine is complex and its different parts are divided under the several chapters. Under most of the subjects there are particular passages which, for one reason or another, need special attention. As stated in the introduction, the Christian Apocalypse, which does not everywhere conform to type, will be taken separately at the end, though particular verses from it are sometimes quoted earlier. One doctrine is the pre-supposition of all the rest, the doctrine of 'the Two Ages'.

In the New Testament the belief that history falls into two Ages is not only ubiquitous, but just taken for granted, the New Testament writers inheriting the idea from the Old, just like the Jewish writers outside the Canon (e.g. 2 Es 6⁹, 7⁵⁰·¹¹²ᶠ, 2 Bar 48²⁸⁻⁴¹). For both Jews and Christians the belief was an axiom. The important terms, as in the Old Testament, are 'age', 'day', and 'end'. Under their discussion the Christian *Differentia* emerges under the term (and idea) 'Parousia', the Christians' word for the Return of Christ. This concept too is axiomatic. The New Testament writers just accept it because they had their Lord's own warrant for it. As everywhere else, however, He and they claim that it is no innovation, but the fulfilment of Old Testament teaching.

The meaning of the term 'Age' (*aion, 103*) is the same as in LXX. The word is distributed through all the various New Testament documents except the Apocalypse, no writer having any pre-eminence. The two Ages are named together in Matthew 12³² and Ephesians 1²¹, one being called 'this age' (e.g. Lk 16⁸, Ro 12²; cf. Mk 4¹⁹, Eph 2², Jn 9³²) or 'the present (*nun*) age' (confined to the Pastoral Epistles—e.g. 2 Tim 4¹⁰, Tit 2¹²), and the other 'the coming (*mellōn, erchomenos, eperchomenos*) age' (e.g. Mk 10³⁰, Eph 2⁷, He 6⁵). In the phrase *eis ton aiona* (*28*) 'age' nearly always means 'the coming age' (e.g. Mk 3²⁹, 2 Co 9⁹, He 5⁶,

1 P 1^{25}, Jn 6^{51}), though three times the 'universe of discourse' gives it the indefinite sense of 'ever' in English (e.g. Mk 11^{14}, 1 Co 8^{13}, Jn 13^{8}). The 'present age' differs from 'the coming age' because the former, being sinful, is 'evil' (cf. Mk 4^{19}, Ro 12^{2}, 2 Ti 4^{10}), while the latter, being the Age of the Kingdom of God (cf. Rev 11^{15}), is, of course, sinless, perfect, and everlasting. 'The god of this age' (2 Co 4^{4}) fronts the 'true God'. Usually it is just taken for granted that one Age is sinful and the other righteous.

The Present Age has, of course, been a long one, and it may be spoken of as a series of 'times' (*chronos*—e.g. Ac 1^{7}, Ro 16^{25}, 1 Th 5^{1}, Tit 1^{2}). *Chronos*, like 'times' in English, denotes particular 'occasions' or 'periods' in history (e.g. Mk 9^{21}, Lk 4^{5}, Ac 13^{18}, 1 Co 7^{39}, He 5^{12}, Rev 2^{21}). The word is also used in such phrases as 'the fulness of the time' (Gal 4^{4}), and 'at (the) last of the times' (1 P 1^{20}; cf. Ac 3^{21}, Jude 18). The Present Age is divided into 'times' because of its vicissitudes. There is no text where *chronos* means 'time' in the modern abstract or philosophical sense. When, in the Apocalypse, an angel takes an oath that 'there shall no longer be a time' (Rev 10^{6}), the context shows that he means that vicissitudes are over. An Age is not a part of 'time', of *history*—that is, of 'time filled with events'—as the term *aion* itself implies. While the first Age is broken up by vicissitudes of weal and woe, there is no breach in the bliss of the second. All this no more than repeats LXX.

It is the same with the plural 'ages' (*aiones*, *55*—Paul *21*, Rev *28*) and with such phrases as 'the age of the ages' and 'the ages of the ages'. As in LXX, all the plural uses are synonyms for *aion*, used just to emphasize length, as in the English phrase 'for ever and ever'. It is natural, therefore, that the phrases should often be used for God (e.g. Mt 6^{13}, Eph 3^{21}, He 1^{8}, 1 P 4^{11}). Paul, wishing to emphasize the length of both Ages, uses the plural of both (Eph 2^{7}, Col 1^{26}). To give only one more example, the writer to the Hebrews is just using four synonyms when he says that the Son reigns 'unto *the age of the age*', that He is priest '*unto the age*', that He was 'manifested at the consummation of *the ages*', and that His 'glory' is 'unto *the ages of the ages*' (He 1^{8}, 5^{6}, 9^{26}, 13^{21}). As with 'age', the meaning of 'ages' in its various phrases just repeats LXX. In the Apocalypse, except in the doubtful text of Revelation 15^{3}, the only phrase is 'the ages of the ages' (*13*). The texts just quoted from Paul and Hebrews, however, refer to

Christ and, therefore, illustrate the persistent *differentia* of the New Testament. This appears, for instance, in passages where God and Christ are put together. When Paul speaks of a 'mystery fore-ordained before the ages' he means 'the mystery of Christ' (1 Co 2⁷ᶠ; cf. Col 1²⁶). It is 'in Christ Jesus our Lord' that God 'purposed the purpose of the ages' (Eph 3¹¹). It is 'through' the Son that God 'made the ages' (He 1²). The 'word of the Lord' 'that abideth unto the age' is the 'word of good tidings' in Christ (1 P 1²⁵). John the Seer, having described the *old* doxology of heaven (and Israel), using the phrase 'to (God) that liveth unto the ages of the ages' (Rev 4⁸⁻¹¹), passes to the '*new* song' of heaven (and Christians), 'new' because it is sung unto 'him that sitteth on the throne *and unto the Lamb* . . . unto the ages of the ages' (Rev 5¹¹⁻¹⁴; cf. 1⁵ᶠ, 11¹⁵). There are several other examples in doxologies—e.g. 'to the only wise God *through Jesus Christ* . . . unto the ages of the ages' (Ro 16²⁷; cf. 2 Co 11³¹) and 'unto (God) in the church and *in Christ Jesus* through all the generations of the ages of the ages' (Eph 3²¹; cf. 1 P 4¹¹, Jude 25). A text in Hebrews seems to mean 'of the *Son* (God saith), Thy throne is God unto the age of the age' (He 1⁸; cf. 13²¹). Christ, as God's vicegerent, is Lord of History in both Ages (e.g. Eph 1²¹). There is negative evidence, as in LXX, that, while *eis ton aiona* and its parallel phrases varied in meaning with the 'universe of discourse', they were the normal expressions for 'for ever'. Of the four other terms mentioned under the discussion of LXX renderings of '*olam*, one, *aenaos*, does not occur in the New Testament, *aei* (*7*) and *dia pantos* (*10*) always refer to the Present Age, and there is only one exception under *pantote* (*42*) (1 Th 4¹⁷). When the first Christians wanted to say 'for ever', the natural phrase was *eis ton aiona*.

The use of the adjective *aionios* (*69*—Paul *21*, John *23*) in the New Testament varies from the Septuagintal in two ways. First, *aionios* is never used to describe *God* for there was no need to use it of Him. It is perhaps not accidental that the writer to the Hebrews, when speaking of the 'life' that *Christ* now lives, does not describe it by *aionios*, but *akatalutos* ('indissoluble'—He 7¹⁶; cf. 1²). In the New Testament the word is always used about *men*. Even in 1 Timothy 6¹⁶ the probable meaning is that it is for men to render 'glory and power' perpetually to God. Second, in the New Testament *aionios* never refers to the past or present parts of history, but always to the future. Its 'universe of discourse' is always 'the Coming Age'. This implies or at least suggests that it always means 'everlasting', and not merely 'enduring', as sometimes in LXX. The word only occurs once in the Apocalypse (Rev 14⁶).

As in LXX, *aionios*, like *aion*, is a quantitative term. If, however, the noun that accompanies it is qualitative, the whole concept is thereby qualitative too. For the Christian doctrine of everlasting life the crucial point is that certain qualitative nouns carry with them *per se* a quantitative everlastingness. What the qualitative dominant is appears for the whole New Testament in John 3¹⁶⁻²¹, ³¹⁻⁶. Here it is 'whosoever *believeth on (the Son)*' who has 'everlasting life'. The word for 'life', *zoē*, is easily the best single word to describe the quality inherent in belief in Christ. There is no need to expound the whole passage. It begins by describing those who 'believe' and so do not 'perish', and ends by describing the disbeliever—for *apeithōn* denotes the man who, when Christ challenges him to '*believe*', refuses to '*obey*' (cf. Ac13⁴⁶)—upon whom the 'wrath of God abides'. As shown in *The Bible Doctrine of Sin*, this is the Unforgiven Sin—or rather, the Sin that is *per se* Unforgivable. Christian Faith, just because it is faith *in Christ*, is intrinsically everlasting. Here is the Christian *differentia* under *aionios*. It is not remarkable, therefore, that *wherever* the word occurs in the New Testament the context refers either to 'faith in Christ' or the refusal of it. In a few instances the reference to faith is a little remote, but it is there. In 2 Corinthians 4¹⁸ the phrase 'things unseen' refers back to the 'eternal weight of (believers') glory'; in Hebrews 6² the words 'eternal judgement' look forward to the description of apostates—i.e. one kind of disbelievers—in verses 4-6; in 1 John 3¹⁵, while men who 'hate' are 'murderers', believers cannot 'hate' for through Christ they have 'passed out of death into life'; in Jude 7 the reference to 'Sodom and Gomorrah' warns Christians that a true believer cannot be 'lascivious' (verse 4). The connexion is least obvious in two Synoptic passages, but in Matthew 18⁸ *Jesus* is teaching *His disciples* how to 'enter into life' (cf. verses 1f), and in Luke 16⁹, where He ironically describes Mammon as a god who opens the door into 'the everlasting tabernacles', He means that, in fact, it is *His* 'gospel of the kingdom' that lifts that latch.

There are only seven texts where *aionios* describes the Future of the *wicked*, and in every one the context relates their fate to their rejection of Jesus. In Mark 3²⁹, as already indicated, it is those who, knowing that the Spirit is telling them that Jesus 'comes from

God', refuse to admit it (and desperately ascribe His 'powers' to Satan), who commit the 'everlasting sin'. Two of the three passages that speak of an 'everlasting *fire*' have been mentioned in the last paragraph (Mt 18[8], Jude 7). In the third the phrase describes the fate of those who have neglected the suffering 'brethren' of the Son of Man, 'ever-lasting *punishment*' being a synonym (Mt 25[41, 46]). In 2 Thessalonians 1st Paul speaks of 'the everlasting *destruction*' of those 'who know not God and obey not the gospel of our Lord Jesus'. As noted above, the 'everlasting *judgement*' of Hebrews 6[2] is to fall upon those who, having been 'enlightened' and having 'tasted' the first-fruits of the Spirit, 'fall away . . . and crucify . . . the Son of God afresh' (verses 4-7). In this series of texts the four words in italics—'fire', 'punishment', 'destruction', and 'judgement'—describe one thing. John does not use the word for the fate of the *wicked*, but takes a negative way, as in 'he that hath the Son hath the life; he that hath *not* the Son of God hath *not* the life' (1 Jn 5[12]). Since His believers 'have *no* life in (themselves)' (Jn 6[53]), 'everlasting life' is *not* for them (Jn 3[36], 5[39f], 1 Jn 3[15]; cf. 5[11]). It may be noted that none of the four italicized nouns, taken *per se*, requires that the adjective *aionios must* mean 'everlasting'. It is remarkable that the word *aionios* only occurs once in the Christian Apocalypse and then in the phrase 'an everlasting gospel' (Rev 14[6]).

For the Future Fate of the *Righteous* by far the commonest phrase is 'everlasting *life*' (*43*). For 'John', who uses no other phrase (*23*), examples will be quoted below. There are nine examples in Paul, but the phrase is rare elsewhere. In the Synoptics, when parallel passages are allowed for, the eight instances reduce to three (Mk 10[17, 30], Mt 25[46]). Acts has only two examples (13[46, 48]), Jude one (verse 21), and the Apocalypse, Hebrews, Peter, and James, none. A few typical texts may be quoted—'What shall I do that I may inherit everlasting life?' (the ultimate answer being 'Follow *me*'—Mk 10[17, 21]); 'everlasting life through Jesus Christ our Lord' (Ro 5[21]); 'he that soweth unto the Spirit shall of the Spirit (who is the Spirit of God's Son as well as of God —Gal 4[6]) reap everlasting life' (Gal 6[8]). The reference of the phrase to the Gospel is ubiquitous.

It is the same where other words occur with *aionios*. Hebrews has the phrases 'everlasting *salvation*', 'everlasting *redemption*', 'everlasting *inheritance*', and 'everlasting *covenant*' (He 5[9], 9[12, 15], 13[20]). Both Paul and Peter speak of 'everlasting *glory*' or 'weight of glory' (2 Co 4¹⁷, 2 Ti 2¹⁰, 1 P 5¹⁰). Four phrases occur once each—'An everlasting *house* not made with hands' (2 Co 5¹), 'everlasting *encouragement*' (*paraklēsis*—2 Th 2¹⁶), 'everlasting *kingdom*' (2 P 1¹¹), and 'everlasting *gospel*' (Rev 14⁶). Philemon will one day 'receive (Onesimus) everlastingly' (Philem 15). Every one of the phrases relates to Christ.

As already indicated, it is in the Fourth Gospel that the doctrine of 'everlasting life' culminates. The writer seems to have deliberaately kept *aionios* for *zoe*, as he uses it with no other word. When he wishes to describe it further, he prefers periphrases. For instance, he does not speak of 'the spring of everlasting water', but of the 'spring of water, leaping up unto everlasting life' (Jn 4¹⁴). Similarly, he speaks of 'fruit unto everlasting life' (4³⁶), 'food that abides unto everlasting life' (6²⁷), 'words of everlasting life' (6⁶⁸). Christ 'gives' it, for the Father has 'commanded' Him to do so (10²⁸, 12⁵⁰; cf. 1 Jn 2²⁵). In several of these phrases the Future Age is in mind, as the word 'unto' (*eis*)—paralleled by *eis ton aiona* (4¹⁴, 10²⁸)—implies, but in other texts the 'believer' already 'has everlasting life' (3¹⁵f. ³⁶, 5²⁴, 6⁴⁷). There is a text that shows the relation between the two sets of texts—'He that eateth my flesh and drinketh my blood *has* everlasting life, and (it follows that) I will raise him up at *the last day*' (6⁵⁴; cf. 11²⁵). While 'everlasting life' does not abolish the gulf between the two Ages it bridges it. But there is more than all this. In other parts of the New Testament there are eight or nine texts where *zoe* means 'the life that now is' (e.g. Lk 16²⁵, 1 Co 15¹⁹, Ja 4¹⁴), but this is not so with 'John'. *Wherever the word occurs in the Fourth Gospel and the Johannine Epistles, whether with aionios (23) or without it (11), it expounds the phrase* 'In him was life' (1⁴)—i.e. it relates to Christ, and, even if *aionios* be absent, the 'life' that *He* gives is everlasting *per se* (e.g. 1⁴, 6³⁵, 10¹⁰, 14⁶, 1 Jn 5¹¹). This implication, of course, has examples outside 'John' (e.g. Mk 9⁴³, Ac 3¹⁵, Ro 5¹⁷, Col 3³, 2 Tim 1¹, Ja 1¹², 1 P 3⁷, Rev 2⁷). The kind of life that Christ gives is the kind that He has. A believer 'has eternal life' because 'As the Father hath life in himself, so also hath he given the Son to have life in himself' (5²⁴, ²⁶). The New Testament writers dealt with LXX words and phrases in two ways—sometimes they used them in the *same* sense as LXX, leaving the *context* to show the Christian *differentia*, as with *aion* and *aionios*, and sometimes they so used a word that the *differentia* gave a distinctive meaning to the word *itself*, as with *zoe* (and *agape* and *pistis*, etc.). The text 'This is life everlasting, that they should know thee, the only true God and him whom thou didst send, Jesus Christ' (17[3]; cf. 1 Jn 5[20]) gives the fundamental idea for the whole New Testament. To 'know God' is to 'have fellowship with God' (1 Jn 1[3]), and through this fellowship the Christian lives a distinctive kind of life, for, since it is in 'the true (God)' (1 Jn 5[20]), it is qualitatively different from all other kinds. It is intrinsically everlasting, for God is everlasting and it is life 'in Him'. The nature of the Christian *differentia* is defined similarly in a culminant text. While any Jew could have said 'This is life ever-lasting, to know thee the only true God', the Christian writer, using his paratactic 'and', adds 'and (this knowledge only comes through) him whom (God) sent, *Jesus Christ*'.[1]

It follows that between the two Ages there is a relation of a given kind. There are many passages that teach that for Christians the first is the organic prelude to the second—for instance, in Philippians 3[8-11], where the word 'resurrection' implies the Coming Age. Or again, the 'completion of the age' is the 'harvest' of the 'seed' that the Son of Man sows in this Age and that grows in it (Mt 13[37-40]). Again, the disciple's blessings 'in this time' are the prelude of 'everlasting life', for they already 'taste the powers of the coming age' (He 6[5]). It is because they 'look for the blessed hope and appearing of the glory of (their) great God and Saviour Jesus Christ' that they 'live soberly and righteously and godly in this present age' (Tit 2[12f]). This organic connexion between the life of the believer in this Age and the next is one of the 'burdens' of the Fourth Gospel. There, of the twelve uses of *eis ton aiona* ten occur in words ascribed to Jesus. These all relate to believers. Four are negative—the believer shall 'never thirst', 'shall not see death', 'shall not taste of death', 'shall not perish', 'shall never die' (Jn 4[14], 8[51f], 10[28], 11[26]). In every case the Greek negative is emphatic (*ou mē*). In the positive texts the believer is 'to live for ever'—unlike a slave, the 'son abides in the home for ever'; Jesus will give the disciples the Paraclete *now* that 'he may be with (them) *for ever*' (Jn 6[51, 58], 8[35], 14[16]). Life *in Christ* is already *qualitatively* distinctive, and *therefore quantitatively* everlasting (cf. 1 Jn 2[17], 2 Jn 2). It is a mistake to take John 17[3] to mean that *zoe aionios* is qualitative and therefore not quantitative; on the contrary it means that 'to know God' is life of such a

---

[1] For a longer examination of the use and meanings of *zoe*, both in LXX and the New Testament, see *The Bible Doctrine of Man*, *sub voce* in the Index of Terms.

quality that it is intrinsically ever-lasting—i.e. both qualitative and quantitative.

In the New Testament, as in the Prophets and Apocalyptists, the Present Age culminates and closes in a final 'Day'. This term, with such phrases as 'in those days', is used in an Apocalyptic way about eighty times. Of these there are seven in Mark, twelve in Luke, fourteen in Matthew, nineteen in Paul, ten in the Johannine books, three in the Apocalypse, and fourteen elsewhere. The word is everywhere used in the Old Testament ways, without explanation. Sometimes, though rarely, it means 'a Day', as sometimes in the Prophets, not '*the* Day'. Often it is called 'the Day of Judgement', and this is everywhere implied. Clearly the belief in a final Judgement was part and parcel of the primitive Christian creed, as it was of Israel's. The Christian *differentia* here is the belief that *Christ* is Judge. Certain words and phrases recur along with 'Day'—it will come 'as a thief' (*kleptēs*, 6), it is 'nigh' (*enggus* and *enggizein*, *14*), and its advent will be 'sudden' (*aiphnidos* and *exaiphnes*, *3*); Christians, therefore, are to 'watch' for it (*grēgorein*, *15*; *agrupnein*, *2*), and not to 'sleep' (*katheudein*, *4*). Instances of these terms are given elsewhere.

The terms *telos* ('end') and its derivative *sunteleia* ('completion') are alternatives for 'day'. As shown above, this use of the terms begins with the Greek versions of Daniel in their rendering of *qetz*. *Sunteleia* may be taken first. It always occurs in the phrases 'the completion of the age' (*5*, all in Matthew) or 'the completion of the ages' (*1*—He 9[26]). In all the passages the context relates the phrase to Jesus. In Matthew 13[39-41, 49], the 'harvest' is 'the completion of the age' when 'the Son of Man sends forth his angels' to reap. In 24[3] 'the sign of thy *parousia*' is equated with 'the completion of the age', and in 28[20], Jesus promises to be with His disciples 'even unto the completion of the age'. In Hebrews 9[26], the present time is 'the completion of the ages' just because in it Christ 'has been manifested'. The use of *telos* with the meaning 'the end of the age' is a little more frequent. Omitting three texts where it may mean 'the end of a man's life' (Ro 6[22], Ph 3[19], 1 P 4[17f]), it occurs fourteen times, or, counting Synoptic parallels as one, ten. It is found in the Synoptics, Paul, Hebrews, First Peter, and the Apocalypse, but not in John. Except in the phrases 'the ends of the ages' (1 Co 10[11]) and 'the end of all things' (1 P 4[7]), it is just taken for granted that 'the end' means 'the end of the age'. References to 'the day of our Lord Jesus Christ' and to

His '*parousia*' occur in 1 Corinthians 1⁷ᶠ, 15²⁴. Both the Synoptists and Hebrews speak of 'enduring unto the end' (Mk 13¹³, Mt 10²², He 3⁶· ¹⁴, 6¹¹), and John the Seer has a parallel text (Rev 2²⁶). Perhaps the phrase 'I am the beginning and the end', used both by God and Christ, should be added (Rev 21⁶, 22¹³). The phrases 'the end is not yet' and 'the end is not immediately' (Mk 13⁷, Mt 24⁶, Lk 21⁹) will be considered later. The ten clearly relevant texts have two things in common—they are addressed to contemporaries, the 'universe of discourse' being *their* lifetime, i.e. it is implied that the writers expect 'the end' within a generation and in every case there is a reference to Christ in the context (i.e. for the writers He and 'the end' go together). Two texts are typical—'The end of all things has come near' (1 P 4⁷); 'Then the end, when (Christ) shall deliver up the kingdom to God and Father' (1 Co 15²⁴).

All the texts quoted under 'day' and 'end' and 'completion' either assert or assume three things—that Christ will return to the earth, that His return will be the dividing point between the two Ages, and that this belief was one of those that dominated the life of Christians. But the evidence for the belief in the Coming of Christ is much wider than the three terms. The exultant Aramaic words '*maran atha*' (1 Co 16²²), repeated in Greek in Philippians 4⁵, seem to have been a Christian watch-word. Then there is the use of two Greek words meaning 'come' (*erchesthai*, *hēkein*). This has examples in many parts of the New Testament. For instance, a phrase from a Psalm (118²⁶), used on 'Palm Sunday' and descriptive of the coming kingdom of God (Mk 11⁹ᶠ), is by Luke used of a future coming of Christ (Lk 13³⁵), and Matthew has the text: 'The Son of Man shall come in the glory of his father' (Mt 16²⁷). Paul applies the text 'There shall come out of Zion the Deliverer' to Christ (Ro 11²⁶), and bids Christians keep the Lord's Supper 'till he come' (1 Co 11²⁶). The writer of Hebrews applies a text in Habakkuk to Christ: 'He that cometh shall come and shall not tarry' (He 10³⁷; cf. 9²⁸, 12²⁶ᶠ). John the Seer has the phrase 'I come quickly' four times (Rev 3¹¹, 22⁷· ¹²· ²⁰). In the supplement to the Fourth Gospel (Jn 21²²ᶠ) it is implied that the disciples took Jesus' phrase 'till I come' to refer to His return to earth. The belief 'Christ is coming' is the ubiquitous New Testament equivalent to the Old Testament belief 'The Kingdom of God will come'. This belief was epitomized in the word 'Parousia'.

The literal meaning of the term is 'presence', but this does not adequately render it either in LXX (*4*), in the passages where it is used in the New Testament of the 'presence' of others than Christ (*7*), or of the 'presence' of Christ at the End of the Age (*17*). The term is everywhere used of the 'presence' of someone *who has not always been present*. In LXX it occurs of Nehemiah's 'return' to Shushan (Neh 2^6 A), of Judith's 'arrival' at Holofernes' camp (Jth 10^{18}), and of the arrival and 'presence' of an invading army (2 Mac 8^{12}, 15^{21}). Paul uses it of the 'arrival' of friends, with the suggestion that, now they have arrived, they will stay for a while (1 Co 16^{17}, 2 Co 7^{6f}); of his own 'presence' with churches from which he is now absent (2 Co 10^{10}, Ph 1^{26}, 2^{12}); and of the 'arrival' of the Lawless One (2 Th 2^9). In the *papyri* the word occurs of 'the visit of some official or a monarch'[2] —for instance, of Hadrian's 'visit' to Egypt, as to other Provinces, to 'put things right'. When a Christian heard the word Parousia he would think both of the 'return' of Jesus, the 'arrival' of the Messiah, and His continual 'presence' thereafter. It was true that He had always been present in and through the Holy Spirit, but now He would come in 'the body of His glory' (cf. the use of 'absent in body' and 'present in spirit' in 1 Co 5^3).

The distribution of the term when used of Christ is peculiar. It occurs six times in the Epistles to the Thessalonians (1 Th 2^{19}, 3^{13}, 4^{15}, 5^{23}, 2 Th $2^{1,8}$) and once elsewhere in Paul (1 Co 15^{23}); Matthew has it four times in one chapter ($24^{3,27,37,39}$); and there are sporadic instances in James 5^{7f}, 2 Peter 1^{16}, $3^{4,12}$, and 1 John 2^{28}. On the other hand, it does not occur, for instance, in Mark or Luke or the Apocalypse or the Epistle to the Hebrews or the Fourth Gospel. This, however, has no particular significance, for, as already shown, the *idea*, as distinct from the *term*, is ubiquitous. Matthew, for example, has no more than added the term to the 'Little Apocalypse' of Mark 13, where it is already the ruling idea, as it is in the Apocalypse of John. Indeed, all the earlier discussions of the 'Day' and the 'End' illustrate the prevalence of the idea. It has two synonyms—*epiphaneia* (*6* —'manifestation'), which has only one example outside the Pastoral Epistles (2 Th 2^8, 1 Ti 6^{14}, etc.), and *apocalupsis* ('revelation'), which under this meaning (*4*) is confined to Paul and Peter (e.g. 1 Co 1^7, 1 P 1^7). But *parousia* is *the* word.

The word gathered to it other ideas beside 'presence'. Among

[2] *ERE*, IX. 636, *sub voce*.

these the fundamental concept is 'victory'. All the rest are *sequelae*. Here it is to be remembered that in the New Testament Christ triumphs initially at the Ascension, finally at the Parousia. At the Ascension final victory was already sure but not yet achieved, as, to use a hint of a parallel, El Alamein in the second World War was the 'turning-point' that led to Berlin. Yet the parallel fails at a significant point. In the interval between the Ascension and the Parousia Christ is not waging war; He is exercising the 'long-suffering' or 'long-temperedness' of God as through the Spirit He gives men a 'last chance' to turn from rebellion to loyalty. This comes out, for instance, in Paul's quotation from Psalm 68^{18} *and* in his variation from it (Eph 4^8). Christ has 'ascended on high,' leading captive the 'principalities and powers' that have hitherto 'lorded it' over men (Col 2^{15}), but He has 'received gifts *for* men', not 'from' them. The 'gifts' are the 'grace' given under various *charismata* to Christians (verses 7, 11f). Paul, to suit his immediate purpose, goes on to say that these are given 'for the perfecting of the saints', but, as his mention of 'apostles' and 'evangelists' implies, they are also given for the evangelizing of the world. Meanwhile God holds His hand, and the final victory is delayed. Here the much-quoted phrase from Psalm 110^1 describes both the delay and its end—'Sit thou on my right hand *Until* I make thine enemies thy footstool' (e.g. Mk 12^{36}, Ac 2^{34f}, He 1^{13}). For the Parousia the appropriate quotation is not Psalm 110^1, with its 'until', but Psalm 8^6—'Thou *hast put* all things under his feet' (1 Co 15^{25}, He 2^{8f}).

To understand the *sequelae* it is worth while to recall what happened when an Eastern king had finally conquered rebels. He would take his seat on a throne, with his exultant troops feasting about him. He had conquered, of course, by force, and alongside his loyal soldiers there would be a mass of captured rebels in chains. There would be a distribution of rewards to the loyal soldiers and of punishments to those who had fought against their lord. There would also be a multitude who had not obviously taken sides and fought, but none the less had been 'for or against'. To use the modern term, these would be 'screened', usually by subordinates, some being punished, some rewarded, and many just set free. It would be to these, and to these only, that the word 'judge' could be applied in the sense 'to decide which are loyal' and which 'rebels'. It is only when the word 'judge' is taken to denote 'reward' and 'punishment' that those who had fought on either side could be said to be 'judged' for there was no need to decide which side *they* had taken. Finally, the king would arrange for the future government and ordering of the reconquered kingdom. *Mutatis mutandis* all this may be applied to the Parousia though the *mutanda* are important. Except in the Apocalypse (Rev 19$^{11-21}$), there is no war at the Parousia for through Christ God then lets loose His omnipotence, and where there is omnipotence, there is no struggle. *Ipso facto* the Almighty is victor on the instant. Even the horrible picture of Revelation 19$^{11-21}$ portrays the pursuit of fugitives rather than the struggle of fight. Under Judgement God does not need, of course, like human kings, to find out which men are good and which bad before He judges, for He knows already. Strictly speaking, from His judgement-seat He does not decide, but declares, which are good and which bad. Again, while human victors cannot reward the loyal who have *died* for them, God raises them from the dead that they may share in His triumph. Finally, unlike human kings, the Son of Man goes on to rule an empire as wide as the world, and to rule it for ever. None the less, in spite of these weighty *mutanda*, the triumph of an Eastern king is the best starting-point for a study of the Parousia. New Testament writers refer to any element in the concept that suits their immediate purpose, taking it for granted that the whole set of ideas is already well known to their readers.

CHAPTER THIRTEEN

GEHENNA AND PARADISE

THE meaning of the terms 'Gehenna' and 'Paradise' may be considered at this point. Under 'Gehenna' there is no doubt about the *derivation* of the word. It is an imperfect Greek (and Latin) transliteration of the Aramaic *gēhinnam* or the Hebrew *gē-hinnom*, 'the valley of Hinnom'. It has been seen that the last was the place where, after Josiah, the great garbage-heap of Jerusalem lay, breeding worms and slowly burning, and that this was almost certainly in Trito-Isaiah's mind when he speaks of an 'undying worm' and an 'unquenchable fire' (Isa 66^{24}).

In the Apocalyptic books the best starting-point is a verse in Second Esdras. In the Revised Version it reads: 'And the pit of torment shall appear, and over against it the place of rest: and the furnace of Gehenna shall be showed and over against it the Paradise of delight' (2 Es 7^{36}). The writer uses 'torment' to refer back to this verse six times in verses 38-84. It would have been better to translate the first relevant phrase by *'lake* of torment' instead of 'pit of torment' and the second by *'oven* of Gehenna' instead of 'furnace of Gehenna', for the other versions show that under the first phrase '*locus*' in the Latin should be '*lacus*', and in the second phrase the Latin word is *clibanus*, which means 'oven', not 'furnace'.

The terms 'lake' and 'oven', of course, do not suit a garbage-heap, but they do suit the crater of an active volcano in a normal eruption—in which there is no cataclysmic outburst such as overwhelmed Pompeii, but a boiling 'cup' of lava that over-spills its lip and a towering cloud of smoke (cf. Ex 20^{18}). This may be called a 'lake' of fire, and also—when it is remembered that the common 'oven' in Palestine was a hole in the ground, without a cover, *in* which the fuel burned[1]—an 'oven' of fire. In the *Book of Enoch* the Patriarch, on his journey to the far West, comes 'to a river of fire in which the fire flows like water and discharges itself into the great sea towards the West' (En 17^5)—i.e. to the part of the Mediterranean where Vesuvius, Stromboli and Etna pour their lava into the sea. In a later chapter (67), as has been

---
[1] See *HDB*, *sub voce*.

seen, when describing the 'burning valley' in the utmost West Noah uses the phenomena of the fall of fire into the sea that attends a *great* eruption. At a later point (90^{24-7}) another of the Enochic writers seems to be referring to this fire in the West when describing the final fate of the 'stars' or Fallen Angels and the 'seventy shepherds' (the post-Exilic priests), and then adds that 'a *like* abyss' was opened 'in the midst of the earth' (i.e. near Jerusalem, where the new 'house' of God is—verse 26), and that into it the 'blinded sheep' (i.e. the other apostates of Maccabean days) were thrown. The writer was perhaps thinking of the great eruption in the Arabah in 'the days of Lot'. To integrate all that the writers of *Enoch* say about Fires of Punishment would need a long discussion. It is sufficient to note that there are at least two, that they are both on earth (and not in Hades), and that, as in Esdras' phrases, the phenomena are volcanic. While both writers would know that the lava came from some subterranean source, called by the Greeks 'tartarus' (cf. Job 41^{23} LXX, En 20^2, 2 Bar 59^{10}, 2 P 2^4), it is not to this but to the crater that the descriptions refer. While Enoch places Gehenna on earth, Esdras declares that no man knows its 'outgoings' any more than he knows the 'springs' of the 'abyss' of waters that envelopes the universe (2 Es 4^7). This seems to mean that at present it lies somewhere outside 'the heavens and the earth'. At the End, however, it moves to earth and 'appears' when all the dead return to *earth* for the final Judgement (2 Es 7^{32f}). It is probably on earth too in the *Assumption of Moses* (10^{10}) for the righteous can *see* the wicked in Gehenna—and gloat. It is clear that 'fire' was now the usual word for the future punishment of the wicked. It had two origins, for the Isaianic phrase 'fire and the worm' was used (Sir 7^{17}, Jth 16^{17}) as well as such a phrase as 'the lake of fire'. Probably in common speech men forgot the dual origins of the idea and used whatever phrase came readily to mind without exactly defining it. This would be the easier when the term was used symbolically, as in James's phrase 'The tongue ... is set on fire by Gehenna' (3^6), though, probably again, many would not clearly distinguish between the literal and symbolic use—like, for instance, most readers of Dante. The 'lake of fire that burneth with brimstone' of the Apocalypse (e.g. Rev 19^{20}) may be a synonym for 'Gehenna', but it is not in Hades (Rev 20^{14}) but on the earth.

Apart from the text in James just named, the word 'Gehenna'

is confined to the Synoptic Gospels (*11*), and there it is always used by Jesus Himself. In Mark it occurs three times in the passage about 'stumbling-blocks' (*skandalon*) (9⁴³⁻⁸). Here it is defined as 'unquenchable fire', and 'to enter into *life*' is the opposite of 'to be cast into Gehenna'. In Luke the one use of the word adds nothing to its elucidation (12⁵). In one text Matthew (*7*) defines Gehenna as 'everlasting fire' (18⁸), and in another he speaks of a man's being 'destroyed' 'soul and body' in Gehenna (10²⁸). The last phrase does not suit the Intermediate State, for the bodies of the dead do not pass there. Similarly, he speaks of the 'whole body' as being 'cast into Gehenna (5²⁹ᶠ). In the arraignment of the Pharisees they are called 'the offspring of vipers'—that is the 'sons of Gehenna' (23¹⁵,³³). All the passages suggest that Jesus is using a well-known term, and there is nothing to indicate that He uses it in any but the current way. There is at least one passage where Gehenna is described but not named—in the phrase 'the everlasting fire, prepared for the devil and his angels' (Mt 25⁴¹). This recalls *Enoch* where the 'fire' for apostates is said to be 'like' the 'fire' for the Fallen Angels and the 'seventy shepherds', but Matthew speaks of one 'fire', not two. It is possible that the 'tormenting flame' in the Parable of Dives and Lazarus (Lk 16²³ᶠ) is the 'fire' of Gehenna. If this is so, two peculiarities appear—first, Gehenna is in *Hades* (verse 23), and second, it denotes the *Intermediate State* of the wicked. This Parable is discussed later. If it be omitted, Gehenna is the place of the punishment of the wicked at the *End*, and probably Jesus' hearers would think that *then*, at any rate, it is somewhere *on earth*, as in *Enoch* and *Second Esdras*. While the term was well-known to Greek-speaking Jews, it does not appear to have been known to Gentiles, for, if it had been, it would probably have been found more often in the New Testament, particularly in the Apocalypse of John.

The term *paradeisos* is found in LXX. It appears to have been borrowed from Persian and occurs as early as Xenophon. It is used of Artaxerxes' 'park' in Nehemiah 2⁸ and of Solomon's supposed 'park' in Ecclesiastes 2⁵. In both texts there is reference to the 'trees' of the 'park'—timber-trees in the first and fruit-trees in the second. For the present purpose the significant passage is Genesis 2⁸ᶠᶠ where LXX has 'the Lord planted a paradise in Eden' (cf. Isa 51³). In LXX the term is not used of the future state of the righteous. This begins in the Apocalyptic literature.

As already seen, in Second Esdras (7^{36}) 'the Paradise of delight', described as 'the place of rest', is set over against 'the lake of torment' and 'the oven of Gehenna'. It is the ancient 'paradise' of Adam (2 Es 3^6), which is to return at the End. Like Gehenna, it lies at present outside the 'heavens and the earth', somewhere beyond the ken of man (4^{7f}). Perhaps it is to be identified with the *promptuaria* in which the righteous dead now 'rest with great quietness', awaiting the resurrection and the End (7^{95}). Like Gehenna, at the End it moves from its unknown site and 'appears' on earth (7^{36}). It is described as 'a paradise whose fruit endureth without decay, wherein is abundance and healing' (7^{123}). In a longer description of its perfect happiness (8^{52-4}) it is added that 'the tree of life' is there and that it lies round a new 'city'. The last detail is a significant addition to the story of Eden.

In *Enoch* Gabriel is the guardian angel of Paradise (20^7). In this book, just as the greater fire (or fires) of punishment lies in the farthest West, so Paradise lies in the farthest East (28^1). On the way to it Enoch, having passed through mountains and deserts, comes to regions where trees of mounting fragrance grow —frankincense, myrrh, mastic, nectar, and so on (Chh. 28-31). Then (Ch. 32) he comes to 'seven mountains' of spices, and so at last to 'the Garden of Righteousness' where there are 'many large trees . . . of goodly fragrance, large, very beautiful and glorious'. Here there grows 'the tree of wisdom' or 'knowledge' 'very beautiful' and 'attractive', of which Adam and Eve ate. In an earlier passage (Chh. 24 and 25), probably misplaced, there are also seven mountains, of which the seventh is one of the thrones of God (25^3). It is circled with 'fragrant trees'. In their midst there is a tree that 'has a fragrance beyond all fragrance, and its leaves and blooms and wood wither not for ever'. This is the 'tree of life'. At the 'great judgement' it is to be 'given to the righteous and holy', being 'transplanted to the holy place to the temple of the Lord, the Eternal King' (25^{4f}). Where Esdras adds a new 'city' to Paradise Enoch adds a new Temple. In both, Paradise, now remote and inaccessible, returns at the End to be the dwelling-place of the righteous.

The accounts of Paradise in three other books may be noted. In the *Testament of Levi* (18^{10}) the Future Priest 'opens the gates of Paradise', removes 'the flaming sword', and gives 'the saints' to 'eat of the tree of life'. In *Second Baruch* one passage (2 Bar 4) describes the City and Paradise, not only as God had from the first meant them to be, but as they *are* through the Era of Sin. They are 'preserved' with God somewhere and He shows them to Adam and Abraham and Moses in turn. Here too Paradise is the place to which the righteous pass at the Judgement. This appears clearly in a later chapter (2 Bar 51), which describes the bliss of the righteous *after* the resurrection (2 Bar 50³). Here they 'behold the world that is now invisible to them', and 'dwell in its heights', like the angels, and there will be 'spread before them the extents of Paradise'. This implies, not that Paradise is *confined* to 'heaven', for the angels' world is 'the heavens and the earth', but that Paradise 'extends' through the whole universe. This is the most splendid account of all. In *Slavonic Enoch* (Chap. 8) the Patriarch 'looks down' from 'the third heaven' on the 'paradise' where Adam dwelt and where God 'rested' on the Seventh Day. It is in this 'great Paradise' that the righteous are to dwell for ever after 'the great judgement' (65⁸⁻¹⁰). Apparently it is on earth somewhere all the time, for Enoch 'looks down' on it from 'the third heaven'. The Apocalyptists agree that the Paradise of Eden still exists, disagree about its present locale, but agree again about its return.

In the New Testament the word 'Paradise' occurs three times, each time as a well-known word. The first instance is in the poignant story of the Penitent Robber (Lk 23⁴²ᶠ). When the Robber says 'Jesus, remember me when thou comest in thy kingdom', he means that he believes that Jesus is the Messiah, who will return to rule in the Kingdom of God, at the End, and he asks for a place in that future realm. Jesus, using a word he would understand, replies: 'Not only at the End—Today'. It follows that Jesus Himself expected to pass to Paradise when He died, and not to any 'Harrowing of Hell'. The writer thinks it not unlikely that Jesus believed in a literal Paradise, but this is not the vital point. Jesus promised to one whom God had 'given him' that *at once* he will be 'with him where he is' (Jn 17²⁴).

In the second passage (2 Co 12²⁻⁴) Paul, speaking of himself as 'a man in Christ', says that 'fourteen years ago' he was 'caught up even to the third heaven', and calls this 'Paradise'. This reflects yet another opinion about its locale. Perhaps Paul refers to it when he says that he 'desires to depart and be with Christ' (Ph 1²³). The third passage runs 'To him that overcometh, to him will I (Christ) give to eat of the tree of life, which is in the Paradise of God' (Rev 2⁷). Here the Seer seems to refer to a Paradise which now exists somewhere, but it is to be remembered that John of Patmos is the greatest exemplar of the Hebrew habit of mingling the symbolic with the literal, as though the distinction were of no consequence. While all three passages refer to Paradise as it is now, this, of course, does not exclude a belief in its return at the End. Indeed, it is likely that when the Seer, having described the 'holy city, new Jerusalem, coming down out of heaven from God' (Rev 21$^{2,\ 9-26}$), adds a description of 'a river of the water of life', with trees, each of them a 'tree of life', on its banks, whose 'leaves' are 'for the healing of the nations', and declares that 'there shall be no more curse' (22$^{1-3}$), he is just describing Paradise, every phrase recalling the account of the Garden either in *Genesis* or in the Jewish Apocalypses or in both. It is under the phrase 'The throne of God *and of the Lamb*' that the Christian *differentia* appears.

CHAPTER FOURTEEN

THE DATE OF THE PAROUSIA

SINCE THE belief in the Parousia of Christ is distinctively Christian, the question of its date, of course, does not arise in the Jewish Apocalypses. But Christ is to return to judge. The question 'When did the Apocalyptists expect that the Judgement would come?' is, therefore, apposite here. There is little or no doubt that they expected it soon, but it is remarkable that they rarely say this in so many words. Esdras' verse 'And therefore is my judgement now at hand' (2 Es 8^{61}) suggests the reason. It is a passing mention of something that was usually taken for granted. The fact is that the whole Apocalyptic literature is the organic outcome of a period when religious men believed that the End was near. This is its *raison d'être*. The Apocalyptic writers spoke to people who lived under 'a certain fearful expectation of judgement'. When preachers of doom live at a time when the final Judgement is not expected for a long time to come, they speak, not of it, but of the punishment that comes when a man dies—i.e. that comes *soon*—as might be illustrated from such preachers throughout the Christian centuries. It is a doom that is *near* that men fear. In Enoch 94-105 there is a long sermon, which might well be taken as typical of the message of the Apocalyptists. It may be compared and contrasted with the great sermon in Deuteronomy 28. A chief point of difference is that the Deuteronomic preacher, unlike the Enochic, did not live in a period when men believed that the End was near. The whole atmosphere of the two sermons is therefore different. In the later sermon 'Enoch', the *ostensible* speaker, begins by using once and again the phrase 'in those (distant) days', but after a while the *real* preacher uses such phrases as 'Be hopeful, *ye* righteous' and 'Woe unto you, *ye* sinners'—not 'In those days the righteous shall hope' and 'In those days woe unto the wicked'—that is, he is addressing his own contemporaries and telling them of the bliss and woe that they themselves, and not the men of a distant future, may expect. For them the Judgement is near. This is the silent axiom of the sermon. There is a similar transition in *Second Esdras*. Esdras himself, the ostensible writer, lived centuries before the real writer, and for the former the Judgement is distant (2 Es 14^{35}), but for the latter it is 'now at hand' (8^{61}). In the Interpolation it seems clear that *an* early End comes with the Messiah, though *the* End is four centuries later (2 Es 7^{28f}). Most of the Apocalyptists, and probably all, believed, along with Paul, that upon them 'the ends of the ages are come' (1 Co 10^{11}). The belief was not confined to the Christians. At the same time it must be remembered that 'near' is a flexible and indeterminate word. When Esdras has been told that the Judgement is near, he still goes on to ask 'At what time?' (2 Es 8$^{61-3}$). Such a phrase as 'The End is near, but indefinitely near' would fairly describe the attitude of the Apocalyptists.

On turning to the New Testament, the teaching of the Synoptic Gospels comes first. Here three preliminary notes may be made. First, the question 'What did Jesus teach about the date of His Parousia?' which involves another question: 'How, if at all, did the teaching and tradition of the church develop in the seventy years or so between the Resurrection of Jesus and *c*. AD 100?' It is generally agreed that the Second Gospel was the first to be written, that Luke came next, and Matthew after Luke. It is likely, therefore, that, if there was any development, Mark will show the tradition at an earlier stage than Luke, and Luke than Matthew. As shown below, the evidence confirms this supposition. Of course, the disciples began with the words of Jesus Himself, but already in Mark there are signs that phrases were added to explain what He had said (e.g. Mk 13$^{14, 37}$). It should be noted that another question, often asked under Luke and Matthew, 'What were the sources of this or that passage?', is not relevant here. Where Luke and Matthew differ from Mark, it is very likely that they both sometimes borrow from an earlier document usually called 'Q' and sometimes use other sources, but, to discover the answer to the question 'What was the tradition in the church, or in the part of it that Luke and Matthew respectively represent?' the important matter is *their* teaching, and not its origins. Whatever these were, the Evangelists, or the churches for which they stand, had adopted it and made it their tradition. Below, therefore, there is no attempt to pick out the sources from which they may have borrowed.

Second, the Synoptic passages that describe the Day or the End sometimes refer to 'the Coming of *the Son of Man*', and, while the meaning of this name is not discussed here, the writer's own opinion about it should be stated. He thinks that, as in Daniel and Enoch, the 'Son of Man' is both an individual person and a societary one, and that, when Jesus uses it, He always means Himself. On this account of the name, to ask 'Does the phrase stand for one man or a community?' is to raise a false question. It is not a matter of 'Either-Or' but of 'Both-And'. This is true both of Peter's word 'Christ' and of Jesus' term 'Son of Man' (Mk 8$^{29, 31}$). Both are names for a 'king', and as already shown, for the Hebrew the terms 'king' and 'people', like 'husband' and 'wife', are correlatives, the one implying the other—with the implication that the one and the other 'go together' in a societary unit.

Third, as the *Sitz im Leben* of the church in Palestine in the seventy years or so between Jesus' death and AD 100 gives the background of all the passages, this should be briefly described. Here the Destruction of Jerusalem in AD 70 is the dividing point. This event is named by all three Evangelists—by Luke in set terms, and Mark and Matthew, using a veiled phrase from Daniel (Mk 13^{14}, Mt 24^{15}, Lk 21^{20}). Before this catastrophe it seems clear that, while there was considerable persecution, especially at first, for the most part 'the church throughout all Judea and Galilee and Samaria had peace' (Ac 9^{31}; cf. 5$^{38-40}$). The other Jews came to tolerate this 'sect', for, when Paul spoke to the people from the 'stairs of the castle', they listened quietly until he claimed that Christ had given him a mission *'unto the Gentiles'* (Ac 21^{40}, 22^{21}). It was because of this claim, and not because Paul was a 'Christian'—a nick-name already known in Palestine (Ac 26^{28})—that the Jews hated this particular man. The new sect had spread rapidly for on the same occasion 'James' and 'the elders' said to Paul, 'Thou seest, brother, how many *myriads* there are among the Jews of them which have believed' (Ac 21$^{18-20}$). With 'the Jewish War' the situation was transformed. The Romans marched, fighting and slaughtering as they went, from Galilee to Masada. The conquest culminated, of course, in the long and terrible siege of Jerusalem and the destruction of the Temple. After this the Romans would, of course, 'rule with a rod of iron'. Among other things they kept a careful eye on all descendants of David, Domitian even decreeing that these should be executed. More terrible than Roman rule, famine and all the other dire dislocations of life in a conquered and devastated country would befall the Jews. Christian Jews would share in all these 'tribulations'. For instance, Hegesippus says that two grandsons of Jude, the brother of Jesus, were taken to Rome—and spared by Domitian because they were too contemptible to punish! This means that the Romans knew that even these two were descendants of David. All the while the Jews sullenly held to their Messianic hope, as the sudden and universal rebellion of Bar-Kokhba at last showed. But while the Christians shared these miseries with other Jews, they also suffered as *Christians*. They were 'hated of all for (the) name's sake.' They had been pacifist in the War, and their fellow-countrymen never forgot this 'treachery'. If for fifty years the other Jews dare not rebel against Rome, they could 'take it out' of Christians, and the 'love of the many waxed cold' (Mt 24^{12}). It will be argued later that John the Seer bears witness that in Jerusalem itself the church perished at this time (though to rise again). Within one family a father or brother who held by the old faith, would 'deliver up' a child or brother who was a Christian. The faithful Christians were *literally* 'hungry' and 'thirsty' and 'strangers' (vagrants) and 'naked' and 'sick' and 'in prison' (Mt 25^{35f}). This long 'tribulation' (Mk 13^{19}) is the background of the 'Little Apocalypse' and its variants.

In the Second Gospel the evidence for the date of the Parousia is found in three passages—two brief (8^{38}–9^1, 14^{61f}), which are taken first along with their parallels in Luke and Matthew; and one of considerable length (Mk 13). The first of the three belongs to the sequel of Peter's Confession, 'Thou art the Christ' (Mk 8^{38}). The word 'Christ' or 'Messiah' implied, in accordance with current thought, that the disciples expected that there would be a Day and that Jesus would be its master. He could therefore speak about the 'coming of the Son of Man' without explaining the phrase (verse 38). While He needed to teach the disciples that 'the Son of Man' must suffer and die, He claimed that He would 'come' in triumph at 'the End'. In Mark the relevant passage runs: 'Whosoever shall be ashamed of me and of my words in this adulterous and sinful generation, the Son of Man shall be ashamed of him when he cometh in the glory of his Father with the holy angels. *And he said unto them*, Verily I say unto you, There be some of them that stand here which shall in no wise taste of death till they see the kingdom of God come with power' (Mk 8^{38}–9^1). The words in italics are important, for they allow a distinction between the 'coming of the Son of Man' and the 'coming of the kingdom with power'. The latter phrase refers to Pentecost. With Jesus the 'kingdom of God' had 'come', but it did not come 'with power' until the gift of the Spirit. In Luke's version, however, the words in italics are left out (Lk 9[26f]), the phrase 'But I tell you of a truth' being used instead and 'with power' being omitted. This *allowed* the identification of 'the coming of the Son of Man' with 'the coming of the kingdom'. Matthew *makes the identification*, reading: 'There be some of them that stand here which shall in no wise taste of death till they *see the Son of Man coming in his kingdom*'. It follows that at least in some churches Christians had made up their minds that the Parousia would occur within a life-time. This is a typical example of the relation between the three Synoptic Gospels under the present subject.

In Mark's second short passage (14[62]) Jesus replies to the High Priest's question 'Art thou the Christ, the Son of the Blessed?' with the words: 'I am: and ye shall see the Son of Man sitting at the right hand of power, and coming with the clouds of heaven.' The High Priest would know quite well that there was a current opinion that 'the Son of Man' was another name for 'the Christ', and that it was commonly believed that there would be a 'general resurrection on the last day', when God would judge mankind. What outraged him and 'the chief priests and the elders and the scribes' (verse 53), was Jesus' quiet but confident claim that *He* was 'the Son of Man' who would 'sit at God's right hand' in the Judgement. At this he cried out 'blasphemy' and rent his clothes. The Christian *differentia*, of course, appears here. Luke, in his rather longer account (Lk 22[67-70]), ascribes the High Priest's question to the whole 'council' and adds that Jesus not only claimed to be 'the Christ' and 'the Son of Man', but 'the Son of God'. All three names were sometimes synonymous in the current Apocalyptic literature (e.g. in Enoch), as the members of the 'council' would all know. Matthew too (26[63f]) has all three names. Both Luke and Matthew add the words 'from now' (*apo tou nun, ap'arti*) to Jesus' saying, but in different ways. Luke omits 'Ye shall see' from Mark, while Matthew retains it. Luke's version, 'From now the Son of Man shall be sitting on the right hand of the power of God', describes what is to happen *now* (and to continue)—not, as in Mark, merely what will happen at the Judgement. It is quite possible that Luke's version goes back to Jesus, but more likely that in it the *church* gives expression to the *whole* of its faith about the Session. Matthew confusingly conflates the two accounts of the words.

The long passage in Mark (Ch. 13), often called 'The Little Apocalypse', opens with a question asked by Jesus' first four disciples when He sadly foretold the Destruction of the Temple—'When shall these things be? And what shall be the sign when all these things are about to be accomplished?', 'these things' being the Destruction of the Temple (verses 2-4). Luke has practically the same question (21[7]), but Matthew has 'When shall these things be? and what the sign of thy *parousia* and the completion of the age? (24[3])—that is, he *assumes* that the Destruction of the Temple and the Parousia are not far apart. It would be *his* question that the harried Christians would ask in the 'tribulation' *after* the Fall of Jerusalem—and it is *Matthew's* question that *Mark* answers in the first part of Ch. 13 (verses 5-13) and, for the most part, in its last part (verses 22-37). Between them he gives Jesus' answer to his *own* question (verses 14-21). This arrangement is found also in Luke and Matthew. In whatever way it is to be explained, it is clear that even when Mark wrote, the church took the War, the Tribulation and the End to be three parts of a single whole. Yet in Mark it seems possible to separate the answers to two different questions, 'What did *Jesus* say about the Jewish War?' and 'What did *He* say about the "tribulation" that accompanied and followed it, and about the End?'

Jesus begins His answer to the question about the War (verses 14-21) with a cryptic phrase from Daniel, 'the abomination of desolation', under which He tells the disciples what the 'sign' of the Destruction of the Temple will be. He bids those of His disciples who are in Judea when it comes to 'flee to the mountains'. He goes on to say that then there will be 'days' of an unexampled 'tribulation' for all Jews, but adds that 'for the elects' sake'— that is, for His disciples' sake—God will 'shorten' the 'days' of the War. In the first part of His answer to the question about the End (verses 5-13), Jesus urgently warns His disciples that 'the end is *not yet*' and that they must not take such things as 'wars and rumours of wars' as its signs. Then He tells them that, as to 'themselves', they must expect ruthless persecution, both from Jews and Gentiles—from the latter because before the End the 'gospel must be preached' unto them all! He promises the disciples the help of the Holy Spirit as they answer the charges against them, but He warns them that they will be 'hated of all men', even those in their own homes that are not His disciples, '(for His) name's sake' (cf. Lk 12⁴⁹). Finally, He gives them His word that 'He that endureth to the end, the same shall be saved'. In this passage the dominant idea is 'Endure, endure, for the End is not yet'.

In the remainder of the passage (verses 24-37) it is likely that verses 29-31 originally referred to the Jewish War, and that the phrase 'This generation shall not pass away until all these things be accomplished' refers to this, but these verses are embedded in others that relate to the End. This is a clear sign that the Christians came to link together the War and the End. The phrases 'This generation shall not pass away until all these things be accomplished' and 'Of that day or that hour knoweth no one, not even . . . the Son', taken together, were interpreted to mean 'The End will come within a generation', even though Jesus Himself did not know the exact 'day or hour'. It would be the easier to draw this conclusion because Jesus went on to say 'Take ye heed, watch and pray, for ye know not when the time (*kairos*) is', and, adding a parable in which He compares them to bondmen whose lord is away and Himself to their lord, warned them that He *might* come 'suddenly' at any 'hour'. In this passage His message to them is 'Watch', a word which He uses six times, just as earlier it is 'Endure'.

Finally, there is the passage (verses 24-7) in which Jesus describes the Coming of the 'Son of Man' with its cosmic upheaval. It is introduced by the phrase 'But *in those days, after* that tribulation', which suggests, though it does not say, that the End will follow the Tribulation quickly. On the other hand, there is the phrase 'Then shall *they* (not 'ye') see the Son of Man coming in clouds', but probably 'they' here means 'men generally'. It is assumed that by then there will be 'elect' everywhere under 'heaven' (verse 27). Taking the whole chapter together, it is plain that Jesus warned His disciples that the End *might* come while they were alive, but did not say 'It *will*', for He Himself did not know when it would come.

To the present writer, it seems possible that there is something more. It is not unlikely that Jesus, like other men, formed what can only be called 'opinions', which lay *outside* the message that He had 'received' from the Father (cf. Jn 17⁸). Since the purpose of the Gospels is to record His *message*, it is natural that His *opinions* should rather be implied than stated. There is an example in His belief, common to the Jews and other nations, that the earth has a dome (or set of domes) called 'heaven' (or 'the heavens') above it, and Hades and the Abyss below it. The latter concept has an example in the implications of a paragraph in the Little Apocalypse (Mk 13$^{24-7}$). Similarly, as the writer thinks, the Little Apocalypse *implies* that, while Jesus very emphatically declared that the Father had not told Him when the End would come, His *opinion* was that it would come within a generation or two. There are particular phrases that give this impression. For instance, there are the words, 'These things (wars and so on) are the beginning of *travail*' (verse 8)—'travail' denoting 'an agony that ends in joy'—(cf. Jn 16$^{20-2}$)—but the agony is relatively short. Again, the phrase 'he that endureth to the end, the same shall be saved' (verse 13) follows the phrase '*Ye* shall be hated of all men for my name's sake', and the natural meaning is 'He, among *you*, that endureth to the end'. Or again, the phrase, 'In those days, after that tribulation' (verse 24), does not naturally mean 'after a series of generations'. Similarly, the parable of the Bondmen watching in the Night (verses 35-6) would not suggest to Jesus' hearers a 'night' of centuries. To use modern terms, the writer thinks that in the Little Apocalypse Jesus said two things *in the name of God*—'I do not know when the End will come', and 'It is your business and the business of all during the Tribulation to endure and watch, for the End *may* come in your day'—and *implied* an *opinion*, 'For myself I *think* that the End will come soon'. The disciples added the opinion to the message, shortening it into 'The End *will* come soon'. As the rest of this chapter shows, a two-fold conviction ruled the thought of the first-century Christians: 'We do not know when the End will come, but we do know that it will come soon.'

The passage in Luke parallel to Mark's Little Apocalypse is 21$^{5-26}$. He omits, however, the Parable of the Waiting Bondmen, having placed it earlier and elaborated it (12$^{35-48}$). Similarly, he anticipates the reference to the 'coming of the Son of Man' with a longer, explanatory passage (17^{22}-18^8). Under all these three passages his interpretations of Mark, and variations from him, will be noted, his agreements being taken for granted.

It is assumed here that, while Mark wrote before the Jewish War, Luke wrote after it. It follows that some things that were future for the former were past for the latter. It will be convenient to take first Luke's variations from Mark which for Luke were past, and then those that were still future. Under the first group Luke, while retaining the word 'desolation', interprets the Danielic phrase 'abomination of desolation' to mean the 'encompassing of Jerusalem with armies', for he knew that, in fact, no heathen idol had been erected in the Temple, and this is what the writer of Daniel had meant by the phrase (21[20]). He knew that many Jews had been slaughtered and others expelled from Palestine, and that the Gentiles were 'treading Jerusalem under foot' (verse 24). He omits Mark's passage about the 'shortening of the days' for in the eyes of contemporary Christians they already seemed long. He also omits the phrase 'the beginning of travail' perhaps because this seemed to suggest that for the *whole church* sorrow would end in joy, emphasizing rather that only those who 'endure' will 'gain their lives', and only those who 'take heed' against the ways of their neighbours will 'prevail to escape . . . and to stand before the Son of Man', for, as usual after a national catastrophe, many of the survivors lost all hope and wallowed in the pleasures of a moment (verses 17, 34, 36). Yet the 'days' of the War and after are just days of 'retribution' and 'wrath' (verses 22f).

Under the things that were still future in Luke's day he has some significant alterations. For Mark's 'the end is not yet' he has 'the end is not immediately' (*eutheōs*) (verses 9f). Again, he says 'When ye see these things coming to pass, know ye that the kingdom of God is near', adding that 'all things will be accomplished' within a generation (verses 31f). He admits indeed that there were those who mistakenly said 'The time has come close' (verse 8), and says that the 'day' will surprise all men like the 'sudden' snap of a trap, yet he implies that his readers will themselves live to 'stand before the Son of Man' (verse 34-6). He tells them: 'When these things begin to come to pass . . . *your* redemption is near' (verse 28). Omitting Mark's sentence, 'the gospel must first be preached unto all the Gentiles', he declares that the 'day' will be a 'day' for 'all that dwell on the face of all the earth' (verse 35). Clearly the churches, or some of them, had made the deduction which, as already shown, lay open in Mark: 'We do not know the exact time when the End will come (cf. Ac 1[6]), but we do know that it will come soon.' Further, Luke puts all these phrases on the lips of Jesus, and, very significantly, omits the saying: 'Of that day or that hour knoweth no one . . . not even the Son.' Probably, taking it to mean 'Jesus Himself did not know the precise moment, but He knew that the End is near', he omitted it because it might mislead others. If it be claimed that he learnt his beliefs from Paul, not just taking over those current in the churches, the answer, as will appear later, is that Paul himself held the belief 'We do not know when—but soon', and taught accordingly. Both believed, of course, that they were interpreting Jesus' words aright.

As previously mentioned, Luke omits the Parable of the Waiting Bondmen in his version of the Little Apocalypse because he has already included a parallel passage (12^{35-48}). In it the 'lord' is not returning from 'another country', as in Mark, but bringing home his bride. The chief novelties, however, refer to what he does on arrival. Here the passage falls into two parts. The first (verses 35-40) declares that he will himself wash the feet of the *faithful* bondmen (verse 37)—a thing incredible! The second (verses 41-8) declares that the *unfaithful* will be scourged till they are 'cut in two' (i.e. in a modern phrase, 'lashed to the bone'), and then dismissed to the lot of 'unbelievers' (*apistos*), or rather 'disbelievers', who have heard the Gospel but refuse it (as verses 54-9), spoken to 'the multitudes', show). The misery of the unfaithful bondmen is set over against the glory of the faithful.

In this passage there falls the text: 'The servant who knew his lord's will, and made not ready, nor did according to his will, shall be beaten with many stripes but he that knew not, and did things worthy of stripes, shall be beaten with few stripes' (verses 47f). Here Jesus states and accepts a usual rule. Among *His* 'bondmen', however, there were none who 'did not know'. In answer to Peter's question Jesus says, in effect, 'I am speaking to *you* (and not now to 'the multitudes'—verse 54), and I do tell *you* what my will is, as you well know' (cf. Jn 15^{15}). It follows that *your* responsibility is great, specially great, and that, if you fail me, your punishment will be correspondingly great. None of *you* will be able to claim that he did not know. So, for *all* faithless men among my disciples, it is 'many stripes'. This is consonant with the concluding sentence, which says nothing of those to whom 'little is given', but 'to whomsoever *much* is given, of him shall *much* be required, and to whom (men) commit *much*, of him they will ask the *more*' (verse 48). This, an instance of emphasis by parallelism, is the burden of the whole passage. In brief, it runs: 'Peter, my disciples, and you among them, all *know my will*; remember what this means if a disciple is faithless.'

Luke has his own passage about the Coming of the Son of Man (Lk 17^{20}–18^8), though it includes details found in other contexts in Mark and Matthew and Luke himself. Under this passage it is possible to construct what might be called 'Jesus' programme'. He tells the Pharisees that *their* business is not to be asking when the Kingdom of God will come but to take the opportunity of entering into it now, for with Him it is already here in its essence (verses 20f). Then, addressing His disciples (verse 22), who *are* entering into it, He sets out what is to come. If the events named be put in chronological order, He foretells that first, He will suffer, for 'this generation' will reject Him (verse 25). Next, the birds of prey will gather at Jerusalem (verse 37). The War of AD 70 is now the prelude of the End (cf. verses 31–5, 19^{41-4}, 23^{29f}). Then there will follow a time when the hard-pressed disciples will long that He were still with them (verse 22). To borrow Mark's phrase, They will cry unto God to 'shorten the days', for it will seem to them that he is too 'long-tempered' with sinners (18^7). They pray that He will 'vindicate' them and do them justice (*ekdikein*), their prayer, like the Importunate Widow's, being for justice to themselves rather than the punishment of their persecutors. Spite 'the look of things', God will 'vindicate them with speed' (18^8), for the Son of Man will come like an unexpected flash of lightning (17^{24}). He will be 'revealed' (verse 30), in the Apocalyptic sense of that word—i.e. He has meanwhile been hidden. During this hidden period sinners will be as heedless of their doom as the sinners in the Days of Noah or Sodom (17^{26-9}). The warnings that refer in Mark to the Siege of Jerusalem, are now transferred to the Parousia (verses 31–5). Let no disciple 'look back', like Lot's wife, for he is now settling the answer to the question: 'Shall I gain life or lose it on the Day?' (verses 32f). While the chief subject of the passage is the Tribulation, other events only being mentioned in passing, the War, the Tribulation and the Day are again taken closely together.

Before relating the Parable of the Pounds (19^{11-27}), Luke describes the exact situation when it was spoken. Jesus was on His last journey to Jerusalem, and by now there were many who believed that He was the Messiah, in their sense of the term (Lk 18^{38}, 19^{38}, Jn 6^{15}). Among these some, at least, 'supposed that the kingdom of God would appear (*anaphainesthai*) on the spot' (*parachrema*, a favourite word with Luke). Probably the Twelve themselves hoped for this. To deny it Jesus told a story of 'a certain man of birth (who) went into a far country to receive for himself a kingdom, and to return'. Three of the Herods had gone to Rome to seek a kingdom, and Jesus' hearers would catch the allusion. This means that there would be an interval before He returned as king. Meanwhile Jesus divides His hearers into 'bondmen' and 'citizens'. The latter 'hate' Him and reject His kingship. This exactly suits the *Sitz im Leben*, for the Jews fell into two classes, those who were in some sense His adherents and the great majority, who rejected him though they were all the time '*his* citizens' by right. On His return, while the latter will be slain 'before him' (verse 27), He will discriminate between his 'bondmen'. While He has been away He has entrusted each of them with a sum of *His* money to use for Him. Three are described —two who use it aright, though with varying zeal, and one who commits the sin of 'doing nothing'. The first two are given discriminated but unexampled rewards, 'bondmen' becoming vicegerents! The third, having done nothing, is just left with nothing. Here Jesus teaches that, while He is absent, His disciples are not only to 'endure' and 'watch', but be about His business. It is again the interval before He returns that is the main topic. It is not a very long interval, for He returns while 'citizens' and 'bondmen' are still alive.[1]

Matthew's version of the Little Apocalypse (Ch. 24) is not a conflation of Mark 13 and the passages in Luke 12 and 17, but there are a few points that may be mentioned. As already noted, to the disciples' question 'When shall these things be?' Matthew adds 'and what the sign of thy *parousia* and of the completion of the age?' (verse 3). Here he introduces the term '*parousia*', and assumes that the War, the Tribulation and the Day are just parts of one whole. He retains Mark's 'Of that day and hour knoweth no one, not even . . . the Son' (verse 26), and emphasizes the fact that the *disciples* too did not know the 'day' and 'hour' (verses 42, 44, 50). He has Mark's 'the end is not yet' (verse 6), and agrees with him that it will not come until 'the gospel of the kingdom (has been) preached' to 'all nations' (verse 14), yet

---

[1] In Luke's second book, the Acts of the Apostles, there are only two passages that relate to the Coming of the End, as distinct from the End itself. One (2^{18-21}) occurs in a speech of Peter and is taken with his First Epistle. The other (1^{6-8}) might be called 'Jesus' watch-word for the Church in the Interval'. He teaches the Eleven that it is not for them 'to know the times or the seasons', but to be His 'witnesses' from Jerusalem 'unto the uttermost part of the earth'. Yet, while He leaves the length of the Interval open, He just assumes that (at the Parousia—verse 11) He will restore the kingdom to Israel.'

believes that it will come within a generation (verse 34), and places the *Parousia* '*immediately*' after the tribulation' (verse 29; cf. Lk 21⁹). In other words he teaches: 'We do not know exactly when the End will come, for Jesus Himself did not know—but He told us that it will come soon.' He says more than Mark under 'all the nations', substituting the phrase (verse 9) for Mark's 'all men' in 'Ye shall be hated of all men', declaring that the Gospel will be preached 'in the whole world for a *testimony* to all the nations' (verse 14), and adding that at the Parousia 'all the tribes of the earth will mourn' (verse 30) because they have not listened to it. The *speed* of the Gentile Mission in Matthew's day lies behind these texts. He has 'hypocrites' for Mark's 'unfaithful' bondmen and depicts their utter remorse when their 'lord' comes under the vivid words 'the weeping and gnashing of teeth' (verse 51). Except for one text in Luke (13²⁸), this phrase is peculiar to Matthew (8¹¹ᶠ, 13⁴². ⁵⁰, 22¹³, 24⁵¹, 25³⁰). It always relates to the Judgement at the Parousia.

Matthew adds a whole chapter (25) to his version of the Little Apocalypse. This contains two Parables and a description of the Judgement of the Son of Man. The last is discussed later. The two Parables have much in common. Both have phrases about the *delay* of the End. In the Parable of the Talents the lord of the bondmen returns 'after *much* time' (verse 19), and in that of the Virgins there is that *rara avis*, a '*lingering* bridegroom' (verse 5) He lingers so long that *all* ten Virgins 'nod and fall asleep'! The fault of the Foolish Five is not that they sleep, but that they have taken it for granted that the bridegroom would come before their lamps need more oil—which, no doubt, a bridegroom usually did. The two parables are also alike in the upshot (verses 10-12, 21, 23, 30)—the faithful disciples join in the marriage feast in the first case, and in 'the joy of (their) lord' in the second; on the other hand, the Foolish Virgins are 'shut out' from the marriage feast, the bridegroom refusing to 'know them', and the 'unprofitable bondman' is 'cast into the darkness outside, where there is the wailing and the gnashing of teeth'. Probably the homely origin of the last phrase emerges here. In such a village as Nazareth most families lived in a one-roomed house, gathering after sunset around its lamp. If a lad proved intolerably 'fractious', to get rid of him there was nothing to be done except 'to cast him into the darkness outside', the haunt of dogs and demons. Here, in mingled terror and temper, he would 'wail and gnash his teeth' as only an Easterner can. The chief difference between this parable and Luke's Parable of the Pounds, of course, is that here the two faithful bondmen, while their capacity varies, have the same zeal —and therefore the same reward. The *motif* of both parables is 'Be faithful though the End *delays*'—yet it is assumed that both 'virgins' and 'bondmen' will live to see it.

Matthew transfers a part of Mark's Little Apocalypse to Jesus' earlier commission to the *Twelve* (10$^{16-23}$). Here there is nothing novel except the last verse: 'Ye shall not have gone through the cities of Israel till the Son of Man be come.' This seems to imply that in the Tribulation the Apostles evangelized Palestine, fleeing from one village to another. The verse is a clear proof that some churches, at least, believed that Jesus Himself had taught that the End would come before the Apostles all died. In the exposition of the Parable of the Tares (Mt 13$^{36-43}$), which is peculiar to Matthew, Jesus gives His first description of the End in that Gospel. Here the 'harvest' (cf. Mk 4^{29}) is the 'completion of the age', and 'the angels' are the ministers of the Son of Man's Judgement. Under the fate of the wicked the phrases used are 'the furnace of fire' and 'the wailing and gnashing of teeth'; the righteous are to 'shine forth as the sun in the kingdom of *their Father*'. There is no universal Fatherhood of God when the End comes. In another passage (23$^{37-39}$), Jesus' Lament over Jerusalem, Matthew only repeats Luke (13^{34f}), but, while the latter puts it *before* Palm Sunday, the former places it *after* that triumph. This may mean that Luke refers the words 'Ye shall not see me till ye shall say, Blessed is he that cometh in the name of the Lord' to Palm Sunday, while Matthew applies them to the *Parousia*. There remains the unique phrase that closes Matthew's Gospel—'Lo, I am with *you* every day even unto the completion of the age' (28^{20}). Here 'You' means 'the eleven disciples' (verse 16), and it is once more implied that the End will come within their lifetime. The conclusion seems clear—that, while Mark only leaves the way open to the belief that Jesus foretold that the End would come at an unknown date but within a generation, Luke adopts this belief, and Matthew just takes it for granted again and again.

Paul has passages about the Parousia in the Epistles to the Thessalonians, which are among his earliest letters. In the First Epistle he again and again implies that he expected it during the lifetime of some of his Thessalonian converts and indeed, during

THE DATE OF THE PAROUSIA

his own life (1 Th 1^{10}, 3^{13}, 4^{13-18}, $5^{1-11, 23}$). The significant 'Watch' occurs in 5^6 (cf. 1 Co 16^{13}, Col 4^2). In the Second Epistle he repeats this (2 Th 1^{7-10}), but also specifically discusses the date (2 Th 2^{1-12}). Here he says, in effect, 'It will come *soon*, brethren, as I told you, but it is not *now* impending (*enistanai*), as I also told you, for before the Parousia of Christ there will be another Parousia, the Parousia of "the Man of Lawlessness, the Son of Perdition", and with it a "falling away" (*apostasia*) of believers' (cf. Mt $24^{10, 12}$). This sinister Parousia is delayed because there is something and someone that 'holds it back (*katechein*), as I told you too.' To understand this veiled reference to the Apostle's oral teaching, it is necessary to recall the historical situation as Claudius' reign neared its end. Though this Emperor was not a strong man, he did his best to rule by the Roman Law that had already served Paul, and no doubt other Christians, well. It was Claudius who had appointed Gallio pro-consul of Achaia and Gallio helped Paul about the time when the two Epistles were written. Roman Law had been the strength of the Republic and Empire, but, as men who could read 'the signs of the times' would clearly see, it was now threatened by the Army. It was the Praetorian Guard that slew Tiberius; an insult to one of its tribunes had led to the murder of Caligula; and it was the Guard that secured the succession of Claudius. Now the question of the succession was rife in Rome, with the ruthless Agrippina plotting for her son Nero. But, while the Guard was on the spot, the main armies, each under its own commander, were far away on the frontiers. Paul foresaw that one of these commanders would seize the Empire—as ultimately happened. The Apostle, however, expected that this man would pay no heed either to Roman or Jewish Law, and so he called him 'the Man of Lawlessness'. He would be 'brute force' incarnate, like the Empires that the writer of Daniel called 'Brutes', and like Epiphanes (cf. Dn 11^{36}). He would set up his image in the Temple as both Daniel and Jesus had foretold (Mk 13^{14}) and as Caligula had threatened to do. Paul, writing before AD 70 does not need, like Luke who wrote after it, to reduce 'the abomination of desolation' to the 'encompassing of Jerusalem with armies'. He does not know who this 'Man of Lawlessness' will be, for he has not yet been 'revealed' (*apokaluptein*), but he will be Satan's minion. When *his* Parousia has come, the Lord's will follow, and Christ will 'slay him with the breath of his mouth' and 'bring him to naught' (cf. Isa 11^4). All this is the 'mystery of lawlessness' which has already begun 'to work'—a 'mystery' to which Christians have the clue. The upshot, in secular terms, will be the destruction of the Roman Empire and the beginning of the Reign of Christ. To declare this openly would, of course, have been treason. If the Jews at Corinth had been able to charge Paul with such a doctrine, Gallio would 'have cared' indeed! In this passage Paul says in Christian terms that an Age of Iron will precede the Age of Gold. Second Esdras (5^{1-12}) and Enoch (90^{1-19}, 91^{2-7}), have similar passages in Jewish terms. Yet Paul does not fix a definite date—e.g. Vespasian's victory over his three rivals—but only commits himself to an indefinite 'soon'. As a Jew Paul would watch the Jewish situation as well as the Roman. In Caligula's time there had been a long and blood-stained struggle in Alexandria because the Gentiles had demanded that a statue of the Emperor should be set up in the synagogues and Claudius had to deal with a later Jewish appeal to arms there. In Palestine itself the time of Claudius was the hey-day of the Zealots, and there were wars on one side of the Jordan between Jews and Gentiles, and on the other between Jews and Samaritans—with Rome crushing both. Again, Josephus tells of an insurrection under Theudas, and Philo of an outbreak at Jamnia because the Gentiles set up an altar there to the dead and 'divine' Caligula. Paul, taking all the Roman and Jewish 'signs of the times' together, and no doubt thinking also of the world-wide famine under Claudius (Ac 11^{28}), which probably befell just about the time when he wrote to Thessalonica, concluded that Jesus' prophecy of the events that would precede the Parousia had begun to come to pass and were the 'beginning of travail' (Mk 13^{7f}). Although Mark had not yet written, it seems clear that Paul knew of these prophecies. The Day would come as 'suddenly' 'as a thief' but would not surprise Christians for they are awake and 'watching' (1 Th 5^{2-7}).

In his later Epistles Paul continues to expect the Parousia 'quickly' (Ro 16^{20}). In one passage, using 'salvation' for the Parousia, he declares that this is no time to 'sleep' for 'the night is far spent, and the Day has come near' (Ro 13^{10-12}). In another he applies the belief that 'the time is shortened' to married life, since the 'fashion of this *kosmos* passeth away' (1 Co 7^{29-31} cf. 10^{11}). In a third he expects that his readers will themselves still be joining in the Lord's Supper when (Christ) comes (1 Co 11^{26}). In a fourth he implies that he and the Corinthians will be alive when 'the trumpet sounds' (1 Co 15^{52}). In a fifth he looks forward to 'glorying' in his converts, and they in him, 'on the Day' (2 Cor 1^{14}). In a still later Epistle, written when he was awaiting his trial and possible condemnation before Caesar, while he realizes at last that he *himself* may not live till the Day comes, he still believes that his *readers* will be alive to welcome it, for 'the Lord is near' (Ph 1$^{6, 10, 20-2}$, 4^5). Similarly, expecting that, when 'Christ is manifested', the Colossian Christians too will be 'manifested in glory' (Col 3^4), he gives no hint that they will die and rise again before this happens, and he claims, in effect, that Jesus' prophecy that 'the gospel must first be preached to all the nations' (Mk 13^{10}) has now been fulfilled (Col 1^{23}). In the First Epistle to Timothy either he or one of his school implies that he will die, leaving Timothy behind, but also that the latter will live till the *epiphaneia*, though its exact date is still obscure (6$^{13-15}$). Finally this is implied in the Second Epistle, in the paragraph where the Apostle writes his own epitaph (4$^{1, 6f}$).

There is the same teaching or presupposition in other New Testament books. In the Epistle to the Hebrews there is one verse (10^{25}) that declares that its readers 'see the Day drawing nigh', and another (10^{37f}) where the author, speaking like Isaiah and Second Esdras of 'a very little while' (Isa 26^{20}, 2 Es 16^{52}), and applying a passage from Habakkuk to Christ, declares: 'He that cometh shall come and shall not tarry' (Hab 2^{3f}). In view of this, it is clear that when this author says 'it is appointed unto men once to die' (9^{27}), he does not mean that his *readers* will all die. Indeed, he refers to them, or some of them, under the phrase 'Them that expect' to 'see' Christ on His return. He is urging that, since it has been the fate of *all men, since the first sin*, to die and pass to judgement, therefore Christ died to 'bear the sins' of believers and so bring *them* 'salvation' instead of 'judgement'. James, telling the wicked rich, on the one hand, that they are living in 'the last days' and that 'a day of slaughter' is to be theirs, assures believers, on the other, that though their days of 'patience' are still going on and on, 'the Parousia of the Lord has come near', and 'the judge standeth before the doors' (5$^{1-11}$). The First Epistle of Peter has the phrases 'the end of the times' and 'the end of all things has come near' (1^{20}, 4^7), and its writer speaks again and again of the 'glory' and 'joy' and 'grace' that await his readers—summing them under the phrase 'a salvation' whose apocalypse is 'ready'

(1^5; cf. 4^5) at 'the *apocalupsis* of Jesus Christ' ($1^{7, 11, 13}$, 4^{13}, 5^4; cf. 2^{12}), without any hint that they may die before it comes. Jude, believing that his readers are living in 'the last time (*chronos*)', expects that Christ will 'set (them) face to face with his glory... in exceeding joy' (Jude 18, 24). John of Patmos has the phrase 'I come quickly' three times in his last chapter (Rev $22^{7, 12, 20}$; cf. 1^3). The present writer thinks that the Seer expected the Parousia, or, in his own phrase, that 'the Lamb would take his stand on Mount Zion' (Rev 14^1), seven hundred years after 588 BC, the date he assigns to Nebuchadnezzar's capture of Jerusalem. This would place the Parousia in AD 112.[2]

In the Fourth Gospel there is one relevant passage in 16^{16-24}, and one in the appendix (Ch. 21). In the first the operative phrase under the present subject is 'a little while'. There are three earlier passages where it occurs, and in all of them the phrase means either the period from the time of speaking to Pentecost or a part of it. At the Feast of Tabernacles Jesus says to 'the Jews': 'Yet a little time (*chronos mikros*) I am with you, and I go unto him that sent me' (7^{33}). The last words are Jesus' account of the Ascension (cf. 14^{28}, 20^{17}). For *Him* this is here the limit of the 'little time', though for *them* it would be the Crucifixion. Later Jesus says to 'the multitude', 'Yet a little time is the light among you' (12^{35}), with a similar meaning (cf. 9^5). Again, speaking to the Twelve He says, 'Yet a little while (*mikros*) and the world beholdeth me no more; but ye behold me'—meaning that they would 'behold' Him in the Spirit from Pentecost onwards, as the context shows (16^{16-20}). In the passage relevant here (16^{16-24}), this suits the first verse, 'a little while and ye behold me no more; and again a little while, and ye shall see me', as the preceding verses show (verses 7-15), but in verses 17-24, where the disciples, or some of them, fall to discussing 'What does He mean when he says "A little while"? We know not what he saith', another meaning seems to emerge. In Jesus' reply to this question it is possible to apply verses 19-22 to the 'three days' between the Crucifixion and the Resurrection, but not to the period between the Last Supper, when Jesus was speaking, and Pentecost. After the Resurrection

---

[2] The writer has given his reasons for this in an article entitled 'The Three Woes of the Apocalypse', printed in *The London Quarterly and Holborn Review* for January 1942. Under this account the number 'six hundred and sixty and six' (Rev 13^{18}) not only stands for 'Nero' *redivivus*, but also for the 666th year after 588 BC—i.e. AD 78, the year when the Seer wrote.

the Eleven did not 'weep and lament' for they 'saw the Lord' again and again. After His final disappearance at the Ascension there were ten days before Pentecost, but, according to Luke, they then 'returned to Jerusalem with great *joy*' (Lk 24^{52}). On the other hand, verses 19-24 do describe their plight between Pentecost and the Parousia. During this period the disciples were, in effect, asking one another all the time: 'What did He mean by "a little while"?' In the meantime they were in 'tribulation' or 'anguish' (*thlipsis*), like a woman in travail (Jn 16$^{21, 33}$). This was a current word for the condition of Christians until the Parousia (e.g. Ac 14^{22}, Ro 5^3, 2 Cor 1^4, Col 1^{24}, 2 Th 1^6, He 10^{33}, Rev 1^9), and it went back to the Little Apocalypse (Mk 13$^{19, 24}$; cf. Mt 24^9). There were Old Testament precedents for the phrase. In Haggai (2^6) the Hebrew (though not the Greek) declares that 'in a little while' the End will come. In Jeremiah 51^{33} the phrase is used of the imminent Doom of Babylon. For John the Seer 'Babylon' meant 'Rome' (e.g. Rev 14^8), and probably for other Christians too (cf. 1 P 5^{13}). The most pertinent passage, however, is Isaiah 26$^{16-21}$. Here LXX has the phrase 'a little while' (*mikron hoson hoson*), and with it *thlipsis*, an agonized description of a woman in travail, and a promise of a joyful resurrection of the righteous dead 'in that day' (verse 21)—i.e. the Day will bring blessing, not only to the faithful Hebrews who are alive on the Day, but to those that have died. But this passage in Isaiah not only has the phrase 'a little while', but uses 'travail' as ground of *hope*. The word is quite common to describe utter woe, but usually it describes the woes that come upon the *wicked*, for whom there is no coming 'joy' (e.g. Isa 13^8, Jer 4^{31}, Mic 4^{9f}, 1 Th 5^3). The writer of Second Esdras—perhaps thinking of Isaiah 26^{16ff}, for he has the phrase 'for a moment'—none the less uses 'travail' for the 'evils' that will befall the wicked (16^{38f}). Jesus, on the other hand, is speaking to the faithful, and promises them 'I will see you again, and your heart shall rejoice'. In the Little Apocalypse Mark too uses 'travail' to describe the prelude to the End (Mk 13^8), in a passage (verses 7-13) where the chief subject is the sufferings of *believers* which will end in the joy of 'salvation'. It is at least likely that in John 16^{19ff} the writer, quoting some word of Jesus to the Eleven, applies it to 'those who shall believe through their word' (17^{20}; cf. 10^{16}). If the scholars are right who claim that 'John' sometimes takes words of Jesus in two senses, believing both to be true, this passage would furnish an instance. Of course, this interpretation assumes that 'John' believed in the Parousia, but, while he does not use the word in his Gospel, he has the idea ($6^{39f, 44, 54}$; cf. 1 Jn 2^{28}). To summarize, and to include the rest of Ch. 16, he is saying: 'We are enduring the Tribulation, which the Lord said was to be the prelude to the End, even as travail is the prelude of childbirth; we do not know, however, how long our "little while" will be, but we do know that Christ came forth from the Father, that He has gone back to the Father, and that, even amid our Tribulation, He is wielding a Victor's power—and that is enough.'

From the parallels with Mark suggested above it follows that 'John' and his fellow-disciples knew of the current Christian tradition of Jesus' prophecy of the end. Indeed, it is almost incredible that they should not. In the appendix (21^{20-3}) it seems to be implied that the other Christians, at any rate, had taken the sentence 'This generation shall not pass away until all these things be accomplished' to apply, not only to the period till the Destruction of Jerusalem (as it may originally have done), but to the longer period that would end with the Parousia. It seems clear too that, as the writer of the Fourth Gospel was the last survivor of that 'generation' (21^{24}), his fellow-Christians believed that 'the Lord would come' while he was alive. This belief was reinforced by a story that he had told them in which Jesus had used the words 'If I will that he tarry till I come.' It is possible that the 'disciple' had warned them that this might be a wrong deduction. At any rate, when he too died, they tried to solve the problem by noting that the words did not explicitly say that 'John' would live till the Parousia. It will be shown later that another interpretation is possible. In the story itself, while the survivors are left bewildered, it is implied that they still believe that 'the Lord will come'. It is one more piece of evidence of the puzzle that attended this belief without destroying it, right through the first Christian century. Meanwhile the Christians suffered, as 'John's' use of such a phrase as 'the world hateth you' shows (Jn 7^7, $15^{18f, 23-5}$, 17^{14}; cf. Mk 13^{13}).

The First Epistle is 'Johannine' whether it was written by 'John' or not. The writer uses the word 'Parousia' itself defining it by the phrase 'if he is manifested (*phaneroun*)' (1 Jn 2^{28}; cf. 3^2), a term that he also uses for the Incarnation (e.g. 1^2, 3^5). The significant thing here is the word 'if (*ean*)', for the phrase means 'if he appear while we are alive we shall be like him'. For the first time a New Testament writer thinks it possible that all his readers may die before the Parousia. None the less (2^{18-22}) he says emphatically, 'Little children, it is the last hour'—i.e. he is sure that the Parousia is near, giving as the reason 'even now there have arisen many antichrists'. These are men who 'went out from us', for they now 'denied that Jesus is the Christ'. Their heresy seems to be further defined by the implication that they denied that 'Jesus Christ is come in the flesh' (4^{2f})—that is, they were Docetists. The writer says 'ye have heard that antichrist cometh' (2^{18}; cf. 4^3), as though Christians had been given the coming of Antichrist as a 'sign' of the End. Where this does not exactly tally with what Mark says about 'false' Messiahs (Mk $13^{6, 21f}$), probably Christians thought it like enough to Mark's 'signs' to class it with them, as Paul did 'the Man of Sin'. It is clear, in any case, that at the end of the first century Christians still believed that the Parousia was near, though they now thought that it *might* not come within their generation.

Twenty or thirty years later, however, in the Epistle called 'Second Peter', it is clear that at last there were Christians who asked: 'Is the Parousia near after all?' The writer implies that Peter was now near death (1^{14f}), and that there were now many 'false teachers', whose 'swift destruction' 'lingereth not' and 'slumbereth not' (2^{1-3}). These (3^{3-13}) seem to have misled the 'mockers' who asked: 'Where is the promise of his Parousia? (i.e. 'What about those "signs" now?' The fathers (i.e. all the first generation of Christians) have fallen asleep (and it was confidently expected, was it not, that Christ would come before that happened). (The plain fact is that) All things go on and on as they have done since the beginning of the creation.' To paraphrase from the writer's reply the things pertinent here, he says: 'Remember that once before God suddenly destroyed the world by water. He will do so again by fire, as the Scriptures say. Remember too, however, that for Him there is no difference between a day and a millennium. He has withheld His hand for a long time to give you a longer opportunity of repentance, but His Day will come, and will come like a "thief". Since it may come any time, it is your business to live as men who expect it. Indeed, if you repent and are faithful and ready, you can even hasten the Parousia of the Day.' At the beginning of the Epistle the author, speaking as Peter, and having reminded his readers at length of their high calling (1^{1-12}), asserts

(1^{13-18}), 'We did not follow cunningly devised fables, when we made known unto you the power and Parousia of our Lord Jesus Christ', and recalls, not the Resurrection of Christ, but the Transfiguration, for the latter anticipated the *manner* of the Parousia more nearly than the Resurrection did. But while the writer is certain that there will be a Parousia, he believes that, while it may come quickly, it may be postponed for a millennium. This, of course, contradicts the uniform creed of the church of the first century, and it is in reference to this subject that the writer says that in Paul's letters there are 'some things hard to be understood, which the ignorant and unstedfast wrest, as also the other scriptures, unto their own destruction' (3^{15f}). In other words, this writer believed that, when the earlier writers spoke of the 'nearness' of the Day, they must have meant something different! This has been the normal belief of the Church for nineteen centuries, though the accounts given of the 'something different' have varied and none of them has been satisfactory. Most Christians have believed that, while there will be a Parousia, it is distant, even very distant, however difficult it may be to fit this in with the New Testament evidence. Whenever, however, a historical crisis has arisen at all similar to that in New Testament times, there have been those who have asserted that *this* is the time of the Parousia—i.e. *mutatis mutandis*, they have followed the precedents of Daniel and Enoch. Both kinds of Christians have assumed that the New Testament writers could not be mistaken, and that *somehow* they must be right. It is better to admit that the first Christians were mistaken in their belief that the Parousia was near. On a review of the whole evidence, it may be said that the New Testament writers believed, like the Apocalyptists, that the Judgement was near, but indefinitely so.

CHAPTER FIFTEEN

THE STATE OF THE DEAD

IN THE INTERVAL between the Ascension and the Parousia many, both good and bad, would die, even though the Parousia were to come soon. The Christians, like others, would ask the question: 'What is happening to them *now*?' They gave different answers for three different kinds of people. It will be convenient to summarize these answers before going into detail. First, some of their own company, led by Stephen and James, passed away. Here the Christian *differentia* operated. The first to die in the new community was Jesus Himself. Of course His death was in some capital ways unique—e.g. He was only dead for 'three days', and then 'appeared during forty days', and then took the Throne. None the less, *mutatis mutandis*, the state of the dead believer was to be like His Master's—or, in the Johannine phrase, they would be 'with Him where He is'. Second, there would be those who had heard the Gospel before they died and refused to accept it, and with them those, like Ananias and Sapphira, who, having accepted it, had been faithless. These would pass into a different state—not, however, because they had sinned, but because they had refused to be saved from sin. To define this state the Christians retained the Jewish account of the state of sinners after death. Third, there were the many who died between the Ascension and Parousia without hearing the Gospel, and with them the multitudes on multitudes who had died since Adam. Here the Christians followed the current Jewish account—there is a miserable state for the wicked and a happy one for the good. In the whole account some details from current Jewish Apocalyptic were added to the doctrine with which the Old Testament concluded. Apart from these details, however, the Christians, following Jesus Himself, accepted the teaching of the Old Testament except where the Christian *differentia* over-rode it. In other words, this doctrine conforms to the New Testament type.

To come to the relevant passages, these fall into two classes. In the first either the 'body' or the 'soul' or the 'spirit' is mentioned. This means that the writer is conscious of the trichotomy of the Bible concept of man (e.g. 1 Th 5^{23}), and implies that he thinks of death as the disintegration of the three elements which together make a man. In the other class there is no mention of any of the three, the writer just calling the dead man 'he'. As already noted, this has many parallels both in the Old Testament, in other Jewish books, and in modern speech. Here the writer is not thinking of trichotomy. Sometimes, however, if he were asked 'Which of the three elements in human nature do you mean?', he would be able to give an answer, just as men can today. While the concept that at death a man disintegrates into 'body', 'soul' and 'spirit' may be blurred, it is not abandoned. It follows that, as the three are separate in the Intermediate State, the dead, so long as they are in that State, even though they are good men, are not all that men ought to be, for, throughout the Bible, every one of the three elements is integral to human nature. Though the division is not rigidly followed, the passages that name the 'body', the 'soul', the 'spirit' are taken first and then those where trichotomy is sub-conscious, or even forgotten. The findings under the first class bear upon those under the second.

The question 'What happens to the *body*' falls into two—'What was done with the body?' and 'What happened to it afterwards?' The answer to the first just repeats the Old Testament. The custom was to bury all corpses (Lk 9^{60}, Mt 27^7, Ac 5$^{6, 10}$). No doubt this still illustrated the old Hebrew respect for the body that God had made. While there is a hint that some bodies were buried in the modern way (Lk 11^{44}), others were laid in caves, which might be wholly or partly 'hewn out of a rock' (Mk 15^{46}), and it is implied that this was counted the better way (Mt 27^{60}). As might be expected, such a phrase as 'His body was buried' does not occur. The type is '*He* was buried', as it is today, even though the body only is meant.

After burial the body, of course, decayed, suffering the kind of 'destruction' (*phthora*) called 'corruption'. When Paul calls 'man' 'corruptible', he means man's body just as clearly as when he uses the phrase 'this corruptible' (Ro 1^{23}, 1 Co 15^{53f}; cf. Wis 9^{15}). Again, there are the texts where Peter and Paul's application of Psalm 16$^{8-11}$ to Jesus (Ac 2$^{27, 31}$, 13$^{34-7}$). The Psalm does not mention the body, but Peter, of course, interprets aright when he says 'His *flesh* did not see corruption'. The implication is that all other men's bodies, of course, decay—for instance, as Paul says, 'David . . . . saw corruption' (Ac 13^{36}). There is an implicit

THE STATE OF THE DEAD 159

reference to something other than the body, for *it* does not 'see' its own corruption. This is a simple instance of implicit trichotomy. It is true that in two passages—Matthew 10[28] and in the Pericope of Skandala ('stumbling-blocks'), which occurs three times (e.g. Mk 9[43-8])—the body does not decay in the grave but passes to Gehenna, but probably these passages speak of its state *after* the Parousia, not before it. They are therefore taken later. While the rest of the body perished by corruption, the bones would remain (cf. Mt 23[27], He 11[22]). Under the doctrine of the '*body*' after death the New Testament just repeats the Old except when it speaks of the body of Jesus.

What happened to a man's *psyche* when he died? Here the findings of earlier chapters may be recapitulated. In the Hebrew Bible every dead man's *nephesh* passes to Sheol, whether he is good or bad, Sheol being a dark underground realm where he is helpless. In the Apocrypha new ideas appear, the emphasis being on the fate of a *wicked* man's *psyche*. In Sirach it suffers in Hades by 'fire', the last verse in Isaiah being transferred to the underworld. In Wisdom, similarly, the wicked man's *psyche* suffers 'torment' in Hades. Sirach says nothing of the fate of a *good* man's *psyche* after death, though he implies that his fate differs from that of a bad man's (21[9f]). Wisdom, saying that the 'souls' of good men are 'in the hands of God', seems to imply that they do not go to Hades at all. The Book of Enoch has little to say of 'souls', but one text consigns the 'souls' of the wicked to 'great tribulation in Hades' (103[7]). In Second Esdras, which does not distinguish between the 'soul' and 'spirit', the *anima* or *inspiratio* 'wanders in torment' after death (7[80]) on its way to the *infernus*, but the 'souls of the righteous' are in *promptuaria* or 'garners' (14[9]), and not in Hades. So far as the evidence goes, the common opinion of the period was that a wicked man's 'soul' passes to punishment at death, but that all is well with a good man's *psyche*, though there is not a uniform account of its habitat.

The relevant New Testament texts relate to two subjects—what happens in the moment when a man dies and what happens afterwards. At the moment of death he 'loses his *psyche*' (Mk 8[35]), God 'asking it back' from him (*apaitein*, Lk 12[20]). To 'seek' a man's *psyche* is to seek to kill him (Mt 2[20]). Probably the phrase 'to divide *psyche* and *pneuma*' (He 4[12]) describes a division thought to happen at death. To say 'his *psyche* is in him' (Ac 20[10]) is to say 'he is still alive'. The verb *ekpsychein* ('to give up the *psyche*') occurs three times (Ac 5[5, 10], 12[23]). (The English rendering 'to give up the ghost', used for this verb and *ekpnein* ('to give up the breath' or 'expire'—Mk 15[37, 39]), is inexact under both verbs, for 'ghost' means 'spirit'.)

The passages that describe what happens to a man's *psyche after* the moment of death also begin with Mark 8[35]. Those who 'lose' their *psychae* for Christ's sake 'save' them after death (*sozein*). His faithful followers will 'win' their *psychae* by patience (*ktasthai*, Lk 21[19]); 'the *pneuma* and *psyche* and *soma*' of a true believer will be 'kept' till the Parousia' (1 Th 5[23]); for those that 'have faith' there is no future 'destruction' (*apoleia*) but the 'gaining' (*peripoiēsis*) of the *psyche* (He 10[39]); 'the engrafted word' is 'able to save the psyche' (*sōzein*, Ja 1[21]; cf. 5[20]); the 'end (*telos*) of faith' is 'the salvation of the *psyche*' (1 P 1[9]; cf. 2[11]); as Christ is the *episcopos* of the *psychae* of Christians, they may confidently, when called to martyrdom, 'commit their *psychae* . . . unto a faithful Creator' (1 P 2[25], 4[19]). The implicit doctrine of the whole series of passages is clear. Under the concept of disintegration, a man, whether good or bad, parts with his *psyche* at the moment of death, but, if he is a Christian, it will be safe in the 'keeping' of a Faithful Creator and it will reappear embodied at the Parousia.

But where does God 'keep' the souls of the righteous dead? In Acts 2[29-31] Peter seems to imply that, apart from the soul of Jesus, the answer is 'in Hades'. This word is found ten times in the New Testament. It is remarkable that it does not occur in any Epistle. As in Jewish books, it always denotes the place where the dead are now, not the place where they will be after the End. Capernaum is to be 'brought down into Hades'—i.e. cease to be (Lk 10[15]). Dives passes to Hades as soon as he dies (Lk 16[22f]). When Matthew says that 'the gates of Hades shall not prevail against the church' (Mt 16[18]), he means that it will last unto the Parousia, spite all that death can do to Christians—or, as the writer takes the phrase, in spite of the fact that Jesus Himself is to die (cf. Ac 2[27, 31], Rev 1[18]). It is *before* the End that 'Death', with his henchman 'Hades', will 'kill' a quarter of mankind (Rev 6[8]). Finally, there is the statement that at the Parousia 'Death and Hades', having yielded up their toll of dead men, will themselves be 'cast into the lake of fire' and cease to be (Rev 20[13f]). It need hardly be said that 'hell' is a mistranslation for 'Hades'. It is the realm to which *every* man's *psyche*, whether he be good or bad, passes at death. There is an exception in the Apocalypse, where the Seer says that the '*psychae*' of the martyrs are now 'underneath the altar' in heaven (6^9; cf. 20^4). Here the author of Wisdom had probably, under the phrase 'the *souls* of the righteous are in the hands of God', anticipated the Seer, but this is because these two writers are dichotomists not distinguishing between the *psyche* and the *pneuma*, and as the one is exceptional among Jewish writers, so is the other among Christian. Both Peter and Paul silently take it for granted that *all psychae* pass to Hades at death (Ac 2$^{29-31}$, 13$^{35-7}$). This was the normal Jewish belief and the Christians retained it. It does not follow, of course, that the 'souls' of good men and bad fare alike in Hades, but, as it happens, the passages that describe the difference do not use the word *psyche*. They are therefore taken later.

On passing to the passages relating to the 'spirit' of dead men, it may be premised that the *pneuma*, as well as the *psyche*, was thought to have some kind of tenement, quite distinct from the 'body' of a man in this life. In Luke 24$^{36-43}$ the Evangelist says that when Jesus appeared in the Upper Room the Eleven 'supposed that they *beheld* a spirit'. To show them that He is not such a 'spirit' Jesus points to His 'flesh and bones', implying that a 'spirit's' tenement lacked *these*. Nor could a 'spirit' eat, as He does. No doubt the word 'apparition' (*phantasma*—Mk 6^{49}) is a synonym for 'spirit'. Here the New Testament agrees with the Old, as with current ideas among many peoples at all times.

Under the question 'What happened to a man's "spirit" when he died?' there are ten passages that name the *pneuma*. The antecedent Jewish evidence may again be epitomized. To use convenient modern terms, the Hebrew, having been dichotomist until the Exile, became thereafter trichotomist, adding 'spirit' to 'soul' and 'body' as a constituent in human nature. At death the 'spirit' left a man, passing, like 'breath', back into a kind of undifferentiated fund—i.e. ceasing to be an *individual* spirit. (There is one exception, in a dichotomist passage in *Ecclesiastes*.) The same belief obtains in the Apocrypha. In extra-Canonical Jewish literature the writer of *Second Esdras* is dichotomist, but *Enoch* is trichotomist. The evidence of *Enoch* needs special notice. This book is pre-eminently 'The Book of Spirits', and its writer is far more interested in the 'spirits' of the dead than in their 'souls'. Indeed, he often uses 'spirit' for 'a man'. His book gives the first clear evidence of a capital change in concept. For him a dead man's 'spirit' does not lapse into any undifferentiated fund, but *remains individual*. In the part of the *Book of Enoch* called '*Journeys*' the 'spirits' of bad men pass to three Hollows in the far West, suffering variously there, while, under what is probably an interpolation, the 'spirits' of good men dwell in a Hollow of Bliss (Ch. 22). In *Parables*, however, the 'spirits' of the good, after a moment's sleep, pass into happy 'dwellings' or 'resting-places' at the 'end of the heavens' (En 39^{3-8}; cf. 41^{2-4}). *Parables* says nothing of what befalls the 'spirits' of the wicked. In the whole of Enoch no 'spirit', whether good or bad, passes to Hades. In *Second Esdras*, however, where 'souls' and 'spirits' are identified, those of the bad, after a period of wandering in misery, find their way to *habitacula* in the *infernus*, while those of good men pass to their own proper *habitationes*—the happy *promptuaria* which the wicked seek in vain ($7^{84-6, 95-7}$). It may be added that in both books all 'spirits' have some kind of form or tenement distinct from their buried bodies, but exercising many of its functions, as a 'ghost' does in popular thought today.

In the New Testament there is, of course, no doctrine of 'Hollows' and this part of Enoch may be ignored. The pertinent point here is that the New Testament writers agree with *Enoch*, as against the Old Testament, that 'spirits' remain *individual* after death. Such phrases as 'the spirits of righteous men made perfect' (He 12^{23}) and 'the spirit . . . saved in the day of the Lord Jesus' (1 Co 5^5) show this, and, indeed, it is everywhere implied. Again, there is no doubt that, apart from the Apocalypse, the New Testament is trichotomist. The writer to the Hebrews, for instance, speaks of 'the dividing of soul and spirit' (He 4^{12}) and Paul of 'spirit and soul and body' (1 Th 5^{23}). Unless 'soul' and 'spirit' are different Paul could not have distinguished between 'the body that suits the soul (*psychikos*)' and 'the body that suits the spirit (*pneumatikos*)' (1 Co 15^{44}). As has been shown, at death the soul passed to Hades. What befell the spirit?

As in all the antecedent evidence, at death the spirit *leaves the body*. This appears in the texts 'Her spirit returned' (Lk 8^{55}), 'Jesus . . . yielded up his spirit' (Mt 27^{50}), and 'The body apart from the spirit is dead' (Ja 2^{26}), as well as under all the passages relevant to the question taken next: 'What befell the spirits of *good* men when they died?' Here the first text is Jesus' words: 'Father, into thy hands I commend my spirit' (Lk 23^{46}). No

Christian has ever doubted that Jesus' spirit passed to His Father. Peter expresses this in the words 'made to live in spirit' (1 P 3^{18}) and its indubitable ground appears in the phrase, probably from a sung creed, 'found to be righteous in spirit' (1 Ti 3^{16}). With Stephen's prayer 'Lord Jesus, receive my spirit' (Ac 7^{59}), the Christian *differentia* appears. Here too Christ is the vicegerent of God. While the martyr's body and soul 'fell asleep' (verse 60), his spirit went to company with his Lord. The writer to the Hebrews says the same and more in the phrase 'the spirits of righteous men made perfect'. This is a part of the splendid passage beginning 'We *have come* to Mount Zion' (He 12$^{22-4}$), the perfect tense requiring that the passage describes the company gathered *now* at the Heavenly Jerusalem, not Heaven after the Parousia. The phrase 'the general assembly and church of the firstborn' probably describes the righteous 'of old time', from Seth onwards, while 'the spirits made perfect' are the Christians who have died and so come to 'Jesus', their 'Mediator'. It seems to the present writer that there is a parallel passage in First Peter, and that when Peter says 'the gospel was preached also to the dead' (1 P 4^6), he refers to dead *Christians*, who had heard and accepted the gospel before they died. This suits the next phrase, 'Judged according to men in (the) flesh, but live according to God in (the) spirit', for this is probably a reference to the Christian creed quoted in 1 Timothy 3^{16}, Christians being compared, *mutatis mutandis*, with their Lord.

In the three passages last quoted it is implied that Christ does not 'receive the spirits' of dead *sinners*, that these are not 'perfected'; and that they do not 'live according to God'. But this negative evidence does not answer the question '*Where* do the spirits of the *wicked* go when they die?' There is no evidence unless it be under the phrase 'spirits in prison' (1 P 3^{19}). So far as the word 'prison' goes, the phrase might refer to Hades, for Hades has 'gates' and 'bars' (Isa 38^{10}, Jon 2^6, Wis 16^{13}, Mt 16^8). But there were other prisons and difficulty arises with the term 'spirits', for, in the New Testament, outside the Apocalypse, it is the *psyche*, and not the *pneuma*, that passes to Hades. Where, then, is the prison? The answer may perhaps be found in a passage in the Book of Enoch (Ch. 67). Certain of its phrases suggest that Peter was referring to it, or to a current Apocalyptic story that it exemplifies.

There are four links between the brief reference in First Peter and this chapter. First, the chapter in Enoch (inserted from an *Apocalypse of Noah*) relates to 'the days of Noah' (verses 1-3). Here, where Peter has 'while the ark was preparing', the passage in Enoch has 'the angels are making a wooden (building)'. Second, Enoch 67 is a description of a prison in which God first 'imprisons' (verse 4) the Fallen Angels and then 'the kings and the mighty and the exalted and those that dwell on the earth' (verse 8). Third, the later part of the chapter (verses 8-13), may be summarized as an account of 'spirits in prison', the 'spirit' occurring three times of the 'spirits' of the men who suffer there (verses 8f). Fourth, Peter's phrase 'Christ . . . , being quickened in the spirit, in which also he went and preached to the spirits in prison', has a parallel in the phrase 'deny the Spirit of the Lord' (verse 10), for to 'deny' is to 'reject preaching'. This means that Peter ascribes this preaching to the pre-Incarnational Christ, but other passages refer divine actions in the past to Him (Gal 4^4, He 1^{2f}, 11^{26}, Jn 8^{38}).

A brief account of the chapter in Enoch may now be given. The 'prison' is a huge valley of boiling waters in the far West—beyond the ocean or 'abyss'. It has nothing to do with Hades. The description builds on the phenomena that attend a volcanic eruption, where lava both falls from the sky into adjacent 'waters' and rivers of fire pour into them. In consequence they boil, with a reek of 'sulphur'. It is into this valley, the 'prison' of the Fallen Angels, that at the Flood all the dead, body and spirit, pass. It is meant for 'the healing of the body but for the punishment of the spirit' (verse 8)—i.e. its purpose is purgatorial. It succeeds in this purpose, at least with some of its victims. In later days it is peculiarly the destiny of 'the kings and mighty', against whom the Book of Enoch, in other parts, shows a special animus. In the course of time, however, the 'waters cool'—as with the waters, for instance, of the Bay of Naples when the lava has ceased to teem. The living 'kings and mighty' observe this, and concluding that the valley has lost its terrors, persist in their high-handed sin. Yet, declares Michael, this is their folly for 'they will not see and will not believe that those waters will change and become a fire which burns for ever' (verse 13). This seems to mean that there will be no purgatory for these men, but everlasting fire. There are phrases in the chapter that are obscure. In particular, it is sometimes difficult to be sure whether the writer is speaking of the 'kings and mighty' of Noah's time or of later days. But there can be small doubt about the general teaching. There is an old purgatory in the far West that will become a hell.

On the basis of the comparison is seems to be possible to suggest a connexion between the phrase 'spirits in prison' and its context. Peter was writing to Christians who were suffering the severities of a Roman persecution. Apparently they were sometimes facing the same 'punishments' as thieves and murderers—i.e. scourgings and death (1 P 4^{15f}). Probably the Apostle's reference to 'few' (3^{20}) means that some had flinched and that all found it hard to stand firm. Peter writes to encourage them 'in the Lord'. He seems to make three comparisons between them and the 'spirits in prison', saying, in effect, 'Those sinners of old time suffered even worse than you do; Christ went and preached to them "in spirit" even as He preaches to you "in the Spirit"; since they, or some of them, obeyed His message, even *their* sufferings proved at last a blessing—as *yours* will prove to you if you are faithful.' Then, with a sudden turn to another 'type' in the ancient story, he says: 'Like Noah, you were saved by water when you confessed Christ in baptism, as you yourselves know when you interrogate your "conscience toward God". Hold on to this salvation, for even though He permits you to be persecuted, Christ is already ruling from the throne, and through Him you will conquer at last.' It is true that in this exposition much is 'read between the lines', but this is so on *any* exposition of this passage. In any case, the Petrine passage has no answer to the question, 'Where do the *spirits* of dead sinners now go?', unless it be, 'They pass into a valley in the far West, which was once a valley of boiling and purgatorial waters, but is to become a valley of everlasting fire'? The fact is that Peter is neither asking nor answering nor considering the question. As in the Old Testament, so in the New, there is nowhere any answer to it, 'spirit' here contrasting with 'soul'.

From this survey of the passages where the 'body' or 'soul' or 'spirit' of a dead man is mentioned it follows that it is quite wrong to speak as if a man passes *whole* at death into an 'Intermediate State'. When a man dies, he disintegrates, and the body, the soul, and the spirit have each its own fate, even though on occasion each of the three parts may be called 'he'. It appears too that for the *wicked* dead the New Testament doctrine repeats that of Jewish books (apart from Second Esdras). For the *good* man—i.e., in New Testament thought, the 'believer'

—Christ makes *the* difference here as elsewhere, yet, so far as this allows, the Jewish doctrine is retained. It is modified, not abandoned.

To turn to the second class of passages, where trichotomy is forgotten, or at most sub-conscious, a beginning may be made with the word 'sleep' (*koimasthai, 13; katheudein, 2*). It has been seen that this word goes back right to the beginning of the Old Testament, and that the idea that the dead are 'asleep' was never lost. It was used both of the good and the bad, but far more frequently of the good. Though the question 'Which part of the dead man sleeps?' was not explicitly answered, it seems clear that the concept was that both the *nephesh* or 'soul' and the 'flesh' or body slept. In the New Testament, apart from Jesus' words 'The child is not dead, but sleepeth' (Mk 5[39]), the words for 'sleep', when they refer to the dead, are always used of good men. Matthew uses one of them when speaking of dead 'saints' and Luke (or Paul) has the phrase 'David . . . fell on sleep' (Ac 13[36]), but they are more commonly used of dead Christians, as of Christ Himself (1 Co 15[20]). Stephen 'fell asleep' under a hail of stones (Ac 7[60]); in one passage Paul, speaking of dead Christians, uses the phrases 'they that fall asleep', 'the dead in Christ', and perhaps 'they that are fallen asleep through Jesus', as synonyms (1 Th 4[13-16]; cf. 5[10]), and in another he has 'they that have fallen asleep in Christ' (1 Co 15[18]; cf. verses 6, 51); in the Fourth Gospel Lazarus has 'fallen asleep' (11[11]); the writer of Second Peter, speaking apparently of the Christians of the first generation, has the phrase 'since the fathers fell asleep' (3[4]). In view of this evidence, it is probable that when Paul writes, 'If the husband be fallen asleep, (his widow) is free to be married to whom she will' (1 Co 7[39]), he is speaking of a believing husband, and this suits the context. It is not adequate to take these passages to refer to the 'body' alone. When the first Christians, speaking of their dead, used the ancient Hebrew word 'sleep', they used it in the old Hebrew way, not stopping to ask whether they meant 'body and soul', but none the less meaning 'both'—even though they are now separate. For instance, Stephen was asleep, body and soul, now. But, while using the Hebrew idea, the Christians adopted it under the usual *differentia*. Christ was 'the first-fruits of them that are asleep' and His disciples, when they die, 'fall asleep in Christ', awaiting resurrection (1 Co 15[18, 20]). This is very far different from the belief of the *chasidim* that the 'sleep' of death was endless and hopeless.

It has already been seen that Jesus once used the term 'Paradise' to describe the state of a believer when he dies and, by implication, His own state. There are quite a number of synonyms for it. In the Synoptic Gospels the instances again fall in Luke, where there are three. One of these, the phrase 'everlasting tabernacles' (Lk 16^9), has a parallel in Second Esdras (2^{11}). The second is the phrase 'Abraham's bosom' or 'bosoms' (Lk 16^{22f}). This was a current Rabbinic phrase for the place, near to God, to which righteous Jews passed as soon as they died.[1] It uses the symbol of a banquet (but not the 'Messianic Banquet'), where a favoured guest sat on the right of the host. It is plainly symbolic, for Luke uses the plural 'bosoms', and, of course, it was not possible for *all* righteous Jews to sit in the place of honour. It would be from his place at this banquet that Abraham 'saw (Jesus') day' (Jn 8^{56}) The third Lucan passage is the phrase 'for all are alive to (God)' (Lk 20^{38}). Here, as the context shows, it is the 'sons of God', who are all *now* 'alive', even though men call them 'dead'.

In the later New Testament there is a passage that describes the present abode of the righteous dead in some detail (He 12^{18-24}). Here it is likened, not to a paradise or a banquet, but a city. The writer begins with a contrast between Mount Sinai, on which God had sat terribly alone, and 'Mount Zion', where He sits girt with the faithful. This mountain is 'the city of the living God, the heavenly Jerusalem' (cf. Gal 4^{26}). Here it should be recalled that in the Old Testament, as throughout the ancient East, the King and his City go indissolubly together, the City being the place of his throne. Many of the Old Testament Prophets and all its Apocalyptists expected that *at the End* there would be a new *city*, the capital of the Kingdom of God. With them it is on earth, as also in *Enoch* (e.g. Ch. 26). There grew up a belief, however, that *already* it exists, though not yet on earth. In Second Esdras ($13^{6f, 35f}$) the Messiah 'carves' for himself 'a great mountain' called 'Sion', in a region beyond 'Ezra's' sight, *before* the End. Earlier (7^{26}) 'Ezra' writes 'the bride shall appear, even the city coming forth, and she shall be seen, that *now is withdrawn* from the earth'. It is into this heavenly 'tabernacle', 'not made with hands', that the true High Priest has *already* entered (He $9^{11, 24}$), and in it that He shares with God the throne of the *hilasterion*

[1] *HDB*, vol. i, p. 18.

that is, the throne of mercy and reconciliation (He 1^{13}, 9^5). For the author of *Hebrews*, as in the Old Testament, the King, the throne, the shrine and the City go indissolubly together, God hallowing the Throne, the Throne the shrine, and the shrine the City. For him, as for some Jewish writers, the perfectly 'holy city' is *at present* in heaven. It is on a mountain *there* to which Christians have already 'come near' as the ancient Israelites 'came near' to a very different kind of mountain ($12^{18, 22}$). Elements in this architectonic concept emerge again and again throughout the Epistle. Whether its writer know of the Platonic 'heaven' of 'ideas' or not, he is in the Jewish succession—with the usual Christian *differentia*. It has already been noted that in the splendid description of 'the city of the living God' in Hebrews 12^{22-4} it is the '*spirits*' of righteous men made perfect' that are named. No doubt it is the 'spirits' of 'the first-born' too that are meant, and, of course, 'the myriads of angels' are 'spirits'.

The writer of the Apocalypse also believed in a 'holy city', but it is to be the home of the good at the End, not now (Rev 21^2). For the present 'dead saints' dwell in 'rest' and praise in the symbolic heaven which the Seer has described in Chh. 4 and 5. Coming from all nations, they 'are before the throne', God 'spreads his tabernacle over them', they 'hunger no more, neither thirst any more', the Lamb is 'their shepherd', and 'God wipes away every tear from their eyes' (Rev $7^{9, 13-17}$). It is true that here the Seer is describing 'those who have washed their robes and made them white in the blood of the Lamb', and that he is thinking primarily of those who have died in 'the great tribulation' (cf. 20^4), giving these martyrs a place nearer the throne than others, but there can be no doubt that he believed that all who 'die in the Lord' pass to heaven (cf. 14^{12f}). (Yet it has to be added that he describes the martyrs as pleading with God for retribution upon their persecutors and that they are promised that it is near (6^{9-11}).) He does not speak anywhere of the righteous men of the past, for this was no part of his subject, but no doubt he believed that these 'servants of our God' (7^3) were also in heaven.

The variety of these names for the Intermediate State suggests that they are all symbolic. How can this State be literally a Paradise, a city, a banquet and so on, all at once? It is probable that when such terms were used, the speakers did not usually *recollect* that they were symbols—any more than people do today when, for instance, they speak of 'loyalty to the throne' or 'the flag'. On examination, none the less, they are found to be symbolic—but symbolic of something *real*.

In Paul there are three relevant passages, and in all he goes behind symbols. Having once expected that he would be alive at the Parousia and *then* to be 'for ever with the Lord' (1 Th 4^{17}; cf. 1 Co 15^{52}), he later recognized that he might die before it and go to be at once 'at home (*endēmein*) with (Him)' (2 Co 5^8). Later, he came to 'desire' that he might die soon and so 'escape (*analuein*)' from 'life in the flesh' and 'go to be with Christ', which is 'very far better' (Ph 1^{22f}; cf. 2 Ti 4^{6-8}). 'With Christ' is the heart of the matter and explains all symbols.

In the Fourth Gospel the first passage, already mentioned in passing, is 8^{52-7}. Here Jesus, using the term 'dead' in two senses, implies that in the higher sense Abraham is not dead, for he did not 'die in (his) sins'. He is in the place to which Jesus is Himself 'going' (verse 21). In 11^{23-5} Jesus uses the word 'die' in the same two senses. When, in answer to Martha's word, 'I know that (Lazarus) shall rise again', Jesus says, 'He that believeth on me, though he die (in the lower sense), yet shall he live, and whosoever liveth and believeth on me shall never die (in the higher sense)', He teaches that for a dead believer there is already life, as with Abraham. In John 12^{25f}, where there is an explicit contrast between 'life (*psyche*) in this world' and 'life (*zoe*) everlasting', Jesus says, 'Where I am, there shall also my servant be', God 'honouring' him in this way. In 13^{36} Jesus promises Peter that he shall 'follow (him) afterwards'. This does not mean that Peter will meet Christ at the Parousia, for this is not 'following', but as soon as he is martyred (21^{28f}). John 14^{2-4} is the culminant and explanatory passage. Here Jesus does not mean that He will 'prepare a place' for the Disciples after His return at the Parousia, for He is 'going away' to do this *now*. He is going 'to the Father' (e.g. $16^{5, 28}$, $17^{11, 13}$), and therefore to 'my Father's house'. This is another name for Paradise, the implication being that His Father is also the disciples' Father (cf. 20^{17}). In it there are 'many dwellings' (*monē*), a phrase paralleled in the 'resting-places' described at length in *Enoch* (39^{4-8}), and in the *promptuaria* of Second Esdras (e.g. 4^{35}). The word 'many' probably silently corrects two current beliefs. First, there was a Jewish belief that very few would be saved, pitifully illustrated in *Second Esdras* (e.g. 7^{70}, 8^3), and in the Pharisees' saying: 'This multitude which knoweth not the law are accursed' (Jn 7^{49}). Secondly (cf. Lk 13$^{23-30}$), there was probably a Christian belief that Jesus, when He was asked, 'Lord, are they few that be saved?', had, in effect, replied: 'Yes, few.' He did say (Lk 13$^{23-30}$) that few of those who heard Him 'teach in their streets' during His lifetime would consent to be saved, but He added that many, chiefly Gentiles, will be saved at the Parousia. So far 'John' has only said in his own way what other New Testament writers had already said, but, with the words 'If I go and prepare a place for you, I come again and will take you unto myself, that where *I* am, *ye* also may be' he adds a climax. When one of the Eleven (or any Christian 17^{20}) dies, Jesus Himself will *at once* come to take him home, not waiting for the Parousia. This may be the key to the phrase 'till I come' in 21$^{21-3}$. The disciples had taken it to refer to the Parousia, and were puzzled when the Beloved Disciple died like the rest of the Eleven, but they had misunderstood the phrase 'till I come'. When Peter said, 'Lord, and this man what?', Jesus replied 'What is that to *thee*? do *thou* follow me', the preceding words meaning 'If I will that this man abide (here) till I come (for him when it is *his* time to die)'. He is to live longer than Peter (and the others), but not till the Parousia. Finally (17^{24}), it is likely that the sentence 'Father, I will that ... where I am (these) may be with me, that they may behold my glory, which thou hast given me' refers to the Intermediate State, for there are a number of references to the 'glory' that Christ received at the Ascension. When the Fourth Gospel was written the disciples had begun to take it for granted that most Christians, if not all, would die before the Parousia, even though they did not banish this to a very distant future, and they were therefore specially interested in the Intermediate State. It will be noticed that in John, as in every other reference to the state of the righteous dead before the Parousia—except the satirical passage, Luke 16$^{20\text{ff}}$—all centres in Christ. To be 'with Him' is the sufficient definition of Paradise. Jesus' word, 'Where I am, there shall ye be also' (Jn 14^3; cf. 12^{26}, 17^{24}), is the root of the matter for believers from the Penitent Robber onward. This fellowship is *diaparousian*,[2] for when He leaves Paradise to return in glory, so do they (1 Th 3^{13}). Since they then pass to a still better realm, it is proper to use the phrase 'Intermediate State' of the righteous

---

[2] This unusual word is defined in Chapter 19 as 'Apocalyptic but not only Apocalyptic'; it refers to events and experiences which connect with the Parousia and continue after it. [T.F.G.]

who have died. It will be seen that in New Testament times there was a very widespread belief in such a state. It seems all but certain that it was the Intermediate State of the 'spirits' of the righteous, though the word only occurs twice in the passages. None of them suggests 'sleep', which was the state of the 'souls' of the good.

Under the question 'What befalls the wicked who die before the Parousia and Judgement?', there are very few relevant texts. In the Synoptics there is the text 'Be not afraid of them which kill the body, and after that have no more that they can do. But I will warn you whom ye shall fear; Fear him, which after he hath killed hath authority to cast into Gehenna' (Lk 12^{4f}). In the Matthaean parallel (10^{28}) there are changes that seem to refer this saying to punishment at the Judgement. As the word 'Gehenna' seems usually to denote this later punishment, it is examined in the next chapter. If the Lucan text refers to the Intermediate State of the wicked, it means that for them there is punishment by fire immediately after death—as in the story of Dives and Lazarus, which needs longer notice (Lk 16$^{19-31}$).

As has already been seen, the phrase 'Abraham's bosom' is to be taken symbolically. This raises the presumption that the rest of the story is symbolical too, and, on examination, this proves to be so. The Rich Man passes to Hades, the huge cavern in the earth, which is far too distant from the Intermediate State of the Blessed, under any of its names, for a conversation to pass between an inhabitant of the one and an inhabitant of the other. Probably the 'fire' and the 'great gulf' are symbolical too. Further, while, as shown earlier, a denizen of Sheol or Hades, *nephesh* or *psyche*, has some kind of tenement, which resembles a 'body' in some ways, this is to be compared to the tenement of a 'ghost' in today's thought, and 'ghosts' do not 'thirst', as Dives does. The passage is symbolical, but this does not mean that it can be ignored. It symbolizes something real and terrible. For instance, the phrase 'a great gulf fixed' is described as an impassable gulf. Again, there is no hint of anything purgatorial in the 'torment' of the 'flame'. It is a mistake to try to mitigate the terror of the story.

Is it to be attributed to Jesus Himself? The present writer doubts this—not, however, because he thinks that Jesus never said terrible things, but for other reasons. The chief is the *kind* of symbolism used. It may be called 'artificial', in the sense that, as just shown, it does not describe anything that could, in fact, happen. There are examples of this 'artificial symbolism' in such books as Second Esdras (e.g. 7^{6-8}, 13^{8-11}) and the Apocalypse of John (e.g. 1^{13-16}, 21^{16}). But, outside the story of Dives and Lazarus, Jesus never uses it. His symbolism may be called 'natural'. For instance, many a sower went forth to sow and sowed on four kinds of soil, and virgins did, in fact, go forth to meet bridegrooms. There are two other peculiarities. As often pointed out, Jesus nowhere else uses a personal name for a character in a story, as He does 'Lazarus'. Again, He nowhere else takes it for granted that a *poor* man is *ipso facto* a good man, as with Lazarus —not even in the Lucan Beatitude, 'Blessed are ye poor', for this is addressed to His 'disciples' (Lk 6^{20}). If, for these reasons, the story is not to be ascribed to Jesus Himself, it is an example of the teaching current in the early Church about the Intermediate State of the wicked. As already shown, the Parable probably describes Gehenna. If so, it is the only passage where Gehenna is quite clearly placed in Hades, and the only one where it is quite clearly the place to which the wicked pass as soon as they die. In any case, its message is that, if one man sees another in need and, being able to help him, neglects to do so, this is a terrible sin. It is quite likely that *this* message went back to our Lord Himself. However reluctantly one may reach it, probably the most likely conclusion is that the story is based upon something momentous that Jesus said, but expressed in a form that was current among contemporary Jews. This, of course, means that Jesus' own words are unknown.[3]

Finally, there is the saying in the Fourth Gospel—'I go away, and ye shall seek me, and shall die in your sin: whither I go, ye cannot come' (8^{21}; cf. 7^{34}). This is spoken to 'the Jews' who, shutting their eyes to the truth, resolutely reject Him. It is the negative application of the Christian *differentia*. A man's attitude to Christ decides his fate, he 'will not' (5^{40}) at last becoming 'he cannot'. 'Darkness' has no fellowship with 'light'. There is, of course, no reference to '*honest* doubters'.

Outside the Gospels there is, first, Peter's reticent phrase 'that (Judas) might go to his own place' (Ac 1^{25}). It has been maintained earlier that the phrases 'spirits in prison' and 'preached

---

[3] Few New Testament scholars would agree that the story does not belong to the genuine teaching of Jesus. One view is that our Lord has here appropriated a well-known tale, giving it His own new conclusion and application. [T.F.G.]

to the dead' (1 P 3^{19}, 4^6) are not relevant here. In the latest New Testament book there is the text 'The Lord knoweth . . . how to keep the unrighteous under punishment unto the day of judgement' (2 P 2^9), but the phrase may refer to living sinners, and this suits the context better. While the text in Hebrews 'It is laid up for men once to die, and after this (cometh) judgement' (*krisis*) (9^{27}) describes the lot of all men, good and bad, it warns the wicked of a dread future. The word 'judgement' may be referred either to God's decision about men at the moment of death or to the judgement at the Parousia. The former seems the likelier, though the very similar phrase in 2 Esdras 14^{35} relates to the latter, being followed by the words 'when we shall live again'. Apart from the story of Dives and Lazarus, the evidence about the state of the wicked when they die before the Parousia is meagre, but it cannot be denied that under all the texts, even under Peter's phrase 'He went to his own place', there is the suggestion of a fearful fate.

CHAPTER SIXTEEN

THE PAROUSIA: RESURRECTION

THERE IS no doubt that the idea of 'resurrection' was common among the Jews in New Testament times—and that there was no agreement about it. While there are few references to it in *Enoch*, the last of the seven Archangels that are appointed to 'watch' over the parts of the universe is 'Remiel, one of the holy angels, whom God hath set over *those who rise*' (20^8). This implies that the concept of a resurrection was current, that the writer accepted it, and that not every dead man would 'rise'. No doubt the phrase 'those who rise' describes the righteous, as in the phrase 'The righteous shall arise from sleep' (92^3). Elsewhere, in the part of the book called *'Parables'* Enoch is assured that the angels have a list of all the righteous dead—whether they have been buried, or have perished in the desert, or were devoured by beasts or fish, in order that they 'may return and stay themselves on the day of the Elect One; for none (of them) shall be destroyed before the Lord of Spirits, and none can be destroyed' (61^{1-5}). Also in *'Parables'* there is the curious verse: 'And in those days shall the earth also give back that which hath been entrusted to it, And Sheol also shall give back that which it hath received, And Abaddon shall give back that which it owes' (51^1). This seems to teach that all the disintegrated parts of a dead sinner will reunite and rise again. In the very few relevant passages in Enoch, therefore, the writer of 'Parables' teaches a universal resurrection, but other writers the resurrection of the good only. The fact is that what may be called 'the school of Enoch' was interested, not in the 'body' or the 'soul', but in 'spirits', a term that is used alike of angels, demons and men, and occurs over two hundred and fifty times, and God Himself is 'Lord of Spirits'. For this school men, when alive, are embodied 'spirits', and, when dead, 'spirits' with some kind of tenement. At the Judgement 'spirits' do not 'rise again' but move about, as, for example, in Ch. 108. But the few scattered references to a resurrection show that in the school there were those who believed in a resurrection of the righteous only and those who taught that all, good and bad, rise again. The references are few because, throughout the *Book of Enoch*, the writers are speaking to their contemporaries through ancient 'Enoch', and they expected *them* to be alive when the End came.

It is different with *Second Esdras*. Here the Messiah, chief among the Jews whom the Most High hath 'kept unto the end', after he has destroyed Rome, 'will set' certain people (apparently the wicked Jews) 'alive in *his* judgement' and 'destroy them' before he begins his guardianship of 'the rest of my people' until 'the coming of the end, *the* day of judgement' (2 Es 12$^{30-4}$). In the Interpolation (7$^{28-32}$) the Messiah reigns for four hundred years at the end of this Age—and dies. Then 'the world shall be turned into the old silence seven days, like as in the first beginning, so that no man shall remain'. This universal death will be followed by a universal resurrection—'And the earth shall restore those that are asleep in her, and so shall the dust those that dwell therein in silence, and the chambers (*promptuaria*) shall deliver up those souls that were committed unto them'. This is a singular passage, but it teaches a universal resurrection, as in '*Parables*'. In some other Jewish books, however, it is only the righteous who rise, as in other parts of *Enoch*. For instance, in the *Psalms of Solomon* it is just taken for granted that at the End the wicked remain in the 'darkness' and 'flame of fire' of Sheol (3$^{13-16}$, 13$^{9-11}$, 14^{6f}, 15$^{6-15}$, 16$^{1-3}$), but they that 'fear the Lord' will be 'visited' and 'rise to life everlasting' (3^{14,16}; cf. 13^{9}, 14^{6}, 15^{8,15}). In *Second Baruch* (Chh. 29, 30, 49-52) a Messiah rules for a happy, long, but not endless period at the end of the present Age; then, when the next Age begins, the righteous, who have 'fallen asleep in hope', rise again with the bodies in which they died, in order that they may recognize each other. These, however, are later 'glorified' into the 'splendour' and 'beauty' of immortal life. Meanwhile the 'souls' of the wicked 'waste away' and then 'depart to be tormented'. In the *Testament of Benjamin* it is only the righteous who rise, but here the righteous include some Gentiles, a rare phenomenon (10$^{5f, 9f}$). Other Jewish books could be quoted, but these specimens will suffice to show both that resurrection was a normal element in Apocalyptic and that there was no uniform opinion about it. It looks as if the prevalent belief was that only the righteous 'rise again', the idea being that resurrection is the proper prelude to everlasting *life*. The wicked continue to exist but do not 'live'. It may be added that a reference in *Jude* (verse 9) shows that there was a common belief that at Moses' death his *nephesh* passed, not to Sheol, but to 'heaven', and that Michael took his 'body' there. The reference is to a pseudepigraphical book called 'the Assumption (*analēpsis*) of Moses'. *Mutatis mutandis*, he is classed with Enoch and Elijah.

The belief in the resurrection was a subject of hot contention between the Pharisees and Sadducees, the former accepting it and along with it a belief in angels and spirits, while the latter rejected both beliefs (Ac 23[6-9]). Josephus has two passages that speak of the differences between the two sects—'(The Pharisees) believe that souls have an immortal vigour in them, and that under the earth there will be rewards and punishments, according as they have lived virtuously or viciously in this life; and the latter are to be detained in an everlasting prison, but that the former shall have power to revive and live again; on account of which doctrines they are able greatly to persuade the body of the people' (*Ant.* XVIII. i. 3); '(The Pharisees) say that all souls are incorruptible; but that the souls of good men only are removed into other bodies, but that the souls of bad men are subject to eternal punishment. But the Sadducees . . . take away the belief of the immortal duration of the soul, and the punishments and rewards in Hades' *Jewish War* II. viii. 14).[1] Paul, like Josephus, bears witness that the great mass of the Jews agreed with the Pharisees in accepting the doctrine of the resurrection (Ac 26[6-8]). When Josephus says that 'the souls of good men only are removed into other bodies', he implies that the bad take their old bodies with them into Hades. He does not use the terms 'resurrection' and 'judgement', perhaps because he is keeping to terminology familiar to Gentile readers, but there is no doubt that the Pharisees believed in both. The quotations given above from the *Psalms of Solomon* and *Second Esdras*, books which are usually regarded as representing Pharisaic teaching, prove this (though the quotations also suggest that the Pharisees differed on some points among themselves). All

---

[1] Another quotation from Josephus should be mentioned though it is difficult to reconcile with the two given above. This inconsistency may well reflect the uncertainties and hesitations which existed in Pharisaic circles of the time. The quotation comes from *Jewish War* III. viii. 5, where Josephus gives as Jewish teaching the doctrine that the souls of the righteous 'receive as their lot the most holy place in heaven, from whence, in the revolution of ages, they are again sent into pure bodies'.

A complete treatment of the subject would have to take into account Rabbinic sources, as well as the apocalyptic and pseudepigraphic literature which is mostly drawn upon here. [T.F.G.]

this shows that Apocalyptic ideas were rife in Jesus' day, though there was no one accepted opinion about them.

Under terminology there are here three verbs, with two cognate nouns. In its active voice one verb, *egeirein*, literally means 'to rouse from sleep' (e.g. Mk 4^{38}), and in the middle and passive voices 'to come awake' (e.g. Mt 1^{24}). Its cognate noun, *egersis*, occurs once (Mt 27^{53}). Under the meaning 'to awake from the dead' it is used fifty-three times of the Resurrection of Jesus and twelve of the resurrection of others at the Parousia, of which ten belong to 1 Corinthians 15. The second verb is *anistanai*. It has both an intransitive use, where it literally means 'to stand up' or 'to rise up' (e.g. Mk 1^{35}), and a transitive, where the literal meaning is 'to make to stand up' or 'to raise up' (e.g. Ac 9^{41}). Its cognate noun is *anastasis*. Except in one text, where its literal meaning appears in metaphor (Lk 2^{34}), the noun always means 'resurrection' (*41*). There are fifteen *texts* where the verb refers to the 'resurrection' of Christ, and twenty-six where it denotes the 'resurrection' of others. Of twenty *passages* relating to the latter three belong to the Synoptics, four to Acts, five to Paul (including the one use of *exanastasis*—Ph 3^{10f}), two to Hebrews, two to First Peter, and four to John. Etymologically the adverb 'up' (*ana*) belongs to *anistanai* and not *egeirein*, but in use the two verbs are synonyms. For instance, they occur in parallelism (Lk 11^{31f}), and *anastasis* is used as the noun corresponding to *egeirein* (e.g. Mk $12^{18, 26}$, 1 Cor 15^{12}). The third verb is *zōopoiein* (to 'make to live', 'quicken'). In every relevant text (*10*) it is used of the giving of life *to the faithful*, not to all. The wicked do not rise to live. Most of the texts are Pauline (e.g. Ro 4^{17}, 8^{11}, 1 Co 15^{22}, 2 Co 3^6), but the word also occurs in John 5^{21} and 1 Peter 3^{18}, and outside the list, there is the explanatory phrase in John 6^{63}—'It is the spirit that quickeneth'. Apart from Revelation 11^1, which is irrelevant, none of the three verbs is found in the Apocalypse, and *anastasis* only in one passage (Rev. 20^{5f}).

The phrase *anastasis ek nekrōn* literally means 'resurrection from among (*ek*) dead (people)', but Paul uses it in parallel with 'resurrection *of* dead (people), (1 Co 15^{12f}). The former occurs in five relevant passages (Mk 12^{25}, Lk 16^{31}, 20^{35}, Ac 4^2, He 11^{19}), the latter in nine (e.g. Ac 17^{32}, Ro 1^4, He 6^2), and the phrase 'resurrection of *the* dead' twice (Mt 22^{31}, 1 Co 15^{42}). These uses of *nekros* raise the question 'What does *nekros* mean—the whole man, or some part of him, body or *psyche* or spirit?' There are passages where the body is meant (e.g. Mt 8^{22}, Ro 8^{10}, Ja 2^{26}), but there is no doubt that usually *nekros* (*128*) means 'the whole man' (e.g. Mk 6^{14}, Lk 16^{30}, Ro 14^{9}, 2 Ti 4^{1}, He 6^{2}, 1 P 4^{5}, Jn 5^{25}). It follows that, in spite of the trichotomy current among them the first Christians often thought of a dead man as a unity—just as people do now, in spite of the dichotomy current today. Normally trichotomy was ignored when men spoke of 'resurrection'. This may be compared with the 'blurred psychology' named earlier. It follows that the words '*egeirein*, and *anistanai* and *anastasis* are not used in a completely literal sense. *Egeirein* ('rouse') suits the word 'sleep', which, as has been seen, is itself used both of the body in the grave, of the *psyche* in Hades, and in a general sense, trichotomy being ignored. *Anistanai* ('rise up') suits the body exactly, and perhaps the word was used for this reason. It suits also the return of the *psyche* from Hades, but it does not literally suit the 'spirit', at any rate of the righteous, for, as shown above, their 'spirits' are in Paradise, which is a part of 'heaven'. There can be no doubt that Paul, who uses the phrase 'spirit and soul and body' of Christians whom he expects to be alive at the Parousia (1 Th 5^{23}), would have used it too of those of them who had already died. It follows that the attempt to interpret the phrase 'the resurrection of the dead' to mean 'the survival of the spirit only', in some wholly 'spiritual' state, has no basis in the New Testament. The idea would have seemed altogether inadequate to the New Testament Christian, for, with the Old Testament in his hands, he believed that the body is 'good'—so good that without it a man would be an incomplete man. For him to 'get rid of the body' would not have seemed a boon, but a disaster. Yet, as will appear later, he did believe that he would 'get rid' of the present *imperfections* of the body, for it would be 'transformed'. At the Parousia the dead Christian would return *to earth*—his spirit and soul and body, which had been parted at death, would be reunited—and once again he would be a 'whole (man)' (*holoklēron*—1 Th 5^{23}).

On examining the passages in the New Testament where 'resurrection' is mentioned, it will be found that the word, and even the phrase 'the resurrection of the dead', are used in two senses, which ultimately found expression in the two phrases 'the resurrection of life' and 'the resurrection of judgement' (e.g. Jn 5^{29}). The first of these phrases denotes a resurrection of the *righteous only* —or rather, in the environment of the preaching of the Gospel, of 'believers' only—and the second the resurrection of *all men*, sometimes with special reference to the wicked or to disbelievers in the Gospel. This means that the Christians, led by Jesus, agreed, at least in a general way, with the Pharisees, except at the crucial point. They too believed in a universal 'resurrection of judgement', but they 'proclaimed *in Jesus* the resurrection of the dead' (Ac 4^2)—the last phrase here meaning 'the resurrection of life'. Again, it was at *His* Parousia that the resurrection of all—which includes, of course, the resurrection of the righteous—would occur. It may be added that the New Testament does not answer every question that can be asked about the Resurrection —e.g. 'What about the bodies of the saints of ancient days of which only bones, at most, remain? How can they be said to "rise again"?' Perhaps the first Christians were wise enough to say sometimes 'We do not know' (cf. 1 Jn 3^2). In the end it comes to this, of course, with every doctrine under the sun, including the doctrines of science. A doctrine that explains everything is, *ipso facto*, untrue.

Though Jesus does not often speak of the resurrection, both ideas appear in His teaching. His use of the phrase 'rise up in the judgement' (Lk 11^{31f}), without explanation, shows both that the concept was current and that He Himself accepted it. Here He is saying that the Queen of Sheba and the Ninevites, having used the small opportunities offered to them, will rise from the dead and 'condemn' the men of His own day who have refused the culminant opportunity offered by and in Himself. The latter will be amazed to see certain *Gentiles* among those of the dead who rise. It is probably, though not necessarily, implied that *all* the dead rise. This conclusion is reinforced by the text 'It shall be more tolerable in that day for Sodom than for that city' (Lk 10^{12}), since this implies the resurrection to judgement of the men of Sodom.

There is no doubt, however, about another passage, where the resurrection is itself the subject of discussion and not just named under another subject (Mk 12^{18-23}). Here the Sadducees bring Jesus one of their favourite arguments against the doctrine of the resurrection—'If a dead woman was married seven times in this life, whose wife will she be when she rises again?' In reply Jesus quotes 'Moses', partly perhaps because the Torah was the only canon of the Sadducees, but still more to show that the belief in resurrection follows from the fundamental Hebrew account of the nature of God. He shows that the doctrine of the Covenant had from the first guaranteed it (even though the Hebrews had failed to perceive this). God's words at Sinai, 'I am the God of Abraham, and the God of Isaac, and the God of Jacob' (Ex 3^6) pledged Him to the Three Forefathers and, of course, with them to every faithful Israelite. To abandon them at death would be to break the Covenant. What sort of a god is it that does that? Death cannot foil God. As to the Sadducees' particular query, the answer is that in the resurrection the faithful have a body, but one that has no physical sex, for it is like the body of the angels. This would not seem a bizarre doctrine to men who believed that angels were inhabitants of the same universe as men and sometimes mingled with them. As has been seen, there is a partial parallel in *Second Baruch*. But Jesus' argument does not apply to the wicked, being based on the axiom 'God and the righteous go together'. Luke's additions make this very clear, for in them it is the righteous who 'are accounted worthy to attain to that age and the resurrection from the dead' and are 'sons of God, being (therefore) sons of the resurrection' (Lk 20^{35f}). It follows that when he says 'All live to (God)' (verse 38), he means 'all the righteous'. Jesus nowhere says explicitly that those of His disciples who died before the Parousia—and He expected that there would be some (e.g. Mk 13^{12})—would 'rise again', but, as later New Testament books show, their fellow-disciples would know that they were 'sons of the resurrection'. A man who 'lost his life for (Christ's) sake' would 'find it' (Mk 8^{35})—as also a man who *lived* his life for the Name.

In the *Acts of the Apostles* the Resurrection of Jesus is, of course, a leading theme, and, as already seen, to 'proclaim in Jesus the resurrection of the dead' was its sequel (Ac 4^2), the phrase 'in Jesus' limiting the meaning to 'believers'. The Christians had their own argument: '*He* is risen; *we* shall rise.' As it happens, all the other references to the resurrection of the dead fall in Paul's speeches. In the account of his speech at Athens it seems clear that the phrase 'the resurrection of the dead' refers to Jesus' resurrection (Ac 17^{31f}), though its sequel for believers may be implied. In the speech before the Sanhedrin (23^{1-6}) Paul sides with the Pharisees against the Sadducees, and the phrase 'the *hope* and resurrection' suits the righteous only. In the speech before Agrippa the context seems to require that the word 'hope' again means 'hope of resurrection' and the declaration that Christ rose 'first' confirms this (26$^{6-8, 23}$). On the other hand, in the speech before Felix, Paul, in a telescopic sentence, speaks both of this 'hope' and of 'a resurrection both of the righteous and unrighteous' (24^{15}).

In his Epistles Paul twice writes of the resurrection at some length (1 Th 4$^{13-18}$, 1 Co 15$^{12-58}$). His cursory references may be grouped with the second passage. In the first he deals with a question that had arisen at Thessalonica: 'What will happen at the Parousia to Christians who die before it?' Paul replies: 'They are only asleep, and through Jesus God will bring them back with Him when He returns.' Living believers will meet Him *and them* on their descent through 'the air', and then all Christians will be 'for ever with the Lord' in His Kingdom on earth. The passage says nothing at all about the resurrection of the wicked. In the second passage Paul is facing the heresy of certain Corinthian Christians. These were saying: 'There is no resurrection of the dead' (1 Co 15^{12}). Nothing is known of the heresy except what the Apostle implies in his answer. Probably it was of Greek origin, for in Paul's day there were Greeks who despised the *body*, and in verses 35ff it is clear that he has 'the resurrection *of the body*' in mind. Perhaps the heretics were like such later teachers as Hymenaeus and Philetus, who said that 'the resurrection is past already' (2 Ti 2^{17f}). For this they may have referred to Paul's own teaching that in believers' baptism there was already what might be called 'a spiritual resurrection' (Ro 6^{3f}, Col 2^{12}). This, of course, only shows that, for Paul as for 'John', 'now' and 'then' go together as the sequel to Roman 6^{3f} shows, but the heretics may have claimed that baptismal resurrection was the *only* resurrection. It seems likely that the Corinthian heresy is to be classed with the notions that ultimately crystallized into the Docetic Heresy, which denied the worth of the body. To return to 1 Corinthians 15, Paul's answer to those who deny the resurrection, like his Master's, deals only with the resurrection of *believers*. He prepares the way for his argument by a paragraph where, declaring that the belief in the (physical) resurrection of Jesus was an integral part of the Christian *kerugma*, he gives six examples of those who had 'seen' the Risen Christ (1 Co 15$^{1-11}$). Next (verses 12-19) he urges that if there is no resurrection of

Christians, the whole Christian *kerugma* is 'vain', for, here as elsewhere, Christ and Christians go indissolubly together (e.g. Ro 6⁵, 1 Co 6¹⁴, 2 Co 4¹⁴). Reversing the usual argument 'We shall rise for He rose' he says: 'If we do not rise, neither did He.' It is like saying 'Where there is fire, there is heat' and deducing 'Where there is no heat, there is no fire'. Next (verses 20-8) the Apostle shows that a belief in the resurrection is integral to the wider belief that Christ will at last make 'the whole universe' (*ta panta*) into the Kingdom of God—for the universe includes the body. As the argument relates wholly to the resurrection of *believers*, verse 22 is to be taken to mean: 'Just as all who die do so because they are "in Adam" (cf. Ro 5¹²), so all who rise and live (*zoopoiein*), do so because they are "in Christ".' As already seen, *zoopoiein* is not used of the resurrection of the wicked. Next (verses 29-34) the Apostle, declaring that his own zeal roots in the resurrection hope, reproaches the Corinthians for dallying with the heresy. It is after this long prelude that the Apostle comes to grips with the heretics' favourite question: '*How* are the dead raised? And with *what manner (poios) of body* do they come?' (verse 35).

While the transitions are not sharply marked, Paul's long answer falls into three parts. In the first (verses 35-49) he deals with the question, 'What will happen to the bodies of dead Christians at the Parousia?'; in the second (verses 50-2) with the question, 'What will happen to the bodies of Christians who are alive then?'; and in the third (verses 53-7) with both. Behind the whole passage there lies the axiom: 'God will do as it pleases Him' (verse 38). In the first of the three paragraphs the Apostle uses three analogies—with seeds, with flesh, and with 'glory'. Under the first he points out that, when a grain of wheat is sown, the 'body' that it has had grows into another kind of body, the latter only being 'made to live (*zoopoiein*)' if the former dies. So a dead Christian's present body dies that another kind of body may be 'made to live'. The second and third analogies occur together— there are varieties of 'flesh' in men and animals, and varieties of 'glory' in the stars—that is, among the angels, for Paul clearly shared the current belief that the stars display the 'glory' of the bodies of their inhabitants, the angels. The Christian's resurrection body is to be like theirs, as Jesus had taught (Mk 12²⁵). Reverting to the comparison with seeds, Paul next draws contrast after contrast between the earthly and heavenly kinds of body.

The first is 'destructible' but the second 'indestructible' (cf. 1 P 1^{23}₁); 'dishonour' is the lot of the first, but 'glory' of the second; instead of 'weakness' there is 'strength'; finally, 'if there is a body that suits the *psyche*, there is also a body that suits the *pneuma*'. Probably 'animal' is the best rendering of *psychicos*, here, for not only do men share *psyche* with animals (cf. Gn 2^{19}, Rev 8^9), but, 'animal' suits two, at any rate, of the three other texts where the word occurs (1 Co 2^{14}, Ja 3^{15}, Jude 19). Here there are two contrasts basing on Genesis 2^7—first, the *psyche* links all men with 'the first man' for they live the kind of life that *he* lived, but the *pneuma* links Christians with the 'last Adam', for He makes them to live (*zoopoiein*) in the way that *He* lives; and second, two different kinds of body distinguish these two kinds of 'life'—as Adam's body, being made of earth, passed into 'dust' (*choïkos*) at death so will the bodies of those that are like him; but the 'second man', since He 'belongs (*ek*) to heaven', has a 'heavenly' body, and so will those have who through Him become 'heavenly' beings. Having borne the 'image' (*eikōn*) of the man of dust (cf. Gn 2^7, 3^{19}, 5^3), believers will bear the 'image' of the Man of heaven.

At this point (verse 49) Paul, now using the term 'we', passes to the question: 'What about the bodies of those who are *alive* at the Parousia?' Bodies of 'flesh and blood', since these are 'destructible', and 'mortal', cannot 'inherit the kingdom of God'. When, at the End, Christ comes to inaugurate His Kingdom on earth (verses 23f), the bodies of believers who have not fallen 'asleep' will be 'changed' into something else (*allassein*) in the flash of an eye, their present 'destructible' and 'mortal' bodies 'putting on' 'indestructible' and 'immortal' bodies, like those with which *dead* believers 'rise'. The word 'put on' (*enduesthai*) describes the method of 'change', as another passage shows at some length (2 Cor 5$^{1-5}$). Here the present irksome 'tabernacle' or 'tent' (*skēnos*), a dwelling that is temporary by its very nature, is contrasted with 'a building', which is naturally lasting (cf. He 11^{9f}). The former is 'earthly' but the second heavenly, having its type, 'everlasting in the heavens', in the body that Christ 'put on' at the Ascension. The 'putting on' of this new 'dwelling' (*oikētērion*) means the 'swallowing up' of the old one as the Christian passes from death to life.[2] From the time when God gave Christians

---

[2] For the *present* 'putting on' of 'the new man' in Ephesians 4^{24}, Colossians 3^{10}, see *The Bible Doctrine of Man*, pp. 228, 233f. It is there claimed that these texts relate, not to the new body, but to its form (*eikon*).

His Spirit, He has been 'working away upon' (*katergazesthai*) them for this very purpose. A text in another Epistle, defining the 'putting on' by the term 'change the outward fashion' (*metaschēmatizein*), summarizes the Apostle's doctrine in a single phrase—'the Lord Jesus Christ, who shall fashion anew the body of our humiliation, that it may be conformed (*summorphos*, cf. Ro 8[29]) to the body of his glory' (Ph 3[21]). The 'image' of Adam passes into the 'image' of Christ (1 Co 15[49]; cf. Gn 5[1-3]). The present body is destroyed by transfiguration, not by annihilation. So, in 1 Corinthians 15, the Apostle, now embracing both living and dead Christians in his triumphant conclusion (verses 53-7), cries: 'We are victors over death for its "sting" is gone.' Under the word 'sting' (*kentron*), which means a 'serpent's sting', there is probably another allusion to the story of Genesis (3[1, 15]). Death, and with it 'sin' and 'law', is helpless to harm the Christian. Far from being 'of all men most pitiable', Christians are men who, by the gift of God in Christ, will live for ever.

It is only Paul who says much under the question: 'What kind of body is the body of those who live in the new universe?' His answer includes the Pharisaic assertion, as given by Josephus: 'At the resurrection the righteous will have new bodies.' It also includes Jesus' teaching that the righteous will have bodies 'like the angels', for 'angels' are 'spirits', and the Apostle teaches that the new body will be *pneumatikos*, one that 'suits spirit'. But he crowns his teaching with the Christian *differentia*. The new body will be 'conformed to the body of the glory' of the expected 'Saviour, the Lord Jesus Christ' (Ph 3[20f]). Unlike many modern Christians, when the first disciples thought of Christ as He now is and always will be, they thought of Him as embodied. 'We shall be like him, for we shall see him even as he is' (1 Jn 3[2]). Only men who are like Christ in body as well as in spirit, will be at home in the new universe.

In the *Epistle to the Hebrews* 'the resurrection of the dead' is mentioned as one of the six commonplaces of the faith (6[2]), the phrase probably meaning 'the resurrection of *all* the dead'. Elsewhere this writer has two references (11[19, 35]), the second recalling the story of the Seven faithful Sons in 2 Maccabees 7. In several books—*James*, *Jude*, the two *Epistles of Peter* and the three *Epistles of John*, the writers have no occasion to refer to the resurrection at all. All of these, however, except *Second* and

Third John, mention the Parousia, and to believe in this was to believe in the resurrection. For the writer from Patmos there are two resurrections. At the first (Rev 20⁴⁻⁶) it is the faithful in the Great Tribulation who rise and, apparently in answer to the prayer of 6⁹⁻¹¹, 'live and reign with Christ a thousand years'. At the end of this millennium the rest of the dead rise to be judged (20¹²ᶠ). The first resurrection is near, the second distant. This, of course, is a unique concept.

As usual, the Fourth Gospel illuminates the implications of the other books. The starting-point is the text: 'As the Father raiseth the dead and quickeneth (*zoopoiein*), even so the Son quickeneth whom he will' (Jn 5²¹). The Greek does not say that 'the Father quickeneth *them*', as in the English versions. As already shown, *zoopoiein* is never used of the resurrection of the *wicked*. When the Johannine use of *zoe* (life) and '*zēn*' (live) is remembered, it is surely certain that in John 5²¹ *zoopoiein*, when used of the Father, means, not 'gives life to *all*', but, as with the Son, 'gives life *to whom he will*'. A later verse runs: 'The hour cometh, and now is, when the dead shall hear the voice of the Son of God, and *they that hear* shall live.' Here, as usual with 'John', 'now' and 'then' go together, as the use of the future tense shows (cf. 14¹⁹). The text is the first instance of the characteristic Johannine phrase 'to hear (Christ's) voice' (*7*). Disbelievers do not 'hear' it (5³⁷); it is believers who 'hear' and follow, as sheep follow their shepherd (10³⁻⁵, ¹⁶, ²⁷ᶠ). 'Hear' is a synonym for 'believe'. Jesus' last use of the phrase is definitive—'Every one that is of the truth heareth my voice' (18³⁷). He that 'listens' and obeys will 'never perish', for God in Christ will see to that (10²⁷ᶠ). The story of Lazarus, whether historical or not, is a 'sign' of the coming resurrection of disciples, for it is when Jesus cries to Lazarus 'with a loud voice' that 'he that was dead (hears and) comes forth', body and all. The resurrection of the body is the completion of the present immortality within (11²⁴ᶠᶠ). In the Fourth Gospel Jesus' message is that *believers* will 'rise' unto the consummation of the 'life' that is already theirs. It is they, and they only, whom the Father and Son (and Spirit 6⁶³) 'quicken', both now and at the End. Yet the idea that *all* men will rise occurs too—perhaps by intrusion in order that this doctrine may not be overlooked— 'The hour cometh, in which all that are in the tombs shall hear (the Son's) voice, and shall come forth: they that have done good, unto the resurrection of life; and they that have practised ill, unto the resurrection of judgement' (Jn 5^{28f}). (In this text it may be noted both that the phrase 'hear his voice' is not used in the Johannine way, and that the verb 'come forth' is preferred to the usual verbs for 'rise again.') To sum up, throughout the New Testament the doctrine that all rise to judgement is present, but only as the dark background of the *kerugma*. On this subject, as on others, John epitomizes the *kerugma*: 'I am the resurrection and the life; he that believeth on me, though he die, yet shall he live, and whosoever liveth and believeth on me, shall never die' (11^{25f}).

CHAPTER SEVENTEEN

THE PAROUSIA: JUDGEMENT

It goes without saying that in the Jewish Apocalyptic books the belief in a Final Day of Judgement is universal. No Judgement, no Apocalyptic. For Esdras God 'prepared' it when He made the world (2 Es 7⁷⁰). With the belief in judgement there go two others, which usually are not so much asserted as assumed or implied. First, the Final Judgement is universal. No man, whether Jew or Gentile (and, notably in Enoch, no evil *angel*), escapes it. Second, it is ethical. The criterion of Judgement is: 'Is this man a good man or a bad man?' The criterion applied to angels as well as men. This is one of the main themes in *Enoch*. In *Second Esdras* the writer bewails the results of the criterion for men. Under its rigidity only a handful can be saved. The chief points for examination under the subject in the Apocalypses are: 'Are all Gentiles wicked?', 'What of the Jews?', and 'Is there a vicegerent Judge?' The common belief of the Apocalyptists is that all Gentiles are wicked. For this belief there was obvious ground in the state of the Hellenistic world, but, in addition, for Jews idolatry itself was a horrible, and indeed, the primary sin (e.g. Ex 20³ᶠ, Wis 13-15, Ro 1¹⁸⁻³²), and idolatry was the mark of the Gentiles. Enoch's description of the 'consummation of unrighteousness' in 91¹⁻¹⁰, for instance, ends with the destruction of idols and temples, and his account of the terror of 'the nations' on the Day defines their 'sin' as idolatry (99⁴⁻⁹). In Second Esdras there is a terrible account of the words of the Most High as He speaks in His 'splendour' 'to the nations' on 'the day of judgement' ere they pass to 'fire and torments' 7³⁷⁻⁴³. Yet there is an exception to the belief that all Gentiles are wicked in the Testament of Benjamin (10⁵ᶠ·⁹ᶠ). Here there are Gentiles, living and dead, who are the Lord's 'chosen' and judged righteous on the Day. Again, there is a passage in Enoch (50²ᶠ) where some Gentiles, though hitherto wicked, 'repent' on the Day and 'forgo the works of their hands' (i.e. idols). These are 'saved', though without 'honour'. In *Second Baruch* (Ch. 72) there is another variant. Here the Messiah 'gives up to the sword' the Gentile nations who have 'ruled over' and oppressed Israel, but the other nations will be 'spared' in order that they may be 'subjected to' Israel and serve her. This recalls the teaching of 'survival unto servility' in *Deutero-* and *Trito-Isaiah*, and can hardly be called 'salvation'. Finally, in *Enoch*, there are passages where Gentiles repent and turn to the Lord *after* the Day, for, however inconsistently, there were Apocalyptists who assumed that then the world would still be populated much as it was before the Day. This idea appears in four different documents included in *Enoch*. In *Watchers* one of the items in the cleansing of the earth from 'all unrighteousness' after the Judgement is that 'All nations shall offer adoration and shall praise me, and all shall worship me' (En 10^{18-22}). In *Parables*, after the Judgement (47^3) 'that Son of Man' is to be 'the light of the Gentiles', as in Deutero-Isaiah, and 'All who dwell on earth shall fall down and worship before him, And will praise and bless and celebrate with song the Lord of Spirits' (48^{2-5}). In *Dream Visions* where the Messiah is symbolized as a 'white bull', 'born' after the Judgement, the Gentile nations, symbolized as 'beasts' and 'birds' of prey, are 'transformed' and themselves become 'white bulls' (90^{37f}). Finally, in the *Apocalypse of Weeks*— where a 'week' is seven 'days' of seventy years each—there are two Judgements. The first, called '*a* judgement', falls in 'the eighth week' (the writer's own day), 'a sword' of victory being given of God to the righteous (91^{12}), but the final 'great everlasting judgement' of the *angels* falls at the end of the 'tenth week'—i.e. about a millennium later. Before it, in the 'ninth week', when men see that it is coming, 'all mankind shall look to the path of uprightness' (91^{12-17}). It looks as if this concept was common to the school of Enoch. It does not teach 'universalism', in the modern sense of the term, for it only applies to those who are alive. All four passages express the belief that in the ultimate kingdom of God there can be neither sin nor sinner.

This belief requires that *after* the Day all *Jews* too will become righteous, for it applies to 'all who dwell on the earth' (En 48^{2-5}; cf. 91^{12-17}). But it is everywhere taken for granted that *before* the Day there are both righteous and wicked Jews. There seems to have been a current notion that every *Jew*, good or bad, would be saved (cf. Lk 3^8), but this has no example in the Apocalyptic books, for it ignores ethics, and all Apocalyptists are ethical theists. Some, at least, of the Pharisees, believing that a man is not righteous unless he keeps the whole Law, deduced that only a few would be saved (Jn 7^{49}; cf. Lk 13^{23}). The Pharisee who wrote

THE PAROUSIA: JUDGEMENT 189

Second Esdras cries out against this doctrine again and again, particularly in 7^{45}–8^3, but he cannot escape the conclusion: 'There be many created, but few shall be saved' (2 Es $8^{1,3}$; cf. $7^{47f,60f}$, 9^{14f}). The Apocalyptic books were addressed to Jews, and the underlying challenge of many a passage is 'Ye Jews, look to the Judgement! Are ye righteous or wicked?' For instance, this is the *motif* of the 'Prelude' to *Enoch* (Chh. 1-5).

The *Apocalypse of Weeks* is not the only document in which the writer looks forward, first to '*a* day' and then to '*the* day', as with some of the Old Testament Prophets, but in the other documents the interval between the two is not two 'weeks' but short. For instance, in Esdras' 'Vision of the Eagle' or Rome (2 Es 11^1–12^{39}), the 'time of *her* end' (*ejus tempus*) and '*the* end' are distinguished (12^{21}). Between them the 'Messiah', having executed '*his* judgement', rescues the 'rest of my people' and 'makes them joyful unto the coming of the end, even *the* day of judgement' ($12^{32, 34}$). Yet the judgement itself is near ($8^{18, 61}$). The idea that there are 'first judgements', leading to the Final Judgement, occurs also in the *Zadokite Fragment* (9^{53}) and the *Psalms of Solomon* (Ch. 2). In the latter book Pompey's capture of Jerusalem in 63 BC had been *a* day of judgement on Israel, though the Final Judgement is still to come (Pss Sol 2^{37}, 15^{13}).

God Himself, of course, being King, is Judge. In some books, however, though not in all, He judges through or with a vicegerent. In discussions of this subject the term 'Messiah' is sometimes used for the vicegerent, but here it will be kept for the passages where the writers themselves use it or its translation 'the anointed'. There are books where there is no mention of any vicegerent, but here the *argumentum ex silentio* varies in force. None is mentioned, for instance, in the Greek Apocrypha, but here, under the subjects of almost all the books, any mention would be surprising, though, if the writers of *Wisdom* and *Second Maccabees* believed in a vicegerent, there would perhaps have been a reference to him in such passages as Wisdom 4^{18}–5^{23} and 2 Maccabees 7. The *argumentum ex silentio* is strong in such descriptions of the future realm of God as occur in the *Assumption of Moses* (10^{1-10}) and the *Book of Jubilees* (1^{29}, 23^{27-31}). Of the seven documents into which the *Book of Enoch* is usually divided, four—the 'Prelude', 'Watchers', 'Journeys', and 'Luminaries'—do not mention a vicegerent, but their subjects hardly require it. In 'Dream Visions' one appears under the figure of a 'white bull'

(En 90³⁷ᶠ), and in one of the 'Fragments' in the phrase 'I and my Son' (105²), but the doctrine has no prominence. It is quite different in 'Parables'. Here the 'Elect One' and the 'Son of Man' are frequent names for a vicegerent, and the 'anointed' is mentioned twice (48¹⁰, 52⁴). There are four passages where the Elect One shares both in the Judgement and future Kingdom of God (45³⁻⁶, 49, 51³⁻⁵, 61⁸⁻¹²), and it is the same with the 'Son of Man', if the passages that describe him be taken together (46, 48, 69²⁶⁻⁹, 71¹⁴⁻¹⁷). The same ideas underlie the passing references to 'The Lord of Spirits and his Anointed' (48¹⁰) and 'The dominion of His Anointed' (52⁴). 'The Anointed' was evidently a current name for the vicegerent that needed no explanation. It means 'Messiah', but not necessarily 'the Davidic Messiah', for it and 'anoint' are occasionally used in the Old Testament, sometimes literally and sometimes metaphorically, of any king, priest or prophet, whom the LORD has appointed (1 K 19¹⁵ᶠ, Isa 45¹, 61¹, Lv 6²⁰, Ps 105¹⁵). There has been much discussion about the relation of these three names to each other. The subject cannot be pursued here, but to the present writer it seems likely that they are synonyms, for their functions are the same and they all occur in the same document. He also thinks that they all describe a man—and not an angel, as does the phrase 'one like unto a son of man' in Daniel. The 'white bull' of 'Dream Visions' (90³⁷ᶠ) differs from them because he is 'born'— which may mean 'appointed king' (cf. Ps 2⁶ᶠ) after the Judgement (verse 20) and therefore shares not in it, but only in the future Kingdom. So far as the text goes, this is also true under the phrase 'I and my Son will be united with them for ever' in 'Fragments' (105²). Here too there may be a reference to the Second Psalm, but not necessarily to a Davidic interpretation of it. In *Enoch*, therefore, under 'the Elect One' and 'Son of Man' there is abundant evidence of a belief in a human vicegerent, with some references to him as 'Messiah', though probably not as a Davidic Messiah.

In Second Esdras the vicegerent is called *unctus*, 'anointed', and, according to the Syriac version he is 'of the seed of David' (12³²). He has 'as it were the likeness of a man' (cf. Dn 7¹³), and *is* a 'man' (not an angel as in Daniel) (13³·¹²·³²). God calls him 'my Son' (13³²·³⁷·⁵², 14⁹). This name probably refers back to the Deuteronomic description of the heir of David (2 S 7¹⁴). The writer of Second Esdras believed both in a human and a Davidic

Messiah. Yet he is a unique man, for the Most High has been 'keeping' him 'for a great season' in the place to which Esdras and those like him are to go 'until the times be ended' (13^{26}, 14^9). According to other parts of the book this place is the *promptuaria* or 'garners' in which the 'souls' of the few righteous spend the intermediate state between death and resurrection (e.g. $7^{32, 95}$). Even among them the Son is unique, for there is no hint that he had already lived and died, as they had, and he comes to earth before the Resurrection to prepare the way for the Judgement. He is 'pre-existent' in the sense that he has lived 'for a great season' as a 'soul' in the *promptuaria* before he is born of David's line. In any case the Son is a man who lives elsewhere before he comes to earth.

In two of the Visions the Messiah plays a large part. The first is the Eagle Vision (11^1–12^{39}). Here the writer first goes into great detail in a symbolic description of the last days of the Roman Empire (11^{1-35}), which is Daniel's 'fourth kingdom' (12^{11}). Only a remnant of its power is left. Then (11^{36}–12^3), there appears 'a lion as it were roused out of the wood roaring', who is the Messiah (12^{32}). Probably he is the Lion of Judah, the reference being to the description of that tribe, in an early song, as a 'lion's whelp' that pounces and 'takes the prey' (Gn 49^9). The Lion denounces the Eagle, telling him that, by the decree of the Most High, his 'times are ended' (11^{38-46}). Immediately the remnant of Roman power 'appears no more', 'the whole body of the eagle is burnt', and Esdras awakes from his dream in 'ecstasy' (12^{1-3}). Here the Messiah is little more than the Voice of God. Through him, when the set time is come, God just speaks—and there is no more Rome. After this the Messiah, having judged his own people, guards the faithful and joyful Jews until 'the day of (universal) judgement' (12^{32-4}).

In the next Vision (Ch. 13) the writer gives an account of this universal judgement. In it (13^{1-13}) the Messiah, God's 'Son', appears as a Man-out-of-the-Sea—i.e. a man of unsearchable origin (verse 52). He sweeps through the air upon 'a mountain' that he 'graves' in an unknown place to meet a 'multitude' that musters to fight him 'from the four winds of heaven'. This multitude is 'all the nations' (verse 33), and the 'mountain' is the new Sion that takes the site of the old one (verses 35f). He uses no weapon but pours out of his mouth 'as it were a flood of fire', so that 'upon a sudden' 'of an innumerable multitude' nothing is left but 'dust of ashes'. Finally, 'the same man calls unto him another multitude that is peaceable'. These are the faithful among the exiled of the Ten Tribes (verses 40-2), who now join their brethren 'within the holy border' of Palestine (verse 48). This Judgement on the Nations seems clearly to be the Last Judgement. In it the Messiah is vicegerent victor rather than vicegerent judge. It is assumed that all the Gentiles are his enemies, and it is only faithful Hebrews who survive (cf. 12$^{32-4}$).

Some other accounts of the vicegerent may be mentioned. In the Interpolation (2 Es 7$^{28-32}$) 'my Son Christus' is 'revealed with those that be with him' (in the *promptuaria*) and rejoices with the surviving Jews for four hundred years. Then, like all other men, he dies before the 'seven days' of silence come. No doubt he shares in the ensuing resurrection, but he is not named further. In *Second Baruch* (29 and 30) there is another example of a Messianic reign of limited length, though it 'lasts long' (40^3). In the *Psalms of Solomon* (17$^{23-51}$) there is an account of a Davidic Messiah, with no hint that he is other than a man, his reign apparently belonging to the present Age. It is the same in the *Testament of Judah* (Ch. 24), but in the *Testament of Levi* (Ch. 18) the vicegerent is a scion of Aaron, not David. In the *Assumption of Moses* (10$^{1-10}$) and the *Book of Jubilees* (23$^{27-31}$; cf. 1^{29}) there are descriptions of the future Age without any vicegerent at all. The belief in a Davidic Messiah, who will emerge to conquer at the end of the present Age, while not universal seems, however, to have been general. Again, the use of the phrase 'Son of Man' and others like it as synonyms for 'Messiah' seems to have been common. It follows that the identification was not first made by Jesus (Mk 8$^{29, 38}$). It was in contemporary use. This has an important bearing upon the question 'What did He mean by the phrase?' —but to discuss this does not belong to the present subject. From this survey it is clear that the ideas of 'judgement' and 'Messiah', like that of 'resurrection', were 'in the air' in the days of Jesus and the Apostles. No doubt the words were in general use. The very varieties in the accounts given of them show that they were discussed, and that people wanted to know about them. The Apocalypses, however bizarre they seem today, are examples of the way in which demand created supply.

With this background it is clear that Jesus and His followers did not need to tell the Jews that there is a Judgement. In accordance with the Christian *differentia*, however, the immediate criterion of judgement is no longer 'Is this man a good man or a bad man?' but 'Is this man a believer in Christ or a disbeliever?' Under this criterion men fall into the two classes of 'those who are being saved' (*sōzein*), and 'those who are perishing' (*apollunai*). For Christians, as distinct from Jews, it is the first class that are 'the saints' and who 'are not condemned' (Jn 3^{18}). Two comments need to be added. First, while all men are sinners without Christ, through the grace of God in Christ the 'believer' has become, or is becoming, a good man. The old criterion, therefore, has not lapsed, but takes a new form. At the Judgement men are still divided into the good and the sinful, for a man's refusal to believe in Christ and do His will, when he knows he ought, is the Sin of Sins. Second, while the new criterion sufficed for men who have heard the Gospel, it clearly did not apply to those who had not yet heard it. What about them? There is New Testament evidence, especially in Romans 1 and 2, that here another criterion applies—'Has this man done the best that he knows—according to "the law of nature" for the Gentile, and "the law of Moses" for the Jew?' This is a brief summary of doctrines fully discussed in the writer's earlier volumes on the *Bible Doctrine of Salvation* and the *Bible Doctrine of Sin*. It is pertinent to recall them here because of their relevance to the doctrine of Judgement.

In the New Testament the doctrine of Judgement is implicit in many passages where the words 'judge' and 'judgement' do not occur, as will appear below, but the number of the uses of *krinein* ('to judge') and its cognates will sufficiently show how common the concept is. The passages where the terms refer to man's 'judging' are, of course, omitted, but all those where God or Christ judges are included, whether they refer to the Parousia or not. The list is *krinein* ('to judge', *48*—Paul *11*, Rev *10*, Jn *11*); *kritēs* ('a judge', *7*); *krisis* ('judgement', *39*), and its synonym *krima* (*23*—Paul *12*); *katakrinein* ('to condemn', *8*); *katakrima* ('condemnation', *3*), and its synonym, *katakrisis* (*1*); *anakrinein* ('examine (in order to judge)', *1*—1 Co 4^4); and *dikaiokrisia* ('righteous-judgement', *1*—Ro 2^5).

With *krinein* there go *ekdikein* and its noun *ekdikesis*. These are usually rendered by 'avenge' and 'vengeance', but the words embody rather the idea of 'doing justice'. For the noun English has the term 'retribution', but for the verb 'vindicate' is the nearest equivalent. Apostolic writers twice (Ro 12^{19}, He 10^{30}) quote the saying 'Retribution is mine, I will repay, saith the LORD' (Dt

32³⁵) to forbid Christians to 'hit back' when persecuted. This accords with Jesus' word bidding His followers to 'turn the other cheek' when wronged (Mt 5³⁹ᶠ). It is with this background that the difficult Parable of the Importunate Widow, where Jesus speaks of retribution, should be considered (Lk 18¹⁻⁸). Is it not likely that, when He used the strange figure of the vociferous woman, He meant that God's 'elect'—whoever these may be —ought not to be clamorous for retribution on their enemies, but leave that to God? And, when He says, that God will 'do retribution speedily', is He not referring to the coming Destruction of Jerusalem (cf. Lk 21²²) and speaking sorrowfully? It was only a day or two later that He wept over the city (Lk 19⁴¹). The doctrine that 'Retribution is mine, saith the Lord' is not a joyful doctrine. At least in his earliest Epistles Paul did not here rise to his master's level (2 Th 1⁶⁻⁸), and, as will appear more fully later, still less did John of Patmos, who represents the martyrs as eager for retribution (Rev 6¹⁰) and exulting when it comes (Rev 19¹⁻³).

In the Synoptic Gospels the *terms krinein* and its cognates are rare (7), but the *idea* of Judgement is never far away. Indeed, under the meaning 'to declare which men are good and which are bad' it pervades much of Jesus' teaching for He often implies: 'This kind of man is righteous, and that wicked.' Under the other meanings of 'judge' a very large part of the evidence falls under the many Parables of Judgement. Of these there are at least eighteen—one being peculiar to Mark (13³⁴⁻⁷), eight to Luke (12¹⁶⁻²¹, ³⁵⁻⁸, ⁴²⁻⁸, 13⁶⁻⁹, 14¹⁵⁻²⁴, 16¹⁻¹³, 18¹⁻⁸, 19¹²⁻²⁷), and seven to Matthew (13²⁴⁻³⁰, ⁴⁷⁻⁵⁰, 18²³⁻³⁴, 20¹⁻¹⁶, 22¹⁻¹⁴, 25¹⁻¹³, ¹⁴⁻³⁰). One—which refers primarily to the Judgement of AD 70—is common to all three (Mk 12¹⁻¹²), and Luke and Matthew share another (Lk6⁴⁷⁻⁴⁹). In some instances two Parables are so nearly alike that they may be variants of one, but in this list they are counted separately.

These eighteen Parables fall into four classes—(*a*) there are four where God Himself is King-Judge; (*b*) eleven where the Judge is a Householder, or, better, 'the Master of the House' (*oikodespotes*); (*c*) two where the concept of 'judgement' is present without mention of a judge (the Parables of the Drag-net in Mt 13⁴⁷⁻⁵⁰, and of the Two Houses in Lk 6⁴⁶⁻⁹); and (*d*) one, the Parable of the Wicked Husbandmen (Mk 12¹⁻⁹), where the judge is owner of the vineyard. A king, of course, is *ipso facto* judge of his subjects. It is assumed that, also *ipso facto*, the 'master of the house' is judge of his bondmen (*doulos*) for he is their 'lord' (*kurios*). It is important to remember that neither king nor householder judges in the same limited way as the judge in a modern law-court. Where the last merely decides whether a man is guilty or innocent of a particular crime, punishing him if he is guilty, a king 'judges' *all* his subjects, whether good or bad, often taking account of the *whole* of their conduct, and distributing *rewards* as well as punishments, as also does a 'master of the house' with his bond-men.

The four Parables in the Judge-King group (*a*) are those of the Rich Fool (Lk 12^{16-20}), the Importunate Widow (Lk 18^{1-8}), the Two Debtors (Mt 18^{21-35}), and the Marriage Feast (Mt 22^{1-14}). Here, as already stated, God Himself is judge. It is *He* who challenges the Rich Fool; the Parable of the Importunate Widow ends with the question 'Shall not *God* vindicate?' and that of the Two Debtors with 'So shall *my heavenly Father* do unto you'; it is *God* who makes the Marriage Feast and judges both the guests who make excuses and the man without a wedding garment. Yet, while God is judge, in three of these four Parables there is a reference to *Christ*. In the Parable of the Two Debtors the Judge is '*My* Father'; under the Importunate Widow God's 'own elect' are *Jesus*' persecuted followers; under the Marriage Feast the *King's son* is bridegroom. In all these Parables the King's question, in effect, is: 'How have you treated My Son?' The one Parable in the fourth class (*d*), that of the Wicked Husbandmen (Mk 12^{1-9}), may be added, for they kill the owner's '*beloved son*'. It is the same with one of the Parables under (*c*), that of the Two Houses, for in it all depends on the hearer's reaction to '*my* words' (Lk 6^{47}). Under the groups (*a*), (*c*) and (*d*) only the Parables of the Rich Fool and the Drag-net are unrelated to Jesus.

To the 'Householder-Judge Group' (*b*) there belong the three Parables of the Watching Bondmen (Mk 13^{34-7}, Lk $12^{35-8, 42-8}$), the Parable of the Pounds (Lk 19^{12-26}), the Parable of the Ten Virgins, where the householder 'shuts his door' (Mt 25^{1-13}), the Parable of the Labourers in the Vineyard, where the vineyard goes with the household (Mt 20^{1-16}; cf. 21^{28}), the Parable of the Talents (Mt 25^{14-30}), the Parable of the Tares, where the 'field' goes with the household (Mt 13^{24-30}), and the Parable of the Barren Fig-tree (Lk 13^{6-9}), the Parable of the Unjust Steward (Lk 16^{1-13}), and Luke's version of the Marriage Feast (14^{15-24}).

In the first six of these eleven Parables the Householder-Judge is evidently Christ. In one of the next four, the Parable of the Tares, a later verse (Mt 13^{27}) attests this, and in a second, the Parable of the Labourers, the preceding verses do so (Mt 19^{29f}; cf. 20^{16}). In view of this list it is all but certain that Christ is the Householder also in the next two, the Parables of the Barren Fig-tree and the Unjust Steward, even though, taken alone, they give no evidence whether the 'householder' is Christ or God. It is only in Luke's variant of the Marriage Feast that God is clearly the 'householder'. In Parables of Judgement Jesus liked to compare Himself to a 'householder-judge'. This preference is consonant with the fact that until Palm Sunday He did not publicly claim to be 'Christ, a king' (cf. Mk 8^{30}). It seems clear that He loved to think of Himself and His disciples as a household. He had not yet taken the throne. None the less, there is a Householder Parable where He expects one day to be king and when that time comes, to act like a king (Lk 19$^{15, 17-19, 27}$). In this and a number of other Parables the Householder sets His 'bond-men' a responsible task, and then takes account of their faithfulness or unfaithfulness at its *end*, and, as Jesus' interpretation of the Parable of the Tares shows (Mt 13$^{39-41}$), this end is 'the completion of the Age' at the Parousia of 'the Son of Man'.

Another feature common to most of these Parables is that, while the *oikodespotes* is 'lord' all the time, he is at present an absentee. In the Parables of the Pounds and Talents he has gone 'into another' and 'far country' (Lk 19^{12}, Mt 25^{14}). In four other Parables his absence is implied (Lk 12$^{36, 43}$, Mt 20^8, 25^5). The same idea appears in the Parables where the host awaits his guests at the 'great supper' (Lk 14$^{17, 24}$) and the Sower of 'good seed' awaits the harvest (Mt 13$^{26, 30}$). For the disciples this meant that, while there was a sense in which Jesus was present with them between the Ascension and the Parousia (Mt 28^{20}; cf. Jn 14^{18}), there was also a sense in which He was absent—for He was not fully present until He appeared *bodily*.

Another noteworthy feature is that the 'bondmen' of the household are four times divided into two classes, the faithful and unfaithful (Lk 12$^{35-40, 41-7}$, 19$^{11-26}$, Mt 25$^{14-30}$). It is the same in the Parable of the Virgins (Mt 25$^{1-13}$). In two of these Parables the *faithful* disciples eagerly await the Bridegroom's return (Lk 12^{35}, Mt 25^1), and in two others they zealously do the work that He has appointed them (Lk 12^{43}, 19$^{16-19}$, Mt 25$^{20-5}$). Until the

Parousia disciples' duties were to 'watch and work'. Unfaithful disciples, under various phrases, fail the *oikodespotes* in both duties. While the disciples who 'do their lord's will' would, of course, be good men, for His will is a moral will, it is not morality that is the basic criterion of judgement, but, as with those who reject His claims outright the question 'What do ye about Christ?' 'What is your personal relationship to Him?' is fundamental. Jesus is not discussing 'Judgement in general' but the Judgement of those who hear the Gospel—and usually of those who are at least nominally, disciples. The fundamental question again is: 'How do men treat Christ?' This is the question that each man must answer at the Parousia, for these Parables are Parables of the End.

The phrase 'Son of Man' occurs four times under these Parables (Lk 12^{40}, 18^8, Mt 13^{37}, 19^{28}). This anticipates and justifies the statement in the Fourth Gospel: '(God) gave (the Son) authority to execute judgement because he is Son of Man' (5^{27}). It also leads up to Matthew's account of the Last Judgement when 'the Son of Man shall ... sit on the throne of his glory' (25^{31-46}). This is not a parable, though there are symbolic phrases in it, but a description of an event. There have, of course, been various interpretations of the passage. Here the writer confines himself to giving his own. Its *differentia* does not fall under the phrases 'everlasting punishment' and 'everlasting life' (verse 46), for these have parallels in Jewish literature, and they may even be an editorial addition. The *differentia* falls under the account of the two classes into which 'all the nations' will fall at the Judgement. It is wrong to take this phrase to mean that Christ is judging each 'nation' as a single whole, for everywhere else each man answers for himself at the Judgement (e.g. Ro 14^{12}), and, indeed, the use of the phrase elsewhere shows that it just means 'all those who are Gentiles' (e.g. Mk 11^{17}, Mt 10^5). Again, there is no question of the Judge's needing to *find out* which men are to be put on the 'right' or 'left'. He already knows this, as the *initial* division into 'sheep' and 'goats' shows. The purpose of the passage is to reveal the *ground* on which men have already been assigned their doom.

In addition to the two kinds of Gentiles, symbolized as 'sheep' and 'goats', there is a third class called 'these my brethren'. In the Synoptists apart from the tests where the word 'brother' means 'son of the same parents', there are three uses of the term. Under one it seems at first to be implied that '*all men* are brethren', but the real implication is 'all men ought to be brethren—and are not' (e.g. Mt 5$^{22-4}$, 7$^{3-5}$; cf. Lk 15^{32}). Under the second it is Jesus' disciples that are called each others' 'brethren' (e.g. Mt 10^{21}, 23^8). Under the third Jesus speaks of '*my* brother' or '*my* brethren'. Here there are three texts. In two the phrase 'my brethren' means 'my disciples' (Mt 12^{49}, 28^{10}), and in the first of these Jesus adds His own definition of the phrase, 'Whosoever shall do the will of my Father which is in heaven, he is *my* brother. . .'. In harmony with this the phrase 'these my brethren' under the Last Judgement means 'my disciples' and applies to a wider saying: 'He that receiveth you receiveth me . . . and whosoever shall give to drink unto one of these little ones a cup of cold water only in the name of a disciple (i.e. because the 'little one' is a 'disciple'—cf. Mk 9^{41}), he shall in no wise lose his reward' (Mt 10$^{40-2}$).[1] In the final judgement 'the Son of Man' and His 'brethren' 'go together' just as 'one like unto a son of man' and the 'saints' 'go together' in Daniel 7$^{13f, 18}$.

The immediate application of the passage appears if the point at which Matthew puts it is noted. In Chapters 24-5 he takes Mark's account of the Little Apocalypse, adding other teaching on the same subject, as is his wont. In particular he interpolates the Parables of the Virgins and the Talents. If these be omitted, it appears at once that for Matthew the Last Judgement is just the conclusion of the Little Apocalypse—Matthew 25$^{31\text{ff}}$ linking readily with 24^{51}. As already shown, the background of this Apocalypse is the *Sitz im Leben* of the disciples in Palestine between the Fall of Jerusalem and the Parousia. After the Fall Gentiles crowded into Palestine, finding the surviving Jews still persecuting the Nazarenes (cf. 1 Th 2^{14}). Many of the latter would *literally* be wandering 'hungry and thirsty', knocking at the doors of the 'stranger' Gentile asking shelter. Many, again, would be 'sick' or 'in prison'. Those who succoured them would run such risks as the modern inhabitants of an 'occupied country' ran in both the World Wars when they helped escaped prisoners or refugees. It is to such men that the Judge says: 'Inasmuch as ye did it unto one of these my brethren, even these least, ye did it unto me.' Is it impossible that a persecuted Christian would pass

---

[1] Disciples, of course, are 'brethren' because they have one Father in Heaven. Other men are potentially 'sons of God', but not actually so until they 'believe'. The underlying idea is 'fellowship', and this fellowship, like all others, requires the free consent of *both* the parties to it. The biblical teaching about 'the Fatherhood of God' is fully examined in *The Bible Doctrine of Man*.

on the Judge's pledge to some Gentile who befriended him? Mark significantly prefixes the word 'He that is not against us is for us' to the saying about a cup of cold water (Mk 9⁴⁰ᶠ). The Palestinian Gentile fell under the principle clearly implied in Luke 12⁴⁸: 'To whomsoever little is given, of him shall little be required.' In the particular *Sitz im Leben* the regular New Testament division of men into 'believers' and 'disbelievers' is qualified. It was enough that a Gentile 'outsider' should merely be kind to a helpless Christian. Of course, here too the principle involved has many applications beside this one, but it is to the historical situation in Palestine in a particular period that Matthew's account of the Last Judgement immediately refers. It is just taken for granted that 'these my brethren' do not need to be judged. Because the 'Son of Man' and His disciples 'go together', the latter are *ipso facto* safe at the Judgement. Matthew, as elsewhere, deals with the historical situation as he knew it in Palestine after AD 70, but generalizes from it, writing as though '*all* the Gentiles' were in a situation like that of Gentiles in Palestine in his own day. While, however, the details are those of a particular situation, the basic criterion of judgement, 'For Christ or against Him?', did apply to all Gentiles who had heard the Gospel. This passage, with Mark 13 and others in the Synoptics, shows that the first disciples declared: 'Vicegerent, say they? *We* know that there is one, and *we* know who he is.'

In the Acts of the Apostles the term *krinein* is only used three times of the Last Judgement (10⁴², 17³¹, 24²⁴ᶠ). The complete evidence, however, includes much more than these texts. It begins with Peter's quotation from Joel on the Day of Pentecost, for this ends with the words: 'Before the Day of the Lord come, That great and notable Day, And it shall be that whosoever shall call on the name of the Lord shall be saved' (Ac 2²⁰ᶠ). Here the Apostle just takes it for granted that *Jews* (verse 14) believe in a Last Judgement. His distinctive message is that it is Jesus who will sit to judge, for God has made Him 'both Lord and Christ' (verses 34-6). This is implicit in other texts (e.g. 15¹¹, 20³², 26¹⁸). Behind them all there is the message that Peter summarizes in the words: 'He charged us . . . to testify that this is he which is ordained of God to be the Judge of quick and dead' (10⁴²). The Jews believed in a Last Judgement; the Christian *differentia* is that the Risen Jesus will be Judge. On the other hand, when

Paul is telling the *Gentile* Felix what 'the faith in Christ Jesus' is, he begins by '*reasoning* of righteousness and self-control and *the judgement to come*' (24^{25}), and when he is preaching to the Gentile Athenians, he needs to tell them first something that Jews assumed, '(God) hath appointed a Day in the which he will judge the world in righteousness'—then adding 'by the man whom he hath ordained; whereof he hath given (a ground for) belief (*pistis*) to all men in that he hath raised him from the dead' (17^{31}). No doubt this is Luke's summary of a longer exposition. Jesus' teaching that He must die and rise again had only puzzled the Disciples while He was on earth. Among other things they had not understood its bearing upon His teaching that He would be Judge at the End. Now this is clear. For the Apostles the belief in Jesus' Judgement now bases on the belief in His Resurrection. From Pentecost onwards the Church believed that the Risen Jesus sits at God's right hand, awaiting His final triumph and ready to judge (Ac 2$^{33-6}$).

What the Apostles preached to outsiders, as Acts shows, they just took for granted when they wrote letters to *Christians*, for a belief in the Judgement was one of the 'elements' of their creed (cf. He 6^{1f}). Consequently the writers of Epistles only mention judgement when they are dealing with some subject to which it is pertinent, and then without more exposition than that subject requires. This appears clearly in the Pauline Epistles. Here there are eight passages under *krinein* or a cognate, and one under *bēma* ('judgement seat'). The Apostle refers three times to the final Judgement of *God*—once as Judge of the Kosmos (Ro 3^6), once as Judge of those who sin against the State (Ro 13^2), and once as his own Judge on the Day (2 Ti 4^8). There are two passages where *both* God and Christ judge (2 Th 1$^{3-10}$, Ro 2$^{3-16}$). These are taken later. In the other four *Christ* alone is named. Two declare that He knows all the secrets of men (1 Co 4^{4f}, 1 Ti 5^{24f}; cf. Ro 2^{16}). In another (2 Co 5^{9f}) Paul reminds his readers that, when they 'all will appear before the judgement-seat (*bēma*) of Christ', their works will show whether their lives have been 'well pleasing to the Lord'. In the fourth text Paul 'charges' Timothy 'in the sight of God and of Jesus Christ who shall judge the quick and the dead' to be faithful to his ministry (2 Ti 4^{1f}). In the two last passages works are the evidence of faith. Paul draws out this doctrine in 2 Thessalonians 1$^{3-5}$. Here the 'faith' of the Thessalonian converts, having already 'grown exceedingly', has already shown itself in the Christian way-of-life, and therefore they will be 'counted worthy of the kingdom of God' (cf. the use of 'grace', the correlative of 'faith', in verses 11f). The verses are part of a passage (2 Th 1^{3-12}) that refers to the immediate situation in Thessalonica, setting the disciples over against their 'persecutors'. The latter, like the former, have heard the Gospel but do not 'obey' it—i.e. Believers and Disbelievers are set over against each other. Both belief and disbelief show themselves in 'works', and, at 'the revelation of the Lord Jesus from heaven', God will judge both by what their 'works' show them to be. While the Lord Jesus will be 'glorified in his saints', only one item in the ensuing fate of believers is mentioned—'release' (*anesis* —cf. 2 Co 2^{13}, 7^5) from the continual tension that 'patience' under 'persecution' imposes. On the other hand, Paul gives a lurid description of the future fate of the persecuting Disbelievers. Its details belong to the Section on 'Rewards and Punishments'. For Paul the persecution of his recent converts does not raise the question 'Why does God allow this?' for their 'patience and faith' under it are, for him, themselves a 'proof' (*endeigma*) that God will do them justice at the Epiphaneia of Jesus. His converts are ringing true to the coming test. 'Why do the righteous suffer?' is not a *New* Testament problem.

There remains the most important passage in Paul (Ro 2^{12-16}). This needs to be studied in relation to the whole doctrinal part of the Epistle (1^{18}–11^{36}). Behind all this there lie the concepts of 'judgement', in the sense of 'condemnation' (*katakrinein*—e.g. 2^1, 5^{16}), and 'salvation', the former being more prominent in the earlier part of the eleven chapters and the latter in the later part. The concept of Judgement emerges with the word 'God's wrath is revealed from heaven against all ungodliness and unrighteousness of men' (1^{18}), and culminates in the text 'All have sinned' for 'all have come short of the glory of God' (3^{23}). Within the mass of men Paul, in effect, distinguishes six classes—two kinds of Gentiles, two of Jews, and two of 'Christians'. With some of these six classes he deals explicitly, with others implicitly. Again, he distinguishes three kinds of 'law' (*nomos*)—for all Gentiles there is 'the law written in their hearts, their conscience bearing witness therewith' (2^{15}; cf. 1^{20f}); for all Jews there is the Law of Moses (2^{17}; cf. 3^2); and for all Christians there is 'the law of the Spirit of life in Christ Jesus' (8^2), called elsewhere 'the law of

Christ' (Gal 6^2). In the Judgement all *Gentiles* will be judged by 'the law of conscience', all Jews by the Law of Moses, and all Christians by 'the law of Christ'. Here, however, a qualification needs to be made—under this classification Paul means by 'Gentiles' and 'Jews' those of both classes who have *not* heard the Gospel. Of the two kinds of such *Gentiles* the first are the great multitude who, sinning against the Law of Conscience, have committed the horrible catalogue of sins enumerated in 1$^{24-32}$. Rome would be rife with such Gentiles. Here Paul matches Juvenal. But there were other Gentiles, for whom Seneca and Epictetus might stand, who ordered their lives according to what they knew of God. This does not mean that they *never* transgressed the Law of Conscience, but that their normal way-of-life corresponded to their knowledge of what God requires of men. They are '*doers* of law' and will be 'justified . . . in the day when God judgeth the secrets of men, according to my Gospel, by Jesus Christ' (2$^{13, 16}$). For the other Gentiles, who have sinned against the Law of Conscience, 'the wrath of God is revealed' (1^{18f}).

Of the two kinds of *Jews* Paul delineates the worse kind as he argues with him throughout Romans 2. Apparently there were Jews in Rome who were no better than the worst of the Gentiles (2$^{1-3}$), and others who, while they did not fall into such enormities as unnatural vice, yet failed to keep the Ten Commandments (2^{21f}). All of these sinners boasted that they were better than the Gentiles because in the Law of Moses God had given them a higher law than the Gentiles knew, and set themselves up to teach their ignorant heathen neighbours (2$^{17-20}$). Their criterion was knowledge, not life. It looks as if, as in Luke 3^{7f}, they claimed that all Jews would be safe at the Judgement because, however they lived, they belonged to the Chosen People. Behind the Apostle's argument with these men there is a certain impatience with their folly. He tells them that at the Judgement they will fare worse than the better kind of Gentile just because they knew the will of God better than he (2$^{12f, 18}$). Paul does not explicitly deal with the better kind of Jew—the man who did his best to keep the Law of Moses and who lived therefore on a higher level than the average Gentile—but he deals with him implicitly when he comes to write of Abraham (4^{1f}). While the Patriarch, of course, knew neither the Law of Moses nor the Law of Christ, he nevertheless 'knew God' so intimately that he could be 'called the friend of God' (Ja 2^{23})—and, trusting Him, he did what God told him to do (even on Moriah). His way-of-life resulted from his trust in *God*. He could not be said to 'believe on the Lord Jesus Christ', but he lived according to what he did know of God. The writer to the Hebrews applies the same criterion to all faithful Jews throughout the centuries past (He 11). It may be applied to Paul himself before his conversion. Being a sincere Pharisee, he kept every detail of the Law of Moses (Ac 26^{4f}). If he had died then, surely he would have been 'on the right hand' at the Judgement. There were Jews who, trusting God, lived according to the Law of Moses. This does not mean that they never broke a commandment, but that their way-of-life was of a certain kind.

Of the two kinds of men who claimed the name '*Christians*' the worse appear in Romans 6. There were already antinomians who used the shallow argument: 'There is no reason why we should not sin for every sin gives God the opportunity of forgiving a sinner for Christ's sake.' In answer Paul bursts out with an indignant 'Never! (*mē genoito*)' (6$^{2, 15}$), not troubling to draw out the dire fallacy of the antinomian claim, but describing the other and true kind of 'Christian'—the man who bears 'fruit unto sanctification' (6^{22}). This, again, does not mean that he never sins at all, but that his way-of-life will exhibit the 'fruit' or inevitable outcome of his faith in Christ—as already described under the passage in Second Thessalonians, or, to quote a later text in Romans: 'There is therefore now no condemnation (*katakrima*) to them that are in Christ Jesus' for they '*walk* not after the flesh, but *after the Spirit*' (8$^{1, 4}$).

To sum up, one of the purposes of Romans 1-11, especially in its earlier part, is to make manifest 'the righteousness of the judgement of God' (*dikaiokrisia*—2^5). Paul does this under what may be called 'the Criterion of Opportunity'. Since little is given to Gentiles, from them little will be required; since more is given to Jews, from them more will be required; since most is given to Christians, from them most will be required. On the Day (2^{16}) Christ will judge each man according to his use of *his own* opportunity. While the Synoptic teaching about judgement is limited to the immediate *Sitz im Leben*, Paul explores the whole subject. None the less, in Paul as in the Synoptics, for those who hear the Gospel Christ's offer of salvation from sin and entrance into the Kingdom is the climax of opportunity. To reject it is the Sin of Sins. Often in the New Testament men fall into two classes,

Believers and Disbelievers. This applies the Criterion of Opportunity to the particular situation in which preachers of the Gospel found themselves. Their hearers either accepted or rejected the Gospel that they preached. The division into Believers and Disbelievers is just the greatest example of the universal principle that judgement is according to opportunity. It is a fearful thing to preach the Gospel, for men may reject it.

It has already been noted that the writer to the Hebrews counts a belief in 'everlasting judgement' as part of the alphabet of the faith and therefore does not discuss it (6^{1f}). Yet he has references to this doctrine when the context requires it. For instance, there is the passage, already discussed, in which he describes the gathering of the faithful dead in a glad intermediate state (12^{23}). It is glad because, while God 'the judge of all' is there, with Him there is 'Jesus', whose 'blood' avails for salvation (cf. 10^{22}). Another text reminds readers that God will judge sins against marriage (13^4). In another there is a Judgement which follows death (9^{27}). Finally there is the terrible passage where the writer warns apostates (10^{26-31}). Since 'retribution belongs' to God, and since God 'will judge (even) his (own) people', for apostates there is a 'certain fearful expectation of judgement and a fiery jealousy (*zēlos*)' that is about to 'eat up the adversaries' (cf. 12^{29}). 'It is a fearful thing to fall into the hands of the living God.'

In the *Epistle of James* there are illustrations of two points already taken—God alone is Judge, for He alone 'is able to save and to destroy' (4^{12}), and Christians are judged under the Criterion of Opportunity—all Christians by the perfect 'law of liberty', which is their high monopoly (2^{12f}; cf. 1^{25}), and Christian 'teachers' because they have greater responsibilities—and greater opportunities—than the taught. There is a longer passage (5^{8-12}) that warns against the judgement that awaits both those who, failing to be 'patient' in the sense 'long-tempered' (*makrothumein*), 'let fly' at others, and those who, failing to 'endure' (*hypomenein*), 'let go' their faith. 'Why sin in these ways?' asks James, when the Parousia and the Judge are 'at the doors'. In the *First Epistle of Peter*, the writer, reminding his readers that 'the Father' will 'judge every man according to his work', without showing any favour to *any* kind of man (1^{17}), applies this principle to Christians, both living and dead (4^{5f}), for, as there are now different kinds of men claiming the name 'Christian', it is 'time for judgement to begin at the house of God' (4^{12-16}; cf. 2^{20f}). The true Christian is to trust a 'faithful Creator' to vindicate him when he 'appears' before Him at the Judgement, even as He vindicated Christ Himself at His resurrection (2^{21-23}, 4^{18f}). In this Epistle there is the only New Testament example of the idea of 'visit' to denote 'final judgement' which is so common in the Old Testament. It falls under the phrase 'the Day of Visitation' (*episcopē*) (1 P 2^{12}).

The Epistle of Jude speaks of nothing but two kinds of 'Christians', and is chiefly a vehement polemic against libertine teachers, who preached the antinomianism first described in *Romans*. The writer's message to them is 'At the End you will be judged indeed'. Crying out against them because they 'rail at dignities' (verse 8), he himself rails at them! He rehearses against them the stories of Judgement in the Pentateuch and Enoch's account of the present and final doom of the Fallen Angels, adding the latter's tremendous prophecies of the ultimate fate of sinners (cf. En 1^9, 5^{4f}, 27^{26}). On the other hand (verses 20-5), God through Christ will set the faithful 'before the presence of his glory without blemish in exceeding joy'.

In the *Second Epistle of Peter* the second chapter, of course, is a variant of Jude. Under Judgement the writer makes two additions. First, he explicitly treats the distinction between faithful Christians and libertines as an instance of that between the 'righteous' and 'unrighteous' (2^{5-9}), and second, he appeals to the Criterion of Opportunity, declaring that the libertine 'Christians' would have been better men if they had never heard of Christ! (2^{20-2}). The whole Epistle might be called 'The Epistle of the Parousia', for this is the dominant concept throughout.

In the Apocalypse of John the idea of judgement is everywhere. There is a difference, however, between the two parts of the book. In the first part (Rev 1-3) the Christ judges the several churches in the sense that He decides and declares what in them is good and what bad. The ideas of punishment and reward are subordinate to this. In the second and longer part (4-22), on the contrary, it is usually assumed that already men are divided into 'saints' and sinners, and the chief idea under 'judge' is 'punish'. As the book proceeds, Judgement under this definition looms nearer and nearer. The period of the Third Woe, within which the writer lives, might almost be called 'the Era of the Imminent Judgement'. Yet even here it is not until the eve of the 'seven last plagues' that the word rings 'The hour of (God's) judgement is come' (14^7; cf. verse 11). The description of these 'plagues' fills rather more than four chapters (16^1–20^6). Here nothing more is attempted than to make some notes on this passage and its sequel (20^{7-15}).

As the sequel shows (20^{11-15}), the Seer teaches that there are two Judgements to come, one imminent and the other a thousand years away. It is the first, however, that engrosses his mind, for he spends almost as many chapters on it as he does verses on the second, which, strictly speaking, is the *last* Judgement. The idea that between the imminent Judgement and the last there is an interval of about a thousand years occurs also in the latter part of the *Apocalypse of Weeks* (En 91^{12-17}), but there are many differences in detail. In *Second Esdras*, again, as in some Old Testament Prophecies, there is *a* Day and *an* End, separated by a long interval from *the* Day and *the* End. The first is the Day and End of the Eagle (Rome), as distinct from '*the* End' (2 Es 12^{21}). Similarly the Messiah executes *a* 'judgement' as distinct from *the* Judgement (12^{33f}). The idea that there are 'first judgements', which lead to the final Judgement occurs also in the *Zadokite Fragment* (9^{53}), and in the *Psalms of Solomon*. Pompey's capture of Jerusalem had been *a* Day for Israel, though the final Judgement is still future (Ps Sol 2^{37}, 15^{13}). When the Seer taught a doctrine of two Judgements, separated by a millennium, he was just adapting a current but flexible concept to his own uses.

In the account of the First Judgement (Rev 16^6–20^6) there are a number of scattered but significant references to the fate of the saints under the term 'happy' (*makarios*)—they are 'happy' even if they die (14^{13}), happy if they are ready for the Day (16^{15}), 'happy' because they are 'bidden to the marriage supper of the Lamb' (19^9), 'happy' because they have a part in the first resurrection' (20^6). But these passages are hardly more than parentheses. The main subject of the first Judgement is the doom of the wicked. The 'everlasting gospel', an earlier title of the whole account, is the message that now at last God is vindicating His rule in judgement (14^6). To the little, scattered and persecuted churches this was 'good news'!

The structure of the passage describing the Seven Last Plagues (15^1–20^6) is irregular. Angels pour the 'plagues' from seven 'bowls' or 'vials' (16^1). The first four angels pour woes upon nature—the earth, the sea, the rivers, and the sun (16^{2-8}). With the fifth vial the doom of Rome begins (16^{10f}), and with the sixth that of the 'kings of the whole earth', special mention being made of the nations of the Parthian Empire (16^{12-16} cf.; En 56^{1-8}). The Euphrates is dried up that they may pass to the West (cf. 2 Es $13^{43f, 47}$). The armies gather at Har-Magedon—i.e. the Pass of Megiddo, often a critical point in the old struggles between the two empires on the Tigris-Euphrates and the Nile. Here *the nations* are left, not to reappear as the principal subject till 19^{19}. Under the 'seventh vial' (16^{17-21}), the writer leaves them to concentrate on 'Babylon the great' (Rome), who is now, with matchless *meiosis*, 'remembered in the sight of God'. She is figured as a 'beast' or 'brute' (13^1, etc.), like alien empires in other Apocalypses (e.g. Dn 7^3, En $90^{2, 9f}$; cf. 2 Es 11^1). The Seer turns aside for two chapters and more (17^1–19^{10}) to spend himself upon her fate. These recall and surpass Ezekiel's oracles against Tyre (27-29). Here what must almost be called the 'gusto' of the Seer's description reaches its height. This appears not least in the joy with which the martyrs, the 'altar' in heaven, the inhabitants of 'heaven' and the 'saints' and 'apostles' and 'prophets' all greet the righteous doom of the wicked (15^{2-4}, 16^7, 18^{20}). This joy culminates in the 'Hallelujah' of 'the great multitude in heaven' whose voice is the 'voice of many waters' (19^{1-6})—and the 'Hallelujah' is the prelude to 'the marriage supper of the Lamb' (19^7)! The horrors over which they rejoice need not be detailed here. It is very difficult to call this whole passage Christian.

It is possible that 19^{11}–20^6 is to be taken under the seventh vial (16^{17-21}), but, whether this is so or not, it is remarkable that, apart from the phrase 'the marriage supper of the Lamb' ($19^{7, 9}$), there has so far been no mention of the Vicegerent. All that has happened has its source in the 'smoke from the glory of God and of his power' that fills the opened 'temple of the tabernacle of the testimony in heaven' ($15^{5, 8}$)—i.e. 'the words of *God*' are being 'accomplished' (17^{17}). But with 20^{11-16} the Vicegerent takes charge. He has three names—He is 'Faithful and True' to his promise that He will vindicate the saints (cf. 6^{9-11}); He is 'the Word of God'—i.e. He is God's warrior, as in *Wisdom* 18^{15f}; He is 'King of Kings and Lord of Lords'. 'Heaven is opened' and He rides forth at the head of the armies of heaven, mounted on white horses, 'conquering and to conquer' (cf. 6^2). His 'garment is dipped in blood', for the Lamb is also a 'lion' (5^5). He comes to 'smite the *nations* and rule them with a rod of iron'. Against him 'the Brute and the kings of the earth'—who were left at Har-Magedon (16^{16})—muster their armies, but there is no real battle, for before the clash the carnage is sure (verses 17-19). Then the Brute and those that bear his name are 'cast alive into the lake of fire'; the rest of the alien armies are slain; and 'the dragon, the old serpent, which is the Devil and Satan' is bound in 'the abyss' (not 'hell') for a thousand years. In *Enoch*, similarly, the Fallen Angels are prisoned in a furnace in the Far West at the time of the Flood (En 18^{11-16}, 21^{1-6}), though their spirits sally forth from it (En 19^1). Next (Rev 20^{4-6}), the 'souls' of the martyrs return to earth, judge all who are left alive (for, while armies might be exterminated in an Eastern war, as in 19^{21}, peoples were not) and 'reign with Christ for a thousand years'. The martyrs share Christ's rule, as the 'saints' in Daniel share the rule of 'the one like unto a son of man' (Dn $7^{14, 27}$; cf. Rev. 11^{15}, 22^5). But over whom do they rule? The natural answer is 'over the wicked'. This means that in the millennium there are still wicked people in the world. Yet this is not certain, for the Greek word for 'reign' (*basileuein*) can be used of the 'reign' of the saints in a world where *all* are saints (Rev. 22^5; cf. 2 Ti 2^{11f}), the word apparently meaning that they will 'do what they will, as a king does'. Their 'service is perfect freedom' (cf. verse 3). After the millennium Satan is loosed, deceives 'Gog and Magog'—i.e. the barbarians beyond civilization in 'the four corners of the earth' (cf. Ezk 38 and 39)—and leads them in the very last war. This seems to complete the story of Har-Magedon, for they assault 'the beloved city', Jerusalem. Again there is no real battle, for 'fire' just falls upon them from heaven and 'devours them' (cf. 2 Es 13^{9-11}). Then the Devil and these, his last myrmidons, are flung into 'the lake of fire' and 'tormented for ever' (cf. En 91^{15}). Finally, the 'great white throne' of the unnamed God appears on earth; all the dead, good and bad, rise to judgement; there is no more 'death' or 'Hades'; the 'lake of fire' more than does their worst work. But, it is taken for granted, there remain those whose names are 'written in the Book of Life'. For them there is forthwith a 'new heaven and a new earth' (21^1).

In this account of Judgement the Vicegerent, of course, is Christ and the saints are His faithful followers, but otherwise there is hardly anything that cannot be paralleled, more or less exactly, in the Jewish Apocalyptic writers. A few examples have been given above in references to Jewish books. The Seer uses the same Apocalyptic apparatus, if the phrase may be used, as they do. Like each of them he uses it in his own way, but it comes from a kind of common stock, as with the 'properties' of a theatre. Was the Seer a Jew who had become a Christian and who was ready to lay down his life for his new faith, but who, none the less, had not altogether 'cast out the old leaven'? Perhaps the delay in the admission of his book to the Canon is significant here.

Under the *Gospel and Epistles of John* the latter may be taken first. In them there is only one example of the use of a term within the group under *krinein* and its cognates. If Christians 'love' as they ought to 'love', they will 'have boldness in the day of judgement' because 'in this world' they are 'as (Christ) is' (1 Jn 4^{17}). Like the solitary reference to the Parousia, where the word 'boldness' also occurs (1 Jn 2^{28}), this text shows that 'John', or at any rate the Christians of his school, shared the beliefs of other Christians about the Future. Whether John 5^{28f} is an intrusion or not, its phrase 'the resurrection of judgement' may be added here. Everywhere else the Fourth Gospel describes a *present* 'judgement' —'*Now* is the judgement of this world: *now* shall the prince of this world (a phrase that links with Apocalyptic) be cast outside (it)' (Jn 12^{31}). The text illustrates this writer's own type of 'realized eschatology'. The ruling idea emerges first in 3^{17-21}. There is no 'condemnation' (*krinein*) for the 'believer', but the disbeliever has already been 'condemned'. The writer's favourite figure explains why. The 'believer' sees 'the light of the world' in the Son and seeks it; the disbeliever sees the same 'light', and, 'hating' it, turns to 'the darkness' that he 'loves'. While God 'sent not the Son into the world to condemn the world', disbelievers 'condemn' themselves. The same ideas appear in two other passages (9^{39}, 12^{46-8}). Those who will not 'see', refusing the light, blind themselves. Persistently to refuse to use the Opportunity of Opportunities, which is Christ, is gradually to lose the capacity to use it. To 'behold' Jesus is to 'behold' God, and to 'refuse' Jesus means 'condemnation at the last day' (another Apocalyptic phrase). All this only expounds Synoptic teaching (e.g. Mt 10^{14f}, 11^{20-4}). As in the three earlier Gospels there is the appeal to Isaiah 6^{10} (Jn 12^{39f}). God 'blinds' disbelievers because He has decreed that they shall blind themselves. Sometimes 'the Son' is said not to 'judge', and sometimes to do so, but this is no more than a verbal contradiction, for it only illustrates the truth that 'the Son can do nothing of himself, but (only) what he seeth the Father doing' (5^{19}). In Judgement, as elsewhere, the Son is vicegerent. The climax of this Gospel comes when the disbelievers 'lift up' the Son of Man on the cross, thereby 'lifting him up' to the throne (12^{32}, etc.) Here, as elsewhere, the Paraclete continues the work of Christ —'When he is come, he will convict the world ... of sin because they believe not on me, ... of judgement because the prince of this world hath been judged' (16^{8-11}). While 'John' was no doubt one of the Christians for whom some of the details in the Church's account of the Parousia, the 'last day', and the Last Judgement, were symbolic, he does not silently discard the belief in the event called the End, but it lays bare its spiritual basis. Here, while he had predecessors in Paul and the writer to the Hebrews, he is a consummator. The Fourth Gospel depicts a tragedy. In Shakespeare's tragedies *Macbeth* and *Lear* the two kings are judged already in the first Acts by what they are, but this does not preclude a fifth Act. The last Act is only sequel, yet it is climax. Through the story of Jesus and His contemporaries 'John' is preaching to his own contemporaries, and to them the relevant message is 'You are being judged *now* by what you do with Christ *now*'. Here too, all else is sequel, yet the sequel is climax. It will be seen that the doctrine of Judgement, not often preached today, runs right through the New Testament as well as the Old.

If the findings of the last chapter be included, the New Testament doctrine of Judgement may be summarized as follows— There is a continual Judgement going on all the time in the sense that men are being divided into 'good' and 'bad'; for those who die before the Parousia there is a final judgement at the moment of death, both for good men and bad, in the sense that all are then sentenced, the first to bliss and the second to woe; for those who are alive at the Parousia the final sentence falls when Christ comes.

CHAPTER EIGHTEEN

AFTER THE PAROUSIA: THE FUTURE OF THE WICKED

ON THIS sinister subject the writer of *Second Esdras* adds nothing to the two phrases 'the lake of torment' and 'the oven of Gehenna' (7^{36}), which have already been discussed. This is in marked contrast to his long account of the Intermediate State of the wicked (as of the righteous). It looks as if the latter were his own account, while he shared a common opinion about the 'lake' or 'oven'. It will be remembered that in this book the dead rise to join the living for the Judgement, and that most of the Jews and all the Gentiles are wicked. It may be mentioned that, so many are the myriads of the Gentiles, that the Day of Judgement, such a Day as has never been, lasts 'a week of years' (7^{37-44}). In this book, as in other Apocalypses and Prophets, there are terrible 'tokens' or 'signs' (with or without the word) that prelude the Judgement (5^{1-13}, 9^{1-3}; cf. Mk 13^4, Rev 6^{1-8}, etc.).

In the *Book of Enoch*, on the other hand, very much is said about the ultimate fate of the wicked. While the general concept does not differ from that of *Second Esdras*, probably some of the details were peculiar to the Enochic school. The book opens with a Prelude (Chh. 1-5), which describes, particularly in Chapters 1 and 5, the main purpose of the whole book. Speaking of the men who 'will be living in the day of tribulation'—i.e. in the real writer's own time—'Enoch' divides them into two classes, 'the elect and righteous' and 'the wicked and godless', and describes their different fates when the Judgement comes. He contrasts these under the pairs of terms 'perish' and 'live', 'execration' and 'joy', 'curse' and 'forgiveness'. Here *all* the righteous, on the one hand, and *all* the wicked, on the other, are taken together. This is not so in the rest of the book. There the *wicked* are taken in various classes according to the particular subject in hand—the Fallen Angels or 'Watchers', the Giants, 'the Kings and the Mighty' (who seem to be the rulers of the Gentile 'powers' from Noah to the Judgement, standing societarily for their peoples), the 'Seventy Shepherds' (the post-Exilic High Priests), the wicked Jews, and the Gentiles considered as individuals. These will be taken in order. It has been seen above that the writers of *Enoch*, taking it for granted that there will be Gentiles and Gentile nations in the world *after* the Judgement, teach that these will at length worship and serve the Lord. Here the fate of those who 'perish' *at* the Judgement is in question. While the various writers differ in a good many ways, the underlying ideas are broadly the same. *Journeys* describes a fire in the utmost West for the Fallen Angels—apparently farther West and worse than the fire of their Intermediate State—where they are 'imprisoned for ever' (En 21^{7-10}). In *Watchers* after 'seventy generations' (from Noah) these Angels are cast into the 'torment' of the 'prison' of an 'abyss of fire' (10^{12f}; cf. 14^{4f}). It is implied that their sons, the Giants, join them there (10^{11-15}). In *Dream-Visions* they pass at last to 'the place of condemnation' and are thrown into 'an abyss, full of fire and flaming, and full of pillars of fire' (90^{24}). Three words summarize the accounts—'prison', 'fire', 'everlasting'. *Parables* describes the final lot of the 'kings and the mighty' who are alive when the Judgement comes. 'They will perish', for 'their life is at an end' and 'on the day of their anguish and affliction' all 'trace' of them will be lost (38^{1-6}); laden with 'chains', they will be 'cast into the abyss of complete condemnation' and share the 'fire' that the Angels are preparing for the Watchers (53^3–54^5; cf. 52). *Dream-Visions* describes the fate of 'the seventy shepherds'. The good Angels 'bind' them and they join the Fallen Angels in the 'abyss, full of fire, and flaming, and full of pillars of fire' (90^{20-7}).

Under the fate of the wicked Jews, as has been stated, the writers tell their contemporaries what *their* fate will be, but no doubt they would have said the same, *mutatis mutandis*, to wicked Jews of other generations. Here a chapter in *Fragments* (98) is a good guide to the whole teaching. At long last the righteous will exult over their persecutors, for these will die a sudden death and their corpses will lie unburied; chief of all, their 'spirits' will be 'cast into the furnace of fire'. In *Parables*, being unable to 'look upon the face of the Holy', they will be 'driven from the face of the earth', and it would be good for them if 'they had never been born' (38^{1-6}). In *Dream-Visions* 'the blinded sheep'—the apostates who *will not* see—are cast, bodies and all, into a 'fiery abyss', which lies 'in the midst of the earth' (i.e. near Jerusalem) (90^{24-7}).

The fate of the Gentiles, considered as nations, has been described under 'the Kings and the Mighty', who stand for them.

The Gentiles are not often taken as individuals, for the book was not written for them, but in one of the *Fragments* (Chh. 99 and 100) there is an account of the fate both of Gentiles and wicked Jews 'in those days'. Here the former are described as 'they who worship stones and graven images . . . and worship impure spirits and demons . . .' (99$^{6-9}$). This describes *all* the Gentiles and describes them as *sinners*, for idolatry is the worst of sins. When the 'Day of Destruction' comes, they will flee in terror, even leaving their children behind (99^{4f}). In 99$^{10-16}$ the writer turns to the Jews, dividing them into the righteous and the wicked. In 100$^{1-9}$ the writer then describes the fate of all the wicked, Gentile and Jew. First they turn on one another in civil war, 'and the horse shall walk up to the breast in the blood of sinners'. Then the Angels will gather all the dead sinners from 'the secret places' of Sheol, and 'the most High will arise . . . to execute great judgement amongst sinners', meanwhile appointing 'guardian' Angels over the righteous, who will 'have nought to fear' after their 'long sleep'. But the 'day of strong anguish' will bring 'woe' to the sinners who have persecuted the righteous, for 'in blazing flames, burning worse than fire, shall ye burn'.

There are many other details under the subject of the fate of the various sorts of wicked men, for some of the writers give themselves to this subject with gusto, but enough, no doubt, has been said. It will be noticed that throughout all the various accounts, the concept of punishment by 'fire' is constant, and that, where this is located, it is placed in the far West or near Jerusalem, not in Hades. The whole account explains what the *Prelude* means by 'perish' and 'execration' and 'curse'.

In the New Testament, as in all the earlier Hebrew literature, whether canonical or not, a sharp distinction is made between the ultimate fate of the wicked and the righteous respectively. Apart from longer passages this expresses itself clearly in the use of certain contrasting terms. These are not Apocalyptic *per se*, though in use, as the context sometimes shows, they may take flavour or colour from the current Apocalypticism. Under the fate of the wicked most of the terms are rare, but they were all in common use at the time, as LXX and the Apocalypses show, and, just because they are used without explanation, they show what convictions were current in the Church. The first is 'Cursed' (*katarasthai*), which only occurs once, but then on the lips of the

Son of Man (Mt 25⁴¹; cf. He 6⁸). Probably *anathema* should be added, though this may refer to a 'curse' that falls in this life (e.g. Ro 9³, 1 Co 16²²). *Katathema* seems to be a synonym (Rev 22³; cf. Zec 14¹¹, LXX). Another of the terms is 'Woe' (*ouai*—*37*), a chief passage being in Luke's version of the Sermon on the Mount (Lk 6²⁴⁻⁶; cf. 11⁴²⁻⁷). As the phrase 'in that day' (verse 23) shows, Jesus is here speaking of the 'Woes' of the End, and, as the phrase 'Woe unto *you*' shows, He is addressing His contemporaries (where, for instance, the 'rich', as a class, rejected Him). In John's Apocalypse the word is used both of a series of three 'Woes' that precede and accompany the End (Rev 8¹³, 9¹², 11¹⁴), and of Rome in particular (18¹⁰,¹⁶,¹⁹). Another term is 'wrath', which usually renders both *orgē* (e.g. Lk 3⁷, 1 Th 1¹⁰, Ro 2⁵, Rev 6¹⁶ᶠ; cf. Jn 3³⁶), and its synonym *thumos*, though the latter is only relevant once outside the Apocalypse (Ro 2⁸, Rev 14¹⁹, 15¹, etc.). The word rendered 'vengeance' (*ekdikēsis*) means 'retribution' (e.g. 2 Th 1⁸, He 10³⁰). Two rare terms mean 'punishment', *kolasis* (Mt 25⁴⁶) and *timōria* (He 10²⁹). There are several where 'death' (*thanatos*) describes the final fate of the wicked (e.g. Ro 6²³, 8⁶, He 2¹⁴ᶠ, Ja 5²⁰, 1 Jn 3¹⁴)—clearly as a state, not an event that passes. The only relevant texts under *penthos* ('mourning') and *ponos* ('weary pain') are in the Apocalypse (Rev 18⁷ᶠ, 16¹⁰ᶠ). The most frequent terms are *apollunai* and its noun *apōleia*. Under the former there are relevant texts both under the rendering 'destroy' (e.g. Mt 10²⁸, Ja 4¹²), and, more frequently, 'perish' (e.g. Ro 2¹², 2 Co 2¹⁵, 2 P 3⁹, Jn 3¹⁶). For *apōleia*—better rendered by 'destruction' than 'perdition'— there are four examples (Mt 7¹³, Ph 3¹⁹, Rev 17⁸, Jn 17¹²; and for its synonym *olethros*, 2 Th 1⁹). What is left of the wicked is only the ruins of a man. As in LXX these two words denote 'ruin', not 'annihilation' (cf. Mk 2²², 1 Co 10⁹, Jn 11⁵⁰). There is a terrible account of this 'destruction' in Luke 20¹⁶⁻¹⁸. Here Jesus speaks of a 'stone' that falls upon a man and 'scatters him as dust', using the word found in Dn 2⁴⁴ (Theodotion) where the kingdom of God 'scatters' the pagan kingdoms, just as the stone 'made without hands' crushes the great Image into pieces as small as chaff. The seven texts where the adjective *aionios* is used in relevant texts may be added—it occurs three times with 'fire' (Mt 18⁸, 25⁴¹, Jude 7), and once each with 'sin' (Mk 3²⁹), 'punishment', 'destruction' (2 Th 1⁹), and 'judgement' (He 6²). There is nothing to suggest that it has any other meaning than in

LXX and in other New Testament passages—namely, that, as shown earlier, it means 'belonging to the (future) age', an 'age' that in the mind of all Jews was everlasting. Behind the whole series of terms there are two axioms, inherited from the Old Testament—first, that a wicked man, having chosen to sin and remain in sin, is responsible for his own doom; and, second, that God inflicts the doom or, to speak in a modern way, that He has so made the universe that for such a man the doom is inevitable. The whole series of terms is anticipated in such books as *Enoch*.

It will be seen that the phrases just examined describe the *state* of the wicked after the Judgement, but say nothing of the *place* to which they pass. In the Synoptic Gospels there are three accounts of place and state taken together. The first falls under the words 'Gehenna' and 'fire', which have already been noticed. The adjectives 'everlasting' and 'unquenchable' occur with 'fire' (e.g. Mt 25^{41}, Mk 9^{43}), and the latter is described as 'the furnace (*kaminos*) of fire' (Mt 13^{42}). Jesus and the Baptist say that fruitless trees are 'cast into the fire' (Lk 3^9, Mt 7^{19}); the former saying the same of 'tares' (Mt 13^{30}) and the latter of 'chaff' (Lk 3^{17}). Jesus speaks of 'the everlasting fire prepared for the devil and his angels' (Mt 25^{41}). This phrase, as has been shown, has parallels in *Enoch* (e.g. 21^{7-10}, 23^{1-4}). It implies that, while 'the devil and his angels' (of whom the 'demons' are the lowest grade) are busy on earth now, the place of their doom is already 'prepared' and after the Judgement they will plague the world no more. In all this there is nothing that cannot be paralleled in Jewish books, and, if the story of Dives and Lazarus be discounted, as suggested earlier, there is nothing to show whether the 'fire' is in Hades or on earth. On the whole, with *Enoch* and *Second Esdras* in view, the latter is the more likely.

As in Isaiah 24^{21f} and *Enoch*, the place to which the wicked pass is also called a 'prison' (*phulakē*), notably in the Parable of the Two Debtors (Mt 18^{23-35}). Here 'prison' is the destiny of the unforgiving, of whom Jesus speaks as severely as of 'stumbling-blocks'. As 'ten thousand talents' would equal more than 'a million of money', Jesus' hearers would know that a prisoned bond-man could never 'pay the last mite'. The last phrase also occurs in a Lucan Parable of 'prison' (12^{59}). In Matthew the jailors are called 'torturers' (*basanistēs*). The use of the word 'torment' or 'torture' in *Wisdom* and *Second Esdras* has been noted above. In the New Testament the word and its cognates are confined to the Synoptics (*7*) and the Apocalypse (*10*). Once it is a 'flame' that 'tortures' (Lk 16$^{23,\ 28}$), but among the Jews the usual 'torture' was by the scourge (e.g. Dt 25$^{1-3}$, 2 Co 11^{24}). It was so severe that *derein*, 'to flay', is the Greek word for it. Probably *dichotomein* ('to cut in two'—Lk 12^{46}), is a synonym, for sufferers by scourging have often said that the lash seems to do just this. This word appears in the Parable of the Faithful and Unfaithful Bondmen (Lk 12$^{42-8}$). Though the word 'prison' does not occur here, it seems to be implied that the Unfaithful Bondmen are sent to one. The jailors first scourge them and then their 'lot is appointed with the disbelievers.' The wilfully sinful are beaten with 'many stripes' and the culpably ignorant with 'few'.[1] Here all do not suffer alike but none escape the one 'appointed lot'. It would often happen that scourging, more or less severe, was the prelude to prison.

The third account falls under the phrase 'the wailing and gnashing of teeth'. It occurs, for instance, of those who are 'cast forth outside' when others gather at the feast of 'the kingdom of God' (Lk 13^{28}). There are five other examples, all in Matthew (8^{12}, 13^{50}, 22^{13}, 24^{51}, 25^{30}). In two of these the phrase 'the darkness outside' is added (22^{13}, 25^{30}). The words ring like a current phrase, which seems to be drawn, not from books, but from village life. In such a village as Nazareth most of the houses had only one room, as a saying of Jesus implies (Mt 5^{15}). When darkness fell, the family would gather around the one lamp in the one room. If a child were so persistently quarrelsome as to be an 'intolerable nuisance', the father would at last seize him, open the door, and thrust him into 'the darkness outside' with the dogs and the demons. In a one-roomed house, how else get rid of him? The lad would then 'wail' as only an Easterner can, and 'gnash his teeth' in fright and fury. Every village would know the sound. The phrase might be used with 'furnace of fire' (Mt 13^{50}), and, apparently, of prisoners (Mt 24^{51}). It does not, *per se*, require that punishment is everlasting.

If these three accounts are taken literally, it is not easy to harmonize them. Indeed, it seems clear that the second and third, if not wholly symbolic, contain symbolic elements. It may be so too with the first. But it cannot be denied that, if they are

---

[1] In *The Bible Doctrine of Sin* the writer has shown why he refers this text (with Lv 5^{17}, Nu 15$^{29-31}$) to *culpable* ignorance.

symbolic, they are symbols of a state as terrible as the symbols. It should be noted that, so far as they have been described above, there is nothing specifically Christian about them. Any Rabbi might have spoken similarly of 'fire' and 'prison' and 'the darkness outside'. The distinctive element appears in the word 'Depart *from me*', spoken by the Son of Man to those whose fate is 'the fire' (Mt 25^{41}). In the same way the Unfaithful Bondmen are 'scourged' and cast into prison because they have been unfaithful to the Householder, and the Householder is Jesus (Lk 12^{46}). It is the same with 'the unprofitable bondman' who is 'cast into the darkness outside' (Mt 25^{30}). Similarly, it is those who 'have eaten and drunk in his presence' upon whom the Householder 'shuts the door', saying 'I know not whence ye are; depart from me' (Lk 13$^{25-7}$), and it is the Bridegroom who tells the Foolish Virgins, when 'the door is shut', 'I know you not' (Mt 25$^{10-12}$). It is in the place given to Jesus that the accounts have their differentia. It is here, and here only, that the Synoptic evidence is distinctive. The rest is Jewish.

In the New Testament *Epistles* there is no mention of a place of punishment except in Jude and Second Peter. In both the immediate reference is to the fate of the Fallen Angels. The passages show the influence of the Enochic school. In Jude these Angels are 'being kept in everlasting (*aidios*) bonds (*desmos*) under darkness (*zophos*) unto the judgement of the great day' (Jude 6; cf. 13). There can be little doubt that this is also the place of 'everlasting fire' assigned to Sodom and Gomorrah (verse 7; cf. 23). In Second Peter this place is called 'Tartarus', and the phrase 'pits (*seiros*) of darkness' appears (2 P 2^4; cf. verse 17). There is no hint that the place is Hades. On the contrary, the texts harmonize with the descriptions of 'the fire in the West' in the Book of Enoch. They also repeat the teaching of *Weeks* that it is at the Great Judgement that the Fallen Angels will be finally judged. It does not follow, of course, that the two New Testament writers accepted every detail in Enoch—for instance, they may not have placed the 'fire' in the West. Both writers imply that wicked men will share the lot of these Angels under the phrase 'for whom the blackness of darkness hath been reserved for ever' (Jude 13, 2 P 2^{17}). It will be noticed that the three leading items in the description—'fire', 'darkness', and 'bonds' or 'prison'—are those found in the Synoptic Gospels, though in the latter 'darkness' does not seem to derive from the Jewish books.

In the *Apocalypse of John* the fate of the wicked after the second and universal resurrection is described in the words: 'But for the fearful, and unbelieving, and abominable, and murderers, and fornicators, and sorcerers, and idolaters, and all liars, their part shall be in the lake that burneth with fire and brimstone; which is the second death' (21^8). There can be little doubt that this description covers all sinners, and not only the vilest, for all the unconverted Gentiles were 'idolaters', and a parallel phrase runs: 'There shall in no wise enter into (the City) anything unclean ... but only they that are written in the Lamb's book of life' (21^{27}; cf. 22^{14f}). The phrase 'the lake that burneth with fire and brimstone' describes the crater of an active volcano. It is to be remembered that Vesuvius was active for several years before the final outburst of AD 79, and its crater would be perpetually boiling. This 'lake of fire' exists after the 'new heaven and new earth' appear (21^1). Earlier references give further particulars. It was no new 'lake', for into it the 'Beast' the 'false prophet' and 'Satan' were imprisoned during the Millennium, to be released again at its end 'for a little while' and then flung back into it 'for ever and ever' (19^{20}, $20^{1-3, 7-10}$). At the second Resurrection 'Death and Hades' were cast into it (20^{14})—i.e. the first death had gone, for the second had come. Clearly this is symbolic, and furnishes a good example of the way in which this writer ignores the difference between the literal and symbolic. Clearly, too, the 'lake' is not another name for 'Hades', for the latter is thrown into it. If certain texts are taken together it follows that the 'lake' may also be called 'the pit of the abyss' (9^{1f}, 19^{20}, 20^1). The first of these passages is the prelude of the 'First Woe' (9^{1-11})—that is, as the present writer thinks, the period of the Captivity. All this recalls the Enochic account of the Prison of the Fallen Angels, where the word 'abyss'—the *Tehom* or 'deep' which surrounds and underlies the earth—occurs once and again. In another passage, as soon as the Lamb appears on Mount Zion (14^1), all the living who bear 'the mark of the beast' are 'tormented' (*basanizein*) in His 'presence' with 'fire and brimstone ... and the smoke of their torment goeth up for ever and ever' (14^{10f}). Probably this does not mean that 'the pit of the abyss' is near Zion for in *Enoch* there is a passage which first describes the 'fiery abyss' into which the 'stars', or Fallen Angels, and the 'seventy shepherds' are

THE FUTURE OF THE WICKED   219

thrown, and then 'a *like* abyss' for the 'sheep' who will not see, which is near the Temple (90$^{24-6}$). It is all but certain, however, that the 'lake of fire' is somewhere on earth. The ruling terms in these passages—e.g. 'fire', 'prison', 'abyss', 'torment', 'for ever and ever'—are just those of *Enoch*.

As already indicated, there are no such descriptions in the Epistles of Paul, in James, in *Hebrews*, in *First Peter*, and in the Gospel and Epistles of John. It does not follow, of course, that the writers of these books repudiated Apocalyptic descriptions. Paul's phrase 'in flaming fire' (2 Th 1^8)—and possibly John's phrase 'they cast (fruitless branches) into the fire' (15^6)—suggest the opposite. None the less, as illustrated above, it is true that when these writers need to refer to the punishment of the wicked, they prefer such terms as 'retribution', 'death', and, in particular, 'destruction'—that is, terms that are not *per se* Apocalyptic, and that describe a *state* and not a place. It is the state that is the fundamental fact.

So far references to the Christian *differentia* have, as far as possible, been deliberately avoided. This has been done to show that, in the rest of the New Testament, as in the Synoptic Gospels, there is nothing *apart from Christ*, that is original in the teaching. The writers use ideas current among the Jews of the time. On this subject this means that in Apocalyptic passages they repeat ideas found in Jewish Apocalyptic rather than in the Old Testament. While here these books are like the Synoptic Gospels, at another point there is a difference. In the Synoptic Gospels the King-Judge or Householder-Judge not only judges the wicked but awards their punishment. This is not explicitly so in the other writings. There Christ is not said to allot punishment; so far as the words used go, it just comes. This is so even in the Apocalypse. There while 'the King of Kings, and Lord of Lords' (Rev 19^{16}) himself inflicts the terrible societary punishment on the sinful world before the millennium begins, under the judgement of individuals at the second Resurrection He is not named (Rev 21^8). This difference, of course, does not mean that the Church repudiated the teaching of its Lord, for the substance of the Synoptic Gospels was already the canon of the Church. While Christians believed both that punishment was the expression of 'the wrath' of God, and that it was the wicked man himself who 'treasured up for himself wrath in the Day of wrath' (Ro 2^5), it was the second belief that was the burden of their preaching. In particular, their message to disbelievers was that they would 'perish' because they 'thrust' the Gospel 'from (them) and judged (themselves) unworthy of everlasting life' (Ac 13[46]). The Apostolic writers, with the Old Testament behind them, took it for granted that sinners would be punished; their message was that God had found a way to save men from punishment. To reject His offer was to crown their sins—and, *ipso facto*, punishment would follow. The Apostolic Epistles were written to Christians and not addressed to sinners, but if their references to punishment may be taken to indicate the nature of their preaching to Gentile 'outsiders', it follows that it normally took the form 'Punishment is sure unless you believe in Christ. Therefore, believe!'

To this account of 'the Future of the Wicked' it needs to be added that they *lose* all the blessings which, as the next chapter shows, God gives to the Righteous. It is, of course, impossible to over-estimate this loss. None the less the negative word 'loss' is not a complete account of the New Testament teaching. 'Depart from me' is a negative phrase, but 'into everlasting punishment' is positive. There can be no doubt that Jesus' hearers would take it so, and He knew that they would. Similarly, when the Apostolic writers speak of 'the wrath of God', they do not mean something negative. Mere negation, indeed, implies extinction, and extinction is not a biblical concept. To the present writer it seems impossible, if the evidence is considered objectively, to deny that there is a doctrine of 'everlasting punishment' in the New Testament.

CHAPTER NINETEEN

AFTER THE PAROUSIA: THE FUTURE OF THE RIGHTEOUS

WHILE the *Book of Enoch* is a strange miscellany, there is no doubt what its final editors took to be its chief message. This is 'The Future Blessedness of the Righteous'. Its opening verse runs: 'The words of the *Blessing* of Enoch, wherewith he *blessed* the elect and righteous, who will be living in the Day of Tribulation, when all the wicked and godless are to be removed.' This, of course, means that 'Enoch' declared how *God* would bless the righteous (cf. Dt 33^1). The ruling ideas in the concept of 'blessedness' may be illustrated by two quotations from the Prelude. When the 'Holy Great One' comes to judge, 'With the righteous he will make peace, And will protect the elect, And mercy shall be upon them. And they shall all belong unto God, And they shall be prospered, And they shall all be blessed. And he will help them all, And light shall appear unto them' (1^8); 'There shall be salvation unto them, a goodly light.... But for the elect there shall be light and grace and peace, And they shall inherit the earth. And then shall be bestowed upon the elect wisdom, And they shall all live and never again sin.... And the years of their joy shall be multiplied, In eternal gladness and peace, All the days of their life' (5$^{6-9}$). The whole just draws out the meaning of the Old Testament phrase: 'They shall be my people, And I will be their God.' Not only the items in the passages should be noted, but their perspective—the 'righteous' are loyal to God: therefore He is loyal to them; therefore theirs shall be perpetual 'joy in the Lord', and prosperity and peace. First the spiritual; then, as its inevitable accompaniment, the physical.

There are numerous parallel passages in other parts of the book, the lot of the righteous being set in contrast, as in the Prelude, with the lot of the wicked. Some passages add details, and examples of these may be given. In 10^{16}–11^2 there is a description of the 'planting of righteousness' in the earth, the word 'plant' being used literally as well as symbolically. 'All desirable trees shall be planted' in the 'whole earth', and each 'measure of seed' shall bear a thousand-fold, for God 'will open the store-chambers of blessing which are in the Heavens'. Then the righteous 'shall live till they beget thousands of children, And all the days of their youth and their old age shall they complete in peace'. Here, as apparently in the Prelude (5⁹), the righteous are not immortal, but elsewhere 'the days of their life shall be unending, And the days of the holy without number', for they live 'in the light of everlasting life' (58³,⁶). Here 'light' is used in a symbolic-*cum*-literal sense. It is both 'the light of the sun' and 'the light of uprightness'. In another text the righteous themselves 'shine as the lights of heaven' (104²). There are several passages that describe, not the 'whole earth', but its centre, the Temple. In this 'blessed place' there is a 'holy mountain' (26¹ᶠ), where 'the merciful bless the Lord of Glory . . . for (His) mercy' (27³ᶠ). The 'old house' is 'folded up' and taken away, and God 'brings' (probably from heaven) a 'new house greater and loftier than the first', in which the 'sheep' (the Israelites) and 'all the beasts' and 'birds' of prey (the converted Gentiles) 'assemble' until 'it holds them not' (90²⁸ᶠ,³³ᶠ). A later text runs: 'A house shall be built for the Great King in glory for evermore' (91¹³). As already noted, the 'fragrant tree' of life is to be 'transplanted to the holy place, the temple of the Lord', where, on a 'high mountain', there is 'the throne of God' when 'he shall come down to visit the earth with goodness', and 'the fruit (of the tree) shall be for food to the elect', its 'fragrance' passing into their 'bones' as they enter with joy 'into the holier place' (25³,⁵ᶠ). In such passages it is peculiarly clear that the future Paradise is *on earth*. There are also passages where there is a reference to the rule of the Vicegerent. In one the Elect One, sitting 'on the throne of glory', 'dwells among' the righteous (45³ᶠ), and in another God declares: 'I and my Son shall be united with them for ever' (105²). In the former there is also the detail that 'their places of rest shall be innumerable' (45³; cf. Jn 14²). In another passage, when the Elect One has 'chosen the righteous and holy' from among those who have risen from the dead, the 'mountains' and 'hills' leap with delight, and the faces of the angels light up with joy (51²,⁴; cf. Lk 15⁷). In another text the 'lot' of the righteous is 'abundantly beyond the lot of the living' (103³), and in another there is the interesting detail that new 'books' of faith and joy will be given to the righteous to guide their lives (104¹²ᶠ). In all the passages, even through the veil of translation and retranslation, there gleams delight. The delight, however, is in the retribution done on the wicked as well as in the blessings of the righteous. In practically all the passages the two themes mingle. There is, indeed, one passage where 'Enoch' cries to the wicked, 'Oh that mine eyes were waters that I might weep over you', but even here the dominant phrase is a passionate 'Woe unto you!' (95^{1-7}; cf. 97^6, 98^9, 99^1), and elsewhere the wicked in their doom are to be 'a spectacle for the righteous' that they may 'rejoice over them' (62^{12}; cf. 27^{3f}). One can only say that this is a 'natural feeling' at a time when the wicked flourish and have long been triumphing over the righteous (e.g. 97^{7-9}, 98^{11-15}, 99^{1f}).

In Second Esdras there are not very many references to 'The Future of the Righteous'. The phrase, 'The coming *saeculum* shall bring delight to few, but torment to many' (7^{47}), gives the reason. The writer's long argument is about the 'many', not the 'few'. Yet the passages are significant. There is a future 'reward' for the righteous (8^{33}), who 'shall see my salvation in my land' (9^8), for 'the world' is theirs and 'for them it (was created)' (9^{13}). For Esdras himself and the few like him 'paradise is opened, the tree of life is planted, the time to come is prepared, plenteousness is made ready, a *city* is builded, and rest is allowed, goodness is perfected, wisdom being perfect beforehand, the root (of evil) is sealed up . . . weakness is done away, death is hidden, hell and corruption are fled into forgetfulness, sorrows are passed away, and, in the end is shewed the treasure of immortality' (8^{51-4}; cf. 7^{113f}). Here the writer seems to imply that 'paradise', the intermediate home of the righteous, will descend to earth when the future *saeculum* begins. The writer's chief contribution to the present subjects falls under 'the city'. One passage runs 'the *bride* shall appear, even the city coming forth, and she shall be seen that now (exists but) is withdrawn from the earth' (7^{26}). The 'Vision of the Mourning Woman in the Open Field' (9^{26}–10^{54}) is an account of the true 'Sion, the mother of us all' (10^7). When the angel interprets it (10^{40-55}), it appears that the city has existed somewhere from the Creation, 'no offering being offered in her'. In Solomon's day she appeared in Jerusalem, but there her 'son', the Davidic line (cf. 2 S 7^{14}), typified as a 'bridegroom', dies, and Jerusalem is destroyed. Yet this is not the end of Sion. God will rebuild her in 'the brightness of glory and the comeliness of beauty', but this will be in the open field, where there is not even the foundation of a building—where, indeed, no *man* can build any lasting building. None the less, Esdras is not to fear, for *God* will build the true Sion (and Temple) with a 'beauty and greatness' that no human eye can fully compass. Probably Esdras does not mean that the site will be new, but that the present Jerusalem must become like a 'ploughed field' (Mic 3^{12}, Jer 26^{18}) before the Lord can build the true Sion on the old site. There is the same teaching under different symbols in the 'Vision of the Man from the Sea' (13^{1-50}). Here this vicegerent who is God's 'Son' (13^{32}), 'graves himself a great mountain' in some unseen region and 'flies up upon it' (13^{6f}) to conquer the nations. Then (13^{35}) he is to 'stand upon the top of the mount Sion, and Sion shall come and shall be shewed to all men, being prepared and builded, like as thou sawest the mountain graven without hands' (13^{35f})—i.e. made by God (cf. Dn 2^{34}) through His vicegerent. As always, the Temple and City go together, but while 'Enoch' says most about the Temple, 'Esdras' concentrates on the City. Under this subject the other Jewish books add little, but a passage in the *Testament of Dan* (5^{12}) about the New Jerusalem may be mentioned, and several references to 'everlasting life' in the *Psalms of Solomon* (e.g. $3^{14, 16}$).

There is evidence that in the time of Jesus this future state was commonly epitomized under the phrase 'The Kingdom of God'. For instance, one, 'sitting at meat' with Jesus, 'said unto him, Blessed is he that shall eat bread in the Kingdom of God' (Lk 14^{15}), and Joseph of Arimathea was one of those who were 'awaiting the Kingdom of God' (Mk 15^{43}). The cry of the crowds on Palm Sunday 'Blessed is the kingdom that cometh, (the kingdom) of our father David' (Mk 11^{10}) shows that both the belief and the phrase were common. Jesus Himself sanctioned the belief of the crowd, however vague and immature it was, for He had Himself arranged for the simple pageant (Mk 11^{1-6}), and He refused to 'rebuke' these very weak 'disciples' (Lk 19^{39f}). There are quite a number of other texts that imply that the phrase was current in an eschatological sense (e.g. Mk 14^{25}, Lk 1^{33}, 11^2, 12^{32}, 13^{28f}, 22^{29f}, 23^{42}, Mt $13^{41, 43}$, 20^{21}, 25^{34}). In this list there are no texts that may be brought under 'realized eschatology'—i.e. the idea that 'the kingdom' is both present and future. The Jews, Jesus Himself, and Christians, shared the belief that, when this Age is over, there will be another Age, the Age of the perfect Kingdom of God. The Christian *differentia*, as always, lies in the affirmation that it is Jesus who is Messiah. The difference that this made was, of course, very great, but, in the main, it involved completion, not contradiction. So far as the current Jewish concept went, its chief ingredients were that there is to be a Kingdom of God where all are righteous, that His Messiah will rule in it, and that it will be inaugurated by a 'feast' (cf. 2 Es 2^{38}). All these ideas were Christian too. Under the term *basileia* the primary idea is the *kingship* of God, as always, but the difference between this Age and the next lies in the character of those who are His *kingdom*. Now there are no rebels, but every man is enthusiastically loyal. Kingship over rebels is an imperfect kingship; it is only when every man does the will of God freely that even His kingship is perfect. Under *basileia* in this use there is a third idea. A perfect life requires a perfect environment. There must be 'a new heaven and a new earth', which is God's perfect 'kingdom' in what can only be called a geographical sense. God, men, the universe, are the three elements in the concept.

The texts named above are taken from the Synoptic Gospels. In the rest of the New Testament there are similar texts—notably Paul's words 'Then the end, when (Christ) shall deliver up the kingdom to God, even the Father' (1 Co 15^{24}; cf. 2 Ti 4$^{1, 18}$, 2 P 1^{11}), and the Seer's declaration, 'The kingdom of the *kosmos* is become (the kingdom) of our Lord and of his Christ' (Rev 11^{15}; cf. 12^{10})—but they are few. This is probably because Jesus' doctrine of the Kingdom was already well known in the churches and for their practical purposes there was no need to do more than refer to it. But there is another group of words that bears on the subject—the words 'heir' (*kleronomos*) and 'inherit' (*kleronomia*) and their cognates. The word 'inherit' occurs in the Synoptic Gospels, though only three times. In one (Mk 10^{17}) the Young Ruler asks 'What shall I do to *inherit eternal life?*', and the phrase is synonymous with 'enter into *the kingdom of God*' (Mk 10$^{25, 30}$). Clearly the idea that the future is an inheritance was current at the time. In Matthew 25^{34} the words 'inherit' and 'kingdom' occur together: '*Inherit the kingdom prepared for you from the foundation of the world.*' Jesus is 'the heir' and He shares His 'inheritance' with His 'brethren' (cf. Lk 20^{14}), for it is 'the meek' who 'inherit the earth' (Mt 5^5). With this background it is practically certain that, whenever the Apostolic writers use any of the words in the group they mean that Christians 'inherit *the kingdom*'. The word 'kingdom', indeed, appears in several of the passages (1 Co 6⁹ᶠ, 15⁵⁰, Gal 5²¹, Eph 5⁵, Col 1¹²ᶠ, Ja 2⁵).

Paul's doctrine of the Inheritance appears first in Galatians 3¹⁶⁻⁴⁷. Everything that he adds in later Epistles is implicit here. The argument of the passage is complex, but under 'inheritance' it may be summed in a few assertions—God gave a promise of an inheritance to Abraham and his seed; the true 'seed', and therefore the heir, is Christ; he shares His inheritance with those who, through His Spirit, become 'sons (and therefore 'heirs') of God'. In Romans the doctrine is summarized in the exultant phrases, 'If children, then heirs! Heirs of God! And joint-heirs with Christ!' (8¹⁷), and the 'inheritance' is 'the world (*kosmos*)' (4¹³). In Colossians, believers, having been 'translated into the kingdom of the Son of (God's) love', are 'meet to be partakers of the inheritance of the saints in light' (1¹²ᶠ; cf. Ac 20³², 26¹⁸). It is from Christ that Christians 'receive the recompense of the inheritance' (Col 3²⁴). In Ephesians, believers are themselves 'the inheritance' of God in Christ, the Spirit is 'an earnest' of their inheritance, and Gentile believers are 'joint-heirs' with Jewish (1¹¹,¹⁴,¹⁸, 3⁶). In Titus the 'inheritance' is defined as 'everlasting life' (3⁷). Paul's doctrine is trinitarian.

In the Epistle to the Hebrews, since the 'Son' is 'heir of all things' (1²), in Him an everlasting 'promise' of an inheritance stands 'immutable' to all 'men of faith', past and present (6¹⁷, 9¹⁵, 11⁷,⁹; cf. 4¹,⁹). For James those that love God are 'heirs of the kingdom' (Ja 2⁵); Peter, besides defining the 'inheritance' as 'indestructible, unspotted and unfading', reminds his readers that women are 'joint-heirs' of the grace of life' (1 P 1⁴, 3⁷), and for the Seer 'he that overcometh' is God's son and heir (Rev 21⁷). There are also four stern warnings against the loss of the Christian inheritance (Gal 5²¹, 1 Co 6⁹ᶠ, Eph 5⁵, He 12¹⁶ᶠ). The doctrine of Inheritance is almost ignored today, but for the first Christians there was thrill and glow in the word.

A discussion of some of the chief terms that describe the future *state* of the righteous follows, and then there is an account of the geographical concept of the future kingdom. Most of the terms that describe the future *state* describe an *experience*. It may be noted that, as the title of the chapter indicates, it is taken for granted that those who 'inherit the kingdom' are *righteous*. With this word there go others—'holy' and 'pure' and 'perfect'.

The use and meaning of these words have been examined in *The Bible Doctrine of Man*. When describing the Future Kingdom the New Testament itself usually makes the same assumption. In it 'holiness' and its outcome 'righteousness' are prerequisites for entry into the Kingdom. It assumes that they continue through the Parousia and are consummated in it. For instance, Jude, asserting that Christ 'is able . . . to set (believers) before the presence of his glory without blemish' (verse 24), assumes that, if they are faithful, He will do so.

Under the passages that describe the *state* or experience of the righteous, a beginning, as with the wicked, may be made with Matthew's account of the Judgement. Here the phrase 'Come, ye blessed of my Father' stands over against 'Depart from me, ye cursed' (Mt 25[34, 41]). The former phrase, of course, introduces the Christian *differentia*. The Son of Man is the 'king' who uses the words, and, as the present writer thinks, at least from the story of Caesarea Philippi onward, the name 'Son of Man' stands for 'Jesus'. It is He who is God's vicegerent—that is, He and His 'Father' go together; when He says 'Come', all else follows. To be with Him is 'heaven'. This differentia will emerge once and again under various terms. It will be enough here to give typical illustrations from the various parts of the New Testament. 'The Son of Man . . . shall send forth the angels and he shall gather together his elect from the four winds' (Mk 13[26f]); '(The lord of those bondmen) shall gird himself, and shall make them sit down to meat, and shall come and serve them' (Lk 12[37]); 'So shall we ever be with the Lord' (1 Th 4[17]); 'Then shall ye also be manifested with him in glory' (Col 3[4]); 'Christ . . . shall appear a second time . . . to those that wait for him, unto salvation' (He 9[28]); 'To set you before the presence of his glory without blemish in exceeding joy' (Jude 24); 'The Lamb which is in the midst of the throne shall be their shepherd' (Rev 7[17]); 'Where I am, there shall also my servant be' (Jn 12[26]); 'We shall be like him, for we shall see him even as he is' (1 Jn 3[2]). The variety in expression only illustrates the wealth of the idea.

The Son of Man calls the righteous 'Ye *blessed* of my Father' (Mt 25[34]). The state of the redeemed is a state of 'Blessedness' or 'bliss'. There are two words, both in Hebrew and Greek, rendered by 'blessed'. This is unfortunate, for the words have distinct uses. In the Old Testament one word, *baruk*, is almost confined to God (e.g. Ex 18[10], Ps 28[6]), and the second, *ashrey*, almost to man (e.g. Ps 1¹). The first means 'blessed' and the second 'happy' as with the two Greek words, *eulogētos* and *makarios*. Here too the first is generally used for God and the second for man, but in the text quoted, *eulogēmenos*, a cognate of *eulogētos*, is used of *men*.[1] The righteous are 'the blessed of the Blest'. What this means appears fully in the Matthaean Beatitudes (5²⁻¹²). Here the word rendered 'blessed' is *makarios* ('happy'). As Luke's version shows, it is the opposite of 'woe'. Every Beatitude illustrates the one truth, 'He is happy who is blessed', and it is their latter parts, not the former, that define 'blessedness'. The 'blessed' are those whose is the Kingdom, who inherit the earth, and so on. All the Beatitudes are *diaparousian*—that is, they are Apocalyptic, but not only Apocalyptic. The word 'happy', of course, denotes 'joy'. The belief that in the Future Age there will be 'fulness of joy' has, of course, many other illustrations—e.g. in the thrill of the splendid Doxology of the Lamb (Rev 5¹¹⁻¹³). There are other examples in the feasts that follow the 'lord's' return in the Householder Parables and in the marriage-feast of the King Parables and of the Lamb (Rev 19⁷⁻⁹). They are 'happy' (*makarios*) who are bidden to it. The Future Kingdom is a happy kingdom.

In an early song, which describes the sending of Christ in Old Testament terms, the last words are 'to guide our feet into the way of *peace*' (Lk 1⁷⁹). It is true that in the New Testament the word 'peace' usually describes an element in the state of believers *now*, the sequence of thought being—peace with God in Christ, peace with oneself, peace with other believers (and, as far as possible now, peace with other men—Ro 12¹⁸). Yet the classical exposition of the complex but unitary concept is in Ephesians 2¹⁴⁻²², where all follows from the first words '(Christ) is our peace', and, as soon as it is examined, it is plainly *diaparousian*. Believers do not cease to be 'fellow-citizens' at the Parousia. On the contrary, it is then that the 'household of God' and the 'holy sanctuary' are perfected, and then that 'the peace of God that passeth all understanding' (Ph 4⁷) is both universal and consummate. There are other *diaparousian* passages (Lk 2¹⁴, Ac 10³⁶, Ro 2¹⁰, 8⁶, 14¹⁷, He 13²⁰, Jn 14²⁷, 16³³). In the Future Kingdom there is unbroken peace.

With 'peace' there goes 'rest'. Here the writer of *Hebrews* is chief expositor (4¹⁻¹¹). Snatching a promise out of the threat

---

[1] *Baruk* is applied to both God and men. *Eulogētos* is used of men as well as God in the LXX, but is never applied to men in the New Testament. [G.W.A.]

in the words 'They shall not enter into my rest' (*katapausis*) (Ps 95^{11}), he interprets '*my* rest' to mean God's 'rest' on the seventh day in the story of creation, a day that God had 'blessed' (Gn 2^{2f}), and, deducing that believers in Christ are to share God's own kind of 'rest', calls it a 'sabbath-keeping' (*sabbatismos*). The phrase, 'Let us give diligence to enter into that rest' (*katapausis*), shows that the writer is thinking of the future lot of the righteous. Christians have not been wrong when they have taken Jesus' own promise, 'And ye shall find rest (*anapausis*) unto your souls' (Mt 11^{29}), in a *diaparousian* way (cf. Rev 14^{13}).

Another of the terms that describe the future of the righteous is 'glory', *doxa*, a concept much neglected now. Its use and meaning in the Bible have been examined in *The Bible Doctrine of Man*. To summarize, 'glory' is the outward expression of true character, the 'spiritual' and 'physical' elements in it not being distinguished. It is used primarily of God; Christ shares it with Him; from Christ it passes to believers at the Parousia. It is the last use that is pertinent here. There are at least eighteen relevant passages, and more if the pertinent uses of its verb, *doxazein* ('to glorify'), are added. In Romans 2$^{4-10}$ Paul has the phrases 'glory and honour and indestructibility' and 'glory and honour and peace'. Elsewhere he writes of 'the obtaining of the glory of our Lord Jesus Christ' (2 Th 2^{14}), 'an everlasting weight of glory' (2 Co 4^{17}), 'the hope of the glory of God' (Ro 5^{2}), 'the liberty of the glory of the children of God' (Ro 8^{21}), 'the riches of the glory of his inheritance in the saints' (Eph 1^{18}), 'Christ in you, the hope of glory' (Col 1^{27}), and 'everlasting glory' (2 Ti 2^{10}). Evidently it is a word in which the Apostle exulted. Its physical side appears in his accounts of the resurrection body (1 Co 15^{43}, Ph 3^{21}). Similarly, the writer of *Hebrews* says that God is, through Christ, 'bringing many sons unto glory' (2^{10}), and Peter speaks of believers' 'praise and honour and glory at the revelation of Jesus Christ' (1 P 1^{7}), repeatedly contrasting their present 'sufferings' with their future 'glory' (1 P 1^{11}, 4^{13}, 5$^{1, 4, 10}$). In the Apocalypse, where the term is frequent for God and Christ, the 'holy city' has 'the glory of God', and the 'nations' and 'kings', now holy, 'bring their glory and honour' into it (Rev 21$^{11, 24, 26}$). As usual, John sums all up—'the glory which thou hast given me, I have given unto them' (17^{22}; cf. 13^{31f}, 17$^{5, 24}$). It is time that this word were something more than a hilarious interjection! The Future Kingdom glows with 'glory'.

There are other terms that describe the future of the righteous (e.g. Paul compares it to an athlete's 'prize' (*brabeion*) in 1 Co 9^{24}, Ph 3^{14}, Col 2^{18}), but only one more is examined here, the most important of all. This is the word *zoe* ('life'). In the phrase 'everlasting life' it obviously refers to the kind of life that belongs to the Coming Age, but, as will appear, the term 'life', when used alone, sometimes does so, and with it the corresponding verb 'live' (*zēn*).

The phrase 'everlasting life' is not frequent in the Synoptic Gospels. In Mark it is confined to the story of the Young Ruler (10$^{17-31}$). In Luke 'a certain lawyer' asks the same question as the Ruler (10^{25}), and Matthew closes the account of the Last Judgement with the words: 'But the righteous (shall go away) into everlasting life' (25^{46}). Two other passages use the word 'life' to mean 'everlasting life', setting it over against 'Gehenna' and 'destruction' (Mk 9$^{43, 45}$, Mt 7^{14}). The story of the Young Ruler brings out three significant features. First, his question 'What shall I do that I may inherit everlasting life?' shows that 'everlasting life' was a *current* phrase for the future of the righteous (Mk 10^{17}; cf. Dn 12^2, Lk 10^{25}, Ac 13^{46}). Next, the words 'inherit' and 'enter into' (Mt 19^{17}) show that the phrase here denotes something altogether *future*, not something that begins now and lasts always—i.e. the *diaparousian* use, which emerges in the later New Testament, was specifically Christian. Third, Jesus' words, 'One thing thou lackest . . . Come, *follow* me' (verse 21), relates 'everlasting life' to discipleship, as does the sequel to the story, where Jesus promises faithful disciples 'everlasting life' in the Coming Age (verse 29). Similarly, at the Last Judgement 'everlasting life' is the meed of those who have dealt well by the Son of Man in the persons of the 'least' of His 'brethren' (Mt 25$^{40, 46}$).

There are Synoptic passages where the verb 'to live' and the noun 'life' (without '*aionios*') denote 'everlasting life'. While these terms are now and then used in the New Testament to describe man's present life (e.g. Lk 16^{25}, 1 Co 15^{19}, Ja 4^{14}), far more often they denote the kind of life that is intrinsically everlasting. For instance, 'to enter into life' (Mk 9$^{43, 45}$) means to 'enter into everlasting life', and 'the way that leadeth unto life' means the 'way that leadeth unto everlasting life' (Mt 7^{14}). The phrases 'man shall not live by bread alone' (Lk 4^4), '(God) is not the God of the dead, but of the living' (Mk 12^{27}), and probably 'not in a man's abundance consisteth his life' (Lk 12^{15}), may be added.

They appear to describe a kind of 'life' that begins here but continues hereafter. Already in the Synoptics the doctrine of the future 'life' is not to be confined to the phrase 'everlasting life', and already the *diaparousian* use begins to emerge.

In the *Acts of the Apostles* the use of the term 'life' is rare (5), but there is a new situation. There are men now who are living a new kind of 'life' and know that they are. The regnant Christ, 'the Prince of Life' (Ac 3^{15}), has given them His Spirit, and this means that they are living a kind of life that, without further definition, may distinctively be called '*this* life' (5^{20}). It is 'given' to Gentiles as well as Jews, for the former, as well as the latter, receive the Spirit (11^{17f}). It is the 'everlasting life' of which the Jews had long talked (13$^{46, 48}$). Clearly it begins now but it is to be perfected at the Parousia. It is an instance of 'realized', but not of 'fully realized', 'eschatology'.

In the other New Testament books thirty-three of the relevant passages contain the phrase 'everlasting life'. With these the unique phrase 'an indissoluble life' (He 7^{16}) may be classed. The phrase 'everlasting life' is found nine times in the Pauline Epistles, seventeen times in the Gospel of John, six in the First Epistle of John, and once in Jude. These passages will be taken first, and then those where 'life' occurs without the adjective.

In four of the Pauline passages the phrase 'everlasting life' certainly denotes the *future* life only—i.e. it is not *diaparousian*. 'Everlasting life' is one of the future boons that Christians 'seek' (Ro 2^7); it is the harvest that they 'reap' (Gal 6^8); they 'hope' for it (Tit 1^2, 3^7). Here it is to be remembered that the *literal* meaning of '*aionios*' is 'belonging to the (coming) Age'. This is also the natural meaning of three other texts—'Grace reigns' in Christians 'unto (*eis*) everlasting life' (Ro 5^{21}); Christians 'believe *unto* everlasting life'; Paul bids Timothy to 'lay hold on everlasting life' (1 Ti 6^{12}; cf. verse 19). Jude's phrase too is '*unto* everlasting life' (verse 21). But in the remaining Pauline text God's 'free gift of everlasting life' is parallel to the phrase 'Ye *have* ... the *end*, everlasting life' (Ro 6^{22f}). This at least looks in the *diaparousian* direction.

In the two Johannine books, on the other hand, the *diaparousian* use is dominant. There are five texts where the believer is said to *have* everlasting life' (Jn 3^{36}, 5^{24}, 6$^{47, 54}$, 1 Jn 5^{13}) and one which implies that it 'abides in him' (1 Jn 3^{15}). In another the 'Jews' claim to 'have' it (Jn 5^{39}). In others the context probably implies the *diaparousia* concept—Jesus 'gives' His sheep 'everlasting life, and (so) they shall never perish' (Jn 10^{28}); the 'Son' 'gives' believers 'everlasting life', and this *is* 'to know' God and 'Jesus Christ' (Jn 17^{2f}); God 'gives' 'everlasting life' to the man who 'has the Son' (1 Jn 5^{11f}); in John 3^{15f} the phrases 'may have' and 'should not perish but have everlasting life' are interpreted in verse 36 where the phrase is '*hath* everlasting life'. Similarly the phrase 'hath everlasting life' in John 6^{47,54} interprets the phrases 'the meat which abideth unto everlasting life' (verse 27) and 'that he that believeth on (the Son) should have everlasting life' (verse 40). Of the remaining texts some do not bear upon the present subject (Jn 6^{68}, 12^{50}, 1 Jn 1^2, 5^{20}). In another the 'spring of water leaping up unto everlasting life' (Jn 4^{14}) admits of a *diaparousian* sense, though it does not require it. Apart from the phrase 'the resurrection of life' in the intrusion (Jn 5^{29}), there are three texts which may be put, though not certainly, on the other side—'He that reapeth . . . gathereth fruit unto life everlasting' (Jn 4^{36}); 'He that hateth his *psyche* in this world shall guard it unto life everlasting' (Jn 12^{25}); 'This is the promise which he promised us, life everlasting' (1 Jn 2^{25}). One Johannine text sums all: 'Because I live, ye shall live also' (Jn 14^{19}). Paul did not find it natural to call 'the life that (he) now (lived) in the flesh' 'everlasting' because of its imperfections; John took it for granted that it is intrinsically so, but added 'it is not yet made manifest what we shall be' (1 Jn 3^2). From one point of view the believer's 'life' now does not 'belong to the (coming) Age' (*aionios*), from another it does. The phrase in Hebrews 7^{16}, 'the power of an indissoluble (*akatalutos*) life' all but defines '*diaparousian*'.

There are very many passages to consider under the noun 'life' (unqualified by any adjective) and the verb 'to live'. This is not remarkable for the burden of the *kerugma* is the 'life that is really (*ontōs*) life' (1 Ti 6^{19}). In Paul there are about forty passages. There are a few that may be taken as referring either to the future life or to life, present and *parousian* (Ro 11^{15}, Ph 2^{16}, 2 Ti 1^{10}). Some others refer more or less certainly, to the future life (Ro 5^{10,17}, 2 Co 5^4, 13^4, Ph 4^3, 1 Th 5^{10}, 2 Ti 1^1). Yet others refer both to the present and the future—as in 'To me to live is Christ but to die is gain' (Ph 1^{21}), 'Your life is hid with Christ in God. When Christ, our life, shall be manifested . . .' (Col 3^{3f}); 'Having promise of the life that now is, and of that which is to come' (1 Ti 4^8). But more than half the Pauline texts refer to life, present and *diaparousian*. There are representative phrases in 'Justification of life' (Ro 5[17]), 'Walk in newness of life' (Ro 6[4]), 'The mind of the Spirit is life and peace' (Ro 8[6]), 'That the life of Jesus may be manifested in our body' (2 Co 4[10]). Under 'to live' there are instances in 'The righteous shall live by faith' (Ro 1[17]), 'Alive unto God in Christ Jesus' (Ro 6[11, 13]); 'Yet I live —no longer I, but Christ liveth in me' (Gal 2[20]); 'To live godly in Christ Jesus' (2 Ti 3[12]). For Paul the distinctively Christian kind of life is intrinsically *diaparousian*, even though this is not so, or hardly ever so, under his use of '*zoe aionios*'.

While it is notoriously impossible to define 'life' in any of its forms, the various *kinds* of 'life' may be distinguished. Paul has left no doubt about the *differentia* of the Christian kind. He relates it to Christ in an almost bewildering way. Christ has 'brought life and indestructibility to light through the gospel' (2 Ti 1[10]), and it is 'by (the Son's) life' that men are 'saved' (Ro 5[10]). Christ *is* the 'life' of Christians (Col 3[4]), and 'the life of Jesus is manifested' in their lives now (2 Co 4[10f]). To them 'to live is Christ' (Ph 1[21]); their life is 'life in Christ Jesus' (2 Ti 1[1]); they 'live godly (*eusebōs*) in Christ Jesus' (2 Ti 2[12]). Again, Christians 'live by the Spirit' (Gal 5[25]). This is the theme of Romans 8[3-17]. There is no room here to expound the wealth of the passage. The words 'life' and 'live' occur three times (verses 6, 10, 12), but behind the whole passage there lies the exultant conviction 'the Spirit is *life*'. Indeed, every text about 'the Spirit' might be quoted, for 'life' is part of the definition of 'spirit', whether in God or man. Finally, 'life in Christ' and 'life by the Spirit' both imply 'life in God'. Christians are no longer 'alienated from the life of God' (Eph 4[18]), for their 'life is hid with Christ in God' (Col 3[3]). The doctrine is trinitarian. It will be noticed that none of the texts just quoted contains the phrase '*everlasting* life'. The Christian life is qualitatively distinct under the *noun*, not the adjective. Where *aionios* occurs it is, as always, a quantitative word. 'Life in God' has a quality that is intrinsically everlasting.

Fundamentally John's teaching is the same as Paul's, but he has his own *nuances*. The chief of these, as already noted, is that he generally uses the phrase 'everlasting life' of the life of Christians *now*. In his Gospel and First Epistle there are twelve relevant texts under *zen* and twenty-five under *zoe* (unqualified), with twenty-three under *zoe aionios*. His starting-point is that already 'In the beginning' 'life' was 'in the *Word*' (Jn 1[1, 4]; cf. 8[12]). This text implies that there is a kind of 'life' that is intrinsically everlasting because of its distinctive quality. There are the texts that open with the words 'I am'—'I am the bread of life' (Jn 6$^{35, 48}$); 'I am the resurrection and the life' (with its *paranomasian* sequel —Jn 11^{25f}); 'I am the way, the truth, and the life' (Jn 14^6). The way to 'live' is to 'eat the flesh of the Son of Man and to drink his blood' (Jn 6^{53f}). The writer wrote his book that 'believing ye may have life in his name' (Jn 20^{31}). Similarly, the subject of the First Epistle is 'That which was from the beginning . . . concerning the Word of life . . . the everlasting (life), which was with the Father, and was manifested unto us' (1 Jn 1^{1f}). Toward the end of the Epistle the writer sums up his message once again—'The witness is this, that God gave unto us everlasting life, and this life is in his Son. He that hath the Son hath the life; he that hath not the Son of God hath not the life' (1 Jn 5^{11f}). The relation of the Spirit to 'life' is not often mentioned, but it is clear. In one text Jesus says 'It is the Spirit that maketh (men) to live (*zōopoiein*)', for 'the words that I have spoken unto you are spirit and (therefore) life' (Jn 6^{63}). The phrase 'to be born of water and the Spirit' describes the new kind of life (Jn 3^5), and in 1 John 2^{27} 'the anointing (*chrisma*)' that 'abideth in you' probably refers to the Spirit.

This introduces the word '*abide*' (*menein*), a term that implies 'love'. In the Gospel it is linked with the Spirit in '(The Father) shall give you another Paraclete that he may be with you for ever (a *diaparousian* phrase), the Spirit of truth . . . for he abideth with you and shall be in you' (Jn 14^{16f}). In the First Epistle the complementary phrase occurs: 'Hereby we know that we abide in him, and he in us, because he hath given us of His Spirit' (1 Jn 4^{13}). Christians 'abide in' Christ and He in them. The word is a favourite with John, there being sixteen relevant texts in the Gospel (ten in 15$^{4-10}$), sixteen in First John, and two in Second John. To 'abide in Christ' denotes an enduring and intimate 'fellowship' (cf. 1 Jn 1^{6f}), but it far surpasses even the enduring and intimate fellowship of home itself, for 'to abide *in*' far surpasses 'to abide *with*'. What it means may be experienced but not explained. With John 'abide' is an intensive alternative for 'live'. In the leading passage in the Gospel (Jn 15$^{1-10}$) the opening words 'I am the true vine' means 'I am the true life'. In this passage the phrase 'to abide in me' occurs five times (cf. 6^{56}), with the alternatives 'abide in the vine', and 'abide in my love'.

There are also the complementary phrases 'If I (abide) in him' and 'If my words abide in you' (cf. 5^{38}, 8^{31}). In the Epistles the phrase 'to abide in him' occurs seven times (e.g. 1 Jn 2^6, 3^6, 4^{13}). There are also the phrases 'abide in the Son and in the Father' (1 Jn 2^{24}), 'abide in the teaching' (2 Jn 9) 'abide in love' (1 Jn 4^{16}), and 'abide for ever' (1 Jn 2^{17}). The complementary truth appears under various words—the 'seed' of God 'abideth' in those 'begotten of God', as do 'the word of God' (1 Jn 2^{14}), the 'truth' (2 Jn 2), 'everlasting life' (1 Jn 3^{15}), and 'God' Himself (1 Jn 4$^{12, 15}$). The corresponding noun, *monē* (abode), appears twice (Jn 14$^{2, 23}$), in complementary ways. On the one hand Jesus and His Father will 'make (their) abode' with them that 'love' and are loved, and on the other Jesus 'goes to prepare' 'many abodes' for His many disciples. The Greek of 1 Maccabees 7^{38} seems to show that the noun was current for the 'abiding-places' of the righteous dead.[2] They pass into 'the Father's house' as soon as they die, but they do not cease to 'abide in God' at the Parousia. In this use the word 'abide', like 'live', is *per se diaparousian*. For 'live' there are culminant texts both in the Gospel and the First Epistle—'This is *life* everlasting that they should know thee, the only true God, and him whom thou didst send, Jesus Christ' (Jn 17^3), 'This is the true God and everlasting *life*' (1 Jn 5^{20}).

In First Peter there are five relevant passages under 'live'. For its writer Christians are already 'begotten of an indestructible seed' unto the 'living hope' of 'an indestructible inheritance' (1$^{3f, 23f}$, cf. 3^7). Alternatively they are 'living stones', who are 'being built up, a spiritual house' (2^5). In the *Apocalypse* there are twelve texts under 'life'—all but one (Rev 21^6) referring to the future, though without the adjective 'everlasting'. Two have the phrase 'the tree of life' (2^7, 22^2), and another 'the wreath of life' (2^{10}); three speak of 'the water of life' (7^{17}, 21^6, 22^1); and five either of 'the book of life' (3^5, 17^8, 20$^{12, 15}$) or 'the Lamb's book of life' (13^8, 21^{27}). The writer of *Hebrews*, in addition to the phrase 'indissoluble life' (7^{16}), has the text 'my righteous one shall live by faith' (10^{38}), and teaches that those who 'submit to the Father of spirits' shall 'live' (12^9). In *James* there is the phrase 'the wreath of life' (1^{12}), and the writer of *Second Peter* speaks of

---

[2] Alternatively, *monē* in 1 Maccabees 7^{38} means 'continuance', 'tarrying', as often in the classics. 'Let them fall by the sword ... and give them not *continuance* (i.e. suffer them not to continue any longer).' [T.F.G.]

'all things that pertain unto life and godliness' (1³). There are, of course, many passages (e.g. under 'save' and 'salvation') where the word 'life' and 'live' do not occur, but which *imply* that there is a distinctively Christian kind of life and that this is everlasting. Every New Testament writer would agree that 'If in this life only we have hope in Christ, we are of all men most pitiable' (1 Co 15¹⁹). The New Testament itself *is* 'The Lamb's Book of Life'.

The *geographical* account of the Future Kingdom may be summed in two sentences—it includes *the universe*, and it centres in a *city*. The first belief is a corollary of monotheism. One God must rule all or He is not the one God. The 'universe' here, of course, is *this* universe. Neither in the Old Testament nor the Jewish Apocalypses nor the New Testament is there anywhere any concept either of a *'merely* spiritual universe' or of a future 'kingdom *in* heaven'. There is no need to say that the phrase 'the kingdom of heaven', or rather 'of the heavens' (Mt 21, Jn 1), is just a synonym for 'the kingdom of God', and does not mean that the future realm is situated 'above'. On the other hand, it is not quite accurate to say that it is 'on earth'—though it includes 'the earth' (Mt 5⁵) —for in the Bible the one universe is 'the heaven *and* the earth'. But, while the future universe is this universe, it may still be called a 'new universe', for it is this universe rid of all the imperfections that belong to the present one. There is no need here to discuss the question, 'Are there any passages where *basileia*, which normally means "kingship", is used to describe the geographical realm ruled?,' for in the New Testament there are four phrases that are undoubtedly names for the universe— 'the heaven(s) and the earth', the *kosmos* (which, unlike '*aion*', is rightly rendered 'world'), (*ta*) *panta* ('all things'), and *ktisis* ('creation')—and, as will appear, under all these there is a doctrine that at the Parousia there will be a new, or rather a renewed, universe.

In the Old Testament, as has been seen, this doctrine culminates in the phrase: 'Behold, I create new heavens and a new earth' (Isa 65¹⁷). The doctrine is not dealt with often or at large there because it is only a sequel to the doctrine of a new *mankind*, which is the architectonic doctrine. This is so also in *Enoch*, with an exception. The writer of *Luminaries* (En 72-82) spends his eleven chapters in describing the present motions of the heavenly bodies (with a warning that in the coming 'days of the sinners' much will go wrong with 'nature', even with the motions of the moon (Chh. 80). It is an exultant description, yet all the while the writer expects a 'new creation' (72^1), which will surpass the present universe in glory. Elsewhere there is the usual perspective. In *Weeks*, after the last Week 'the first heaven shall depart and pass away, And a new heaven shall appear', giving 'seven-fold light', for now men do not sin but there is 'goodness and righteousness for ever' (91^{16f}). Elsewhere this 'passing away' comes by 'transformation', for, *men* being 'transformed', the universe will be 'transformed' too in uninterrupted 'blessing' (45^{4f}, 90^{29}, 108^{11}). In *Second Esdras* after the 'seven days' of 'the old silence', God will 'renew the creation' in the sense that everything that is 'corrupt' or 'destructible' is gone, for righteousness has come—i.e. there is a new kind of *man* ($7^{31, 75, 113f}$). As for any further account of the new creation, the writer is content to say 'And then shall he show them (*his people*) many wonders' (13^{50}).

This is also the perspective of the New Testament, and not least of the Synoptic Gospels. Jesus' primary interest is in men, not in the universe. For the most part He just assumes that where there is the right kind of man God will give men the kind of environment that suits them. The perspective is well illustrated from the Beatitude, 'Happy are the meek, for (being the right kind of *man*) they shall inherit the *earth*' (Mt 5^5). Similarly, the earlier part of the Lord's Prayer, while it implies that there is still to be a universe, 'the heaven and the earth', is fundamentally a prayer that there may be a new kind of men—men who, like the angels, 'hallow' God's name, delight in loyalty to His kingship, and do His will. Other examples of this perspective appear below.

Two rare words that describe the passage to the new universe may be taken next. Both are used as current and well-understood terms. The first is '*palingenesia*' (Mt 19^{28}). Literally it denotes that the universe will 'again come to be (*ginesthai*)' what it was. It may be mentioned that, in the LXX version of the Story of Creation, '*ginesthai*' occurs again and again in a phrase that tolls through the chapter, '*kai egeneto houtōs*' ('and it was so'). Whatever Aramaic words Jesus used, it is to this story that '*palingenesia*' refers, and 'recreation' is a better rendering than 'regeneration'. Just as, in its only other instance, it means 'the changing of a bad man into a good one by 'renewal' (*anakainōsis*—Tit 3^5; cf. Ro 12^2), so in Matthew 19^{28} it means 'the changing of an evil world into a good one'. 'Recreation' is by 'renewal'. The saying, 'When they rise from the dead, they neither marry nor are given in marriage, but are as angels in heaven' (Mk 12^{25}), should be taken with *palingenesia*. As has been seen, 'resurrection' always includes the 'resurrection of the *body*' and it is through the body that man is linked with the universe and part of it. Here Jesus declares that sex, a blessing for the Present Age (Gn 1^{28}), will have no place in the next. At this point the new universe will differ from the old. As has been seen Paul drew out the underlying doctrine in his account of 'the body according to *pneuma*' (1 Co 15^{44}). There is no need to add that, as biology shows that without sex there would be no continuity of *any* kind of life in the present universe Jesus' saying has very far-reaching implications. To attempt to draw them out would be mere guess-work. Just as 'it is not yet made manifest what we shall be' (1 Jn 3^2), so it is not yet made manifest what the universe will be. The old universe, like the bodies of the saints, will be 'fashioned anew' (Ph 3^{21}), not photographed.

The second word is '*apokatastasis*' ('restoration') (Acts 3^{21}). This noun does not occur elsewhere in the New Testament, but its corresponding verb is used of the 'restoration' of the sick to health, of the restoration of a man to his friends, and, in texts more closely apposite, of Elijah's 'restoration of all things' and of the 'restoration of the kingdom to Israel' (Mk 3^5, He 13^{19}, Mk 9^{12}, Ac 1^6). In this word the emphasis is on the fact that the new universe is the ancient universe (however refashioned). The context illustrates the usual New Testament phenomenon. Peter, taking a current concept, puts it 'into subjection' to Jesus.

To turn to the relevant uses of the four names for the universe, a beginning may be made with the old Hebrew name, 'the heaven(s) and the earth'. In the New Testament there are some forty texts where the phrase occurs or is implied (e.g. in the phrase 'as in heaven, so on earth'—Mt 6^{10}). The great majority of these passages use the phrase for the *present* universe—as, for instance, when Jesus says 'Heaven and earth shall pass away' (Mk 13^{31}). Two writers, however, practically quote the Trito-Isaianic text: 'I create new heavens and a new earth' (Isa 65^{17}). The Seer writes, 'And I saw a new heaven and a new earth: for the first heaven and the first earth are passed away', and then expounds what he means by this (Rev 21$^{1-8}$). The prime novelty in this new universe is that now 'the tabernacle of God is with men, and he shall dwell with them, and they shall be his peoples, and God himself shall be with them, their God'—i.e. as the men of the new universe are holy God will dwell with them (cf. verses 26f). *Therefore* those 'first things', death and sorrow, are 'passed away', and God 'makes all things new'. The emphasis throughout the passage is on the word 'new'. Yet the Seer does not mean that the old universe has passed out of existence, as, strangely enough, the reference to 'the lake that burneth with fire and brimstone' shows, for this was a part of the old universe (20^{10}). There is a new kind of men, and therefore everything in the old universe that mars their happiness is gone. This means a new world indeed, for in it there is 'no more death or mourning or crying or pain', 'no more curse', 'no more night' (Rev 21^4, $22^{3, 5}$).[3]

The second quotation is in 2 Peter 3^{13}: 'According to his promise, we look for new heavens and a new earth, wherein dwelleth righteousness.' In the last phrase the writer defines the ground of the novelty. He has been describing (verses 10-12) the passing away of the old 'heavens and earth' in a mighty 'melting' by 'fervent heat'. Here he borrows as much as suits him from the notion, current through the Stoics, that one Age passes into the next by conflagration, and, in particular, that the present Age of Iron passes in this way into the Age of Gold. For Christians, for whom there was no recurrent cycle of Ages, as with the Stoics, but only two Ages, this was the one conflagration. But the Stoic doctrine was that the universe was *remade* by conflagrations, not destroyed. For Christians it is to be remade in 'righteousness'. There is a parallel passage in the *Sibylline Books* (Bk IV, lines 175-92; cf. Bk III, lines 83-90). Here the 'fervent heat' reduces the universe to 'sooty dust' but, none the less, when God 'quenches the fire', He remakes the 'bones and ashes' of men into bodies as before. Then the wicked pass to 'Tartarus and Gehenna' (cf. 2 P 2^4), and the 'godly' live again on earth in 'lovely and pleasant sunlight'. Other passages (Bk III, lines 702-31, 772-9) show that as in the old universe, so in the new one, there are cities and isles and mountains and so on. Once again a Christian writer takes current ideas and subdues them to 'our Lord and Saviour, Jesus Christ' (2 P $3^{2, 18}$). To quote one of a number of later examples, Aquinas did much the same with Aristotelianism.

---

[3] Earlier the Seer has said that 'earth and heaven flee away' when God appears on 'the great, white throne' (20^{11}). Literalistically this means that the Throne and the multitudes round it are left *in vacuo!* But such things do not worry a symbolist.

The words 'heaven' and 'earth' occur with the implication, as distinct from the assertion, that there will be a new universe, in at least three passages in Paul and one in *Hebrews*. In two of the Pauline instances the phrase 'the things in the heaven and the things upon the earth' occurs as a definition of 'all things', another name for the universe, discussed later (Eph 1[10], Col 1[20]). These 'things' are 'summed up' in Christ and 'reconciled' to God in Christ. The third passage runs: 'In the name of Jesus every knee shall bow, of (things) in heaven and (things) on earth and (things) under the earth' (Ph 2[10]). The three texts, *implying* that there is to be a new universe, *state* the ultimate ground of its newness, Christ. Similarly, the writer to the *Hebrews* (12[25-9]), quoting Haggai (2[6]), speaks first of a final 'shaking' and 'trembling' of both 'earth' and 'heaven', and then of a *basileia* 'that cannot be shaken', wherein Christians will 'offer service (*latreuein*) with reverence and awe'. The four passages offer a good illustration of the New Testament perspective. The true King rules over true men—and therefore, as there is hardly need to say, there will be such a universe as suits this *basileia*.

The next word, *kosmos* (*176*), means literally 'an ordered and comely world', but in the great majority of New Testament uses it denotes 'an ordered world that is now disordered'. John, with whom the word is specially common, both expresses and explains the idea in the text, 'He was in the *kosmos*, and the *kosmos* was made by him, and the *kosmos* knew him not' (Jn 1[10]). There are however, two classes of passages that refer to a future and true *kosmos*. First, there is the implication of the phrase '*this kosmos*'. Paul has the phrases, 'The fashion of this *kosmos* passeth away' (1 Co 7[31]; cf. 5[10]) and 'Ye walked according to the age of this *kosmos*' (Eph 2[2]), implying that in another Age there is another *kosmos* that does not pass away. In the Fourth Gospel there are five instances—e.g. 'He that hateth his psyche in this *kosmos*, keepeth it unto life everlasting' (12[25]), 'Now is the judgement of this *kosmos*; now shall the prince of this *kosmos* be cast out' (12[31]), 'My kingdom is not of this *kosmos*' (18[36]; cf. 8[23], 9[39]). Similarly in John's First Epistle: 'As he is, even so are we in this *kosmos*' (4[17]). All these texts clearly expect a better *kosmos*. Second, there are texts that refer to 'the world' as it was once and is to be again—good. Paul calls Abraham, 'the heir of the *kosmos*' (Ro 4[13]), declares that 'the *kosmos*' belongs to Christians (1 Co 3[22]), and uses the interpretative and triumphant phrase: 'God

THE FUTURE OF THE RIGHTEOUS 241

was in Christ, reconciling the *kosmos* unto himself' (2 Co 5^{19}; cf. Ro 11$^{11f.\ 15}$). There are similar texts in the Johannine books. In them Jesus is 'the saviour of the *kosmos*' (Jn 4^{42}; 1 Jn 4^{14}; cf. Jn 12^{47}); He has come to 'bear away the sin of the *kosmos*' (Jn 1^{29}); He is 'the atonement . . . for the sins of the whole *kosmos*' (1 Jn 2^{2}); it was because 'God so loved the *kosmos* that he sent his only begotten Son . . . that the *kosmos* should be saved through him' (Jn 3^{16f}; cf. 1 Jn 4^{9}). Even in Jesus' discourse and prayer at the Supper (Jn 13-17), where the term *kosmos* occurs in the bad sense thirty-nine times and 'the world' is the enfolding enemy, there are the phrases 'that the *kosmos* may believe' and 'that the *kosmos* may know' 'that thou didst send me' (Jn 17$^{21.\ 23}$). It will be seen that John sometimes means the 'world of men' by *kosmos* and sometimes 'the world of men and things', thus illustrating the New Testament perspective. To save the first is to save the second. Christ 'overcomes the *kosmos*' and its present 'prince' by drawing 'all *men*' unto Himself (Jn 16^{33}, 12^{31f}). So with the Seer. At the last 'the *basileia* of the *kosmos* becomes (the *basileia*) of our Lord and of his Christ' (Rev 11^{15}).

The next name, (*ta*) *panta* ('all things'), a synonym, for *kosmos* (e.g. Ac 17^{24}), is far the most frequent in Paul. Under the phrase the Christians shared two beliefs with the Jews. First, both believed that God created 'all things', upholds 'all things', and, as Paul's many prepositions show, is related to 'all things' in as many ways as a non-pantheist can admit (e.g. Ro 11^{36}, Eph 4^{6}, 1 Ti 6^{13}; cf. He 2^{10}). Second, there is to be a 'restoration of *all things*' (Ac 3^{21}), a phrase that presupposes that 'all things' are now far from what they should be. The Christians, under the usual tremendous *differentia*, claimed that the Father had 'delivered all things' unto His vicegerent, Jesus (Mt 11^{27}), both as creator, as upholder and in all other ways. Paul relates 'all things' to Christ under many prepositions, as when he relates the universe to God (e.g. Col 1^{15}). John has passages that recall Matthew's phrase (Jn 3^{35}, 13^{3}), as well as the text 'All things were made by him' (Jn 1^{3}). The writer of Hebrews includes the significant phrase '*heir* of all things' (1^{2f}). Under these phrases and others like them the Apostolic writers refer to two things, both relating directly to the period from the Ascension to the Parousia, and only indirectly to the Future Universe. The first of these is the salvation of believers. For example, Paul, writing that God 'summed up (*anakephalaioun*) all things in Christ' 'unto a dispensation of the fulness of the times (*kairos*)' (Eph 1^{10}), devotes the rest of a long paragraph to a description of the salvation of believers now (Eph 1$^{3-14}$). Similarly, the writer of *Hebrews*, quotes from Psalm 8 a passage that ends with the words 'Thou didst set all things (*hupotassein*) under his feet', and speaks of God as 'Him from whom are all things and through whom are all things' (He 2$^{8, 10}$) in a passage whose subject is 'the author (*archēgos*) of (men's) salvation' *now* (2$^{5-18}$). None the less here he is 'speaking of the coming world (*oikoumenē*)' and of the 'bringing of many sons unto glory' (verses 5, 10). In other words, while the immediate subject in these passages is Christ's use of His power over 'all things' to save men *now*, there is the implication that He will still control 'all things' in the Future Age.

Another long passage (Col 1$^{9-23}$), where Paul speaks of 'the church' (verse 18) as well as of individual believers, illustrates the same phenomenon. But here there is the phrase 'thrones or dominions or principalities or powers'. Under this phrase and similar ones Paul usually means 'the devil and his angels' (Mt 25^{41}). While the list of terms varies, 'principalities (*archē*) and powers (*exousia*)' are a constant element. Though some of the terms are abstract in form, they are all concrete in meaning. In the Colossian passage the Apostle, speaking of all angels, good and bad, declares that 'in (Christ)' and 'through (Christ)' and 'unto (Christ)' they were 'created' like everything else. They were made to be God's agents in the rule of the universe. But, as, for instance, in *Enoch*, multitudes of these persons, for they *are* persons, have rebelled and become the *fons et origo* of the vast disorder of the universe. Christ won the decisive victory over them when He died and rose again (Col 2^{15}), leading their 'captivity captive' (Eph 4^{8})—but, as in many of the wars of history, the enemy struggles for a while after the decisive victory (cf. He 2^{8}). Christians share in the struggle against them, but, if they 'put on the panoply of God' they will 'beat (them) all down and stand' (Eph 6$^{10-13}$). While these passages refer to the period between the Ascension and the Parousia, it is impossible to miss an overtone which the writer of Hebrews puts into words when he says that Christ is 'expecting' (*ekdechesthai*) as a foregone conclusion that his 'enemies' will be 'set down (as) the footstool of his feet' (He 10^{13}). Here, of course, he is referring to a text from the Psalms (110^{1}) which the New Testament writers, led by Jesus, often quote, in whole or in part, to describe the sovereignty of the Ascended

Christ (e.g. Mk 12^{36}, Ac 2^{34f}, Eph 1^{22}, He 2^8, 1 P 3^{22}). To the modern reader, academically wondering whether there are any devils at all, Paul's preoccupation with the 'principalities and powers', like *Enoch's* with the Fallen Angels, seems strange, but the Apostle believed that they are 'the world-rulers (*kosmokratōr*) of this darkness' (Eph 6^{12}; cf. 1 Jn 5^{19}), still active in the disorders, distractions and disasters of the universe. For Paul, as for his contemporaries, the universe is bedevilled—but Christ will deliver it from the bedevilment.

Paul has two passages that directly describe the new universe. In the first of these (*ta*) *panta* occurs seven times and Psalms 110 and 8 are both quoted (1 Co 15$^{23-8}$). The Apostle, since he is writing about the resurrection of Christ and the righteous, includes 'death' under the 'principalities and authorities', as the Rabbis did. At the Parousia there 'cometh the end', when Christ, having 'brought these enemies to helplessness (*katargein*)', crushing their remnant of resistance, will render up the perfected *basileia* to God, Himself triumphantly submitting at its head, for it was the will of God (*dei*) that He should rule as king (*basileuein*) until He had 'put all his enemies under his feet'. When He has accomplished His mission, God will, as in the beginning, be 'all in all'. The Seer has an epitomizing phrase: 'He that sitteth upon the throne' says 'Behold, I make all things new' (Rev 21^5).

The second Pauline passage falls under the fourth name for the universe, *ktisis* ('creation') (Ro 8$^{19-22}$). The passage completes a doctrine whose other ingredients appear in other epistles. The fundamental concept appears in the description of Christ as 'the first-born (*prōtotokos*) among many brethren' (Ro 8^{29}) and 'the first-born from the dead' (Col 1^{18}; cf. Rev 1^5), for the latter clearly refers to something that happened to Christ, 'the first-born of all *creation*' (Col 1^{15}). As the writer of *Hebrews* puts it, at the Resurrection and Ascension God 'brought *again* the first-born into the world of men (*oikoumenē*)' (1^6). It follows that Paul thought of the '*body* of (Christ's) glory' (Ph 3^{21}) as the beginning of a 'new creation'. Next there comes the text, 'If any man be in Christ, there is a new creation' now (2 Co 5^{17})—new because the 'old things pass away' by 'becoming new'. But this 'new creation' is at present incomplete, for it does not include the body. Even those who 'have the first-fruits of the Spirit' 'groan within (themselves) waiting for the adoption, the redemption of (their) body' (Ro 8^{23}). For them there is a 'glory that is (yet) to be revealed'

(Ro 8^{18}). This leads to the relevant passage (verses 19-22). This 'glory' includes a new creation, which will come by a birth from the old creation. In 'earnest expectation' the latter, having been by God's will 'set under (*hypotassein*) vanity' until now, expects to be 'delivered from the bondage of destruction' and to share in 'the liberty of the glory of the children of God'. Meanwhile the 'whole creation groaneth and travaileth in pain together'. Under this phrase Paul seems to have in mind a passage in Trito-Isaiah (Isa 66^{8f}), where the Prophet declares that a new city is coming to birth by the agony of travail of the old city—the underlying idea being: 'If there is no travail, there is no birth; but in *this* travail God will see to it that there is a happy birth.' The order of Paul's thought, as the Christian perspective requires, is—The new creation is 'summed up' in Christ's 'body of glory' at the Ascension; among men it *begins* now spiritually in those who are 'in Christ'—and who are therefore, as James puts it, 'a kind of firstfruits of (God's) creatures (*ktisma*)' (1^{18}); for them it will be *completed* at the Parousia when their bodies become like Christ's (cf. 1 Co $15^{20, 23}$); then God will create a new universe out of the old one to be a fit home for the 'men of his good pleasure'.

The second geographical term, '*city*', is complementary to the first, for, from the rise of Assyria onward, there was a series of 'city empires', culminating in Rome. In this series the capital city not only ruled an empire but epitomized it. Further, in some instances at any rate, the city centred in a temple. A Roman general, for instance, celebrated his triumph at the temple of Jupiter Capitolinus. In their beliefs about the future the Jews put Jerusalem in the place of Rome—and more. Jerusalem was the city of the one God and therefore it was the inevitable capital of His future empire. But the future city would be far different from the present one. It would be the Jerusalem 'that now is' purged and perfected. Alternatively, it would be a New Jerusalem that God would establish on the old site. The site, of course, was Zion, the 'holy mountain', and the city lay around a 'temple' built on the mountain. Where any one of these terms, 'city' and 'mountain' and 'temple', occurs in Jewish books, the other two are usually implied.

In *Enoch* there are two principal passages. The first is in *Journeys* (En 24-27). Only relevant points need be named. In Ch. 24 the writer describes a mountain and a tree, amid others, which is *now* in a remote and unnamed part of the earth. The mountain 'resembles the seat of a throne' and the tree has 'a fragrance beyond all fragrance' (verses 3f). In Chapter 25 Michael explains that the mountain is 'the throne' whereon God 'will sit' *at the End* when He shall come down to visit the earth 'with goodness and the tree is the Tree of Life, whose fruit shall be for food to the elect'. It (and apparently the throne with it), is to be 'transplanted to the holy place, the temple of the Lord', where 'its fragrance being in their bones', they shall 'rejoice' and 'no sorrow or plague or torment or calamity shall touch them'. In Chapter 26 Enoch journeys from this unnamed place to 'the middle of the earth', where there is a 'blessed place' and a 'holy mountain'. This is Jerusalem, which was 'in the middle' of the then-known world (cf. Isa 19^{24}). Apparently this is the present Jerusalem, yet it has two marks of the future Jerusalem—a river flows from 'underneath the mountain' (En 26^2; cf. Ezk 47^{1-12}) and the 'blessed land is entirely filled with trees' (27^1). There can be little doubt that the present Jerusalem is the site to which the throne of Chapter 25 and the Tree of Life are to move at the End.

The second passage closes the last of the *Dream-Visions* (En 90^{28-36}). Here 'a throne is erected in the pleasant land' (90^{20}), the Judgement follows, and then (verses 28f) 'the old house' is 'folded up' and stored away. In its place God 'brings a new house greater and loftier than the first' and 'sets it up' on the old site. Into this first the Jews (the 'sheep') flock. Later (verse 33) the submissive Gentiles (the 'beasts' and 'birds' of prey), now 'good', 'assemble' with them there, and the Lord 'rejoices'. It is God, not man, that builds the new temple.

In *Second Esdras* there is first the phrase 'the bride shall appear, even the city coming forth, and she shall be seen that now is withdrawn from the earth' (7^{26}). This writer concentrates on the city rather than the temple. In two Visions he elaborates the theme. The first is the Vision of the 'Woman in the Field' (9^{26}–10^{56}), interpreted in 10^{40-56}. This might be called 'The Vision of the City' for the 'woman is Sion' (10^{44}). This city stands in a place where no man has laid 'a foundation' and where 'no man's building can stand' (10^{53f}). After it has stood for three millenniums (i.e. from the creation) Solomon builds *a* city, typified as the Woman's 'son', which perishes in 587 BC (10^{46-8}). But *the* City does not perish. It abides indestructible in its solitary place until its time comes. 'Suddenly' the mourning woman's face shines; she utters a 'cry that shakes the earth'; she is gone; and in her place there is 'a city builded with large foundations (10^{25-7}). Uriel bids Esdras gaze on its 'beauty and greatness . . . as much as (his) eyes be able to see' (10^{55}). The implication throughout is that God is the builder of *the* City. In the Vision of the Man from the Sea (13^{1-50}) there are the same ideas under different symbolism. In some far spot beyond Esdras' ken the Man 'graves for himself a great mountain and flies upon it' (verses 6f). Yet it is 'graven without hands' (verse 36)—that is, God has graven it through His vicegerent. The latter alights 'on mount Sion and (the new) Sion shall come, and shall be shewed to all men, being (already) prepared and builded' (verses 36f). At the End a new city, which God has long held in readiness, will stand on the old site. The belief in the New Jerusalem was current in Judaism when the New Testament writers wrote.

A passage in Paul shows that he shared this belief, Christianizing it. Writing to a church in a Roman colony, he says: '*Our Politeuma* (city-commonwealth) is in heaven, from whence also we await a Saviour' (Ph 3^{20}). The implication is that at the Parousia Christ will bring the *politeuma* with Him, for the Apostle goes on to say that Christ will then 'transform' the bodies of the waiting saints to suit their new environment. It looks as if the doctrine of the new commonwealth were a part of Paul's teaching, church by church. For Christians, and perhaps for some Jews, the City is at present 'in heaven', and not in some indeterminate place, as in *Enoch* and *Second Esdras*.

As several passages show, the writer of *Hebrews* too believed in a city, centring in a shrine, which is at present in heaven. He calls the shrine a 'tabernacle', not a temple, for he identifies it with the shrine whose 'pattern' was shown to Moses 'in the mount' (8^5). This is 'the true tabernacle, which the Lord pitched, not man'; it is 'the greater and more perfect tabernacle, not made with hands—that is to say, not of this creation' (8^2, $9^{11, 24}$). Of it the 'tabernacle' on earth is an imperfect 'copy and shadow', which belongs to this 'world' (*kosmikos*) (8^5, $9^{1, 23}$). In 12^{22-4}, as already seen, there is a description of the City and community now in heaven. It is this writer's account of the *politeuma*. Its name is 'Mount Zion, the city of the living God, the heavenly Jerusalem'. The Patriarchs—who lived 'in tents', dwellings with no foundations—were on pilgrimage to it, for it is 'the city that hath the foundations, whose architect and builder is God' (11⁹ᶠ; cf. Isa 28¹⁶). They sought a 'better and heavenly fatherland' (*patris*) whose 'city' God had 'prepared for them' (11¹⁶). Some of the phrases are those of Jewish Apocalyptic, and everything quoted so far might have been written by a Jew. The Christian element appears in the claim that *Christ* is the 'high priest' of the 'true tabernacle' (8¹ᶠ, 9²⁴), and it is in '*Jesus*' that the description of the *politeuma* culminates (12²⁴). It is true that the writer nowhere says that this city and shrine will descend to earth at the End, but a later phrase (13¹⁴) suggests that he (and his readers) took this current idea for granted. After referring to Jesus' crucifixion just outside the earthly Jerusalem, he writes, 'For we have not here a city that abides (i.e. the old perishable Jerusalem is not ours), but we seek for the one that is about to be (*mellōn*)', not 'the one that awaits us in heaven'. It would not be wrong to translate the last phrase by 'We seek for the coming city'. It is the centre of 'the coming (*mellon*) world' of men (2⁵).

In the *Apocalypse of John* there are passages about the present Jerusalem as well as about the new one. Its writer thinks of the former in two contrasting ways. In one passage (Rev 11¹⁻¹³) it is called both 'the holy city' and 'Sodom and Egypt' where Jesus 'was crucified' (verses 2, 8). In this passage it is 'trodden underfoot of the Gentiles' (cf. Lk 21²⁴); in it the 'beast from the abyss' (Rome) slays the 'two witnesses'; after their resurrection an earthquake shatters a 'tenth part of the city' and slays its thousands. None the less for the Seer and for other Christians (Mt 4⁵, 27⁵³; cf. Ac 21²³ᶠ), the present Jerusalem is still 'the holy city', as it had been for the Maccabees in an earlier desecration. Later the Seer calls it 'the beloved city' (20⁹; cf. Sir 24¹¹), and it is on 'mount Zion' that the Lamb takes his stand (14¹) *before* the New Jerusalem appears, just as the vicegerent does in 2 Esdras 13³⁵ᶠ. There can be little doubt that the Seer and his readers believed that the new City would stand on the site of the old. It was another current idea that could be taken for granted.

The *new* City is first mentioned in Revelation 3¹², where it has a 'sanctuary' (*naos*), and is called 'the city of my God, the new Jerusalem, which cometh down out of heaven from my God'. But on this subject the culminant passage is the description that ends the book (21¹–22⁵). Here the writer, like Trito-Isaiah (Isa 65¹⁷ᶠ), passes straight from the 'new heaven and the new earth' to its capital city (21¹ᶠ) and presently gives himself wholly to it (verses 9ff). He delights to accumulate its names, yet there is only one that has no Jewish antecedent. It is 'the holy city', 'new Jerusalem', 'the tabernacle of God' 'the bride'—*and* 'the Lamb's wife' ($21^{2f.\ 9}$; cf. 19^7, Eph 5^{25-7}). The name 'the Lamb' is, of course, the Christian *imprimatur*. On its 'foundations' there are the names of the twelve apostles of the Lamb' (21^{14}); 'the Lord God and the Lamb' are its 'temple' (21^{22}); 'the Lamb' is its 'lamp' (21^{23}); only those enter it whose names are 'written in the Lamb's book of life' (21^{27}); in its midst there is 'the throne of God and the Lamb' ($22^{1.\ 3}$). The long list of jewels denotes its bridal joy (21^{19f}; cf. 21^2), but *the* mark of the City is its holiness. This is depicted in symbol after symbol. The old Holy of Holies was a cube (1 K 6^{20}), the symbol of perfection; now the whole city is a cube (Rev 21^{16})—i.e. it is the new Holy of Holies. This is why there is 'no temple therein' (verse 22), for God and the Lamb are the temple and they are everywhere. In the old Temple, barrier after barrier parted people from God—first the Gentiles were shut out, then Jewish women, then Jewish men, then the Levites, then the priests—and, save once a year when the High Priest entered behind his shield of holy incense, the Holy One dwelt alone in the Holy of Holies. Now men throng about God for they too are holy. Again, every portal is 'one pearl' (21^{21})—i.e. only the pure may enter the city. Its very merchandise is holy, for nothing 'secular' (*koinos*) can enter its ever-open portals—and its merchandise is the merchandise of the world (21^{25-7}), as the merchandise of Rome, the Great Harlot, had been (18^{9-19}). In it God's 'bondmen' 'see his face' and bear 'his name', as is the prerogative of holy men, and their service is 'worship' (*latreuein*) (22^{3f}). This service is 'perfect freedom', for, as the Seer exults to conclude, 'they shall reign for ever and ever' (22^5). Other details might, of course, be mentioned—such as the river and its trees (22^{1f})—and the eating of 'the tree of life' as prelude to entry into the City ($22^{14,\ 19}$)—but, to use the Seer's own epitome, the City has 'the glory of God' (21^{11}).

This passage furnishes the culminant example of two recurrent phenomena. First, there is the intermingling of the literal and symbolic which is characteristic of Apocalyptic. The Seer certainly believed in a literal city, and probably, for instance, in a literal river and literal trees, but not that the walls of the City were literally 'twelve thousand furlongs' high (21^{16})! When he says that the City is a cube he is using a symbol for perfection, as already seen, but the perfection is factual, not merely ideal, and so with his other symbols. They are all symbols of the actual. Second, as already suggested, if the phrases about 'the Lamb' were omitted, there is nothing, even in this splendid passage, that might not have been written by a contemporary Jew of talent. Of course, for the Christian to omit the Lamb would have been like describing the universe without the sun. For him God and the Lamb went together and they are the sun of the City (21^{23}). None the less, the phenomenon noted raises the question: 'Is an Apocalyptic form of the Jewish kind essential to the Christian doctrine of the Future?' Perhaps the Fourth Gospel was a contemporary attempt to answer the question.

CHAPTER TWENTY

THE EVIDENCE FOR UNIVERSALISM

TODAY THE argument for Universalism, or the doctrine that at last every man will be saved, runs, to put it in its briefest form, 'If God is Love, He will not let any man perish at last—let alone suffer everlasting punishment'. This argument approaches the subject from the point of view of the individual, and is fundamentally humanitarian. It has been seen that it is very difficult to find it in the New Testament, and that, on the contrary, in its several parts there is a doctrine of everlasting punishment. None the less there are passages in the New Testament which require the doctrine that all men will be saved—but in these passages the approach is not from the side of the individual, but from that of the future universe. If the implied argument were put in brief, modern, and logical form, it would run: 'The new universe will be perfect; if any sinner survived *in* it, it would not be perfect; if he survived *outside* it, it would not be the universe, for, *ipso facto*, the universe includes everything. The concept of a perfect universe involves "Universalism".' It has already been seen that the Prophets and Apocalyptists all firmly believed that after the Day, God would make a new universe wherein every man would be holy, righteous and happy; indeed in the perspective of their thought God makes the perfect universe *for* perfect men and no others; yet, as will appear below, they did not draw the logical conclusion—'There will therefore be no sinners left, even, for instance, in Gehenna, for that too is part of the universe'. Here it is again to be remembered that these writers were not articulating a systematic theology, but dealing with some immediate and practical subject. None the less, in their writings there are passages which may be said to feel toward universalism. In the New Testament there are passages which are explicitly 'universalist' in the sense that they draw out the doctrine of a complete *universe*—and therefore *imply* 'universalism' in the modern sense— i.e. they imply the doctrine that *every man* will be saved at last. Yet even in the New Testament, there is no passage that faces the logically inevitable question: 'How then can there also be a doctrine of everlasting punishment?'

The antecedents of the doctrine in the Old Testament and Jewish Apocalypses may be briefly noted. In the later Old Testament period, when the Hebrews had risen to the belief that there is only one God, the idea that He will at last rule a submissive world was natural enough, for they lived under a series of huge empires and it was only necessary to extend the meaning of 'empire' to include the world. But the word 'submissive' is important, for all these empires were despotisms, and their rulers, while all supported by loyal armies, held conquered nations down by force. Most Old Testament passages that describe a future world-wide kingdom, ruled by God or a vicegerent, include this use of force (e.g. Isa 49^{22-6}, 60^{9-14}, Mic 7^{14-17}, Ps 2^{8f}, $72^{4,9}$). There are, however, a few passages where the concept of universal *loyalty* in a universal kingdom seems to be implied. Isaiah 2^{2-4} is one of them if, as is likely, the phrase 'many nations' means 'all nations'. In a companion passage (Isa 11^{1-10}) one verse teaches coercion and two others seem to deny its need (verses 4, 9f). The 'Servant Songs' seem to imply that *all* Gentiles will be 'saved' and loyal as well as all Jews (Isa 42^{6f}, 49^{6}). There are also passages that describe a future *Israel* where every Israelite is loyal to the LORD (e.g. Jer 31^{34}, Ezk 36^{27}, Jl 2^{28f}, Isa 60^{21}), and it may be claimed that, while the Prophets are here preaching to Israel, the *grounds* on which they base their forecast are intrinsically universal. Yet all this is no more than adumbration of universalism, not complete exposition. In particular, nothing is said under the question 'What about the wicked *dead*?' Considering the purpose of the Prophets' sermons, why should there be? Yet the concept that in the perfect kingdom everyone is *loyal*, and therefore there is no coercion, is integral to its perfection.

The belief that the one God, having long permitted (and controlled) the sway of alien empires, will at last overthrow them and set up His own universal and ultimate kingdom, is, of course, the axiom of the Apocalyptic literature. In Daniel, to take an example, for the 'Son of Man' and his loyal 'saints' there is the promise 'His kingdom is an everlasting kingdom, and all dominions shall serve and obey him' (Dn 7^{27}; cf. verse 14). Judging by the temper of the whole book, it is all but certain, however, that he exercises this universal sway over others than the 'saints' by coercion. This is the usual concept in Apocalypses. In *Second Esdras*, for instance, God judges the world after the Great Silence, appointing few to Paradise and many to Gehenna (2 Es 7$^{30\mathrm{f}}$). He now exercises universal sway—but, as the Angel says categorically, 'The Most High hath made this age for many, but the age to come for few' (8^1). The 'many' have no part in it. Is their Gehenna inside or outside the universal realm? It is certain that they are not lovingly loyal. Theirs is a realm of coercion. In *Enoch*, as has been seen, much space is given to exultant accounts of the ill habitats of the various evil beings—angels, giants, and men—in the Coming Age, yet, in various parts of the book there are texts that show that after the End there will be sinners outside those habitats who become loyal and righteous (En 10^{21f}, 48^5, 90^{37f}). In the last passage, as noted earlier, there is a direct assertion of the ultimate conversion of the Gentiles, for not only 'all the sheep (Jews) that have been destroyed and dispersed' assemble to worship the one God, but with them 'the (predatory) beasts of the field and birds of the heaven (the Gentiles)', and 'the Lord of the sheep rejoices with great joy'. In the *Testament of Levi* (18^9) and the *Testament of Naphtali* (8^{3f}) too the Gentiles are at last saved. These passages have, not wrongly, been called 'universalist', yet they deal only with the men (and nations) that are *alive* on the earth when the End comes; the fate of the unnumbered dead of the multitude of earlier generations is not within the 'universe of discourse'. It may be noted, on the other hand, that in the New Testament Apocalypse, the dead of the long past are named. At the Second Resurrection all 'the dead stand before the throne' and the wicked among them are 'cast into the lake of fire' (Rev 20$^{12, 15}$). Is this 'lake' within the universe or outside it? Similarly, while all who enter into the City are loyal, there are wicked men outside it (21$^{24-7}$; cf. 22^{15}). Yet the Seer writes: 'The kingdom of the *kosmos* is become the kingdom of our Lord and of his Christ' (11^{15}). Did he believe that in the perfect realm there was a place of everlasting punishment? Perhaps it may be said that Apocalyptists were apt to write as if the future habitat of the wicked were somehow outside the universe.

In the Synoptic Gospels Universalistic passages are rare. Indeed, there are only two. One, the former part of the Lord's Prayer, has already been named (Mt 6$^{9\mathrm{f}}$.) So long as any sinner, whether man or devil, remains, God's name is not being hallowed, His kingdom has not come, His will is not being done, 'as in heaven, so on earth'—and God has failed to answer His children's perennial prayer. It may indeed be said that the realm of 'everlasting fire, prepared for the devil and his angels', to which sinners go at last (Mt 25[41]), is not 'on earth' but 'under the earth'. To the present writer, however, the phrase 'heaven and earth' here presupposed is the whole universe, as elsewhere in Matthew (5[18], 11[25], 24[35]). The other passage is the Parable of the Leaven. It is a 'Parable of the Kingdom'. As has been seen, there are some eighteen such Parables which are also Parables of Judgement. In these Jesus 'individualizes', calling each man to choose for himself whether he will 'enter into' the Kingdom or not, and teaching that his choice on earth decides his fate in the Coming Age. But the Kingdom is, of course, a society, or rather, *the* Society, and at least three Parables—those of the Seed Growing Secretly, the Mustard Seed, and the Leaven (Mk 4[24-9], Mk 4[30-2], Lk 13[20f])—deal with it as a *whole*, without any reference to the individuals that belong to it. In the Parable of the Leaven, the last words are its burden, and they are 'the *whole* is leavened'. The woman's arduous kneading ends in complete success. This is universalism. To these two universalistic passages the term 'the regeneration' (Mt 19[28]) might perhaps be added. While it cannot be denied that in the Synoptists Jesus' emphasis is not on Universalism, but on the dread and final results of each man's present choice, yet Universalism is not absent.

Does Paul teach Universalism? There are passages where he does so, explicitly or implicitly. A beginning may be made with some verses in Romans 11. Here Paul expects that all men, both Jews and Gentiles, will be converted before the Parousia, for he writes that the 'fulness' (*plērōma*) of both will 'come in' (verses 12, 25). Here the Apostle does not merely mean that the great majority of men will be converted, for '*pleroma*' requires the meaning 'the whole', as its other examples show (e.g. Mk 2[21], Ro 13[10], Eph 1[23], Col 2[9]). In the same passage Paul has the word 'lump (of dough)' (*phurama*), perhaps recalling the Parable of the Leaven. There is also the phrase 'the reconciling (*katallagē*) of (the) kosmos' (verse 15). So long as there is sin or a sinner in the *kosmos*, the phrase is inadmissible. Similarly, Paul elsewhere speaks of God as 'reconciling the *kosmos* unto himself in Christ' (2 Co 5[19]) and 'reconciling all things unto himself through (Christ)' (Col 1²⁰), in both instances the context presenting this universal 'reconciliation' as forecast in the 'reconciliation' of believers to God. A like idea occurs in the promise that the *'creation (ktisis)'* is to enter into 'the liberty of the glory of the children of God' (Ro 8²¹). A similar idea appears when 'all things' are said to be 'summed up in Christ' (Eph 1¹⁰). As already shown, the word *panta* ('all things'), does not mean 'things as distinct from persons', but 'the universe, including persons'. The New Testament never isolates 'things'. It will be seen that all these texts, except the first, fall under two of the collective terms for 'the universe', *kosmos* and *panta*. It is possible that a Pauline writer went on to apply the concept to men individually in the texts 'God our Saviour, who willeth (*thelein*) that all men should be saved' and 'the living God, who is the Saviour of all men, most of all (*malista*) of them that believe' (1 Ti 2⁴, 4¹⁰), as though God's purpose of universal salvation were at present only partly accomplished. It will be noted that there is no pertinent text in the Epistles to the Thessalonians, usually counted Paul's earliest extant letters. This may be either because he had not yet reached a universalistic belief when he wrote them, or because one must not expect a reference to every doctrine in every Epistle.

There are four other passages where the Apostle seems to teach Universalism. In them Christ is complete master of the universe from the Ascension onward; until the Parousia He needs to exercise force over some of the beings within it; but when the End comes, it is either asserted or implied that this coercion will end, for everyone will be wholly loyal to the King. In other words, 'perfect kingdom' and 'perfect liberty' are correlative ideas. The first of these passages is 1 Corinthians 15²⁴⁻⁸. This culminates in the universalistic words 'that God may be all in all'. To this end Christ has rendered the 'principalities and authorities' helpless (*katargein*), and so 'put all things in subjection under his feet'. The term for 'put in subjection' is *hypotassein* (*33*), which has a derivative noun *hypotage* (*4*) ('subjection'). These words are used twenty-five times of the 'subjection' of *men* and in every case the idea is of a *'voluntary* subjection'. Indeed, 'submit' and 'submission' would here be better renderings (e.g. Lk 2⁵¹, Ro 13¹, 2 Cor 9¹³, Eph 5²¹ᶠ, 1 Ti 2¹¹, He 12⁹, 1 P 2¹³). It may be claimed, therefore, that in 1 Corinthians 15²⁴⁻⁸ Paul teaches that all *mankind* will be saved because every man will, before the Parousia, submit willingly to Christ. His old enemies, 'the principalities and authorities', who for Paul are the primary source of the repeated sins of men, are now helpless against men, and Christ, himself willingly submitting to God, hands over a perfect mankind to His Father. But what of the 'principalities and authorities'? Is it enough that they are helpless but still sinful? Is Christ 'delivering' a *perfect* 'kingdom' to God if any sinful beings of any sort survive? Today any question about the ultimate fate of evil spirits may seem superfluous because most Christians do not seriously believe that they exist at all, but, in a discussion of *Paul's* doctrine it is pertinent, for he believed firmly in the very active existence of 'the spiritual (hosts) of wickedness in the heavenly (realms)' (Eph 6^{12}). Indeed, he believed that the sinful 'principalities and authorities' are God's creatures just as much as sinful men (Col 1^{16}). It might be suggested that, at the End they too, like Christ their conqueror, 'submit' willingly to God (1 Co 15^{28}), but the passage neither says nor suggests this. 'Demons' submit unwillingly (Lk $10^{17, 20}$). In this passage the doctrines of God and of sin are at this point in unresolved conflict. The one demands universalism, the other denies it.

The same dilemma recurs in Ephesians 1^{20-3}. Here at the Ascension God 'puts all things', including the 'principalities and authorities', under Christ's feet for Christ 'filleth all in all'. But surely Christ does not 'fill' any *sinful* being, whether man or spirit. If, even in the interval between the Ascension (verse 20) and the Parousia, He 'fills all in all', there is no need for the Judgement. Yet it is certain that the Apostle believed in the Judgement. If, however, he means that *at the End* Christ will 'fill all in all', doing so recapitulatorily now (cf. 1^{10}), this is universalism. The third passage is Ephesians 4^{8-10}. Here Christ 'ascended far above all the heavens that he might fill all things'. This is parallel to Ephesians 1^{20-3}. The fourth passage is Philippians 2^{9-11}. Here the whole passage thrills with exultation in the Lordship of Christ (verse 11). God has 'exalted' Christ so that (at the End) 'in the name of Jesus every knee shall bow, of heavenly (beings), and earthly (beings), and (beings) under the earth, and every tongue confess that Jesus Christ is Lord, to the glory of God the Father'. The three kinds of beings are evidently an account of what Paul means by '*panta*'. In classical use *katachthonia* ('beings-under-the-earth') is used of the 'subterranean' gods, but in Paul it seems to describe the beings in Hades, who for him are the souls (*psyche*) of dead men. God puts every kind of being under the universal rule of Christ. Is this rule, while welcome to the good, coercive to the bad? It is possible to argue that the phrase 'confess (*exomologein*) that Jesus Christ is Lord' implies *willing* submission, for the fundamental meaning of the Greek word (which needs various renderings to suit the context) is 'agree' (Lk 22⁶), and this suits nine of the ten passages where the word occurs. For instance, Jesus rejoices to agree with the way of His Father and therefore 'praises (*homologein*)' Him. Praise implies agreement. In other texts men 'confess their sins' and repent—that is, agree that they are sinners and act accordingly (Mk 1⁵, Ac 19¹⁸, Ja 5¹⁶; cf. Ro 15⁹). But in the one passage where *homologein* denotes unwilling agreement (Ro 14¹¹), Paul quotes the same Old Testament text as in the passage under discussion (Ph 2¹¹). It is, therefore, possible that in the latter Paul means that Christ is at last Lord both of the willing righteous and the rebellious sinful. Yet this is unlikely, for this is not perfect lordship. Would Paul rejoice in it? Is it a lordship 'to the glory of God the Father'? The passage is probably universalist like the three others.[1]

In the remaining New Testament books, outside the Fourth Gospel, there are few texts that imply Universalism, but there are some. The writer to the Hebrews calls the Son 'the heir of *all things*' (1²). James speaks of Christians as 'a certain first-fruits of (God's) creatures' (1¹⁸), and the biblical meaning of 'first-fruits' is 'the part that represents *the whole*'. As already seen, the Seer of Patmos has the texts, 'The kingdom of the world is become that of our Lord and his Christ and he shall reign for ever and ever' (Rev 11¹⁵) and 'I saw a new heaven and a new earth' (Rev 11¹⁵, 21⁸). The writer of Second Peter expects God to fulfil His promise of 'new heavens and a new earth, wherein dwelleth righteousness' (2 P 3¹³).

In the Johannine Gospel and First Epistle the doctrine of Universalism takes the form that Christ 'saves' the present evil *kosmos*, with the implication that it thereby becomes a good one. The phrase 'the Saviour of the world' occurs twice (Jn 4⁴², 1 Jn 4¹⁴), and with it the phrases 'the Lamb of God which beareth away

---

[1] A further passage which should be noted is Col 1²⁰, which says that all things in heaven and earth are to be reconciled. [T.F.G.]

the sin of the world', 'I came, not to judge the world, but to save the world', 'He is the atonement for our sins, and not for ours only, but also for the whole world' (Jn 1^{29}, 12^{47}, 1 Jn 2^2). A text containing one of the few Apocalyptic phrases in this Gospel may be mentioned here—'Now is the judgement of this world: now shall the prince of this world be cast outside. And I, if I be lifted up from the earth, will draw all men unto myself' (Jn 12^{31f}). The devil is to be flung out of the universe. Logically, of course, this is a contradiction in terms, for nothing can be outside the universe. But if the phrase 'draw all men' means 'draw successfully', as is probable, the text at least means that all *men* will be saved and the *kosmos* with them. There remains one more passage (17$^{21, 23}$). Here Jesus prays both that His disciples 'may be one ... that the world may believe that thou didst send me' and 'that the *world* may know that thou didst send me'. In this rendering the verbs 'believe' and 'know' lack the full Johannine meaning. In English usage, a man may 'believe' and 'know' something that makes no difference to his life at all, but 'John' knows nothing of such a vain use of the words. In Jesus' prayer to *know* thee, the only true God, and him whom thou didst send, Jesus Christ' is 'life everlasting' (verse 3), and the disciples are those who '*know* that thou didst send me' (verse 25). Again, it is the disciples who have 'received' Jesus' words (cf. Mk 9^{37}), who '*know* of a truth that I came forth from thee', and who '*believe* that thou hast sent me' (verse 8). Clearly here there is no otiose 'knowledge' and 'belief'. Everywhere in the Fourth Gospel (and often outside it), the terms involve the idea of a life lived in accordance with the 'knowledge' and 'belief'. Outside the Prayer there are other texts where 'know' and 'believe' occur along with the word 'sent' as used of Jesus (6^{29}, 7^{28}, 11^{42}; cf. 8^{42}). There can be no doubt that when Jesus prayed 'that the world may believe and know that thou didst send me', He was asking that all men might become disciples. It is not irreverent to say that if the prayer was not answered the purpose of God 'in Jesus' was foiled. It is a universalist prayer, as is the other 'Lord's Prayer', and as all Christian prayer must be. Is Jesus' prayer only partly answered? Yet, over against these texts there lies the contrast between 'believers' and 'disbelievers' which, as has been shown, permeates the whole of the Fourth Gospel, and carries with it the teaching that the fate of inveterate 'disbelievers' is separation from Christ—'Whither *I* go, *ye* cannot come' (7^{34}); 'If ye believe not that I am (He), ye shall die in your sins' (8^{24}). In the Fourth Gospel, as in the Synoptics and the Epistles, the beliefs that the world will be saved and that disbelievers will 'perish' in ruin are held in unresolved tension. There is a Johannine passage where the two doctrines lie side by side without any hint that they conflict (Jn 3^{16-21}). Here, when it is said that God 'so loved the (sinful) world that he sent his only begotten Son that whosoever *believeth* on him should not perish but have everlasting life', it is implied that 'everlasting life' is not for disbelievers. Being 'judged already', they are left to 'perish'. On the other hand, 'God sent not his Son into the world to judge the world, but that the world should be saved through him', and surely He will at last save it.

In an earlier chapter it has been shown that the New Testament teaches everlasting punishment. On a review of the whole evidence, therefore, it follows that throughout that book there are two doctrines which to the human mind are irreconcilable, the doctrine of Universalism and the doctrine that there are those who will not be saved. Some further notes may be added. First, there is no hint that every man will be saved as soon as he dies. The salvation of all *men* is a part of the salvation of the *universe*, and this does not come till the End of the Age. This leaves room for the belief that wicked men are converted in the Intermediate State, but there is no New Testament evidence for this. Second, broadly speaking, the doctrine of Universalism is less prominent in the earlier documents than in the later. Third, the doctrine of doom appears chiefly in passages of warning to the *individual*, the doctrine of Universalism in passages that encourage the *church*.

Is it then to be concluded that on this subject there are two doctrines in the New Testament which cannot both be true? Or is the right conclusion that here there are two doctrines that are both true, though the mind of *man* cannot reconcile them? To use the technical word, is there here an antinomy? There are, of course, antinomies in Christian theology. For instance, no satisfactory answer has ever been reached to the question: 'How can Christ be both God and man?' Yet the Christian, though he cannot rationally harmonize the statements 'Christ is God' and 'Christ is man', believes both, adding that to the mind of God there is no contradiction. It is the same with the doctrine of the Atonement.

> *'Tis mystery all! The Immortal dies:*
> *Who can explore His strange design?*

Again it is the same with the doctrine of the Trinity. Here there are analogies that lead some way to the understanding of what is meant, but none of them leads all the way. Yet, though the Christian cannot logically explain how there can be 'Three Persons (to use the least unsatisfactory word) in One God', He believes in the 'Three in One', and 'One in Three'. Again, under such a phrase as 'God fore-ordains everything that men do, yet men are free', many Christians add yet another antinomy. May there not be one more? It is admitted that all doctrines about God *must* run up into mystery, and antinomy is a form of mystery. Again, in reaching all the admitted antinomies there is the same process. First, scholars collate all the evidence scattered in the different parts of the New Testament, for there is no *system* of theology in the New Testament itself, but only the *data* for one. Next, there is an attempt to summarize and epitomize the *data*. Third, it is found that this results in an antinomy—an assertion of two truths which only the mind of God can harmonize. Under the present subject the same process leads to a like result. At any rate the question may be asked: Is it not possible that under the doctrines of Universalism and its opposite there is yet another antinomy—that is, a truth that seems to the mind of man to contradict itself, but that is harmonious to the mind of God? Mathematicians tell us that parallel lines are not lines that never meet, but lines that meet at *infinity*. 'My thoughts are not your thoughts,' saith the Lord.

INDEX OF HEBREW, GREEK, AND ENGLISH TERMS

abad, abaddon: 40, 56, 59, 87
abyss: 3, 4, 5, 218
abussos: 3
achar, acharith, acharōn: 98, 105
ad: 51
aenaos: 99, 119
agape: 122
Age, the Present: ix, 112, 118
Age, the Future: ix
Age of Righteousness: 5, 112, 114
Age of Sin: 5, 112, 114
Age, the coming: 117
Age of the Kingdom of God: 118, 224
Ages, the Two: 117
agrupnein: 124
aidios, aidiotes: 93, 217
aion, aiōnios: 96ff, 100, 110, 117, 118, 119, 120, 121, 122, 230, 231, 232, 233, 236
aiphnidos: 124
akal: 86
akatalutos: 119, 232
allassein: 183
ammi: 15
anabiosis: 110
anakainōsis: 237
anakephalaioun: 241
anakrinein: 193
analiskein, analuein: 86, 169
anapauein, anapausis: 90, 93, 94, 95, 229
anapsuchein: 90
anaphainesthai: 145
anastasis: 177, 178
anatema: 214
anemos: 87
anesis: 201
anima: 159
anistanai eis: 95, 104, 105, 110, 177, 178
Anointed: 190
apakein: 159
apeithōn: 120
aphthartos, aphtharsia: 87, 93
apistos: 144
apocalupsis: 126, 152
apokaluptein: 149
apokatastasis: 238
apōleia: 87, 89, 91, 160, 214
apollunai: 87, 89, 193, 214
apo tou aionos: 96, 98, 139
archaios: 101
arche: 242
archegos: 242
arrabon: 115
Asaph: 43
Ascension, the: 127
ashrey: 227

bara: 22
baruk: 227, 228
basar: 8, 87
basanistēs, basanizein, basanos: 93, 215, 218
basileia, basileus, basileoin, basileuein: 84, 85, 94, 113, 114, 208, 225, 236, 240, 241, 243
bema: 200
bios: 104
bis: 63
bor: 40, 88, 105
bothros: 88
brabeion: 230
Branch: 24

chasid: 30, 49, 55ff, 72, 75, 93, 95, 106, 109
chasidim: 55, 65, 90, 97, 109, 167
charismata: 127
chazah: 59
chesed: 55, 106
choïkos: 183
choter: 23
chrisma: 234
chronos: 100, 118, 152
City of Righteousness: 69
City of Sin: 69
clibanus: 129
corvée: 27

Day, the: ix, x, 67, 71, 79, 112, 113
Day of the Lord: 6, 16, 17, 18, 20, 67, 79, 83
Day of Aram: 16
Day of Jezreel: 15
Day of Judgement: x, 67, 71, 79, 112
Day of Midian: 15, 23
Day of Nineveh: 16
Day of Salvation: 16, 18, 19, 20, 67, 112
Day of Sisera: 15
Day of Slaughter: 18
Day of Sodom: 15
Day of Wrath: 18
Days, end of: 73
Days of the Lord: 17
Days of Despair: 70
Days of Destruction: 18
Days of Doom: 17
Days of Jerusalem: 18
Days of Punishment: 18
Days of Trouble: 18
death: 32ff, 56, 88
deep: 2, 3
derein: 216
desmos, desmōterion: 105, 217

262 INDEX OF HEBREW, GREEK, AND ENGLISH TERMS

deuro: 95
diagnosis, diagnoskein: 82, 107
diaparousian: 170, 228, 230, 231, 232, 233, 234
diaphtheirein: 86, 87
diaphthora: 89
dichotomein: 216
dikaiokrisia: 193, 203
doulos: 195
doxa, doxazein: 229

earth: 11
egersis, egeirein: 105, 177, 178
eikon: 93, 183
eis ton aiōna: 96, 97, 98, 99, 100, 101, 102, 103, 117, 119, 122, 123
ekdechesthai: 242
ekdikein, ekdikesis: 145, 193, 214
ekleipein: 88, 89
ekpnein: 160
ekpschein: 160
Elect One: 190
elegmos: 91
End of the Age: 113
endeigma: 201
endēmein: 169
Endor, Witch of: 47
enduesthai: 183
engastrimuthos: 48
eperchomenos: 117
epiphaneia: 126, 151
episcopē: 84, 107, 205
Era of Righteousness: 20, 79
Era of Sin: 20, 79, 82, 112
erchesthai: 125
erchomenos: 117
eretz: 11
eschatos: 20, 105
esthein: 86
ethical monotheism: ix
eudokia, eulogētos, eulogēmenos: 91, 228
eusebōs: 233
eutheōs: 143
Everlasting: 31
exaiphnes: 124
exanastasis: 177
exilasma, exilasmos: 65, 109
exodos: 93
exomologein: 256
exousia: 242

faith in Christ: 120
firmament: 1
for ever: 51, 52, 53, 54
future, Old Testament doctrine of: 10, 30, 66
future of the Righteous: 221ff
future of the Wicked: 211ff, 220

Gabriel: 74
gehenna: 38, 129ff, 171, 172, 239

geviyyah: 8, 87
gēy hinnom: 38
gibborim: 89
gigantes: 89, 95
God of Heaven: 76
go'el: 25, 58, 59
grave: 39
grēgorein: 124

Hades: 3, 5, 86ff, 104, 172
hagiazen, hagios: xi, 106
harpagein: 94
Heavenlies: 2
Hell: 39, 92
hēkein: 125
hemera: 83
Hereafter: ix
hilasterion: 167
holoklēron: 178
homologein: 256
hosios: 106
hybris: 108
hypnoun: 90
hypomenein: 204
hypotagē, hypotassein: 242, 244, 254

idiotēs: 93
infernus: 159
inspiratio: 159
ir: 25

judge: 8, 9
Judgement: 8, 9, 187ff
Judgement, Last: 9
Judgement, New Testament doctrine of: 210

kairos: 83, 84, 100, 141, 242
kalah: 18, 74, 83
katachthonia: 255
katakrima, katakrinein: 193, 201, 203
katakrisis: 193
katakurieuein: 65
katallage: 253
katanaliskein: 86
katapasios: 229
kataptheirein: 86
katarasthai: 213
katargein: 243, 254
katathema: 214
katechein: 149
katergazesthai: 184
katesthiein: 86
katheudein: 90, 124, 166
kentron: 184
kerugma: 181, 182, 186, 232
Kingdom: 31, 83, 113, 114
Kingdom of God: 30, 145, 182, 216, 224, 225
kingship: 30, 31, 84, 113, 114, 225, 236
kleptēs: 124

INDEX OF HEBREW, GREEK, AND ENGLISH TERMS 263

kleronomia, kleronomos: 225
koimesis: 90
koimasthai: 90, 166
koinos: 248
kolasis: 214
kosmikos: 246
kosmos: 106, 113, 150, 225, 226, 236, 240, 241, 253, 254, 256
kosmokrator: 243
krima, krinein, krisis, krites: 173, 193, 194, 199, 200, 209
ktasthai: 160
ktisis: 236, 243, 254
ktisma: 244
kurios: 195

lā'ad: 51, 52, 96
lacus: 129
lakkos: 88
Lamb: 248
lanetzach: 51, 52, 96, 100, 101
laqach: 62
latreuein: 240, 248
Latter Days: 73
Leviathan: 3
lo-'ammi: 15, 18
locus: 129
life in God: 233
Lord of Spirits: 174

makarios: 228
makrothumia, makrothumein: 112, 204
malak: 30
mana: 49
man of war: 16
Man of Lawlessness, the: 149
man clothed in linen: 77, 78
maran atha: 125
masger: 105
massah: 70
maveth: 32
Messiah: 190, 191, 192, 225
metaschēmatizein: 184
metatithenai: 94
metzulah: 41
Michael: 75
mone: 169, 235
monstrum: 49
muth: 32, 86

naos: 247
nekros: 177, 178
nephesh: 4, 7, 8, 34, 41, 42, 45, 49, 50, 59, 75, 87, 166, 171
nephashoth: 46, 69
nephilim: 53, 89
neshamah: 7, 8, 35, 87
netzach: 51, 64
nētzer: 23
nomos: 201
nustazein: 90

ob: 48
ochuōrma: 105
oiketērion: 183
oikodespotes: 196, 197
oikoumenē: 242, 243
olām: 51, 53, 96, 98, 99, 101, 119
olethros; 93, 214
ontos: 232
Oracles of the Coming King: 23
orgē: 214
ouai: 214

padah: 65
palingenesia: 237, 238
panta: 254, 255
parachrema: 145
Paradise: 129ff, 131, 167
paraclete, paraklesis: 122, 234
paranomasian: 234
Parousia: 113, 117ff, 135ff, 160, 169, 170, 178, 179, 182, 183, 185, 187ff, 246, 254
patris: 247
peirazein: 93
penthos: 214
peras: 83, 84
peripoiēsis: 160
phtharma: 87
phthartos: 86, 87
phthora: 158
phaneroun: 154
phantasma: 161
phulake: 215
pistis: 122, 200
pit: 39, 40, 58, 88, 89
pleroma: 253
pneuma, pneumatikos: 8, 87, 88, 109, 110, 160, 161, 162, 163, 183, 184, 238
pnoe: 8, 87, 88
politeuma: 246, 247
Prince of Peace: 21
promptuaria: 132, 159, 162, 169, 191, 192
prototokos: 243
psyche, psychikos: 8, 87, 88, 93, 94, 159, 160, 161, 162, 163, 169, 171, 178, 183, 232, 255
Purgatory: 92

qabar: 35
qaddish: 77
qeburah: 35
qedem: 99
qetz: 18, 73, 83, 84

rāphāh: 42
realm: 30, 31, 114
realized eschatology: 114, 231
Rephaim: 42, 45, 50, 56, 89, 95, 105
Remnant, Righteous: 68
resurrection of the dead: 104ff, 184
righteous, future of: 221ff.
Root of David: 24

264 INDEX OF HEBREW, GREEK, AND ENGLISH TERMS

ruach: 1, 8, 34, 35, 75, 87, 88
rule: 30, 113
Rule of God: 80ff, 114, 116

saints of the Most High: 77
sabbatismos: 229
saeculum: 223
sakal: 75
sarx: 8, 87
Second Coming: 113, 136
segullah: 12, 13, 20
seiros: 217
servility, doctrine of: 26
shachath: 40, 86, 88
shakab: 43
sheol: 3, 4, 5, 30, 33ff, 55ff, 88
simpliciter: 74, 78
Sitz im Leben: 137, 146, 198, 199, 203
skandalon: 131
skenos: 183
skia thanatou: 63
soma: 8, 87, 160
Son of Man: 190
Son of Perdition: 149
sower: 7
sōzein: 160, 192
Spirit of God: 8
stone: 77, 78
summorphos: 184
sunteleia, suntelein: 83, 84, 104, 124

tartarus: 130, 239

tehom: 2, 3, 4, 5, 41, 42, 218
teleutē: 84
telos: 83, 84, 101, 124, 160
thanatos: 88, 89, 214
thlipsis: 153
timōria: 214
tzalmaveth, tzalmuth: 63
tzebi: 78
tzemach: 24

unctus: 190

Valley of Hinnom: 38
Valley of Jehoshaphat: 67
Valley of the Lord's Judgement: 67
Visitation: 17

wicked, the future of: 211ff, 220
wind: 1
Witch of Endor: 47

yarēk: 4
yāshēn: 43
Year of Visitation: 17

zelos: 204
zen: 185, 230, 233
zoe: 109, 110, 120, 122, 123, 169, 185, 230, 233
zoopoiein: 177, 182, 183, 185, 234
zophos: 217

INDEX OF SCRIPTURE REFERENCES

THE OLD TESTAMENT

Genesis
1...2, 10
1^7...3
1–11...10
1^{27}...55
1^{28}...238
2^{2f}...229
2^7...39, 183
2^8...131
2^{19}...8, 183
2^{22}...62
3^{19}...183
3^{22}...97
4^{14-16}...10
5^{1-3}...184
5^3...183
5^6...31, 33
5^{21-4}...49
5^{23f}...94
5^{24}...65
6^3...32, 97
6^4...53
6^9–9^{19}...41
6^{13}...83
7^1...11
7^4...34
7^{11}...2
7^{22}...34
8^{21}...11
9^{12}...101
9^{16}...101
10^{8f}...89
11^{1-9}...11
12ff...11
12^3...11
13^{15}...98
14^5...89
15^{15}...43
15^{20}...89
18^{18}...11
18^{23}...11
19^{24}...34
21^{33}...53, 101
22^{18}...11
25^8...43, 44
25^{17}...44
26^4...11
28^{14}...11
35^{29}...44
37^{20-9}...40
37^{35}...34, 40
38^7...34
41^8...8
47^{30}...44
48^{16}...11

49^9...191
49^{25}...2, 3
49^{26}...53, 99
49^{29}...44
49^{33}...44
50^{26}...37

Exodus
1^{5-7}...7
3^{3-15}...12
3^6...180
3^{15}...101
4^{10}...13
13^{19}...37
15^{1-18}...41
15^3...16
15^{4f}...41
15^5...41
15^8...2, 41
15^{10}...41
15^{18}...52, 97
15^{21}...41
15^{29}...41
18^{10}...227
19^{4f}...12
19^6...31
19^8...12
19^{18-20}...5
20^3...18
20^{18}...129
21^6...97
23^{12}...90
23^{20-33}...13
23^{21}...13
24^3...12
24^7...12
27^{21}...101
32...13
32^{13}...97
40^{15}...97

Leviticus
5^{17}...216
6^{20}...190
22^{25}...87
25^{32}...99
25^{34}...53

Numbers
8^{18}...62
13^{33}...89
14^{11n}...13
14^{29n}...13
15^{29-31}...216
16^{28-33}...34

16^{30}...40
16^{33}...41
17^{13}...101
19...36
19^{14}...35
19^{16}...38
24^8...37
24^{14}...105
30^{3f}...8

Deuteronomy
2^{10f}...89
3^{11}...89
4^{24}...86
4^{30f}...15
4^{31}...13
4^{35}...15
4^{37}...13
4^{39}...15
5^{4f}...5
7^6...14
8^7...3
14^2...14
15^{17}...53
23^3...99
24^{20}...62
25^{1-3}...215
26^5...11
26^{14}...36
26^{16-19}...14
28...135
28^{1-14}...14
28^{46}...98
28^{68}...14
30^{1-10}...14
30^4...62
30^{15-20}...14
30^{20}...63
31^{16}...43
32^5...194
32^{22}...50
32^{40}...97
32^{50}...43, 44
33^1...221
33^{13}...2, 3
33^{15}...99
33^{27}...99

Joshua
5^{13}...28
24^3...62

Judges
3^9...14
5^{20}...1

INDEX OF SCRIPTURE REFERENCES

Judges—cont.
7^{20}...28
9^{14}...6
11^{24}...11
15^{14}...8

1 Samuel
1^{22}...53, 98
1^{28}...98
2^6...40
9^3...40, 87
12^{12}...22
13^{13}...53
13^{19-22}...27
15^{29}...51
18^6...25
20^{41}...98
24^3...3
27^{12}...53
28^3...36, 45
28^{3-25}...47
28^{13}...47
28^{21}...47
31^{11-13}...37
$31^{12\text{f}}$...37

2 Samuel
2^{26}...51
3^{31}...36
6^7...34
7^{12}...5, 33, 43
7^{12-16}...15
7^{14}...190, 223
7^{16}...97
7^{18}...98
7^{26}...98
22^6...88
23^5...53

1 Kings
1^{21}...43
1^{31}...53
2^{10}...44
2^{33}...53
6^{20}...248
9^3...97
11^{37}...62
11^{43}...43
12^{17}...25
13^{30}...36
14^{20}...20
14^{31}...43
17^{17}...49
17^{17-24}...49
$17^{21\text{f}}$...49
19^{15}...190
22^{40}...43

2 Kings
2^{1-18}...49
2^3...62
2^{15}...8

$4^{18\text{f}}$...49
4^{18-37}...49
4^{29}...49
8^1...49
8^5...49
9^{34-7}...37
13^{17}...83
$13^{20\text{f}}$...35, 49
15^{38}...43
16^{20}...43
19^{15}...28
23^{10}...38
23^{16}...38
$23^{29\text{f}}$...43
25^{27-30}...14

1 Chronicles
15^2...98
16^{15}...97
17^{14}...31
28^5...31
29^3...12
29^{10}...98
29^{11}...31, 51
29^{28}...44

2 Chronicles
5^{13}...98
6^2...99
13^8...31
16^{14}...35, 36, 45
20^6...31
$21^{19\text{f}}$...36
21^{20}...44
32^{33}...36, 44
33^{20}...44
34^{28}...43

Ezra
3^{11}...98
9^{6-15}...29

Nehemiah
2^6...126
2^8...131
6^2...61
9^5...96

Job
3^5...63
3^{13}...42
$3^{13\text{f}}$...90
3^{18}...102
7^9...34
7^{16}...97
7^{21}...35, 44
8^6...60
9^{31}...40
$10^{21\text{f}}$...63
10^{22}...102
12^{12}...63
12^{22}...63

13...57
13^{15}...57
14...57
14^{1-12}...57
14^{7-15}...44
14^{13-15}...50, 57, 104
14^{16-22}...57
14^{20}...51, 101
16^{16}...63
17^1...58
17^{10-16}...58
17^{13}...45
17^{14-16}...58
17^{16}...56
17^{16-22}...58
17^{27-33}...58
17^{34}...58
19^{25-7}...58, 59, 104
19^{27}...59
20^{11}...35, 43, 44
21^{16-34}...58
21^{23-6}...58
21^{26}...35, 44
22^{15}...101
24^{17}...63
26^5...4, 42
$26^{5\text{f}}$...50
26^6...40, 59
26^7...2
27^3...34
28^3...63
28^{22}...59
31^{12}...89
31^{19}...41
32^{19}...48
33^{18-30}...34
33^{23-8}...59
33^{24}...40
34^{14}...34
34^{17}...102
34^{22}...63
36^7...1, 101
38^{17}...56, 63
41^{23}...130
41^{34}...3
42...58

Psalms
1^1...228
2...29, 108
$2^{6\text{f}}$...190
$2^{8\text{f}}$...251
5^{11}...98
6^4...8
7^{15}...40
8^6...127
9^6...99
$9^{13\text{f}}$...56
9^{15}...40
9^{17}...56
10^{11}...51

INDEX OF SCRIPTURE REFERENCES

Psalms—cont.
10^{16}...99
13...44
13^1...101
13^3...43
15^5...53
16...40, 101
16^4...64
16^6...64
16^{8-11}...158
16^{10}...34, 40, 106
16^{10f}...64
17...60, 61
17^3...60, 62
17^{3-9}...62
17^6...62
17^{10-12}...62
17^{13}...62
17^{14}...62
17^{15}...62
18^{4f}...40
18^{50}...98
19^{1-6}...1
20^1...12
21^4...63
22^{28}...31
22^{29}...56
23...63
23^4...63
24^7...53
25^6...53, 96
27^4...64
28^6...227
28^9...98
29^{10}...97
30^1...60
30^3...60
30^5...60
30^9...40
34^{20}...37
35^{23}...60
37...97
37^{18}...97
37^{27}...97
37^{27-9}...53
37^{29}...99
39^4...83
41^{13}...53
41^{14}...96, 98
42^4...64
42^7...2
44...44
44^{19}...63
45^{17}...99
48^{14}...99
49...110
49^{1-4}...64
49^4...64
49^{6-8}...64
49^8...11
49^9...101

49^{10-12}...64
49^{11}...98
49^{12-20}...64
49^{14}...65
49^{15}...64
49^{17}...65
49^{19}...65, 98
49^{19f}...51, 65
51^{10}...22
51^{16-19}...22
52^5...51
52^{8f}...98
55...44
55^{15}...34
55^{19}...99
58^{12}...101
59^4...60
59^{16}...60
61^4...101
61^8...52, 53
63^9...3
68^{18}...127
69...41
69^1...4
69^{1f}...41
69^{14f}...41
71^1...98
71^{20}...3, 34
72...29
72^4...251
72^9...251
72^{17}...53, 99
72^{19}...97
73...60, 61, 63
73^{12}...97
73^{15}...62
73^{20}...62
73^{24}...62
73^{26}...59, 97
73^{28}...62
74...44
74^1...101
74^3...101
74^{10f}...101
74^{19}...101
76^{3-6}...43
77^2...60
77^6...53, 60
77^7...101
78^{31}...62
78^{69}...53
84^4...64
86^{13}...34
88^{3-6}...56, 60
88^{4f}...56
88^5...42, 43
88^{5f}...44
88^{10}...42, 50
88^{10-12}...56, 60
88^{11}...40
88^{12}...50

88^{13}...60
89^{29}...52
90...32
90^2...96, 98
91^{16}...32, 63
92^7...52
92^9...52
92^{11}...52
92^{13}...64
92^{14}...52
93^2...53
94^{13}...40
95^{11}...229
103^4...40
103^9...51
103^{17}...98
103^{19}...30
104^9...2
104^{19}...1
104^{25f}...3
104^{29f}...35
105^{15}...190
106^9...2
106^{31}...98
106^{48}...98
107^{10-14}...63
107^{18}...56
107^{26}...2
110...29
110^1...127
110^4...97
111^3...52
111^8...52
111^{10}...52
116^3...40
116^{19}...64
118^{1-4}...98
118^{26}...125
119^{44}...52, 97
119^{52}...96
119^{55}...60
119^{89}...53
121^6...1
121^8...53, 98
122^1...64
132^{14}...52
136...53, 98
136^4...98
136^{23-5}...98
139...50, 60, 61, 63
139^1...50
139^{1-12}...61
139^3...61
139^5...50
139^8...45
139^{8-10}...50
139^{13-18}...61
139^{18}...61
139^{19-24}...61
139^{24}...50
141^7...38

TDBH

INDEX OF SCRIPTURE REFERENCES

Psalms—cont.
143...60
143^3...60, 96
143^{5t}...60, 96
143^5...53
143^7...60
143^8...60
145^1...99
145^2...98
145^{11}...31
145^{13}...31, 99

Proverbs
1^{12}...34
2^{18}...42
3^2...63
5^5...56
7^{26t}...56
8^{23}...53, 96
9^{18}...34, 42, 56
10^{30}...97
15^{11}...40, 50
15^{24}...69
21^{16}...42
23^{14}...34, 69
26^{27}...40
31^6...41

Ecclesiastes
1^{10}...99
2^5...131
3^{11}...53
3^{19}...35
9^{1-4}...42
9^{5t}...54
9^{10}...54, 57
12^{1-8}...54
12^7...35
12^8...35

Isaiah
1^{18}...17
1^{26}...20
1^{26t}...25
2^2...20
2^{2-4}...27, 251
2^4...21
5^{14}...34
6^5...22
6^{10}...209
9^{1-7}...23
9^2...63
9^6...52
9^{6t}...21
10^3...17
10^{12}...17
10^{20}...18, 19
10^{20-3}...18
10^{23}...74
10^{33t}...23
11^{1-9}...23, 28
11^{1-10}...251

11^4...149, 251
11^{6-9}...21
11^9...251
11^{10}...28
13^6...16
13^8...153
14^{3-23}...46
14^{9t}...89
14^{9-11}...42, 46
14^{9-20}...46
14^{12}...70
14^{15}...34
14^{19t}...46
14^{26}...17
16^5...22
17^6...18
19^{5-7}...19
19^{24}...245
22^{16}...38
22^{18}...38
24-7...15, 65, 105
24^{1-12}...68
24^5...102
24^{5t}...68
24^{10-12}...68
24^{12}...69
24^{15}...69
24^{21}...68, 105, 215
24^{21-3}...105
24^{23}...69
25^{1-8}...68
25^2...97
25^{5-12}...69
25^8...105
25^9...68
26^1...68
26^{1-4}...69
26^4...98, 102
26^{5t}...68
26^{14}...69
26^{16-18}...68
26^{16-21}...153
26^{19}...35, 45, 69, 75, 76
$26^{19 n}$...105
26^{20}...151
27^{1t}...68
27^{7-9}...69
27^{12t}...68
27^{13}...21
28^{16}...77, 247
29^6...19
29^{17}...16
30^{26}...21
32^{1-8}...23
32^7...21
33^{20}...25, 97
33^{22}...22
34...19
34^2...17
34^{10}...97, 101
35^{10}...25

38^{10}...163
38^{10t}...56
38^{17}...34
40^8...53
40^9...25
40^{28}...53, 101
41^4...98
42^{1-9}...27
42^{14}...99
43^{15}...22
43^{17}...43
44^5...21
44^6...22, 98
45^1...90
45^{14-17}...26
45^{18-25}...27
46^9...53
47^3...62
47^7...53
48^{12}...98
49^{1-6}...28
49^8...16
49^{22-6}...27, 251
51^1...20
51^3...131
51^{4-6}...16
51^6...97
51^7...20
51^9...96
51^{10}...2
51^{19}...19
52^{1-6}...16
52^6...19
52^7...21
52^{13}–53^{12}...28
52^{15}...28
53^{1-6}...28
53^{7-10}...28
53^{9t}...49
53^{11}...28
53^{13}...28
55^{3t}...22
55^{12}...21
55^{13}...16
56^{1-8}...27
57^{15}...52
58^{14}...21
59^{17-19}...27
59^{20}...25
60...16
60^3...26
60^{5-10}...27
60^{9-14}...251
60^{10t}...26
60^{21}...20, 23, 251
61^1...190
61^2...16
62^{11}...16
63^6...51
63^{11}...53
64^4...96

INDEX OF SCRIPTURE REFERENCES 269

Isaiah—cont.
65^4...45
65^{17}...236, 238
65^{17f}...22, 52, 247
65^{20}...22, 23
66^{8f}...244
66^{10-24}...16, 17
66^{12}...21
66^{15f}...19
66^{20}...27
66^{22}...52
66^{23}...17
66^{23f}...27
66^{24}...19, 38, 76, 82, 91, 108, 129

Jeremiah
2^6...63
2^{13}...1
2^{27}...18
3^5...51, 97, 101
3^{16}...19
3^{17}...25, 27
4^2...11, 27
4^{27}...83
4^{31}...153
5^{15}...53
5^{18}...18
6^{16}...101
6^{26}...36
7^{1-11}...17
7^{1-15}...25
7^7...98
7^{31f}...38
7^{32-4}...19
8^{1f}...37
11^4...15
12^3...18
13^{16}...63
15^{2-4}...19
15^8...19
16^{3-6}...37
16^7...36
16^{14f}...19
16^{19-21}...27
17^{25}...77
19^{6-14}...38
20^{17}...102
22^8...17
22^{19}...38
23^{5-28}...24
23^6...24
23^{7f}...24
23^{20}...20, 105
24^7...15
24^{10}...19
25^{11f}...24
25^{15}...17
25^{15-31}...17
25^{17}...17
25^{26}...17

25^{33}...37
25^{34}...36
26^{18}...224
26^{23}...35
27^{6f}...17
28^8...53
29^{11}...21
30^8...19
30^9...22
30^{11}...18
30^{22}...15
31^{10-14}...21
31^{30}...19
31^{33}...20
31^{34}...21, 251
31^{35-7}...20
33^{14-18}...19, 24
33^{16}...20
33^{17-24}...24
33^{25f}...25
34^{4f}...36
34^5...36
35^6...98
36^{30}...38
38^6...40
40^{15}...41
46^{21}...16, 17
46^{28}...18
47^6...28
48^{44}...17
49^8...18
50^4...19
50^{26}...83
51^{13}...18
51^{33}...153
51^{36-44}...19
51^{39}...43, 54, 102
51^{57}...43, 54

Lamentations
5^{19}...97
5^{20}...63

Ezekiel
1...25
1^{26-8}...78
6^5...38
7^{2-6}...18
7^3...83
7^{6f}...17
7^{15}...19
8^{17}...83
9^2...75
9^{4f}...75
11^{13}...18
11^{17}...18
11^{20}...15
14^{11}...15
18^{20}...19
19^4...40
21^5...28

21^7...8
21^{19}...22
21^{28}...18
21^{25}...83
24^{1-11}...38
24^{25f}...18
26^{2f}...17
26^3...17
26^{21}...97
28^8...41
29^{21}...19
31^4...3
31^{15}...34
31^{18}...44
32^{17-32}...46
32^{18f}...47
32^{21}...46
32^{22f}...46
32^{27}...46, 89
32^{27-30}...44
34...70
34^4...40, 87
34^{25}...21
34^{33f}...22
36^{20}...19
36^{25-7}...68
36^{26}...8
36^{26-8}...20
36^{27}...251
36^{28}...15
36^{35}...21
37^{1-14}...49
37^{11}...49
37^{25f}...20
38...208
38^{2f}...17
38^{16}...20, 105
39...208
39^{11-16}...38
43^7...26
43^8...35
44^{25}...35
47^{1-12}...22, 245
48^{35}...25

Daniel
2...73
$2^{4-7^{28}}$...74
2^{28}...73
2^{34}...224
2^{44}...99, 214
2^{44f}...76
2^{45}...77
4^3...31, 102
4^{17}...31
4^{25}...31
4^{32}...31
4^{34}...31, 97, 102
4^{37}...79
5^{10}...97
5^{21}...31

Daniel—cont.
5^{27}...79
6^{10}...78
6^{26}...31
7...73
7^{1}...73
7^{8}...77
7^{9}...77
7^{9-12}...77
7^{9-14}...77
7^{10}...79
7^{13}...78, 190, 198
7^{13f}...77
7^{14}...31, 77, 102, 208, 251
7^{15-28}...77
7^{18}...77, 99, 198
7^{22}...79
7^{26}...79
7^{27}...31, 77, 102, 208, 251
8–12...74
8^{3-12}...74
8^{17}...74, 83
8^{19}...74, 83, 84
8^{25}...77
9^{2}...74
9^{12}...79
9^{21}...74
9^{24}...74, 102
9^{25-7}...74
9^{26}...74, 83, 84
9^{27}...83, 84
10...73, 74
10–12...74
10^{1}...84
10^{5}...74, 75, 78
10^{5-8}...78
10^{9f}...75
10^{10}...75
10^{11}...75
10^{13}...70, 75
10^{14}...73, 105
10^{16}...75, 78
10^{18}...75, 78
10^{18-20}...75
10^{19}...75
10^{20}...77, 78
10^{20f}...75
11^{2-39}...74
11^{6}...83
11^{13}...83, 84
11^{16}...78
11^{27}...74, 83, 84
11^{27-30}...74
11^{29}...84
11^{30-5}...75
11^{31}...78
11^{35}...74, 83, 84
11^{35f}...83
11^{36}...74, 149
11^{40}–12^{13}...75
11^{41}...78

11^{45}...78, 79, 83
12^{1}...75
12^{1-4}...75
12^{2}...30, 35, 44, 79, 102
12^{2f}...53
12^{3}...76
12^{4}...74, 76, 83
12^{5-13}...76
12^{6}...83
12^{6f}...83
12^{7}...78, 83, 97
12^{9}...74, 83
12^{10}...76
12^{11}...78, 95
12^{11f}...76
12^{13}...73, 76, 83, 95

Hosea
1^{4}...16
1^{4f}...15
1^{9}...15
1^{10}...21
2^{1}...15
2^{16}...19
2^{16-23}...18
2^{18}...20
2^{18f}...97
2^{19}...20
2^{21f}...21
3^{4}...22
3^{5}...20, 105
8^{14}...19
9^{7}...17
13^{11}...62
13^{14}...57

Joel
1^{1}–2^{27}...67
1^{4}...67
1^{6-12}...67
1^{13f}...67
1^{15}...67
2^{1}...67
2^{1-11}...67, 68
2^{2}...96
2^{11}...67
2^{12-17}...67
2^{14}...67
2^{18}...67
2^{19-27}...67
2^{25}...67
2^{26f}...97
2^{28}...67
2^{28f}...251
2^{28-32}...68
2^{28}–3^{21}...67
2^{30}...68
2^{31}...67
2^{32}...68
3^{1}...67
3^{1-14}...67

3^{2-8}...67
3^{9-14}...67
3^{14}...67
3^{15f}...68
3^{16f}...68
3^{16-18}...68
3^{20}...97

Amos
1^{3}–2^{16}...17
1^{4}...19
1^{11}...51
2^{1}...38
4^{2}...19
5^{8}...63
5^{18}...16
6^{3}...16
6^{7}...16
6^{10}...38
7^{8}...18
8^{2}...18
8^{9}...19
8^{11f}...18
9^{2}...50
9^{3}...3
9^{9}...17
9^{11}...53, 96
9^{11-15}...29
9^{13}...22
9^{15}...20

Obadiah
9...18
12...18
21...25

Jonah
2–6...2, 4
2^{1}...4
2^{2}...4
2^{2-6}...4
2^{3}...41
2^{3-5}...42
2^{5}...4
2^{6}...53, 56, 163
2^{8}...88
3–6...4

Micah
3^{6}...19
3^{12}...18, 24, 224
4^{1}...105
4^{1-5}...27
4^{5}...52, 53, 97
4^{6}–5^{9}...24
4^{7}...22
4^{9}...24, 41, 153
4^{10}...24
4^{11}...17
4^{13}...26
5^{2}...24

Micah—cont.
5^{2-4}...24
5^3...24
5^4...24
5^5...21
5^{5-9}...24
5^{11}...24
7^4...17
7^{12}...19
7^{14}...96
7^{14-17}...251
7^{16f}...26

Nahum
1^8...18
1^{13}...16
3^{18}...18, 43, 90

Habakkuk
2^{3f}...151
3^6...101

Zephaniah
1^7...16
1^{15}...18
1^{18}...18
3^{10-13}...18
3^{11-20}...19
3^{14}...25
3^{15}...22

Haggai
2^6...153, 240
2^9...25

Zechariah
2^{10}...25
2^{10-13}...28
3^9...28
8^8...20
8^{11-13}...18
8^{12}...22
8^{18-23}...28
8^{23}...19, 28
9–10...70
9^{-14}...66, 70
9^1...70
9^{1-8}...70
9^9...21
9^{9f}...70
9^{12}...70
9^{16}...70
10^{6-12}...70
10^{12}...21
11^5...70
11^{11}...70
11^{12}...70
11^{15-17}...70
12^1...70, 71
12^{1f}...71
12^3...71
12^4...71
12^{5-9}...71
12^6...71
12^8...71
12^9...71
12^{10-14}...71
12^{11}...71
12^{12}...71
12^{14}...71

13^1...71
13^{1f}...71
13^{2-5}...71
13^3...71
13^4...71
13^7...71
13^{7f}...71
13^{8f}...71
14^1...71, 72
14^4...72
14^{4f}...72
14^6...72
14^{6f}...72
14^8...72
14^{8-10}...72
14^9...72
14^{11}...214
14^{12}...72
14^{12-15}...72
14^{13}...72
14^{13f}...72
14^{15}...72
14^{16-21}...72
14^{17}...72
14^{17-19}...72
14^{20}...72
14^{20f}...72
14^{21}...72

Malachi
1^4...98
3^2...20
3^{16f}...20
4^{5f}...20, 107

APOCRYPHA

1 Esdras
4^{38-40}...100
8^{68}...87
8^{85}...100

2 Esdras
2^{11}...167
2^{38}...225
3^6...132
4^7...130, 132
4^{35}...169
5^{1-12}...150
5^{1-13}...211
6^9...117
$6^{12\mathit{n}}$...xii
6^{34}...xii
7^{6-8}...172
7^{26}...167, 223, 245
7^{28}...136

$7^{30\mathit{n}}$...252
7^{31}...237
7^{32}...130, 191
7^{36}...129, 132, 211
7^{37-43}...187, 211
7^{38-84}...129
7^{45-8^3}...189
7^{47}...223
7^{47f}...189
7^{50}...117
7^{60f}...189
7^{70}...169, 187
7^{75}...237
7^{80}...159
7^{95}...132, 191
7^{113f}...223, 237
7^{123}...132
8^1...189, 252
8^3...169, 189

8^{18}...189
8^{33}...223
8^{51-4}...223
8^{52-4}...132
8^{61}...135, 136, 189
8^{61-3}...136
9^{1-3}...211
9^8...223
9^{13}...223
9^{14f}...189
$9^{26}-10^{56}$...245
10^{25-7}...246
10^{40-55}...223
10^{44}...245
10^{46-8}...245
10^{53f}...245
10^{54}...223
10^{55}...246
11^1-12^{39}...189, 191

2 Esdras—cont.
11^{1-35}...191
11^{2t}...117
11^{36}–12^3...191
11^{38-46}...191
12^{1-3}...191
12^{11}...191
12^{21}...189, 206
12^{30-4}...175
12^{31t}...7
12^{32}...189, 190, 191, 192
12^{33t}...206
12^{34}...189, 191, 192
13^{1-13}...191
13^{1-50}...224, 246
13^3...190
13^{6t}...167, 224, 246
13^{8-11}...172
13^{9-11}...208
13^{12}...190
13^{26}...191
13^{32}...190, 224
13^{33}...191
13^{35}...247
13^{35t}...167, 191, 224
13^{36}...246
13^{37}...190
13^{40-2}...192
13^{43t}...207
13^{47}...207
13^{48}...192
13^{50}...237
13^{52}...190, 191
13^{56}...xii
14^9...159, 190, 191
14^{35}...136, 173
16^{38}...153
16^{52}...151

Add. Esther
10^{5-12}...81
10^{11}...82
11^{2-11}...81
13^7...88
16^{16}...85

Wisdom
1^{12}–5^{23}...92
1^{12}...93
1^{13-15}...92
1^{14}...94
1^{15t}...93, 107
1^{16}...93
2^{1-20}...93
2^{-5}...107
2^3...88
2^{6-20}...108
2^{16}...105
2^{22}...93
2^{23}...93
2^{24}...93

3^1...93
3^{1-4}...93
3^3...93
3^7...84, 107
3^{7t}...94
3^{7-9}...84, 108
3^9...94, 106
3^{10-17}...93
3^{17}...105
3^{18}...82, 94, 107
3^{19}...84
4^2...100
4^7...93
4^{7-14}...93
4^{10}...93
4^{10t}...94
4^{10-14}...108
4^{15}...106, 107
4^{15t}...108
4^{16t}...107
4^{18}...100
4^{18t}...108
4^{18}–5^{16}...108
4^{18}–5^{23}...85, 189
5^1...108
5^{2-8}...108
5^{3-14}...93
5^{15}...93, 100
5^{15t}...108
5^{17-23}...108
6^{1-11}...108
6^4...85
6^{18t}...93
6^{20}...85
7^{27}...106
8^{13}...102
9^{15}...86, 94, 158
10^{19}...3
12^1...87
12^{10}...100
12^{14}...87
13^{-15}...187
13^9...100
14^8...86
16^{13}...163
16^{16}...86
18^4...87, 100
18^{12}...86
18^{15t} 207
19^4...84

Sirach or *Ecclesiasticus*
1^1...100
1^2...100
1^3...3
1^4...100
1^{13}...105
1^{13-15}...100
5^7...84
6^{28}...105
7^{17}...91

7^{36}...105
10^{13}...101
10^{16t}...87
11^{28}...91, 95
12^{12}...105
14^{11-19}...90
14^{16t}...91
14^{17}...100
15^6...102
17^{12}...100
17^{27-30}...91
18^{24}...84
19^3...92
21^9...92, 159
21^{10}...105
24^5...3
24^9...100
24^{11}...247
29^{10}...106
30^{18t}...36
33^{23}...84
36^9...100
38^{23}...90
39^{13}...106
39^{24}...106
41^{1-4}...91
41^{9t}...91
42^{21}...100
44–50...106
44^{13}...100
44^{21t}...11
45^{15}...102
46^{12}...106
46^{19}...90
47^{22}...86
47^{23}...90
48^{1-16}...107
48^{11}...107
51^{1-12}...86
51^6...88

Baruch
2^{35}...102
3^9–19...88
3^{11}...88
3^{19}...88
4^8–5^2...102
4^{29}...102
5^8...84

Song of the Three Holy Children
3^5...80
60...80
61...80
64...80
66...80

Tobit
1^6...102
1^{17t}...88

INDEX OF SCRIPTURE REFERENCES

Tobit—cont.
2^{3a}...88
2^{22}...88
3^{1}...88
3^{2}...100
3^{2-6}...29
3^{6}...102
3^{9}...100
3^{11}...100
3^{15}...87
4^{3f}...88
4^{16f}...37
6^{17}...100
13^{1}...84
13^{4}...100
13^{10}...100
14^{4f}...100
14^{10-12}...88
14^{11}...88
14^{11-15}...86

Judith
5^{5-24}...81
6^{2}...81
10^{18}...126
11^{12}...82
13^{20}...102

15^{10}...100
16^{6}...81
16^{17}...82, 92, 130
16^{23}...86

Susanna
$60-2$...86

Bel and the Dragon
$33-42$...81

1 Maccabees
1^{54}...74
2^{24f}...86
2^{42}...109
2^{54}...102
2^{57}...100, 102
3^{42}...87
7^{12f}...55
7^{13}...109
7^{17}...109
7^{38}...235

2 Maccabees
1^{28}...110
2^{17}...85
3^{31}...88, 105

6^{23}...88
7...76, 82, 109, 110, 184, 189
7^{6}...110
7^{8}...110
7^{9}...88, 102
7^{13}...110
7^{14}...110
7^{16}...86
7^{17-20}...110
7^{23}...110
7^{29}...110
7^{36}...110
8^{12}...126
8^{29}...101
8^{35}...86
9^{5}...86
9^{5f}...110
9^{15}...82
12^{39-45}...109
12^{43}...110
12^{45}...90
14^{9}...109
14^{45}...109
15^{6}...82
15^{14-16}...74, 82
15^{21}...126

THE NEW TESTAMENT

Matthew
1^{24}...177
2^{20}...159
4^{5}...27
5^{1-12}...115
5^{2-12}...228
5^{5}...225, 236, 237, 238
5^{15}...216
5^{18}...253
5^{22-4}...198
5^{29f}...131
5^{39}...194
6^{9}...113
6^{9n}...252
6^{10}...238
6^{13}...118
6^{14}...178
6^{49}...161
7^{3-5}...198
7^{13}...214
7^{14}...230
7^{19}...215
8^{11}...147
8^{12}...216
10^{5}...197
10^{14f}...209
10^{16-23}...147

10^{21}...198
10^{22}...124
10^{28}...131, 159, 171, 214
10^{40-2}...198
11^{9}...125
11^{20-4}...209
11^{25}...253
11^{27}...114, 241
11^{29}...229
12^{32}...117
12^{49}...198
13^{24-30}...194, 195
13^{26}...196
13^{27}...196
13^{30}...196, 215
13^{34f}...148
13^{36-43}...147
13^{37}...197
13^{39-41}...124, 196
13^{41}...224
13^{42}...147, 215
13^{43}...224
13^{47-50}...194
13^{49}...124
13^{50}...147, 216
16^{8}...163, 214
16^{18}...160

16^{25}...8
16^{27}...125
18^{1f}...120
18^{8}...120, 121, 131
18^{21-35}...195
18^{23-4}...194, 215
19^{17}...230
19^{21}...230
19^{28}...197, 237, 238, 253
19^{29}...230
19^{29f}...196
20^{1-16}...194, 195
20^{8}...196
20^{16}...196
20^{21}...224
21...236
21^{28}...195
22^{1-14}...194, 195
22^{13}...147, 216
22^{31}...177
23^{8}...198
23^{15}...131
23^{27}...159
23^{32}...131
23^{37-9}...148
24...198
24^{3}...124, 126, 140, 146

INDEX OF SCRIPTURE REFERENCES

Matthew—cont.
24^6...125, 146
24^9...147
24^{10}...149
24^{12}...138, 149
24^{14}...146, 147
24^{15}...136
24^{26}...146
24^{27}...126
24^{29}...147
24^{30}...147
24^{34}...147
24^{35}...253
24^{37}...126
24^{39}...126
24^{42}...146
24^{44}...146
24^{50}...146
24^{51}...147, 198, 216
25...147, 198
25^1...196
25^{1-13}...194, 195, 196
25^5...147, 196
25^{10-12}...147, 217
25^{14}...196
25^{14-30}...194, 195, 196
25^{19}...147
25^{20-5}...196
25^{21}...147
25^{23}...147
25^{30}...147, 216, 217
$25^{31\textit{f}}$...9, 198
25^{34}...224, 225, 227
25^{35}...138
25^{40}...230
25^{41}...121, 131, 214, 215, 217, 227, 242, 253
25^{46}...121, 197, 214, 230
26^{63}...139
27^7...158
27^{50}...162
27^{53}...177, 247
27^{60}...158
28^{10}...198
28^{16}...148
28^{20}...124, 148, 196

Mark
1^5...256
1^{11}...114
1^{35}...177
2^{21}...253
2^{22}...214
3^5...238
3^{29}...117, 120, 214
4^{19}...117, 118
4^{24-9}...253
4^{29}...148
4^{30-2}...253
4^{38}...177
5^{39}...166

8^{29}...137, 192
8^{30}...196
8^{31}...137
8^{35}...159, 160, 180
8^{38}...138, 192
$8^{38}-9^1$...138
9^1...114
9^{12}...238
9^{21}...118
9^{37}...257
$9^{40\textit{f}}$...199
9^{41}...198
9^{43}...122, 215, 230
9^{43-8}...131
9^{45}...230
9^{47}...114
10^{14}...114
10^{15}...114
10^{17}...121, 225, 230
10^{17-31}...230
10^{21}...121
10^{23-5}...114
10^{25}...225
10^{30}...117, 121, 225
11^{1-6}...224
11^{10}...224
11^{14}...118
11^{17}...197
12^{1-9}...194, 195
12^{1-12}...194
12^{18}...44, 177
12^{18-23}...179
12^{25}...177, 182, 238
12^{26}...177
12^{27}...230
12^{34}...114
12^{36}...243
13...126, 138, 140, 199
13^{2-4}...140
13^4...211
13^{5-13}...140
13^6...155
13^7...125
$13^{7\textit{f}}$...150
13^{7-13}...153
13^8...142, 153
13^{12}...180
13^{13}...125, 142, 154
13^{14}...136, 137, 149
13^{14-21}...140
13^{19}...138, 153
$13^{21\textit{f}}$...155
13^{22-7}...140
13^{24}...142, 153
13^{24-37}...141, 142
13^{26}...227
13^{27}...141
13^{28}...142
13^{29-31}...141
13^{31}...238
13^{34-7}...194, 195

13^{35}...142
13^{36}...142
13^{37}...136
14^{25}...114, 224
14^{34}...8
14^{36}...113
14^{53}...139
14^{61}...138
14^{62}...139
15^{37}...160
15^{39}...160
15^{43}...224
15^{46}...158

Luke
1^{33}...224
1^{79}...228
2^{14}...228
2^{34}...177
2^{37}...64
2^{51}...254
3^7...214
$3^{7\textit{f}}$...202
3^8...188
3^9...215
3^{17}...215
4^4...230
4^5...118
6^{20}...172
6^{20-6}...115
6^{24-6}...214
6^{47}...195
6^{47-9}...194
7^{28}...114
8^{31}...3
8^{55}...162
9^{26}...139
9^{60}...158
10^9...114
10^{11}...114
10^{12}...179
10^{15}...160
10^{17}...255
10^{20}...255
10^{25}...230
11^2...224
11^{23}...214
11^{31}...177, 179
11^{42-7}...214
11^{44}...35, 158
12^4...171
12^5...131
12^{15}...230
12^{16-21}...194, 195
12^{22}...224
12^{35}...196
12^{35-8}...194, 195
12^{35-40}...144, 196
12^{35-48}...142, 144
12^{36}...196
12^{37}...144, 227

INDEX OF SCRIPTURE REFERENCES

Luke—cont.
12^{40}...197
12^{41-7}...196
12^{41-8}...144
12^{42-8}...194, 195, 216
12^{43}...196
12^{46}...216, 217
12^{47f}...144
12^{48}...144, 199
12^{49}...141
12^{54}...144
12^{54-9}...144
12^{59}...215
13^{6-9}...194, 195
13^{20f}...253
13^{23-30}...170, 188
13^{25-7}...217
13^{28}...147, 216
13^{28f}...224
13^{35}...125
14^{15}...224
14^{15-24}...194, 195
14^{17}...196
14^{24}...196
15^7...222
15^{32}...198
16^{1-13}...194, 195
16^8...117
16^9...120, 167
16^{19-31}...171
16^{20a}...170
16^{22f}...160, 167
16^{23}...131, 216
16^{25}...122, 230
16^{28}...216
16^{30}...178
16^{31}...177
17^{20}...145
17^{20-18^8}...145
17^{22}...145
17^{22-18^8}...142
17^{24}...145
17^{25}...145
17^{26-9}...145
17^{30}...145
17^{31}...114
17^{31-5}...145
17^{32f}...145
17^{37}...145
18^{1-8}...194, 195
18^7...145
18^8...145, 197
18^{38}...145
19^{10}...113
19^{11-26}...196
19^{11-27}...145
19^{12}...196
19^{12-27}...194, 195
19^{15}...196
19^{17-19}...196
19^{27}...146, 196

19^{38}...145
19^{39f}...224
19^{41}...194
19^{41-4}...145
20^{14}...225
20^{16-18}...214
20^{35}...177, 180
20^{38}...167, 180
21^{5-26}...142
21^7...140
21^8...143
21^9...125, 147
21^{9f}...143
21^{17}...143
21^{19}...160
21^{20}...136, 143
21^{21}...194
21^{24}...143, 247
21^{28}...143
21^{31f}...143
21^{34-6}...143
21^{35}...143
22^6...256
22^{29f}...224
22^{67-70}...139
22^{69}...116
23^{29}...145
23^{42}...133, 224
23^{46}...162
24^{19-24}...153
24^{36-43}...161
24^{52}...153

John
1...236
1^1...233
1^3...241
1^4...122, 233
1^{10}...240
1^{29}...241, 259
3^5...114, 234
3^8...8
3^{15f}...122, 232
3^{16}...214
3^{16f}...241
3^{16-21}...120, 258
3^{17-21}...209
3^{18}...9, 193
3^{31-6}...120
3^{35}...241
3^{36}...121, 122, 214, 231, 232
4^{10}...1
4^{14}...122, 123, 232
4^{36}...122, 232
4^{42}...241, 256
5^{19}...210
5^{21}...177, 185
5^{24}...122, 231
5^{25}...178
5^{26}...122

5^{27}...197
5^{28f}...186, 209
5^{29}...178, 232
5^{37}...185
5^{38}...235
5^{39}...121, 231
5^{40}...172
6^{15}...145
6^{27}...122, 232
6^{29}...257
6^{35}...122, 234
6^{39}...154
6^{44}...154
6^{47}...231, 232
6^{48}...234
6^{51}...118
6^{53}...121, 234
6^{54}...122, 154, 231, 232
6^{56}...234
6^{58}...123
6^{63}...177, 185, 234
6^{68}...122, 232
7^{15}...154
7^{28}...257
7^{33}...152
7^{34}...172, 257
7^{49}...169, 188
8^{12}...233
8^{21}...169, 172
8^{23}...240
8^{24}...258
8^{31}...235
8^{38}...164
8^{42}...257
8^{46}...114
8^{51}...123
8^{52-7}...169
8^{56}...112, 167
9^5...152
9^{32}...117
9^{39}...209, 240
10^{3-5}...185
10^{10}...122
10^{15}...114
10^{16}...153, 185
10^{27f}...185
10^{28}...122, 123, 232
11^{11}...166
11^{23-5}...169
11^{24a}...185
11^{25}...122, 234
11^{25f}...186
11^{26}...123
11^{42}...257
11^{50}...214
12^{25}...232, 240
12^{25f}...169
12^{26}...170, 227
12^{31}...209, 240
12^{31f}...241, 257
12^{32}...210

INDEX OF SCRIPTURE REFERENCES

John—cont.
12^{35}...152
12^{39}...209
12^{46-8}...209
12^{47}...241, 256
12^{50}...122, 232
13–17... 241
13^3...241
13^8...118
13^{31f}...229
13^{36}...169
13^{37-40}...123
14^2...222, 235
14^{2-4}...169
14^3...170
14^6...122, 234
14^{16}...123
14^{16f}...234
14^{18}...196
14^{19}...185, 232
14^{23}...235
14^{27}...228
14^{28}...152
15^{1-10}...234
15^{4-10}...234
15^6...219
15^{15}...144
15^{18f}...154
15^{23-5}...154
16^5...169
16^{7-15}...152
16^{8-11}...210
16^{16-24}...152
16^{17-24}...152
16^{19-22}...152
16^{20-2}...142
16^{19n}...153
16^{21}...153
16^{28}...169
16^{33}...153, 228, 241
17^{2f}...232
17^3...123, 235, 257
17^5...229
17^8...141, 257
17^{11}...169
17^{12}...214
17^{13}...169
17^{14}...154
17^{20}...153, 170
17^{21}...241, 257
17^{22}...229
17^{23}...241, 257
17^{24}...133, 170, 229
17^{25}...257
18^{36}...240
18^{37}...185
20^{17}...152
20^{31}...234
21...152
21^{20-3}...154, 170
21^{22}...125

21^{24}...154
21^{28f}...169

Acts of the Apostles
1^6...143, 238
1^{6-8}...146
1^7...118
1^{11}...146
1^{25}...172
2^{14}...199
2^{18-21}...146
2^{20}...199
2^{27}...160
2^{29-31}...160
2^{31}...160
2^{34}...243
2^{34-6}...199, 200
2^{37}...158
2^{41}...8
3^{15}...122, 231
3^{21}...118, 238, 241
4^2...177, 179, 180
5^6...158
5^{10}...158, 160
5^{20}...231
5^{38-40}...137
7^{59}...163
7^{60}...163, 166
9^{31}...137
9^{41}...177
10^{36}...228
10^{42}...199
11^{14f}...231
11^{28}...150
12^{23}...160
13^{18}...48
13^{34-7}...158, 161
13^{36}...158, 166
13^{46}...120, 121, 220, 230, 231
13^{48}...121, 231
14^{22}...153
15^{11}...199
17^{24}...241
17^{25}...8
17^{31f}...180, 200
17^{31}...199
17^{32}...177
19^{18}...256
20^{10}...159
20^{32}...199, 226
21^{18-20}...137
21^{23}...247
21^{40}...137
22^{21}...137
23^{1-6}...180
23^{6-9}...176
23^8...44
23^9...111
24^{15}...181
24^{24f}...199

24^{25}...200
26^{4f}...203
26^{6-8}...176, 181
26^{18}...199, 226
26^{23}...181
26^{28}...137

Romans
1...193
1–11...203
1^4...177
1^7...233
1^{18}...201, 202
1^{18-32}...187
1^{18}–11^{36}...201
1^{20}...201
1^{23}...158
1^{24-32}...202
2...193, 202
2^1...201
2^{1-3}...202
2^{3-16}...200
2^{4-10}...229
2^5...193, 203, 214, 219
2^7...231
2^8...214
2^{10}...228
2^{12}...214
2^{12f}...202
2^{12-16}...xi, 201
2^{13-16}...202
2^{15}...201
2^{16}...200, 203
2^{17}...201
2^{17-20}...202
2^{18}...202
2^{21}...202
3^2...201
3^6...200
3^{23}...201
4^{1a}...202
4^{13}...226, 240
4^{17}...177
5^2...229
5^3...153
5^{10}...232, 233
5^{12}...182
5^{16}...201
5^{17}...122, 232, 233
5^{21}...121, 231
6...203
6^2...203
6^{3f}...181
6^4...233
6^5...182
6^{11}...233
6^{13}...233
6^{15}...203
6^{22}...124, 203
6^{22f}...231
6^{23}...214

INDEX OF SCRIPTURE REFERENCES

Romans—cont.
8^1...203
8^2...201
8^{3-17}...233
8^4...203
8^6...214, 228, 233
8^{10}...178, 233
8^{11}...177
8^{12}...233
8^{17}...226
8^{18}...244
8^{19-22}...243, 244
8^{21}...229, 254
8^{23}...243
8^{29}...184
9–11...112
9^3...214
9^{11}...112
11...253
11^{11f}...241
11^{12}...253
11^{15}...232, 241
11^{25}...253
11^{26}...125
11^{36}...241
12^2...117, 118, 237
12^{18}...228
12^{19}...193
13^1...254
13^2...200
13^{10}...253
13^{10-12}...150
13^{11}...112, 113
14^9...178
14^{11}...256
14^{17}...228
15^9...256
16^{20}...150
16^{25}...118
16^{27}...119

1 Corinthians
1^7...125, 126
2^{14}...183
3^{22}...240
4^4...193
4^{4f}...200
5^3...126
5^5...162
5^{10}...240
6^{9f}...226
6^{14}...182
7^{29-31}...150
7^{31}...240
7^{39}...118, 166
8^{13}...118
9^{24}...230
10^9...214
10^{11}...124, 136, 150
11^{26}...125, 150
15...110

15^{1-11}...181
15^6...166
15^{12}...177, 181
15^{12-19}...181
15^{12-58}...181
15^{18}...166
15^{19}...122, 230, 236
15^{20}...166, 244
15^{20-8}...182
15^{22}...177, 182
15^{23}...126, 244
15^{23f}...183
15^{23-8}...243
15^{24}...125, 225
15^{24-8}...254
15^{25}...127
15^{28}...255
15^{29-34}...182
15^{35}...182
15^{35a}...181
15^{35-49}...182
15^{38}...182
15^{42}...177
15^{43}...229
15^{44}...162, 238
15^{49}...183, 184
15^{50}...226
15^{50-2}...182
15^{51}...166
15^{52}...151, 169
15^{53}...158
15^{53-7}...182, 184
15^{54}...69
16^{13}...149
16^{17}...126
16^{22}...125, 214

2 Corinthians
1^4...153
1^{14}...151
2^{7f}...119
2^{13}...201
2^{15}...214
3^6...177
4^4...118
4^{10f}...233
4^{14}...182
4^{17}...122, 229
4^{18}...120
5^1...122
5^{1-5}...183
5^4...232
5^8...169
5^9...200
5^{10}...9
5^{17}...112, 243
5^{19}...241, 253
6^2...112
7^5...201
7^{6f}...126
9^9...117

9^{13}...254
10^{10}...126
11^{24}...215
11^{31}...119
12^{2-4}...133
13^4...232

Galatians
2^{20}...233
3^{16-47}...226
4^4...112, 118, 164
4^{26}...167
5^{21}...226
5^{25}...233
6^2...202
6^8...121, 231

Ephesians
1^{3-14}...242
1^{10}...240, 242, 254, 255
1^{11}...226
1^{14}...226
1^{18}...226, 229
1^{20}...255
1^{20-3}...255
1^{21}...117, 119
1^{22}...243
1^{23}...253
2^2...117, 240
2^7...117, 118
2^{14-22}...228
3^6...226
3^{11}...119
3^{21}...118, 119
4^6...241
4^7...127
4^8...127, 242
4^{8-10}...255
4^{11}...127
4^{18}...233
5^5...226
5^{21f}...254
5^{25-7}...248
6^{10-13}...242
6^{12}...243, 255

Philippians
1^6...151
1^{10}...151
1^{20-2}...151
1^{21}...232, 233
1^{22f}...169
1^{23}...133
1^{26}...126
2^{9-11}...255
2^{10}...240
2^{11}...255, 256
2^{12}...126
2^{16}...232
3^{8-11}...123
3^{10f}...177

Philippians—cont.
3^{14}...230
3^{19}...124, 214
3^{20f}...184, 246
3^{21}...184, 229, 243
4^3...232
4^5...151
4^7...228

Colossians
1^{9-23}...242
1^{12f}...226
1^{15}...24, 243
1^{16}...255
1^{18}...242, 243
1^{20}...240, 254, 256
1^{24}...153
1^{26}...118, 119
1^{27}...229
2^9...253
2^{12}...181
2^{15}...127, 242, 253
2^{18}...230
3^3...122, 232, 233
3^4...151, 227, 233
3^{24}...226
4^2...149

1 Thessalonians
1^8...214
1^{10}...149, 214
2^{14}...198
2^{19}...126
3^{13}...126, 149, 170
4^{13-16}...166, 181
4^{13-18}...149
4^{15}...126
4^{17}...119, 169, 227
5^{1-11}...149
5^{2-7}...150
5^3...153
5^6...149
5^{10}...166, 232
5^{23}...126, 149, 157, 160, 162, 178

2 Thessalonians
1^{3-5}...200
1^{3-10}...200
1^{3-12}...201
1^6...153
1^{6-8}...194
1^{7-10}...149
1^8...121, 219
1^9...214
1^{11f}...201
2^1...126
2^{1-12}...149
2^8...126
2^9...126

2^{14}...229
2^{16}...122

1 Timothy
2^4...254
2^{11}...254
3^{16}...163
4^8...232
4^{10}...254
5^{24f}...200
6^{12}...231
6^{13}...241
6^{13-15}...151
6^{14}...126
6^{16}...119
6^{19}...231, 232

2 Timothy
1^1...122, 232, 233
1^{10}...232, 233
2^{10}...122
2^{11f}...208
2^{12}...233
2^{17f}...181
3^{12}...233
4^1...151, 178, 200, 225
4^{6f}...151
4^{6-8}...169
4^8...200
4^{10}...117, 118
4^{18}...225

Titus
1^2...231
2^{12}...117, 123
3^5...237
3^7...226, 231

Philemon
1^5...122

Hebrews
1^2...112, 119, 164, 226, 256
1^{2f}...241
1^6...243
1^8...118, 119
1^{13}...168
2^5...242, 247
2^{5-18}...242
2^8...127, 242, 243
2^{10}...229, 241, 242
2^{14f}...214
3^6...125
3^{14}...125
4^1...226
4^{1-11}...228
4^7...112
4^9...226
4^{12}...159, 162
5^6...118

5^8...117, 121
5^{12}...118
6^1...200
6^{1f}...204
6^2...120, 121, 177, 178, 184, 214
6^{4-6}...120
6^{4-7}...121
6^5...117, 123
6^8...214
6^{11}...125
6^{17}...226
7^{16}...119, 231, 232, 235
8^{1f}...247
8^2...246
8^5...246
9^1...246
9^5...168
9^{11}...167, 246
9^{12}...121
9^{15}...121, 226
9^{23}...246
9^{24}...167, 246, 247
9^{26}...118, 124
9^{27}...173, 204
9^{28}...125, 227
10^{13}...242
10^{22}...204
10^{25}...151
10^{26-31}...204
10^{29}...214
10^{30}...193, 214
10^{33}...153
10^{37}...125
10^{37f}...151
10^{38}...235
10^{39}...160
11...203
11^7...226
11^9...183, 226
11^{9f}...247
11^{16}...247
11^{19}...177, 184
11^{22}...159
11^{26}...164
11^{35}...184
12^9...235, 254
12^{16}...226
12^{18}...168
12^{18-24}...167
12^{22}...168
12^{22-4}...163, 246
12^{23}...162, 204
12^{24}...247
12^{25-9}...240
12^{26}...125
12^{29}...204
13^4...204
13^{19}...238
13^{20}...121, 228
13^{21}...118, 119

INDEX OF SCRIPTURE REFERENCES

James
1^{12}...122, 235
1^{18}...244, 256
1^{21}...160
1^{25}...204
2^5...226
2^{12f}...204
2^{23}...203
2^{26}...162, 178
3^6...130
3^{15}...183
4^{12}...204, 214
4^{14}...122, 230
5^{1-11}...151
5^7...126
5^{8-12}...204
5^{16}...256
5^{20}...160, 214

1 Peter
1^{3f}...235
1^4...226
1^5...152
1^7...126, 152, 229
1^9...160
1^{11}...229
1^{13}...152
1^{17}...204
1^{20}...118, 151
1^{23}...183
1^{23f}...235
1^{25}...118, 119
2^5...235
2^{11}...160
2^{12}...152, 205
2^{13}...254
2^{20}...205
2^{21-3}...205
2^{25}...160
3^7...122, 226, 235
3^{18}...163, 177
3^{19}...xii, 163, 173
3^{20}...165
3^{22}...243
4^5...152, 178, 204
4^6...163, 173
4^7...124, 125, 151
4^{11}...118, 119, 152
4^{12-16}...205
4^{13}...152, 229
4^{17}...124
4^{18f}...205
4^{19}...160
5^1...229
5^4...152, 229
5^{10}...122, 229
5^{13}...153

2 Peter
1^{1-12}...155
1^3...236

1^{11}...122, 225
1^{13-18}...156
1^{14f}...155
1^{16}...126
2^{1-3}...155
2^4...130, 217, 239
2^{5-9}...205
2^9...173
2^{17}...217
2^{20-2}...205
3^2...239
3^{3-13}...155
3^4...126, 166
3^9...214
3^{10-12}...239
3^{12}...126
3^{13}...239, 256
3^{13f}...156
3^{18}...239

1 John
1^{1f}...234
1^2...154, 232
1^3...123
1^{6f}...234
2^2...241, 256
2^6...235
2^{14}...235
2^{17}...123, 235
2^{18-22}...155
2^{24}...235
2^{25}...122, 232
2^{27}...234
2^{28}...126, 154, 209
2^{29}...153
3^2...154, 179, 184, 227, 232, 238
3^5...154
3^6...235
3^{14}...214
3^{15}...120, 121, 231, 235
4^{2f}...155
4^3...155
4^9...241
4^{12}...235
4^{13}...234, 235
4^{14}...241, 256
4^{15}...235
4^{16}...235
4^{17}...209, 240
5^{11}...121, 122
5^{11f}...232, 234
5^{12}...121
5^{13}...231
5^{19}...243
5^{20}...123, 232, 235

2 John
^{2}...123, 235
^{9}...235

Jude
^{4}...120
^{6}...217
^{7}...120, 121, 214, 217
^{8}...205
^{9}...176
^{13}...217
^{18}...118, 152
^{19}...183
$^{20-5}$...205
^{21}...121, 231
^{23}...217
^{24}...152, 227
^{25}...119

Revelation
1–3...205
1^3...152
1^5...119, 243
1^9...153
1^{13-16}...7, 172
1^{18}...160
2...205
2^7...122, 134, 235
2^{10}...235
2^{21}...118
2^{28}...125
3...206
3^5...235
3^{11}...125
3^{12}...247
4...22, 205
4^{8-11}...119
5^5...208
5^{11-13}...228
5^{11-14}...119
6^{1-8}...211
6^2...207
6^8...160
6^9...161
6^{9-11}...168, 185, 207
6^{10}...194
6^{16}...208
6^{16f}...214
7^3...168
7^9...168
7^{13-17}...168
7^{17}...222, 235
8^9...8, 183
8^{13}...214
9^{1f}...218
9^{1-11}...218
9^{12}...214
10^6...118
11^1...177
11^{1-13}...247
11^2...247
11^8...247
11^{14}...214
11^{15}...118, 119, 208, 225, 241, 252, 256

INDEX OF SCRIPTURE REFERENCES

Revelation—cont.
12^{10}...225
13^8...235
13^{18}...152
14^1...152, 218, 247
14^6...120, 121, 122, 206
14^7...206
14^8...153
14^{10f}...218
14^{11}...206
14^{12}...168
14^{13}...206, 229
14^{19}...214
15^1...214
15^1-20^6...206
15^3...118
15^5...207
15^8...207
16^1...206
16^1-20^6...206
16^{2-8}...207
16^{10f}...207, 214
16^{12-16}...207
16^{15}...206
16^{17-21}...207, 208
17^1...9
17^8...214, 235
17^{17}...207
18^{7f}...214
18^{9-19}...248
18^{10}...214
18^{16}...214
18^{19}...214
19^{1-3}...194
19^7...207, 248
19^{7-9}...228
19^9...206, 207
19^{11-21}...128
19^{16}...219
19^{19}...207
19^{20}...130, 218
19^{21}...208
20^{1-3}...218
20^4...161, 168
20^{4-6}...185, 208
20^6...206
20^{7-10}...218
20^{7-15}...206
20^9...247
20^{10}...239
20^{11}...239
20^{11-15}...206
20^{11-16}...207
20^{12}...235, 252
20^{12f}...185
20^{13}...160
20^{14}...130, 218
20^{15}...235, 252
21^1...208, 218
21^{1f}...247
21^{1-8}...238
21^1-22^5...247
21^2...134, 168, 248
21^{2f}...248
21^3...115
21^4...239
21^5...247
21^6...125, 235
21^7...226
21^8...218, 219, 256
21^{9z}...248
21^{9-26}...134
21^{11}...229, 248
21^{14}...248
21^{16}...172, 248
21^{19f}...248
21^{21}...248
21^{22}...248
21^{23}...249
21^{24}...229
21^{24-7}...252
21^{25-7}...248
21^{26}...229
21^{26f}...239
21^{27}...218, 235, 248
22^1...235, 248
22^{1f}...248
22^{1-3}...134
22^3...208, 214, 239, 248
22^{3f}...248
22^5...208, 239, 248
22^7...125, 152
22^{12}...125, 152
22^{13}...125
22^{14}...218
22^{14-19}...248
22^{15}...252
22^{20}...125, 152

OTHER JEWISH BOOKS

Apocalypse of Baruch
4...132
29...175, 192
30...175, 192
40^3...192
48^{28-41}...117
49–52...175
50^3...133
51...133
59^{10}...133
72...187

Assumption of Moses
10^{1-10}...189, 192
10^{10}...130

Ethiopic Enoch
1–5...189, 211
1^8...221
1^9...205
5^{4f}...205
5^{6-9}...221
5^9...222
7^{84-6}...162
7^{95-7}...162
10^{11-15}...212
10^{12f}...212
$10^{16}-11^2$...221
10^{18-22}...188
10^{21f}...252
14^{4f}...212
17^5...129
18^{11-16}...208
19^{1f}...208
20^2...130
20^7...132
20^8...174
21^{1-6}...208
21^{7-10}...212, 215
22...162
23^{1-4}...215
24...132
24–7...244
24^{3f}...244, 245
25...132, 245
25^3...132, 222
25^4...132
25^{5f}...222
26...167
26^{1f}...222
26^2...245
27^1...25
27^3...223
27^{3f}...222
28–31...132
28^1...132
32...132
38^{1-6}...212
39^{3-8}...162
39^{4-8}...169
41^{2-4}...162
45^{3-6}...190
45^{3f}...222

INDEX OF SCRIPTURE REFERENCES 281

Ethiopic Enoch—cont.
45^4...237
46...190
47^3...188
48...190
48^{2-5}...188
48^5...252
48^{10}...190
49...190
50^2...87
51^1...174
51^{2-4}...222
51^{3-5}...190
52...212
52^4...190
53^3-54^5...212
56^{1-8}...207
58^3...222
58^6...222
61^{1-5}...174
61^{8-12}...190
62^{12}...223
67...163
67^{1-3}...164
67^4...164
67^{8f}...164
67^{8-13}...164
67^{10}...164
69^{26-9}...190
71^{14-17}...190
72–82...236
72^1...237
80...237
90^{1-10}...187
90^{1-19}...150
90^2...207
90^{9f}...207
90^{20}...245
90^{20-7}...212
90^{24}...212
90^{24-6}...219
90^{24-7}...130, 212
90^{26}...130
90^{28f}...222, 245

90^{28-36}...245
90^{29}...237
90^{33}...245
90^{33f}...222
90^{37f}...188, 252
91^{2-7}...150
91^{12}...188
91^{12-17}...188, 206
91^{13}...222
91^{15}...208
91^{16f}...237
92^3...174
94–105...135
95^{1-7}...223
97^6...223
97^{7-9}...223
98^9...223
98^{11-15}...223
99...212
99^1...223
99^{4f}...212
99^{6-9}...212
99^{10-16}...212
100...212
100^{1-9}...212
103^3...222
103^7...159
104^2...222
104^{12f}...222
105^2...190, 222
108...174
108^{11}...237

Book of Jubilees
1^{29}...189, 192
23^{27-31}...189, 192

Psalms of Solomon
2^{37}...189, 206
3^{13-16}...175
3^{14}...175, 224
3^{16}...175, 224
13^9...175
13^{9-11}...175

14^6...175
14^{6f}...175
15^{6-15}...175
15^8...175
15^{13}...189, 206
15^{15}...175
16^{1-3}...175
17^{23-51}...192

Sibylline Oracles
Book III:
Lines 83–90...239
Lines 702–31...239
Lines 772–9...239

Book IV:
Lines 175–92...239

Slavonic Enoch
8...133
65^{8-10}...133

Testament of the Twelve Patriarchs
Benjamin
10^{5f}...175, 187
10^{9f}...175, 187

Dan
5^{12}...224

Judah
24...192

Levi
18...192
18^9...252
18^{10}...132

Naphtali
8^{3f}...252

Zadokite Fragment
9^{53}...189, 206

www.ingramcontent.com/pod-product-compliance
Lightning Source LLC
Chambersburg PA
CBHW071935240426
43668CB00039B/1804